Charles Ashbacher

SAMS
Teach Yourself
XML
in 24 Hours

SAMS

A Division of Macmillan USA
201 West 103rd St., Indianapolis, Indiana, 46290

Sams Teach Yourself XML in 24 Hours

Copyright © 2000 by Sams Publishing

International Standard Book Number: 0-672-31950-0

Library of Congress Catalog Card Number: 00-103859

Printed in the United States of America

First Printing: August 2000

03   02   01   00   4   3   2   1

Trademarks

All terms mentioned in this book that are known to be trademarks or service marks have been appropriately capitalized. Sams Publishing cannot attest to the accuracy of this information. Use of a term in this book should not be regarded as affecting the validity of any trademark or service mark.

Warning and Disclaimer

Every effort has been made to make this book as complete and as accurate as possible, but no warranty or fitness is implied. The information provided is on an "as is" basis. The author and the publisher shall have neither liability nor responsibility to any person or entity with respect to any loss or damages arising from the information contained in this book or from the use of programs accompanying it.

ACQUISITIONS EDITOR
Jeff Schultz

DEVELOPMENT EDITORS
Linda Harmony
Laura Williams

MANAGING EDITOR
Charlotte Clapp

PROJECT EDITOR
Elizabeth Finney

COPY EDITOR
Sean Medlock

INDEXER
Sandra Henselmeier

PROOFREADERS
Katherin Bidwell
Maryann Steinhart

TECHNICAL EDITOR
Suresh Sudarsan

TEAM COORDINATOR
Amy Patton

INTERIOR DESIGNER
Gary Adair

COVER DESIGNER
Aren Howell

LAYOUT TECHNICIANS
Ayanna Lacey
Heather Hiatt Miller
Stacey Richwine-DeRome

Contents at a Glance

Table of Contents

About the Author

CHARLES ASHBACHER has led many lives. He started his work life as a construction laborer before he decided to use his head and go to college. Since then, he has been a college instructor, a programmer in physics research, a research scientist, and a software engineer. His current activities are writing, reviewing, editing, teaching community education classes, and serving as a freelance instructor and consultant for his company, Charles Ashbacher Technologies, where he is president and CEO. He is also co-editor of the *Journal of Recreational Mathematics*. When not pushing his favorite old mouse around, he can be found gardening, doing odd jobs for elderly widows, coaching youth sports, or spending time with his children, Katrina, Steven, and Rebecca. You can visit his Web site at http://www.ashbacher.com.

Dedication

To Katrina, Steven, and Rebecca, three reasons to laugh, scream, and groan.
Sometimes they make me do all three in a span of less than five minutes.

Acknowledgments

No statement of credit can fail to include my mother, Paula Ashbacher, who read to me when I was young and recognized long before I did that I was never going to be able to hit a major league fastball or dunk a basketball. Her encouragement of reading and allowing my imagination to roam free has served me very well. Not killing me when she saw my sketches of a bomb also helped.

I also cannot fully express my thanks to Leonardo Lim, chemistry professor par excellence, who is an example to all who aspire to do it right.

Over the years, I have had many students, and they have all had an impact on me. They have forced me to stretch myself to the limits, until I learned that my limits were not what I thought they were.

Finally, I would like to thank the people at Macmillan who put up with me when I did not follow the clearly defined guidelines. Experts all, it was their gentle but firm grip on the carrots, sticks, and other tools of the business that turned my ramblings into a book that I can be proud of.

Tell Us What You Think!

As the reader of this book, *you* are our most important critic and commentator. We value your opinion and want to know what we're doing right, what we could do better, what areas you'd like to see us publish in, and any other words of wisdom you're willing to pass our way.

You can email or write me directly to let me know what you did or didn't like about this book—as well as what we can do to make our books stronger.

Please note that I cannot help you with technical problems related to the topic of this book, and that due to the high volume of mail I receive, I might not be able to reply to every message.

When you write, please be sure to include this book's title and author as well as your name and phone or fax number. I will carefully review your comments and share them with the author and editors who worked on the book.

Email: webdev_sams@mcp.com

Mail: Mark Taber
          Associate Publisher
          Sams Publishing
          201 West 103rd Street
          Indianapolis, IN 46290 USA

Introduction

When someone asks me where to start learning how to program, I always say, "Learn HTML." The software is free, the language is easy to understand, and you can view the results immediately without having to compile the code. Most of this applies to learning XML as well. HTML and XML have the same linguistic "grandfather," so it takes no great leap of insight to understand the basic structure of XML code once you know HTML. Therefore, this book assumes that you're very familiar with HTML.

At the time that this book was being written, Netscape, the second of the two major browsers, was in a state of uncertainty. The company was publicly unclear about the direction it would take after its purchase by AOL, and there was a great deal of doubt about the future of the Netscape browser. Since IE 5 fully supports XML and has the largest market share, we decided to use it exclusively in this book. This also avoids having to continuously point out differences in the support the two have for XML. Finally, IE 5 is available as a free download, so any decision not to use it is personal and not economic.

With few exceptions, the JavaScript language is used to provide the dynamic features of the instructional code. After a great deal of thought, we decided to avoid spending any time introducing or reviewing JavaScript. However, that's not as serious as it may sound. The programs in this book use fairly standard and basic programming structures, so familiarity with any programming language is sufficient. If you're a programming novice and still want to learn XML, grab a good JavaScript reference and start reading. With this book in one hand and a JavaScript manual in another, any reader who's determined to succeed will be able to do so.

So, why is it important to learn XML? There are three answers to this: World, Wide, and Web. Even though the Web has grown at a phenomenal rate and ideas for new uses multiply at a rate that rivals that of bacteria, it's still in its infancy. Naturally, any tool used to perform operations on the Web will be caught up in this rising tide. Within this tsunami is another very powerful trend, electronic commerce or e-commerce. Many projections about the popularity of e-commerce have been much too high because implementing a business on the Web has proved to be more difficult than first thought.

However, despite those problems, there's no doubt that e-commerce has already become a significant part of the world economy. And the driving force behind e-commerce is the ability to easily capture, store, modify, and interpret data in a Web context. XML allows you to do that.

How to Use This Book

Although the 24 lessons in this book are advertised as being one hour each, a concerted effort has been made to apply a finer point to them. When I go places—youth baseball games, buses, plasma donation centers—I often see people with computer materials in their hands. I generally ask them how much time they can spare to study, and the overwhelming answer is not an hour, but 15 to 30 minutes. Therefore, in an attempt to better fit this book into the reality of modern life, the chapters are split into segments, none of which should take more than 30 minutes and most of which can be done in 15 minutes.

In code listings, line numbers have been added for reference purposes. These line numbers aren't part of HTML or JavaScript, so make sure you leave them out when you enter the code.

To get the most out of this book, you should read every part of every chapter, read and understand all the questions, take all the quizzes, and complete all the exercises. To make this easier, the source code for all of the examples is available on this book's companion Web site at `www.samspublishing.com`. Once you've completed this book, you'll have a set of skills that will prepare you for the exciting and dynamic world of using XML to process data on the Web.

Conventions Used in This Book

This book uses different typefaces to differentiate between code and regular English, and also to help you identify important concepts.

Text that you type and text that should appear on your screen is presented in `monospace` type.

`It will look like this to mimic the way text looks on your screen.`

Placeholders for variables and expressions appear in `monospace italic` font. You should replace the placeholder with the specific value it represents.

> A Note presents an interesting piece of information related to the surrounding discussion.

PART I

The Basics

Hour

HOUR 1

Getting Started in XML

In the short history of the World Wide Web, there's a long list of "next great things" that turned out to be more hype than substance. Extensible Markup Language, or XML, is clearly one of these "next great things," but it's too early to tell where the hype ends. However, there's no doubt that Web commerce is here to stay, and XML is a valuable tool in facilitating the exchange of data between systems. It's based on the same principles of markup languages that make HTML work, so it's easy to learn. For these reasons, XML should have some longevity (at least in terms of the Web).

In this hour, you'll learn the following:

- A brief history of markup languages and why XML was created to supplement HTML in the building of Web pages
- The role of XML as a metalanguage
- The basic organization of an XML data file
- The self-documenting features of XML
- The impact of XML on data transfer over the Web

A History of Markup Languages

Markup languages predate the Web by many years, going back to the beginning of commercial publishing. When an editor prepares a manuscript for publication, sections of the text can be *marked up* with notations. For example, the beginning of a section that needs to be italicized would be marked with the letter *I*. To indicate where the italics should stop, the end of the section would be marked as well. Of course, for the sake of clarity, the closing notation would have to be somewhat different than the opening one.

The first formal markup language used to specify the structure of documents was created at IBM in the 1960s. It was known as the Generalized Markup Language (GML) and was used to standardize internal documents at IBM. Later, it was expanded into the Standard General Markup Language (SGML), which became a standard for information presentation that was adopted by many different industries. SGML was adopted as a standard by the International Organization for Standardization (ISO) in 1986. For more information on this organization and access to the documents on the SGML standards, go to the Web site at `http://www.iso.ch/welcome.html`.

Although you've probably never used SGML to create a document, you might be wondering how HTML, which is a subset of SGML, came about. First, you need to understand that today, when you open a browser and enter a Web address such as `http://www.ashbacher.com`, the following three-step process takes place:

1. The browser contacts a directory assistance computer on the Internet to obtain the Internet address of the requested Web page, which is a file written in HTML.
2. If the address is found, the browser contacts the site and requests the file.
3. If the file is available, the site sends it across the Internet to the browser, which interprets the file and displays the contents.

All of this is now quite routine and mostly transparent. However, in the late 1980s this process didn't exist. The inspiration to create such a process occurred at the European Laboratory for Particle Physics (CERN), a high-energy physics research center in Switzerland.

The scientists at the facility were habitually exchanging online papers containing references to other papers. To view the referenced material, it was necessary to perform searches or at least manually open another document. Additionally, the software didn't always display the online papers in the intended manner, due to the problems of writing complex expressions for display on a computer. In light of these problems, Tim Berners-Lee and Anders Berglund, both researchers at CERN, saw the need for a system of electronic document exchange.

The researchers' vision was to create a markup language of notations, or tags, that would be embedded in a document to inform the program used for viewing (the browser) how the text was to be displayed. Tags bounded by the less-than (<) and greater-than (>) characters were created, and the complete set of tags became known as Hypertext Markup Language, or HTML. The browser examines and interprets the HTML tags, using them as a template to determine how the file's contents are to be displayed. This simple yet powerful solution worked so well that Berners-Lee is now considered the inventor of the World Wide Web.

As the Web continues to grow, HTML also continues to change at a rapid rate. The World Wide Web Consortium (W3C) is the organization that maintains and publishes the standards for SGML and HTML and is currently headed by Berners-Lee. For more information about the history of HTML and the latest in standards documents, visit their Web site at http://www.w3c.org.

The Relationship Between HTML and XML

Listing 1.1 demonstrates the basic skeleton of an HTML file.

LISTING 1.1 The Basic Skeleton of an HTML File

```
1: <HTML>
2: <HEAD>
3: <TITLE> </TITLE>
4: </HEAD>
5: <BODY>
6:
7: </BODY>
8: </HTML>
```

The main thing to remember about an HTML file is that the tags divide it into several sections with distinct purposes. As you'll see, XML files share that characteristic.

HTML has proven to be successful beyond anyone's expectations, and Berners-Lee is now considered the person who was most likely to become rich from the Internet but didn't. However, for many complex operations, HTML is limited in what it can express because it was designed almost exclusively to display static text.

XML is the most widely used extension of HTML that has been created as a response to this deficiency. (Chapter 24 discusses some of the other extensions.) XML is itself a markup language, using the same general tag notation as HTML. It allows you to define your own tags, which makes it much more flexible than HTML. The current XML standard is available at http://www.w3c.org.

Well-Formed Documents in XML

HTML allows you to do many things, but the rules are lax in some areas, forcing the browser to fill in the missing pieces. XML is not so forgiving, forcing compliance in the following areas:

- Every opening tag must have a corresponding closing tag.
- A nested tag pair cannot overlap with another tag.
- Tag names are case sensitive.

HTML requires many tags to be paired (for example, a closing tag must appear for each opening tag). However, pairing is optional for some of the tags, and only the opening tag is required. The standard example of this is the paragraph tag (<P>). For example, browsers will accept the following HTML code, which creates three paragraphs:

```
<P>The first paragraph is here.
<P>The second paragraph is here.
<P>The third paragraph is here.
```

When the browser parses this code, the presence of the next paragraph tag is an implicit signal to terminate the previous paragraph. The problem with this implicit signal is that the browser is deciding where the closing tag should be. The isn't always what the author intends.

XML has been designed to eliminate this possibility with the rigid rule that *every* opening tag must have a matching closing tag. This is one of the rules that must be satisfied if a document is to be considered *well-formed*. For example, the well-formed equivalent of the previous example would be

```
<P>The first paragraph is here.</P>
<P>The second paragraph is here.</P>
<P>The third paragraph is here.</P>
```

HTML contains some additional tags that perform operations, rather than marking sections of text for modification. The line break tag (<BR>) is the best example. To satisfy the XML requirement for a pair of tags, the opening and closing tags are combined. In this type of tag, a slash is placed inside the tag immediately before the greater-than symbol. Such a tag is known as an *empty tag*. For example, the XML equivalent of the HTML line break tag is <BR/>.

HTML is also quite lax in allowing tags to appear without satisfying the rules of proper nesting. For example, both of the following lines of HTML code contain tags that aren't properly nested:

```
<STRIKE><BOLD>This is our first example.</STRIKE></BOLD>
<SUP><SMALL>This is our second example.</SUP></SMALL>
```

Both of these lines would be illegal in XML. To be considered well-formed XML code, the closing tag must match the last-used opening tag. For example, the following are the well-formed equivalents of the code of the previous example:

```
<STRIKE><BOLD>This is our first example.</BOLD></STRIKE>
<SUP><SMALL>This is our second example.</SMALL></SUP>
```

These rules have an added benefit when used on hand-held devices, which have a reduced amount of memory. The lax rules of HTML make it a lot harder to program a browser for these devices, because all the extra code that's needed to check for improper nesting and missing end tags leads to a much larger executable. If you avoid the problems of HTML, the code is more likely to fit within the smaller devices.

XML as a Metalanguage

A *metalanguage* is a language used to describe another language. For example, consider the words "noun," "verb," "adverb," and "adjective." These words describe the structure of sentences in most human languages, so they're part of a language used to describe a language. The advantage of a metalanguage is that it can be used to define more than one implemented language.

First and foremost, XML is a metalanguage used to define other languages. To understand this, you need to accept a very general definition of the word "language." For the purposes of this book, consider any form of data in a database to be a language. Since XML can be used to define the form of the data, it's a metalanguage.

As a metalanguage, XML allows you to define your own tags—which provides a significant advantage over basic HTML. When you surround an XML entry with a tag such as `<Message>`, the meaning of the data between the tags is clear. Writing tags to match the specific form of your data makes the code easier to understand and to write. The choice of tag names is often dictated by what the data represents. The only restrictions on the names of the tags are those that you usually find in other programming languages:

- Keywords cannot be used.
- Spaces, punctuation, and other separation characters (such as parentheses, square brackets, and curly brackets) cannot appear in a tag name.
- The underscore (_) and digits can be used, although the first character of a tag name cannot be a digit. An underscore is acceptable as the first character of a tag name.

When you want to use multiple words in a tag name, you can borrow a strategy widely used in programming by combining the words and capitalizing the first letter of each word. For example, if you want to define a tag to represent the amount of money in a customer's bank account, make the tag name `MoneyInAccount`. This satisfies the naming rules and preserves the meaning of the tag.

Your First XML Program

The first example consists of two files, one in XML and the other in HTML. Listing 1.2 shows the XML file; you'll see the HTML file in Hour 2, "Using HTML Files to Display the Data of XML Files." This example, and many other examples throughout this book, will use the basic structure of an email message as a model.

LISTING 1.2   A Simple XML Data File

```
1:<?xml version="1.0"?>
2: <!-- This is our first XML file -->
3: <MESSAGE>
4: <TO>STUDENT</TO>
5: <FROM>AUTHOR</FROM>
6: <SUBJECT>Introduction to XML</SUBJECT>
7: <BODY>Welcome to XML!</BODY>
8:  </MESSAGE>
```

Internet Explorer 5.0 can be used to verify the well-formed properties of XML files. To do so, simply click File, Open in IE to select the XML file. If the file is well-formed, the result will be similar to Figure 1.1.

Let's examine this program in detail. The first line is a description of the file, including the XML specification version number. Although this line isn't required, it should always be included in your XML files. The syntax of this line is very specific. All letters must be lowercase, the question marks must be present, and the version number must be in quotes.

The syntax for comments in XML is identical to that in HTML, so line 2 is a comment.

As is the case in HTML, comments can be more than one line in length.

FIGURE 1.1

The appearance of your first XML file when viewed in IE.

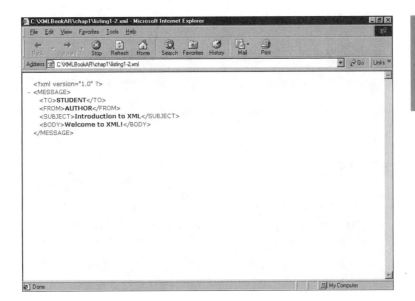

Lines 3 and 8 contain the user-defined tags that delimit the list of data elements. The <MESSAGE> tag pair defines the data type of the file and is the root of the hierarchical structure, shown in Figure 1.2.

In XML, the definition of a structure is known as a *data type*. For example, Listing 1.2 defines the MESSAGE data type as being composed of the TO, FROM, SUBJECT, and BODY elements. Actual code that corresponds to a data type is known as an *object* of that type. In Listing 1.2, lines 3-8 create a MESSAGE object.

FIGURE 1.2

The code for your first XML file in the form of a hierarchical tree.

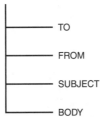

It's not necessary to use uppercase letters for the tag names as long as the opening and closing tags are consistent. For example, the following would be acceptable forms for the tag pairs:

```
<Message>...</Message>
<message>...</message>
<MESSage>...</MESSage>
```

Lines 4 through 7 each define a component of the MESSAGE object. As mentioned before, each of the components must end with a suitable closing tag.

To allow you to gain hands-on experience with XML syntax, the rest of this section describes changes you should make to the XML file. Be sure to change the file back to its original form after each change.

Modify the line

```
<BODY>Welcome to XML!</BODY>
```

to

```
<BODY>Welcome to XML!
```

View the modified file in IE and note the error message. The error informs you that there's no ending <BODY> tag.

Add the following line to the file in front of the line that begins with the <BODY> tag:

```
<CC/>
```

View the modified file in IE. The tag will not generate an error. This illustrates that it's possible for a single tag to represent both the opening and closing tag delimiters.

Remove text from the line

```
<FROM>AUTHOR</FROM>
```

so that it looks like this:

```
<FROM></FROM>
```

View the modified file in IE. The tag will be compressed into the form

```
<FROM/>
```

This operation shows that there doesn't need to be any information inside a tag pair.

Add the following line to the code in front of the line that begins with the `<BODY>` tag:

```
<POSTSCRIPT><NOTE>Enjoy yourself!</POSTSCRIPT></NOTE>
```

View the modified file in IE and note the error message. It tells you that the closing tags aren't in the proper order.

Add the following line to the file:

```
<POSTSCRIPT><NOTE>Enjoy yourself!</NOTE></POSTSCRIPT>
```

View the modified file in IE and note the appearance. In this case, pay particular attention to the indentation of the data elements and the appearance of the red hyphens in front of the `<MESSAGE>` and `<POSTSCRIPT>` tags. This is demonstrated in Figure 1.3.

FIGURE 1.3

The appearance of simply nested XML tags.

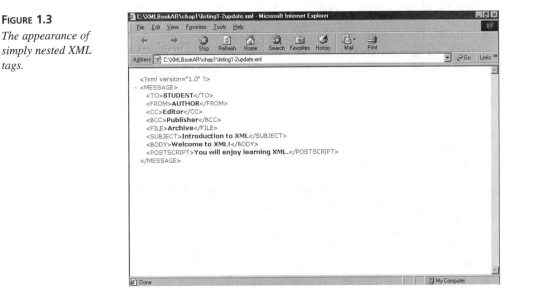

A red hyphen denotes a data element that's a root node, and other data elements branch off from it. The hierarchical tree that corresponds to this file is presented in Figure 1.4.

Finally, modify the `<MESSAGE>` tag to match the following:

```
<MESSAGE.>
```

View the modified file in IE and note the error message.

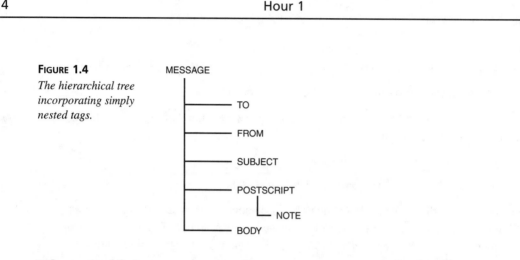

FIGURE 1.4
The hierarchical tree incorporating simply nested tags.

The Self-Documenting Aspects of XML

One enormous advantage of using XML to define the structure of data should be obvious—using tag names of your own creation makes XML files largely self-documenting. Even someone who knows nothing at all about XML can look at the file and make a reasonable guess about what it represents.

This is in sharp contrast to many descriptions of data found in databases, where there's a much steeper learning curve. It also provides a degree of consistency with HTML, the language of the Web. If you have a basic knowledge of markup tags in HTML, you already know a lot about XML.

When you set out to build a database, first you need to describe the form the data takes. Data can be expressed in the form of a hierarchical tree, and it's easy to map trees to XML file structures.

Listing 1.3 is a coded solution to the diagram in XML. The data inside the tags has been added for emphasis and is not required.

LISTING 1.3   An XML File Demonstrating Several Levels of Data

```
 1: <?xml version="1.0"?>
 2: <Memo>
 3: <To>Head of department</To>
 4: <From>Author</From>
 5: <CC>
 6:     <StaffPerson>
 7:         <Rank>Professor</Rank>
 8:         <Name>Jane Jones</Name>
 9:         <Office>101 Maclief</Office>
10:     </StaffPerson>
11: </CC>
12: <Subject>Student scores</Subject>
```

```
13: <Body>
14: Congratulations everyone! Our students averaged over 90 percent on their
    comprehensive examinations. We should be proud of the success
    of our program.
16: </Body>
17: </Memo>
```

1

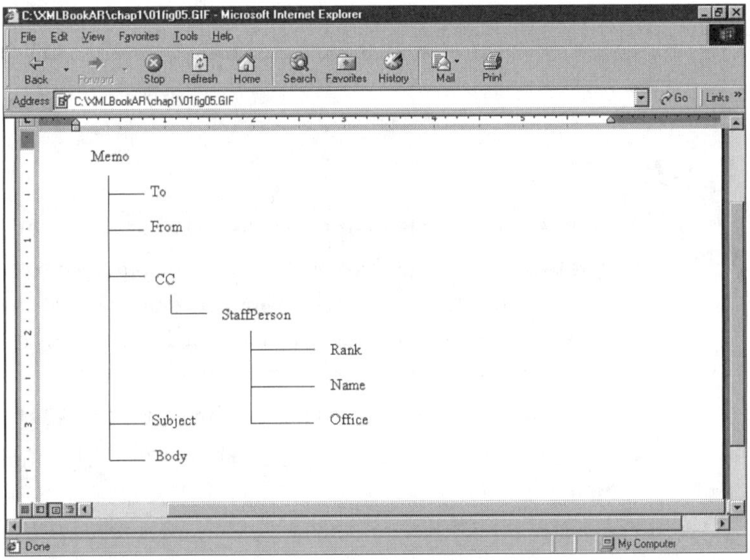

FIGURE 1.5

A hierarchical diagram representing several levels of data.

The Impact of XML

Although email and other text messages are important and make up a significant fraction of the traffic on the Internet, it's the ability to easily and accurately transfer complex forms of data that is making the biggest impact on the growth of the Web. To conduct commerce on the Web, it must be possible to store, retrieve, and process information such as customer profiles and records of purchases on specific visits to a site. XML is an effective metalanguage for describing complex data objects, for two reasons. As stated earlier, the flexibility of creating your own tags makes XML documents largely self-documenting. Furthermore, the way that XML documents are constructed fits in well with our intuitive notions of hierarchies of information.

Summary

HTML and other markup languages arose in response to the need for accurate ways to present and transmit data electronically. Born in a nuclear laboratory, the tags that define the World Wide Web have helped remake the world of data exchange.

In some ways, XML is more restrictive than HTML in how tags can be used to organize information, and those differences were described in this hour. Simple examples of XML files were presented, as well as the hierarchical trees that can be used to describe the data.

Q&A

Q Why is it possible to define your own tags in XML but not in HTML?

A In HTML, the tags tell the browser what to do to the text between them. When a tag is encountered, the browser interprets it and displays the text in the proper form. If the browser doesn't understand a tag, it ignores it. In XML, the interpretation of the tags isn't the responsibility of the browser.

Q How many different data types can be defined in XML?

A Since the number of possible tag names is effectively infinite, there's no upper limit.

Workshop

Quizzes and exercises are found at the end of each hour in this book. They're designed to give you additional practice with what you've learned.

Quiz

1. How long have markup languages been used in the presentation of data?
2. What are the extra rules governing the construction of an XML file versus an HTML file that make it easier to write a program to parse an XML file?
3. Since XML allows you to create your own tags, is it possible to write the data description right into the XML file?
4. XML is an extension of which markup language?

Answers

1. Informal markup languages have existed since the advent of mass printing, although formal ones with standards are of more recent origin.

2. First, all opening tags must have a corresponding closing tag. Second, when a closing tag is encountered, the opening tag that immediately precedes it must be the corresponding opening tag.

3. More than that, proper construction of the tag names means that they describe the data without the need to add any documentation.

4. It's an extension of SGML.

Exercises

1. Construct the corresponding document definition diagram for the following XML file:

```
<?xml version="1.0" ?>
??? It is <!-- filename and not <!- filename
<MESSAGE>
<TO>STUDENT</TO>
<FROM>AUTHOR</FROM>
<CC>Editor</CC>
<BCC>Publisher</BCC>
<FILE>Archive</FILE>
<SUBJECT>Introduction to XML</SUBJECT>
<BODY>Welcome to XML!</BODY>
<POSTSCRIPT>You will enjoy learning XML.</POSTSCRIPT>
</MESSAGE>
```

2. Write an XML file for a simple email message with <TO>, <FROM>, <SUBJECT>, and <BODY> sections.

HOUR 2

Using HTML Files to Display the Data of XML Files

The data contained in an XML file is of little value unless it can be displayed on the Web, and the primary topic of this hour is writing HTML files to do just that. In this lesson, you'll learn a simple way to extract the data from an XML file and use JavaScript to display it in a dynamically created HTML file.

Topics covered in this hour include the following:

- A presentation of the Dynamic HTML features needed to understand the code presented in this hour
- How to write an HTML program that displays the data in an XML file, and why it's advantageous to separate the HTML and XML files
- How easy it is to write HTML code to display the data from multiple XML files

Dynamically Updating the Contents of HTML Tags

Many of the HTML tags are used to surround a section of text and inform the browser to display that text in a certain way. These tags have certain attributes that can be assigned values. For example, the header tags have the align attribute, which can be used to orient the text horizontally.

The following line of code contains the align attribute, which will cause the text within the tags to be aligned on the right side of the line:

```
<H2 align=right>Header text on the right</H2>
```

This works well if static text is the only thing that you want to display; that is, if you place the text between the tags at design time, that's what will always appear in that location. However, for the purposes of this hour, you need to be able to dynamically assign values to the attributes of the HTML tags—in other words, modify the text within the tags while the file is being displayed. This is done by embedding sections of JavaScript code in the HTML, which can change the attributes while the page is being displayed.

You should be familiar with the concept of an HTML *attribute*. In some languages, attributes are known as *properties*.

The key property that you're interested in changing at this point is the innerText property, which corresponds to the text between the beginning and end tags. Therefore, the innerText property will always be a string of characters.

For example, for the line

```
<H2 align=right>Header text on the right</H2>
```

the innerText property of the H2 tag would be the string

```
Header text on the right
```

The short program shown in Listing 2.1 changes the innerText property through the use of JavaScript—which dynamically modifies the text that appears on the screen.

LISTING 2.1   Dynamically Changing the Text of an HTML Tag

```
 1: <html>
 2: <head>
 3: </head>
 4: <body bgcolor="ffffff" >
 5: <span id=span1 style="font-size:16pt">Old text</span>
 6: <script language=JavaScript>
 7: <!--
 8: alert("about to change the text");
 9: span1.innerText="Out with the old and in with the new";
10: //-->
11: </script>
12: </body>
13: </html>
```

2

When you run the program in IE, here's the text that appears in the document window when the alert box pops up:

`Old text`

Notice that after the you click the OK button in the alert box, the text in the document window has been changed to

`Out with the old and in with the new`

Let's look at the program in more detail. Line 5 defines the tag that will be the target of your update. The name span1 is assigned to the ID attribute, which is used to provide uniqueness of reference. Obviously, any particular tag name can be used many times in an HTML file. To be able to refer to a particular tag, you must assign the tag an ID. Later, you'll use the ID to update the tag's innerText property. Line 5 also sets the point size of the text to a value larger than the default.

Line 8 displays a JavaScript alert box that contains the message shown in quotes. Since this line of code appears after the initial assignment of text to the <SPAN> tag, it's executed after the assignment, which halts the execution at that point. This allows you to inspect the text and verify that it has the value that was originally assigned. When you click on the box's OK button, execution will resume.

Line 9 is where the text of the <SPAN> tag is dynamically updated. Note that the ID of the tag is used to perform the update. Also note that the new text is displayed using the 16-point font. This means that the style appearance modifier in the <SPAN> tag isn't executed until after the text in the tag has been changed.

Using an HTML File to Display the Data in an XML File

Although it's possible to embed XML data inside an HTML file, it's strongly discouraged. Once data is placed inside a file, it's essentially eliminated as an option for other programs. Separating the data from the code that processes it allows all programs to access the data and makes your code more generic.

This is especially true when that data is posted on the Web. For all but the most intensive of computations, the bottleneck of working on the Web is the time it takes to transfer information from one point to another. Making small, distinct files leads to faster transfers and less movement of extraneous data.

You might think the same amount of information needs to be transferred regardless of whether that information is contained in one file or two. However, given the bottleneck of data transfer, Web processes are designed to begin executing as soon as sufficient data is available. In the case of small files, it's possible for one of the files to arrive and be used to start the processing while the other is still in the transfer process. In the case of a single large file, the entire file might have to be transferred before processing can occur.

Introduction to ActiveX Controls

Before we get into the actual process of extracting the data from an XML file, you need to learn something about ActiveX controls. These controls are a family of code segments created and supported by Microsoft. Each control is an *object* and (generally speaking) is constructed by combining data and functions. However, it isn't necessary for a control to contain both. For now, all you need to know about objects is that they're entities created by combining variables and functions.

ActiveX controls are commonly used to build Web pages because they can be embedded inside an HTML file. If properly initialized, the functions of a control can then be called from within the page to perform dynamic operations.

As you would expect, ActiveX controls are compatible with IE and usually don't work well with other browsers. Although you'll use an ActiveX control in the next section, there won't be a more detailed explanation of how they're used until Hour 3.

A Programming Example that Displays XML Data

In Hour 1, you created the XML file shown in Listing 1.2. You also spent some time on the construction of hierarchical trees to describe data. The diagram for this XML file is shown in Figure 2.1.

FIGURE 2.1

The hierarchical diagram of the XML file shown in Listing 1.2.

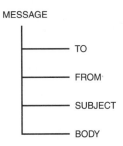

```
MESSAGE
├──── TO
├──── FROM
├──── SUBJECT
└──── BODY
```

Your next step will be to create an HTML file with tags whose definition will allow them to serve as the targets for the assignments of this file's data values.

The file in Listing 2.2 will extract and display the data from the XML file shown in Listing 1.2.

Since you're not specifying a directory location in the line that loads the file, both the XML and HTML files must reside in the same directory. If that's not to your liking, feel free to qualify the path of the XML file.

LISTING 2.2   Extracting and Viewing the Data in an XML File

```
1:<html>
2:<head>
3:<script language=JavaScript>
4:<!--
5:var RootElement1;
6:var xmlDoc1=new ActiveXObject ("microsoft.xmldom");
7:xmlDoc1.load("listing1-2.xml");
8:
9:function StartUp()
10:{
11: if(xmlDoc1.readyState=="4")
12: {
13:  StartLoading();
14: }
15: else
16: {
17:  alert("Loading operation could not start");
18: }
19:}
20:
21:function StartLoading()
22:{
```

LISTING 2.2   continued

```
23: RootElement1=xmlDoc1.documentElement;
24: todata.innerText=RootElement1.childNodes(0).text;
25: fromdata.innerText=RootElement1.childNodes(1).text;
26: subjectdata.innerText=RootElement1.childNodes(2).text;
27: bodydata.innerText=RootElement1.childNodes(3).text;
28:}
29:
30://-->
31:</script>
32:</head>
33:<body bgcolor="ffffff" onLoad="StartUp()">
34:TO: <span id=todata></span><br>
35:FROM: <span id=fromdata></span><br>
36:SUBJECT: <span id=subjectdata></span><br>
37:BODY: <span id=bodydata></span><br>
38:</ body>
39:</html>
```

When you run the HTML file in IE, note that the text of each of the entries in the XML file has been inserted into the proper location.

Line 5 declares an identifier, RootElement1, that will refer to the root of the data defined in the XML file. After assignment, it will refer to the <MESSAGE> tag of the XML file.

A great deal is accomplished in line 6. On the right side of the expression, a new instance of the Microsoft XML document object model ActiveX object is created. This XML object provides the functionality needed to perform all of the operations on the XML file, from opening to reading to updating. After the object is created, it's assigned to the reference name declared on the left.

 An *instance* of an object is where the attributes can be assigned values and the functions of the object can be called. All the components of an object are accessed using the dot notation *NameOfObject.NameofComponentTo Use*.

Once the new xmldom object is created, it needs to be linked to the XML file that's to be read. This is accomplished on line 7, where the XML file to be read is attached to the object and opened.

If the XML data file isn't in the same directory as the HTML file, you need to prefix the filename with the appropriate pathname.

When the command to attach and open a file is attempted, there's always the possibility that it will fail. Files may not exist, may be temporarily unavailable, or may be of the wrong form. To allow you to test for success or failure, the xmldom object contains the readyState property, which is filled with a value as a result of the load operation. This identifier is a string, and the possible values are summarized in the following table.

Symbolic Value	Numeric String	Meaning
Uninitialized	"0"	Object is not initialized with data.
Loading	"1"	Object is loading the data.
Loaded	"2"	Object has finished loading the data.
Interactive	"3"	User can interact with the object even though it's not fully loaded.
Complete	"4"	Object is completely initialized.

The readyState property is tested in the Startup() function. If the file was loaded properly, the function to import and assign the data components is called on line 13. If this doesn't occur, an error message is displayed via an alert box call on line 17. Since no loading is done in that scenario, the innerText properties of the <span> tags will remain empty.

The StartUp() function provides a safety wrapper around the code to transfer the data, so you can make sure the data is available before you try to move it into the HTML file. This is sound programming practice and a graceful way to continue to run the program if the data file's attachment doesn't work properly.

Lines 34 to 37 define the target tags for the assignments of the data values in the XML file. Text labels are associated with each instance of the <span> tag, and unique ID values are assigned. Note that the text is assigned to the tags and that this section is pure HTML code.

All of the data transference is done in the StartLoading() function. Line 23 assigns the root node of the XML file to the RootElement1 reference. This is equivalent to having it point to the file's <MESSAGE> tag. This is demonstrated in Figure 2.2.

FIGURE 2.2

The `RootElement1` *identifier points to the opening* `<Message>` *tag.*

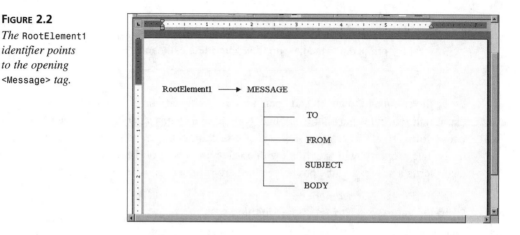

When an XML file is constructed where all components are at the same level, the xmldom object can read the data using array notation. The function used to do this is `childNodes(index)`, where *index* is the number of the item to extract. The numbering of the nodes starts at 0 and proceeds sequentially. The text property is the information between the tags of that data item. Therefore, line 24 extracts the data from the `<TO>` tag, line 25 extracts the data from the `<FROM>` tag, line 26 extracts the data from the `<SUBJECT>` tag, and line 27 extracts the data from the `<BODY>` tag. Once extracted from the XML file, each of the strings is then inserted into the referenced `<span>` tag.

This correspondence between the nodes and the array elements is illustrated in Figure 2.3.

FIGURE 2.3

The correspondence between the components of the XML file and the `childNodes` *array.*

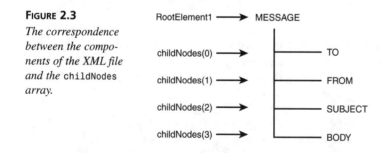

Adding Components to an XML File

If additional entries are added to an XML file, it's only necessary to use additional values when indexing on the `childNodes()` function and add appropriate additional tags in the HTML.

Listing 2.3 contains a file that can be created by adding some additional lines to the XML file that was read previously. The changes to be made are all marked in bold.

LISTING 2.3 Adding Data Elements to the XML File

```
 1: <?xml version="1.0" ?>
 2:
 3: <MESSAGE>
 4: <TO>STUDENT</TO>
 5: <FROM>AUTHOR</FROM>
 6: <CC>Editor</CC>
 7: <SUBJECT>Introduction to XML</SUBJECT>
 8: <BODY>Welcome to XML!</BODY>
 9: <POSTSCRIPT>You will enjoy learning XML.</POSTSCRIPT>
10: </MESSAGE>
```

Listing 2.4 is a modification of the previous HTML file that reflects the changes in the XML file that will be read. All of the changes to be made are marked in bold.

LISTING 2.4 Reading the Data After Adding Components

```
 1: <html>
 2: <head>
 3: <script language=JavaScript>
 4: <!--
 5: var RootElement1;
 6: var xmlDoc1=new ActiveXObject("microsoft.xmldom");
 7: xmlDoc1.load("listing2-3.xml");
 8:
 9: function StartUp()
10: {
11:   if(xmlDoc1.readyState=="4")
12:   {
13:     StartLoading();
14:   }
15:   else
16:   {
17:     alert("Loading operation could not start");
18:   }
19: }
20:
21: function StartLoading()
22: {
23:   RootElement1=xmlDoc1.documentElement;
24:   todata.innerText=RootElement1.childNodes(0).text;
25:   fromdata.innerText=RootElement1.childNodes(1).text;
```

2

LISTING 2.4   continued

```
26:    ccdata.innerText=RootElement1.childNodes(2).text;
27:    subjectdata.innerText=RootElement1.childNodes(3).text;
28:    bodydata.innerText=RootElement1.childNodes(4).text;
29:    psdata.innerText=RootElement1.childNodes(5).text;
30: }
31:
32: //-->
33: </script>
34: </head>
35: <body bgcolor="ffffff" onLoad="StartUp()">
36: TO: <span id=todata></span><br>
37: FROM: <span id=fromdata></span><br>
38: CC: <span id=ccdata></span><br>
39: SUBJECT: <span id=subjectdata></span><br>
40: BODY: <span id=bodydata></span><br>
41: POSTSCRIPT: <span id=psdata></span><br>
42: </body>
43: </html>
```

When you run this HTML file in IE, you can see that each of the data components in the XML file is inserted into its proper location.

Importing the Data from Multiple XML Files

It's a simple matter to import more than one file with the same structure into an HTML file. Basically, you just need to repeat the operation, making sure that the uniqueness of target tag names and variables is preserved.

Listing 2.5 contains an XML file whose structure matches that of the ones used so far. The values of the data components have been changed so that they can be differentiated from the others when read by the HTML files.

LISTING 2.5   The Second File for the Reading of Two XML Files

```
1: <?xml version="1.0" ?>
2: <MESSAGE>
3: <TO>AUTHOR</TO>
4: <FROM>STUDENT</FROM>
5: <CC>Editor</CC>
6: <SUBJECT>Your introduction to XML</SUBJECT>
7: <BODY>I am with you so far.</BODY>
8: <POSTSCRIPT>I am enjoying it so far.</POSTSCRIPT>
9: </MESSAGE>
```

Note that this data has the same structure as that of the other XML files; the differences are in the data values.

The next step is to create a program that will read in the data of both XML files. It will be necessary to create two instances of the xmldom object, one for each file. You'll also create another set of <span> tags in the HTML section to serve as the targets of the extracted data.

Listing 2.6 is a modification of the previous one. It has been altered to read the data from two XML files having the same form. All changes from the previous one are marked in bold.

LISTING 2.6   Reading Two XML Files That Have the Same Form

```
 1:<HTML>
 2:<HEAD>
 3:<SCRIPT LANGUAGE="JavaScript">
 4:<!--
 5: var RootElement1;
 6: var RootElement2;
 7: var xmlDoc1=new ActiveXObject("microsoft.xmldom");
 8: xmlDoc1.load("listing2-3.xml");
 9: var xmlDoc2=new ActiveXObject("microsoft.xmldom");
10: xmlDoc2.load("listing2-5.xml");
11:function StartUp()
12:{
13:
14: if ((xmlDoc1.readyState=="4")&&(xmlDoc2.readyState=="4"))
15:   {
16:    StartLoading();
17:   }
18:   else
19:   {
20:    alert("Process could not start");
21:   }
22:   }
23:   function StartLoading()
24:   {
25:     RootElement1=xmlDoc1.documentElement;
26:     RootElement2=xmlDoc2.documentElement;
27: todata1.innerText=RootElement1.childNodes.item(0).text;
28:    fromdata1.innerText=RootElement1.childNodes.item(1).text;
29:    ccdata1.innerText=RootElement1.childNodes.item(2).text;
```

2

LISTING 2.6 continued

```
30:    subjectdata1. innerText=RootElement1.childNodes.item(3).text;
31:    bodydata1.innerText=RootElement1.childNodes.item(4).text;
32:    psdata1.innerText=RootElement1.childNodes.item(5).text;
33:    todata2.innerText=RootElement2.childNodes.item(0).text;
34:    fromdata2.innerText=RootElement2.childNodes.item(1).text;
35:    ccdata2.innerText=RootElement2.childNodes.item(2).text;
36:    subjectdata2.innerText=RootElement2.childNodes.item(3).text;
37:    bodydata2.innerText=RootElement2.childNodes.item(4).text;
38:    psdata2.innerText=RootElement2.childNodes.item(5).text;
39: }
40://-->
41:</SCRIPT>
42:</HEAD>
43:<BODY onLoad="StartUp()">
44:TO: <SPAN ID=todata1></SPAN><BR>
45:FROM: <SPAN ID=fromdata1></SPAN><BR>
46:CC: <SPAN ID=ccdata1></SPAN><BR>
47:SUBJECT: <SPAN ID=subjectdata1></SPAN><BR>
48:BODY: <SPAN ID=bodydata1></SPAN><BR>
49:POSTSCRIPT: <SPAN ID=psdata1></SPAN><BR>
50:<BR>
51:<HR>
52:<BR>
53:TO: <SPAN ID=todata2></SPAN><BR>
54:FROM: <SPAN ID=fromdata2></SPAN><BR>
55:CC: <SPAN ID=ccdata2></SPAN><BR>
56:SUBJECT: <SPAN ID=subjectdata2></SPAN><BR>
57:BODY: <SPAN ID=bodydata2></SPAN><BR>
58:POSTSCRIPT: <SPAN ID=psdata2></SPAN><BR>
59:</BODY>
60:</HTML>
```

When you run the file, note that the output that appears in the document window is the data from the two message files. This output is illustrated in Figure 2.4.

Line 6 declares the second instance of the xmldom object needed for the second XML file. Lines 9 and 10 create the object and the file's attachment.

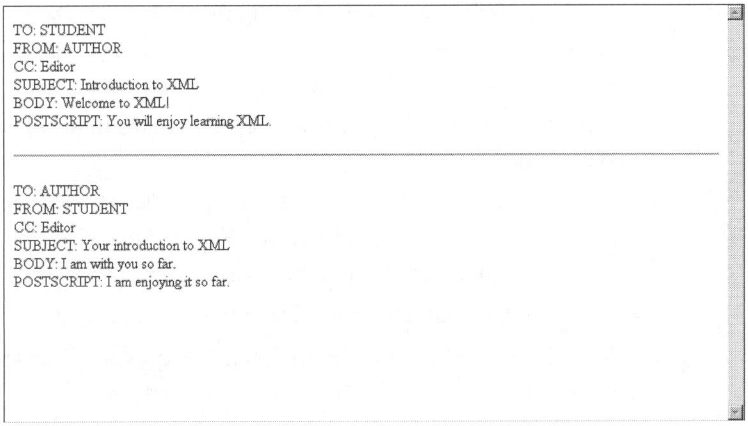

FIGURE 2.4

The output of reading and displaying two files.

```
TO: STUDENT
FROM: AUTHOR
CC: Editor
SUBJECT: Introduction to XML
BODY: Welcome to XML!
POSTSCRIPT: You will enjoy learning XML.


TO: AUTHOR
FROM: STUDENT
CC: Editor
SUBJECT: Your introduction to XML
BODY: I am with you so far.
POSTSCRIPT: I am enjoying it so far.
```

In lines 33 to 38, the second xmldom object is used to extract the data from the file and insert it into the second set of <span> tags.

Lines 50 to 52 create a separation between the two sets of <span> tags, and lines 53 to 58 define the second target set of tags.

Summary

The initial examples of reading and displaying XML data all relied on the dynamic updating of the innerText property of HTML tags. Therefore, your first sample code dealt solely with that. From this, you learned how to read the data using a simple array of nodes. This process works as long as all the nodes are at the same level. Since it's an array, you can easily add more data nodes to the XML file by using larger subscripts on the array and adding more HTML tags as the targets for the data.

Q&A

Q What's the difference between static and dynamic text?

A Static text is placed between the tags when the file is created and is never modified by any process. Dynamic text is assigned to the innerText property of the HTML tag, and the assignment is done when the code is executed.

Q What's the difference between the definition of an object and an instance of an object?

A The definition of an object is the listing of the variable names, as well as descriptions of the functions and what they do. No memory is allocated in the definition, so it's impossible to assign values to the variables. When memory is allocated, the identifiers can then be assigned values and the functions can be called, and you have an instance of an object.

Q What's the main concern when reading more than one XML file from an HTML file?

A The main concern is the usual one: keeping the identifier names unique. In this hour, you used xmlDoc1 and xmlDoc2 as the names of the two XML DOM objects and slight modifications of the HTML tag names.

Q Can ActiveX controls be used in any browser?

A No, they generally work only in Internet Explorer. However, the latest version of Netscape, version 6.0, does provide some support.

Workshop

Quiz

1. What are objects made up of?

    a. Data components

    b. Functions

    c. Comments

    d. All of the above

    e. a and b

2. Why is the <span> tag commonly used as the target of a data insertion?

    a. It's specifically reserved for that purpose.

    b. It has no assigned behavior, so there are no additional effects when it's used.

    c. It's a tag that has been added to HTML to serve as a link to XML data.

3. Why is it considered good design practice to construct your project by using smaller, distinct files?

    a. Smaller entries are easier to understand.

    b. Splitting projects into distinct elements allows the elements to be reused in other applications.

    c. If large files are split into smaller pieces, it's possible for a section to arrive and be used by the application before the remainder arrives.

    d. All of the above.

Answers

1. e
2. b
3. d

Exercises

1. Given the following XML file, write an HTML program that will read this data and insert the contents into properly named HTML tags:

```
<?xml version="1.0" ?>


<Customer>
<FirstName>Jane</FirstName>
<LastName>Reader</LastName>
<Address>100 Main Street</Address>
<City>Anytown</City>
<State_Province>Somewhere</State_Province>
<PostalCode>12345</PostalCode>
</Customer>
```

2. Create another XML file similar to the one in the previous exercise and write an HTML file that will read the data from both of them.

HOUR 3

Objects and XML

In the previous hour, you were introduced to objects, specifically the xmldom object. This hour will explore objects in greater depth, within the context of XML. It will then examine some of the additional functions of the xmldom object and explore other ways to read and examine the data in an XML file. Reading the data from the XML in more than one way gives you more than one perspective on the data and the mechanisms for reading it.

In this hour, you'll learn the following:

- What objects are and how they're related to the structure of XML files
- How to create hierarchical trees that represent HTML files
- The descriptions of the node and nodelist objects and how they're used to extract data from an XML file
- How to create an HTML file that can be used to extract the data from any single-level XML file
- Some of the fundamentals of how to handle errors when reading the data from an XML file

The Relationship Between Objects and XML

In object-oriented programming (OOP), a *class* is the definition of a collection of data and functions enclosed in a common wrapper. The name of the class is the name of the wrapper. When you're working with functions that are contained in classes, it's common to use the word *method* instead. Both terms will be used here.

To better understand the concept of classes, consider a simple oven. It has two properties, one that can be set to either on or off and one that can be set to a temperature. Once these values are set in the initialization, they remain at those values. Therefore, you need some method to change them. There would be two companion methods, one to change the on/off switch and the other to change the temperature setting.

OOP is a very powerful approach to the design and construction of software, and less and less is being built without the involvement of object-oriented techniques. This hour will demonstrate the concepts of OOP as applied to the XML language.

Hour 1 presented an XML email document and a hierarchical tree that represented the structure of the document. (See Listing 1.2 for the document and Figure 1.2 for the hierarchical tree.) The document can also be represented in the form of a template (see Figure 3.1), which is equivalent to the definition in the hierarchical tree. The template represents the model that you're using to define the form of your data. At this level, the word *class* is used to describe the template.

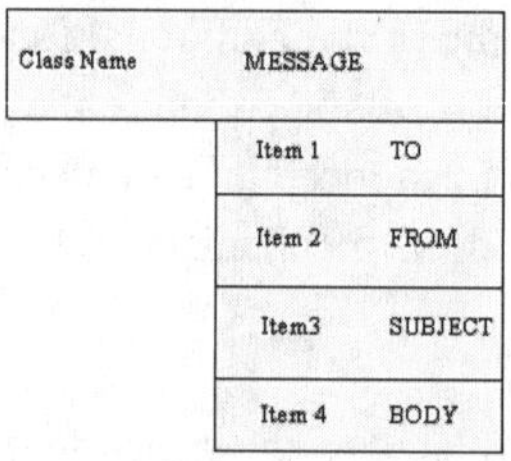

FIGURE 3.1

The abstraction of the message as a class.

Class Name	MESSAGE	
	Item 1	TO
	Item 2	FROM
	Item3	SUBJECT
	Item 4	BODY

Once you have the definition of your class, you can then create instances of it. An instance of a class is where memory is allocated for all of the components of the definition. Therefore, *instances* are the items that you actually manipulate, and an instance of a class is known as an *object*. The act of creating an instance of a class is *instantiation*.

To illustrate these concepts, the XML files shown in Listings 3.1, 3.2, and 3.3 all represent objects constructed according to the template from Figure 3.1. The structure of the three files is identical except for the contents of the data entries.

LISTING 3.1 The First Instance of the Message Class

```
1: <?xml version="1.0" ?>
2:
3: <MESSAGE>
4: <TO>STUDENT</TO>
5: <FROM>AUTHOR</FROM>
6: <SUBJECT>Introduction to XML</SUBJECT>
7: <BODY>Welcome to XML!</BODY>
8: </MESSAGE>
```

LISTING 3.2 The Second Instance of the Message Class

```
1: <?xml version="1.0" ?>
2: <!-- The structure of this file is identical to that of
     the previous one. The only differences are in the contents
     of the data entries. -->
3: <MESSAGE>
4: <TO>AUTHOR</TO>
5: <FROM>STUDENT</FROM>
6: <SUBJECT>Your introduction to XML</SUBJECT>
7: <BODY>I am with you so far.</BODY>
8: </MESSAGE>
```

LISTING 3.3 The Third Instance of the Message Class

```
1: <?xml version="1.0" ?>
2: <!-- The structure of this file is identical to that of the previous two
     listings. The only differences are in the contents of the data entries. -->
3: <MESSAGE>
4: <TO>STUDENTS</TO>
5: <FROM>TEACHER</FROM>
6: <SUBJECT>Continued instruction in XML</SUBJECT>
7: <BODY>Do you follow what I am saying?</BODY>
8: </MESSAGE>
```

If necessary, you can modify the diagrams you used previously to note that an object is being represented, rather than a class. All you need to do is include one or more data values in the diagram. This is demonstrated in Figures 3.2 and 3.3.

FIGURE 3.2

A diagram representing the message of the previous code listing.

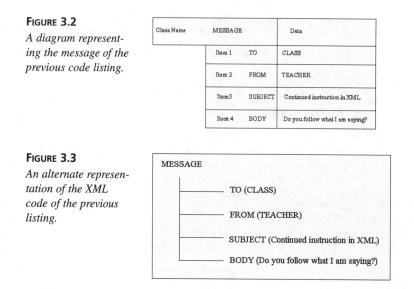

Class Name	MESSAGE		Data
	Item 1	TO	CLASS
	Item 2	FROM	TEACHER
	Item 3	SUBJECT	Continued instruction in XML
	Item 4	BODY	Do you follow what I am saying?

FIGURE 3.3

An alternate representation of the XML code of the previous listing.

MESSAGE

TO (CLASS)

FROM (TEACHER)

SUBJECT (Continued instruction in XML)

BODY (Do you follow what I am saying?)

Creating Hierarchical Trees for HTML Files

In Hour 2, there was a correspondence between the HTML <span> tags and the data in the XML files. Given this relationship, it's possible to construct hierarchical trees to represent the structure of the HTML file. The HTML code from Listing 2.2 is reproduced in Listing 3.4, and the corresponding hierarchical tree is shown in Figure 3.4.

LISTING 3.4　A Simple HTML Listing Needed as an Example to Convert into the Corresponding Tree Structure

```
 1: <html>
 2: <head>
 3: <title> An HTML used as an example to demonstrate the
    corresponding tree</title>
 4: <script language=JavaScript>
 5: ...
 6: </script>
 7: </head>
 8: <body bgcolor="ffffff" onLoad="StartUp()">
 9: TO: <span id=todata></span><br>
10: FROM: <span id=fromdata></span><br>
11: SUBJECT: <span id=subjectdata></span><br>
12: BODY: <span id=bodydata></span><br>
13: </body>
14: </html>
```

FIGURE 3.4

The hierarchical tree for the HTML listing.

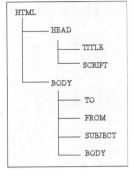

This natural correspondence between the diagrams for the HTML and XML files can and should be used to model the organization of a Web site where XML is used. The common consensus now is that months of planning must be done before you launch an e-commerce site. This amount of preliminary work means that extensive modeling must be done, and these diagrams provide a clear, concise way to do it.

The Node and Nodelist Objects

In Hour 2, you read the data from the nodes in sequence without trying to determine if the node was in the correct position.

Therefore, your next step will be to learn more about some of the objects defined in XML so that you can carry out more robust data manipulation.

When a tree representing the data of an XML file is used, each of the terminal branches is known as a *node* of the tree. When the XML dom object reads the data from the XML file, each of the tag pairs is used by the XML dom object to create an instance of the node class. The node class is defined in the XML dom class, and the node is the basic component of the way the data is represented in memory. The node object has several different properties, and so far you've used only the text property. It's important to note that every tag pair leads to the creation of a node.

Another obvious property that the node object contains is the nodeName property.

For example, if the node is

```
<SUBJECT>Introduction to XML</SUBJECT>
```

then the nodeName property of the node would be SUBJECT. The process of conversion is shown in Figure 3.5.

FIGURE 3.5

The transformation of data into a node.

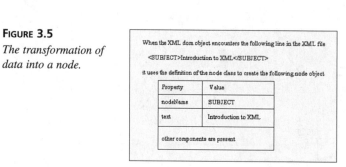

When you were reading the data in the programs in Hour 2, your indices on the array of nodes were hard-coded, as shown in the following snippet of code reproduced from Listing 2.2:

```
todata.innerText=RootElement1.childNodes(0).text;
fromdata.innerText=RootElement1.childNodes(1).text;
subjectdata.innerText=RootElement1.childNodes(2).text;
bodydata.innerText=RootElement1.childNodes(3).text;
```

This requires that you know precisely how many nodes there are in the list. If any attempt is made to read more nodes than are in the list, it's an error. Hard-coding the size of an array is poor programming practice, making the code very dependent on the form of the data.

When the data of the XML file is used to create the nodes corresponding to the tag pairs, all of the nodes at the same level are collected into an instance of the nodeList object. As the name implies, this object type is an ordered aggregation of nodes, so the available properties and methods are those that are used to navigate through the collection. This process is illustrated in Figure 3.6.

FIGURE 3.6

Converting nodes into a nodeList object.

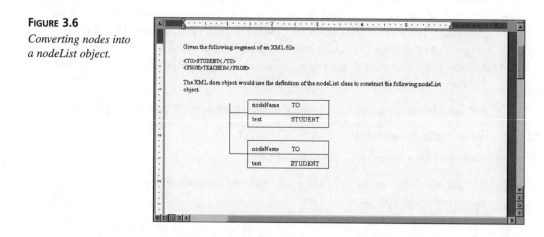

To write more flexible code, you can use the nodeList object. The `childNodes` property of the root element contains an instance of the nodeList object. One property of the nodeList object that can make your code much more flexible is the length property, which stores the number of child nodes that the root node has. Once you have the number of nodes, the list of child nodes can be traversed as an array, avoiding the problems inherent in hard-coding the data extraction. The next section contains an example program that demonstrates these concepts.

Creating a Generic Data Extractor for XML Files

Your next program will perform the same type of data extraction as was done in Listing 2.2. However, this time you'll adapt your traversal to the number of nodes by first determining what the number is and then using a loop to step through the array. Furthermore, the names of the nodes will be extracted and used as the labels. The XML data file that you'll use as your source will be Listing 2.3.

The following code will read the data from an XML file. The first step is to determine the number of nodes in the list of data nodes. Once that's done, a loop is used to step through the array and extract both the name and the contents of the node. These two values are then inserted into tags and placed in the body of the HTML file.

LISTING 3.5 Reading the Data from an XML File Using an Array

```
1:<HTML>
2:<HEAD>
3:<TITLE>Using the Array Properties Of the nodeList to Read
   an XML File</TITLE>
4:<SCRIPT LANGUAGE="JavaScript">
5:<!--
6: var RootElement1;
7:// nodecount will store the number of nodes containing
8:// data in the XML file.
9: var nodecount;
10: var xmlDoc1=new ActiveXObject("microsoft.xmldom");
11: xmlDoc1.load("xmlhour4-1.xml");
12:
13:  function StartUp()
14:  {
15:   if(xmlDoc1.readyState=="4")
16:   {
17:    StartLoading();
18:   }
```

LISTING 3.5 continued

```
19:  else
20:  {
21:   alert("Process could not start");
22:  }
23:    }
24:
25:  function StartLoading()
26:   {
27:// loopindex is the counter used to control the loop
28:// that traverses through the nodes
29:    var loopindex;
30:    RootElement1=xmlDoc1.documentElement;
31: // We now extract the number of nodes in the list
32:    nodecount=RootElement1.childNodes.length;
33:    for(loopindex=0;loopindex<nodecount;loopindex++)
34:    {
35: // This line will write the name of the node to the
36: // body section of the HTML file
37: document.write(RootElement1.childNodes.item(loopindex)
     .nodeName+": ");
38:// This line will write out the contents of the node to
39://  the body section of the HTML file.
40:    document.write(RootElement1.childNodes.
     item(loopindex).text+"<BR>");
41:    }
42:   }
43://-->
44:</SCRIPT>
45:</HEAD>
46:<BODY onLoad="StartUp()">
47:<!-- Since all of the content is now being written from
48: the JavaScript section, it is no longer
49: necessary to put anything here. -->
50:</BODY>
51:</HTML>
```

This code will generate the same output as Listing 2.2 when it reads the data in Listing 2.3. However, this code is much more flexible because the number of nodes and their names are no longer hard-coded.

Note that the <BODY> section of the HTML file in lines 47 through 49 is nothing more than a comment. In this case, you're dynamically writing the contents from the JavaScript code.

On line 32, the number of nodes in the XML file is extracted. On line 29, a variable that controls the loop is declared. A for loop is used to step through the array of nodes, and this loop is defined in lines 33 through 41. Since the code determines the number of nodes for loop control by using the length property, this code will work for an arbitrary number of nodes in the list.

The extraction and writing of the node's name is done on line 37, and the extraction and writing of the text is done on line 40.

Since the code samples the properties to determine the number of nodes and their names, you don't need to change the code to modify the nodes or add additional ones. This is the point of the next example.

Listing 3.6 is Listing 2.3 with two nodes added and a name change.

3

LISTING 3.6   Listing 2.3 with Modifications

```
 1: <?xml version="1.0" ?>
 2:
 3: <MESSAGE>
 4: <TO>STUDENT</TO>
 5: <FROM>AUTHOR</FROM>
 6: <CC>Editor</CC>
 7: <BCC>Publisher</BCC>
 8: <FILE>Archive</FILE>
 9: <SUBJECT>Introduction to XML</SUBJECT>
10: <BODY>Welcome to XML!</BODY>
11: <PS.>You will enjoy learning XML.</PS.>
12: </MESSAGE>
```

Use the code in Listing 3.5 to read this file. Note that the changes in the number and names of the nodes are easily handled.

Error Handling

Error handling is a fundamental part of computer programming and must always be done. This is especially true when you're conducting commerce over the Web with what are, essentially, strangers. When there's a personal face-to-face relationship between buyer and seller, there's a degree of additional credibility that can you can use to recover from errors. This simply doesn't exist in Web commerce. In terms of errors, it's "one and done."

When you're opening files for processing, you need to examine the results of your attempt to open the files to determine if that command has succeeded. The next modification of the previous program will examine the values of some of the properties if the file doesn't load successfully.

Go back to Listing 3.5 and modify the initialization section to match the following. The changes are in bold:

```
    var xmlDoc1=new ActiveXObject("microsoft.xmldom");
alert(xmlDoc1);
xmlDoc1.load("listing3-8.xml");
```

If you run the modified code, you'll see that the message text in the alert box is

```
    [object]
```

This tells you that the minimum criteria for the creation of the xmlDoc1 object were available at the point of creation. Therefore, it was successfully created and object is the same type as the xmlDoc1 variable.

Go back to Listing 3.5 and addthe following line in bold at the indicated location:

```
RootElement1=xmlDoc1.documentElement;
    alert(RootElement1);
```

When you run the modified file, you'll see that the message in the corresponding alert box is

```
    [object]
```

The documentElement property of the xmlDoc1 object is where the data resides. This tells you that not only was the xmlDoc1 object successfully created, but that the data was assigned to the documentElement property.

Go back to Listing 3.5 and modify the filename of the load function so that it attempts to open a file that doesn't exist. Save and run the file again. Note that the message text in the first alert box is still [object], but the message text in the second is now

```
    [null].
```

The program then proceeds to crash because there are no nodes to read.

This demonstrates that when the opening of the program fails, the system assigns the constant null to the RootElement1 object. This constant is reserved for objects that do exist but have no contents that can be read. This allows you to create wrappers around your code that perform a graceful exit when the code is invalid. A simple if conditional where the boolean is a test for the null value is sufficient to avoid crashes with this form.

Modify the `StartLoading()` function in Listing 3.5 to match Listing 3.7. The lines to be added are in bold. The additional lines provide a simple test of the contents of the xmlDoc1 object's documentElement property so that if the data isn't available, no attempt is made to read it. The program simply terminates rather than crashing on a failed data read.

LISTING 3.7 Error Handling by Testing for a Failure to Properly Load the Data

```
 1: function StartLoading()
 2:   {
 3: // loopindex is the counter used to control the loop that
 4: // traverses through the nodes
 5:     var loopindex;
 6:     RootElement1=xmlDoc1.documentElement;
 7:     if(RootElement1==null)
 8:     {
 9:      alert("The root node is null");
10:      document.write("<B><BIG>The data of the XML file
         cannot be accessed</BIG></B><BR>");
11:     }
12:     else
13:     {
14: // We now extract the number of nodes in the list
15:     nodecount=RootElement1.childNodes.length;
16:     for(loopindex=0;loopindex<nodecount;loopindex++)
17:       {
18: // This line will write the name of the node to the body
19: // section of the HTML file
20:         document.write(RootElement1.childNodes.item(loopindex).
            nodeName+": ");
21: // This line will write out the contents of the node to
22: // the body section of the HTML file.
23:         document.write(RootElement1.childNodes.item(loopindex).
            text+"<BR>");
24:       }
25:     }
26:   }
```

Run the file by accessing an existing XML file and attempting to access one that doesn't exist.

The changes and consequences are straightforward. By checking the root node for existence, you can avoid the possibility of fatal errors and gracefully exit without crashing the program.

There are error handling objects that are part of the XML standards, and they should also be used as much as possible. These objects will be examined in Hour 7.

Summary

Object-oriented programming, or OOP, is a software engineering process that offers many advantages over other approaches, and it's used in the IE implementation of XML. This hour started with a brief introduction to the basic principles of applying OOP to XML.

When the xmldom object reads the data from an XML file, each pair of matched opening and closing tags is used to create a node. The nodes at the same level in the hierarchical tree are then collected into an ordered nodeList, which has properties that can be used to move through the list. You used these properties to create an HTML program that reads the data from any HTML file.

Q&A

Q What's the difference between a class and an object?

A The word *object* is often misused when referring to the entities in OOP. A *class* is a definition or a template for how a type of object is to be constructed. There's no memory allocated, so it cannot be used as anything other than a blueprint(An *object* is the result when the class definition is used to create an entity with allocated memory that can be used to store and manipulate data)The term *an instance of a class* is almost synonymous with *object*. It's just a bit more precise.

Q Why is it preferable to use code that can read generic XML files over code that reads only specific files?

A In the interest of efficiency, it's always better to reuse code that's known to be correct. Also, the definitions of data are always changing, so it's much better to use code that requires only minimal modifications when the data is altered.

Q What's the difference between the node and nodeList objects?

A A node is constructed when the xmldom object encounters a set of matching opening and closing tags. The nodeList object is a list of nodes.

Workshop

Quiz

1. The term class refers to what kind of entity?

    a. An object definition

    b. An object that can be updated

    c. A variable

    d. None of the above

2. Is it difficult to construct simultaneous hierarchical trees for XML files and the HTML code that will read them?

   a. Yes, it is. The structure of HTML files makes it difficult to create matching hierarchical trees.

   b. No, it's not. Since both HTML and XML files are built using tag pairs, the trees are very similar.

   c. It's irrelevant because you don't create trees corresponding to HTML files.

   d. Yes, it is. The differences between XML and HTML files are so pronounced that creating simultaneous trees is very hard.

3. While error handling is always important in programming, why is it even more important on the World Wide Web?

   a. Since there's no difference between traditional businesses and businesses on the Web, there's no distinction.

   b. The Web generates more revenue than traditional businesses.

   c. The Web is inherently less personal than a face-to-face relationship with the customer.

   d. There's more competition on the Web.

4. In general, should any container object, such as a file or a root node, be examined before use to determine if it has been properly initialized?

   a. Yes, it's possible to satisfy the minimal criteria for creation even though the object cannot be used.

   b. Yes, the object may not have been created.

   c. Yes. In general, any attempt to use an object that hasn't been properly initialized will cause a fatal error.

   d. All of the above.

   e. a and c above.

Answers

1. a
2. b
3. The best answer is c, although b and d could be true as well
4. The answer is d, and you often have to determine the extent to which the object has been constructed

Exercises

1. Modify any listing of an XML file so it doesn't contain an enclosing initial tag. For example, remove the `<Message>` tags from any listing that contains them. Use Listing 3.5 with the two alert boxes added to read the file. Note the results of the error tests provided by the alert boxes.

2. In Hour 2, you made several modifications to an XML file's tags to demonstrate the types of errors that can be made. Modify an XML file by making some of those same errors, and then use the file as the input into Listing 3.5. Note the form of the errors that are generated.

HOUR 4

XML Data Islands

In general, building a project by creating and combining smaller files makes the application more flexible and maintainable. So far, you've followed that strategy as you've built your examples. However, that's not the only possible approach. This hour will explore ways to insert the XML code directly into the HTML files. When this is done, the XML code is known as an *island*.

It's considered good programming practice to create separate files whenever possible, so you may be wondering why you'd want to insert the XML code into the HTML files. One example is when the amount of code is very small and the overhead of creating an additional file and importing it is just too high. The second example is when the XML code has no reasonable chance of being used in another project. If you have a file that will only be used with another file, it makes sense to bind them together to avoid confusion.

In this hour, you'll learn the following:

- How to insert XML code directly into an HTML file
- How to dynamically update the contents of a node
- Linking the information input via HTML to display the desired list of messages from an XML file

The Basics of XML Data Islands

If you had to guess how XML code is inserted into an HTML file, you'd probably give the logical answer: "Use the XML tag." Which is correct. The XML tag is now supported, and it informs the browser that the contents are to be parsed and interpreted using the XML parser. Like most other HTML tags, the XML tag has attributes. The most important attribute is the ID, which provides for the unique naming of the code. The contents of the XML tag come from one of two sources: inline XML code or an imported XML file.

Using Inline Code in an XML Data Island

When you're creating a program and there's a block of code to be run, there are two ways to make that code part of your program. It can be in an exterior location, such as a file or another part of the program, and can be called from the current location. (This is commonly done when the block is large or is to be accessed from other locations as well.) Or, if the code appears in the current location, it's said to be *inline*.

Listing 4.1 demonstrates the syntax of embedding XML code inside an HTML file.

LISTING 4.1   Embedding XML Code Inside an HTML File

```
 1: <html>
 2: <!-- This is the first example of how to embed XML code
 3:      into HTML files. -->
 4: <head>
 5: <title>First Example of XML Code Islands</title>
 6: </head>
 7: <body bgcolor="ffffff" >
 8: This is before the XML code<br>
 9: <XML ID=message>
10: <MESSAGE>
11: <TO>Student</TO>
12: <FROM>Author</FROM>
13: <SUBJECT>XML Code Islands</SUBJECT>
14: <BODY>This is an example of XML code embedded inside HTML code</BODY>
15: </MESSAGE>
16: </XML>
17: This is after the XML code.<br>
18: </body>
19: </html>
```

When you view this file, the result is rather dull:

```
This is before the XML code
This is after the XML code.
```

The browser has detected the XML code, but it hasn't been instructed how to display the contents. Of course, the solution is to add some JavaScript code that will do that.

Modify Listing 4.1 to match Listing 4.2. The changes are highlighted in bold. Note that the lines of HTML text have been removed.

LISTING 4.2   Displaying the XML Code Embedded in an HTML File

```
1: <html>
2:
3:<!--This is the first example of how to embed XML code
4:    into HTML files. The filename is listing4-2.html. -->
5:
6:<head>
7:<title>Second Example of XML Code Islands</title>
8:<SCRIPT LANGUAGE=JavaScript>
9:<!--
10:function StartUp()
11:{
12: var RootElement1=message.documentElement;
13: var nodecount=RootElement1.childNodes.length;
14: var loopindex;
15:// This will store the current node that has been
16:// extracted for processing.
17: var CurrentNode;
18: var ErrorMessage="Error, data not defined";
19:    if(RootElement1==null)
20:    {
21:     alert("The root node is null");
22:     document.write("<B><BIG>The data of the XML file
       cannot be accessed</BIG></B><BR>");
23:    }
24:    else
25:    {
26:     for(loopindex=0;loopindex<nodecount;loopindex++)
27:     {
28:     CurrentNode=RootElement1.childNodes.item(loopindex);
29:     switch(CurrentNode. nodeName)
30:     {
31:      case "TO":
32:      todata.innerText=CurrentNode.text;
33:      break;
34:      case "FROM":
35:      fromdata.innerText=CurrentNode.text;
36:      break;
37:      case "SUBJECT":
38:      subjectdata.innerText=CurrentNode.text;
39:      break;
```

4

LISTING 4.2   continued

```
40:    case "BODY":
41:    bodydata.innerText=CurrentNode.text;
42:    break;
43:    default:
44:    todata.innerText=ErrorMessage;
45:    fromdata.innerText=ErrorMessage;
46:    subjectdata.innerText=ErrorMessage;
47:    bodydata.innerText=ErrorMessage;
48:    }
49:    }
50:  }
51: }
52://-->
53:</SCRIPT>
54:</head>
55:<body bgcolor="ffffff" onLoad="StartUp()" >
56:<XML ID=message>
57:<MESSAGE>
58:<TO>Student</TO>
59:<FROM>Author</FROM>
60:<SUBJECT>XML Code Islands</SUBJECT>
61:<BODY>This is an example of XML code embedded inside
    HTML code</BODY>
62:</MESSAGE>
63:</XML>
64:<DIV ID=to STYLE="font-weight:bold;color:blue">
65:TO:
66:<SPAN ID=todata></SPAN>
67:</DIV>
68:<DIV ID=from STYLE="font-weight:bold;color:teal">
69:FROM:
70:<SPAN ID=fromdata></SPAN>
71:</DIV>
72:<DIV ID=subject STYLE="font-weight:bold;color:red">
73:SUBJECT:
74:<SPAN ID=subjectdata></SPAN>
75:</DIV>
76:<DIV ID=body STYLE="font-weight:bold;color:magenta">
77:BODY:
78:<SPAN ID=bodydata></SPAN>
79:</DIV>
80:</body>
81: </html>
```

The appearance of the file when viewed in IE is shown in Figure 4.1.

FIGURE 4.1
The embedded XML data.

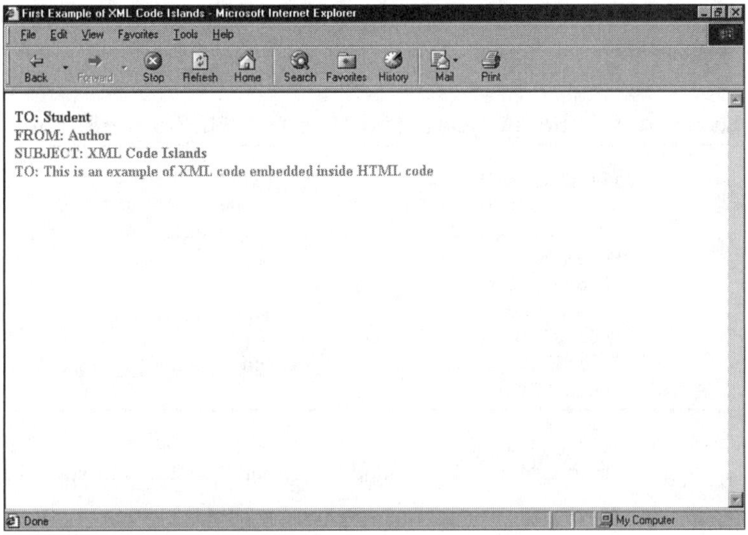

In this case, you go backward and hard-code some of the features. However, since you're using the JavaScript switch statement, modifying the code when nodes are changed is fairly easy. Lines 43 to 47 provide some form of error handling, in the sense that an error message is inserted into every tag. Such errors are generated when a node name is encountered that doesn't match any of the names in lines 31, 34, 37, or 40. This is probably overkill, but that depends on how seriously you take the appearance of a node that's not handled in the switch statement.

Lines 64 through 79 define the targets for the data insertion. In this case, you've wrapped each of the `<SPAN>` tags with a `<DIV>` tag that modifies the appearance of the text.

Go back to listing 4-2.html and modify the line

```
<TO>Student</TO>
```

to

```
<TA>Student</TA>
```

View it in a browser. Note that several error messages are generated. This is because the code assumes that there's a node with the name `<TO>`.

Importing a File into an XML Data Island

Rather than embed the XML data code in the HTML file, in the long term it's much more efficient to create a file and import it. You can easily do so by using the SRC attribute of the XML tag, which is demonstrated in the following exercise.

Listing 4.3 contains the XML data that you'll be importing. The filename for reference is listing4-3.xml.

LISTING 4.3   The XML Data File That You'll Import into Your HTML File

```
1: <?xml version="1.0"?>
2: <!-- This file is the source for the importation of a file
3:      into an XML data island. Filenamelisting4-3.xml -->
4: <MESSAGE>
5: <TO>Student</TO>
6: <FROM>Author</FROM>
7: <SUBJECT>XML Code Islands</SUBJECT>
8: <BODY>This is an example of embedded XML code imported from a file.</BODY>
9: </MESSAGE>
```

Go back to Listing 4.2 and modify the XML section to match the following:

```
<XML ID=message SRC="listing4-3.xml">
</XML>
```

The HTML file will now import the data in Listing 4.3, so that will be the output when it's viewed.

Importing Multiple Files into XML Data Islands

It's possible to import more than one XML file into an HTML file, and this is demonstrated in the following exercise.

Create the XML file shown in Listing 4.4 and save it as listing4-4.xml.

LISTING 4.4   A Second XML File Similar to the First for Importing into the HTML File

```
1: <?xml version="1.0"?>
2: <!-- This file is the second source for the importation of
3:      a file into an XML data island. Filename
4: listing4-4.xml -->
5: <MESSAGE>
6: <TO>Author</TO>
7: <FROM>Student</FROM>
8: <SUBJECT>XML Code Islands</SUBJECT>
9: <BODY>This is a reply to your message about XML data islands.</BODY>
10: </MESSAGE>
```

Go back to Listing 4.2 and modify it to match Listing 4.5. The additions are marked in bold.

LISTING 4.5   An HTML File with Two XML Data Islands That Will Import and
Display Two XML Data Files

```
1:<html>
2: <!!-- This example contains two XML data islands
     so that two XML data files can be imported and displayed.
     The filename is listing4-5.html. -->
3:<head>
4:<SCRIPT LANGUAGE=JavaScript>
5:<!--
6:function StartUp()
7:{
8: var RootElement1=message.documentElement;
9: var nodecount=RootElement1.childNodes.length;
10: var loopindex;
11:// This will store the current node that has been
12:// extracted for processing.
13: var CurrentNode;
14: var ErrorMessage="Error, data not defined";
15: /* The ID name of the XML tag serves as the root node
16:    of the tree. Therefore, the data values of message
17:    can be examined. */
18:    lastURL=message.url;
19:    alert(lastURL);
20:    isValidate=message.validateOnParse;
21:    alert(isValidate);
22:    xmlType=message.xml;
23:    alert(xmlType);
24:    numNodeType=message.nodeType;
25:    alert(numNodeType);
26:    if(RootElement1==null)
27:    {
28:     alert("The root node is null");
29:     document.write("<B><BIG>The data of the XML file
           cannot be accessed</BIG></B><BR>");
30:    }
31:    else
32:    {
33:     for(loopindex=0;loopindex<nodecount;loopindex++)
34:     {
35:     CurrentNode=RootElement1.childNodes.item(loopindex);
36:     switch(CurrentNode.nodeName)
37:     {
38:      case "TO":
39:      todata.innerText=CurrentNode.text;
40:      break;
41:      case "FROM":
42:      fromdata.innerText=CurrentNode. text;
43:      break;
```

4

LISTING 4.5   continued

```
44:      case "SUBJECT":
45:      subjectdata.innerText=CurrentNode.text;
46:      break;
47:      case "BODY":
48:      bodydata.innerText=CurrentNode.text;
49:      break;
50:      default:
51:      todata.innerText=ErrorMessage;
52:      fromdata.innerText=ErrorMessage;
53:      subjectdata.innerText=ErrorMessage;
54:      bodydata.innerText=ErrorMessage;
55:      }
56:    }
57:  }
58: }
59://-->
60:</SCRIPT>
61:</head>
62:<body bgcolor="ffffff" onLoad="StartUp()" >
63:<XML ID=message SRC="listing4-3-3.xml">
64:</XML>
65:<DIV ID=to STYLE="font-weight:bold;color:blue">
66: TO:
67:<SPAN ID=todata></SPAN>
68:</DIV>
69:<DIV ID=from STYLE="font-weight:bold;color:teal">
70:FROM:
71:<SPAN ID=fromdata></SPAN>
72:</DIV>
73:<DIV ID=subject STYLE="font-weight:bold;color:red">
74:SUBJECT:
75:<SPAN ID=subjectdata></SPAN>
76:</DIV>
77:<DIV ID=body STYLE="font-weight:bold;color:magenta">
78:BODY:
79:<SPAN ID=bodydata></SPAN>
80:</DIV>
81:<!-- The following is just separation. -->
82:<br><hr><br>
83:<!-- This is the island that will import the second
84:      file.  Note that the value of the ID differs from 86)
         the previous.-->
85:<XML ID=message1 SRC="listing4-4.xml">
86:</XML>
87:<!-- These are the targets for the data of the second
88:      file. Note that the ID values must be different
89:      from the first. -->
90:<DIV ID=to1 STYLE="font-weight:bold;color:blue">
91:TO:
```

```
92:<SPAN ID=todata1></SPAN>
93:</DIV>
94:<DIV ID=from1 STYLE="font-weight:bold;color:teal">
95:FROM:
96:<SPAN ID=fromdata1></SPAN>
97:</DIV>
98:<DIV ID=subject1 STYLE="font-weight: bold;color:red">
99:SUBJECT:
100:<SPAN ID=subjectdata1></SPAN>
101:</DIV>
102:<DIV ID=body1 STYLE="font-weight:bold;color:magenta">
103:BODY:
104:<SPAN ID=bodydata1></SPAN>
105:</DIV>
106:<SCRIPT LANGUAGE=JavaScript>
107:<!--
108: var RootElement1=message1.documentElement;
109: var nodecount=RootElement1.childNodes.length;
110: var loopindex;
111:// This will store the current node that has been
112:// extracted for processing.
113: var CurrentNode;
114: var ErrorMessage="Error, data not defined";
115: /* The ID name of the XML tag serves as the root node
116: of the tree. Therefore, the data values of message can
   be examined. */
117:    lastURL=message1.url;
118:    alert(lastURL);
119:    isValidate=message1.validateOnParse;
120:    alert(isValidate);
121:    xmlType=message1.xml;
122:    alert(xmlType);
123:    numNodeType=message1.nodeType;
124:    alert(numNodeType);
125:    if(RootElement1==null)
126:    {
127:     alert("The root node is null");
128:     document.write("<B><BIG>The data of the XML file
          cannot be accessed</BIG></B><BR>");
129:    }
130:    else
131:    {
132:     for(loopindex=0;loopindex<nodecount;loopindex++)
133:     {
134:    CurrentNode=RootElement1.childNodes. item(loopindex);
135:     switch(CurrentNode.nodeName)
136:     {
137:      case "TO":
138:      todata1.innerText=CurrentNode.text;
139:      break;
```

4

LISTING 4.5   continued

```
140:    case "FROM":
141:    fromdata1.innerText=CurrentNode.text;
142:    break;
143:    case "SUBJECT":
144:    subjectdata1.innerText=CurrentNode.text;
145:    break;
146:    case "BODY":
147:    bodydata1. innerText=CurrentNode.text;
148:    break;
149:    default:
150:    todata1.innerText=ErrorMessage;
151:    fromdata1.innerText=ErrorMessage;
152:    subjectdata1.innerText=ErrorMessage;
153:    bodydata1.innerText=ErrorMessage;
154:      }
155:    }
156:  }
157://-->
158:</SCRIPT>
159:</body>
160:</html>
```

View the file in IE. Pay very close attention to the contents of the alert boxes, and note that the first file loaded is listing4-3.xml. Knowing the order in which the files are loaded is important if you want to perform some type of simultaneous or sequential processing of the data in the two files. For example, if you're cross-referencing the data between two XML files, the order of examination may be dependent on the order of loading.

The output of the file is demonstrated in Figure 4.2.

Lines 81 and 82 do nothing more than separate the two segments of HTML output. Lines 83 to 158 are a combination of a second set of target HTML tags and the JavaScript code that will extract the XML data and insert it into the HTML tags. The values of the IDs for both had to be modified to avoid a name duplication error.

FIGURE 4.2
Both XML data files.

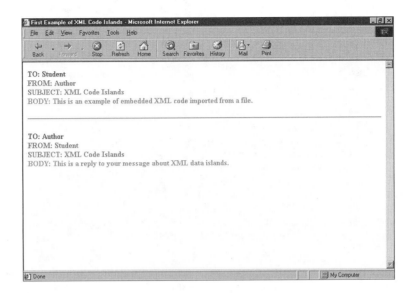

Using XML Data Islands to Update the Contents of a Node

So far, all of the data operations that you've performed on a node have involved extracting the name of the node and the data in the text component. However, the text value of a node is not a read-only property. In the next exercise, you'll use the standard HTML form button element to trigger the updating of the nodes.

Listing 4.6 links the display of the data from an XML file to the clicking of an HTML button. The purpose is to show that your display of data isn't necessarily a passive one, but one that you can control to some extent by interacting with the GUI interface.

LISTING 4.6   Using an HTML Button to Update the Nodes' Contents

```
1:<html>
2:<!-- This is an example of the dynamic updating of the
3:     text property of a node. The filename is
4:     listing4-6.html. -->
5:<head>
6:<SCRIPT LANGUAGE=JavaScript>
7:<!--
8:// These variables are now made global so that we can
9:// access them anywhere in the file.
10: var RootElement1;
```

LISTING 4.6   continued

```
11: var nodecount;
12:function StartUp()
13:{
14: var loopindex;
15:// This will store the current node that has been
16:// extracted for processing.
17: var CurrentNode;
18: var ErrorMessage="Error, data not defined";
19:  RootElement1=message.documentElement;
20:  nodecount=RootElement1.childNodes.length;
21:   if(RootElement1==null)
22:   {
23:   alert("The root node is null");
24:   document.write("<B><BIG>The data of the XML file
      cannot be accessed</BIG></B><BR>");
25:   }
26:   else
27:   {
28:    for(loopindex=0; loopindex<nodecount;loopindex++)
29:    {
30:    CurrentNode=RootElement1.childNodes.item(loopindex);
31:    switch(CurrentNode.nodeName)
32:    {
33:     case "TO":
34:     todata.innerText=CurrentNode.text;
35:     break;
36:     case "FROM":
37:     fromdata.innerText=CurrentNode.text;
38:     break;
39:     case "SUBJECT":
40:     subjectdata.innerText=CurrentNode.text;
41:     break;
42:     case "BODY":
43:     bodydata.innerText=CurrentNode.text;
44:     break;
45:     default:
46:     todata.innerText=ErrorMessage;
47:     fromdata.innerText=ErrorMessage;
48:     subjectdata.innerText=ErrorMessage;
49:     bodydata.innerText=ErrorMessage;
50:    }
51:   }
52:  }
53: }
54://-->
55:</SCRIPT>
56:</head>
57:<body bgcolor="ffffff" onLoad="StartUp()" >
```

```
58:<XML ID=message SRC="xmlhour6-7.xml">
59:</XML>
60:<DIV ID=to STYLE="font-weight:bold;color:blue">
61:TO:
62:<SPAN ID=todata></SPAN>
63:</DIV>
64:<DIV ID=from STYLE="font-weight:bold;color:teal">
65:FROM:
66:<SPAN ID=fromdata></SPAN>
67:</DIV>
68:<DIV ID=subject STYLE="font-weight:bold;color:red">
69:SUBJECT:
70:<SPAN ID=subjectdata></SPAN>
71:</DIV>
72:<DIV ID=body STYLE="font-weight:bold;color:magenta">
73:BODY:
74:<SPAN ID=bodydata></SPAN>
75:</DIV>
76:<!-- The following is just separation. -->
77:<br><hr><br>
78:Click the button to display the characteristics of the
   second message.<br>
79:<FORM>
80:<INPUT TYPE=Button NAME=button1 Value="Click for update"
81:onClick="Update()">
82:</FORM>
83:<!-- These are the targets for the update of the data.
84:     Note that the ID values must be different from the
85:     first. -->
86:<DIV ID=to1 STYLE="font-weight:bold;color:blue">
87:TO:
88:<SPAN ID=todata1></SPAN>
89:</DIV>
90:<DIV ID=from1 STYLE="font-weight:bold;color:teal">
91:FROM:
92:<SPAN ID=fromdata1></SPAN>
93:</DIV>
94:<DIV ID=subject1 STYLE="font-weight:bold;color:red">
95:SUBJECT:
96:<SPAN ID=subjectdata1></SPAN>
97:</DIV>
98:<DIV ID=body1 STYLE="font-weight:bold;color:magenta">
99:BODY:
100:<SPAN ID=bodydata1></SPAN>
101:</DIV>
102:<SCRIPT LANGUAGE=JavaScript>
103:<!--
104: function Update()
105: {
106:  var loopindex;
```

4

LISTING 4.6   continued

```
107:// This will store the current node that has been extracted
108:// for processing.
109: var CurrentNode;
110: var ErrorMessage="Error, data not defined";
111: RootElement1=message.documentElement;
112: nodecount=RootElement1.childNodes.length;
113:  if(RootElement1==null)
114:  {
115:   alert("The root node is null");
116:   document.write("<B><BIG>The data of the XML file
        cannot be accessed</BIG></B><BR>");
117:  }
118:  else
119:  {
120:   for(loopindex=0;loopindex<nodecount;loopindex++)
121:  {
122:  CurrentNode=RootElement1.childNodes.item(loopindex);
123:   switch(CurrentNode.nodeName)
124:   {
125:    case "TO":
126:    CurrentNode.text="All readers";
127:    todata1.innerText=CurrentNode.text;
128:    break;
129:    case "FROM":
130:    CurrentNode.text="Author";
131:    fromdata1.innerText=CurrentNode.text;
132:    break;
133:    case "SUBJECT":
134:    CurrentNode.text="XML Data Files";
135:    subjectdata1.innerText=CurrentNode.text;
136:    break;
137:    case "BODY":
138:    CurrentNode.text="XML data is a dynamic entity
        that can be changed at will";
139:    bodydata1.innerText=CurrentNode.text;
140:    break;
141:    default:
142:    todata1.innerText=ErrorMessage;
143:    fromdata1.innerText=ErrorMessage;
144:    subjectdata1.innerText=ErrorMessage;
145:    bodydata1.innerText=ErrorMessage;
146:   }
147:  }
148:  }
149: }
150://-->
151:</SCRIPT>
152:</body>
153: </html>
```

The initial appearance of this file when viewed in IE is shown in Figure 4.3.

FIGURE **4.3**

*The initial display of
Listing 4.6 before the
button is clicked.*

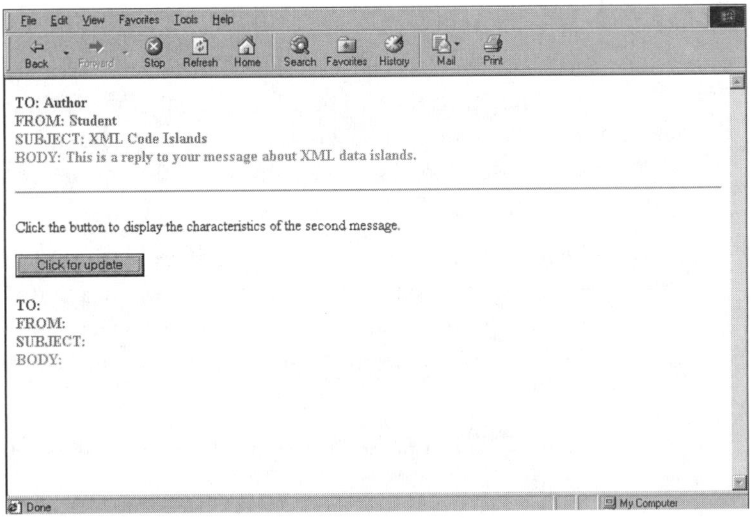

The appearance of the file after the button is clicked is shown in Figure 4.4.

FIGURE **4.4**

*The results of Listing
4.6 after the button is
clicked.*

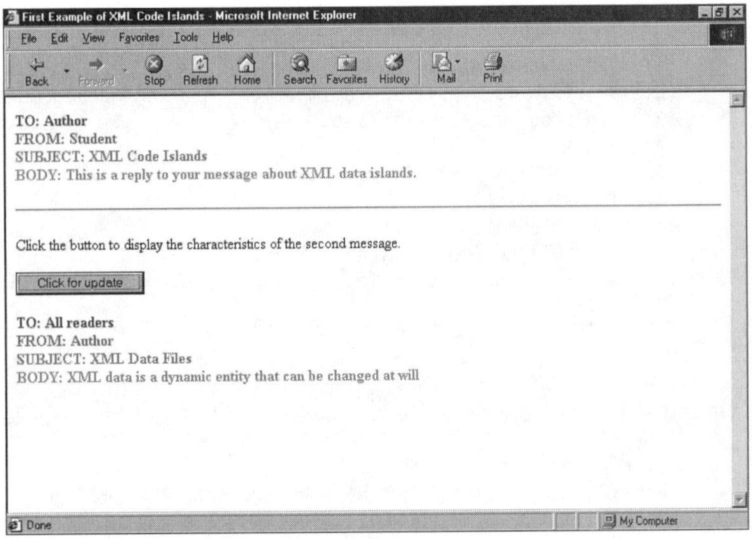

Lines 79 to 83 are the HTML that displays the button and the associated text. In lines 105 to 151, the value of the text property of each of the nodes is modified and then used as the source to update the second set of <SPAN> tags.

Using XML Data Islands to Read Files of Stored Messages

For the final exercise of this hour, you'll simulate the storage and retrieval of a collection of messages. One XML file will be a listing of all of the XML files that contain messages. Each of those files will contain a single stored message. An HTML SELECT box will be used to select the file to open, that file will be opened, and the desired message will be displayed.

This is actually a very typical scenario. Everybody receives email messages, some of which we save and some of which we don't. We tend to archive the important ones on a daily basis for later viewing if necessary. Since you've used XML to define email messages, your data files are in XML. Therefore, this is your first real-world application of XML.

An HTML SELECT box is used to display the archived files. Click on the file to select it.

Create the following XML files and save them under the names listed in the <FILENAME> property in the file.

LISTING 4.7   The First File That Will Be Imported into the Message Reader

```
 1: <?xml version="1.0"?>
 2: <!-- This is a file to be imported into the message reader
 3:      program. Filenamelisting4-7.xml -->
 4: <MESSAGE>
 5: <FILENAME>listing4-7.xml</FILENAME>
 6: <TO>Author</TO>
 7: <FROM>Student</FROM>
 8: <SUBJECT>XML Code Islands</SUBJECT>
 9: <BODY>This is a reply to your message about XML data islands.</BODY>
10: </MESSAGE>
```

LISTING 4.8   The Second File to Be Read into the Message Reader

```
 1: <?xml version="1.0"?>
 2: <!-- This is a file to be imported into the message reader
 3:      program. Filename listing4-8.xml -->
 4: <MESSAGE>
 5: <FILENAME>listing4-8.xml</FILENAME>
 6: <TO>Editor</TO>
 7: <FROM>Author</FROM>
 8: <SUBJECT>The XML Book</SUBJECT>
```

```
 9: <BODY>Great progress has been made.</BODY>
10: </MESSAGE>
```

LISTING 4.9   The Third File to Be Read into the Message Reader

```
 1: <?xml version="1.0"?>
 2: <!-- This is a file to be imported into the message reader
 3:      program. Filename listing4-9.xml -->
 4: <MESSAGE>
 5: <FILENAME>listing4-9.xml</FILENAME>
 6: <TO>Associate Editor</TO>
 7: <FROM>Editor</FROM>
 8: <SUBJECT>The XML Book in Progress</SUBJECT>
 9: <BODY>From author: Great progress has been made.</BODY>
10: </MESSAGE>
```

LISTING 4.10   The Fourth File to Be Read in by the Message Reader

```
 1: <?xml version="1.0"?>
 2: <!-- This is a file to be imported into the message reader
 3:      program. Filename listing4-10.xml -->
 4: <MESSAGE>
 5: <FILENAME>listing4-10.xml</FILENAME>
 6: <TO>Copy Editor</TO>
 7: <FROM>Associate Editor</FROM>
 8: <SUBJECT>The XML Book in Progress</SUBJECT>
 9: <BODY>Get ready to edit some copy.</BODY>
10: </MESSAGE>
```

4

This series of files will serve as the collection of stored messages.

Create the file shown in Listing 4.11 and save it as listing4-11.xml.

LISTING 4.11   The XML File That Stores the Filenames of All Archived Messages

```
 1: <?xml version="1.0"?>
 2: <!-- This file is the source file for all of the XML files
 3:      that are used in this exercise. Filename
 4: listing4-11.xml -->
 5: <MESSAGELIST>
 6: <MESSAGE>listing4-7.xml</MESSAGE>
 7: <MESSAGE>listing4-8.xml</MESSAGE>
 8: <MESSAGE>listing4-9.xml</MESSAGE>
 9: <MESSAGE>listing4-10.xml</MESSAGE>
10: </MESSAGELIST>
```

This file is a simple list of the filenames of the saved messages.

Listing 4.12 is the HTML file that will allow you to access an archived email message.

LISTING 4.12   The HTML File to Access the Archived Email Messages

```
 1:<html>
 2:<!-- This is the file that will allow the user to select
 3:    a filename from a list of saved messages. After the
 4:    selection is made, the message file is opened and
 5:    displayed for viewing. The filename is
 6:    xmlhour4-12.html. -->
 7:<head>
 8: <title>Program to extract the contents of e-mail
    messages in a list</title>
 9:</head>
10:<body bgcolor="ffffff">
11:<!-- This XML file is the list of filenames of the saved
12:    messages. -->
13:<XML ID=messagelist SRC="listing4-11.xml"></XML>
14:<SCRIPT LANGUAGE=JavaScript>
15:<!--
16:/* The following section will dynamically create an HTML
17:    SELECT object and fill the options with the entries
18:    In the list of files in the MESSAGELIST XML file. */
19:    document.write("<h3>Select the XML file to load and
        then click the Load File button to open it</h3>");
20:document.write("<BR>");
21:document.write("<SELECT Name=Select1>");
22:    RootElement1=messagelist.documentElement;
23:    if(RootElement1==null)
24:    {
25:     alert("The root node is null");
26:     document.write("<B><BIG>The data of the XML file
        cannot be accessed</BIG></B><BR>");
27:    }
28:    else
29: {
30:// We now extract the number of nodes in the list
31:    nodecount=RootElement1.childNodes.length;
32:    for(loopindex=0;loopindex<nodecount;loopindex++)
33:    {
34:     str1="<OPTION ";
35:     str1=str1+"VALUE="+RootElement1.childNodes.
        item(loopindex).text;
36:str1=str1+">"+RootElement1. childNodes.item(loopindex). text;
37:     str1=str1+"</OPTION><BR>";
38:     document.write(str1);
39:     }
```

```
40:    }
41:document.write("</SELECT><BR>");
42:document.write("<FORM>");
43:document.write("<INPUT TYPE=button Name=button1
44:Value='Click to load file' onClick='LoadFile()'>");
45:document.write("</FORM><BR>");
46:/* End of section that creates the HTML SELECT object. */
47:function LoadFile()
48:{
49:/* The ActiveXObject will be the one that links to the
50:    message to be read. We load the filename that was
51:    selected. */
52:    var xmlDoc1=new ActiveXObject("microsoft.xmldom");
53:    xmlDoc1.load(Select1.value);
54:    if(xmlDoc1.readyState=="4")
55:    {
56:    // loopindex is the counter used to control the loop
       that traverses through the nodes
57:    var loopindex;
58:    var RootElement1;
59:    var nodecount;
60:    RootElement1=xmlDoc1.documentElement;
61:    if(RootElement1==null)
62:    {
63:     alert("The root node is null");
64:     document.write("<B><BIG>The data of the XML file
       cannot be accessed</BIG></B><BR>");
65:    }
66:    else
67: {
68:// We now extract the number of nodes in the list
69:    nodecount=RootElement1.childNodes.length;
70:    for(loopindex=0;loopindex<nodecount;loopindex++)
71:    {
72:// This line will write the name of the node to the body
   section of the HTML file
73:document.write(RootElement1.childNodes.item(loopindex).
   nodeName+": ");
74:// This line will write out the contents of the node to
75:// the body section of the HTML file.
76:document.write(RootElement1.childNodes.item(loopindex).
   text+"<BR>");
77:    }
78:    }
79:    }
80:    else
81:    {
82:     alert("Process could not start");
83:    }
```

4

LISTING 4.12   continued

```
84:}
85://-->
86:</SCRIPT>
87:</body>
88: </html>
```

View the result in IE. The initial appearance is shown in Figure 4.5.

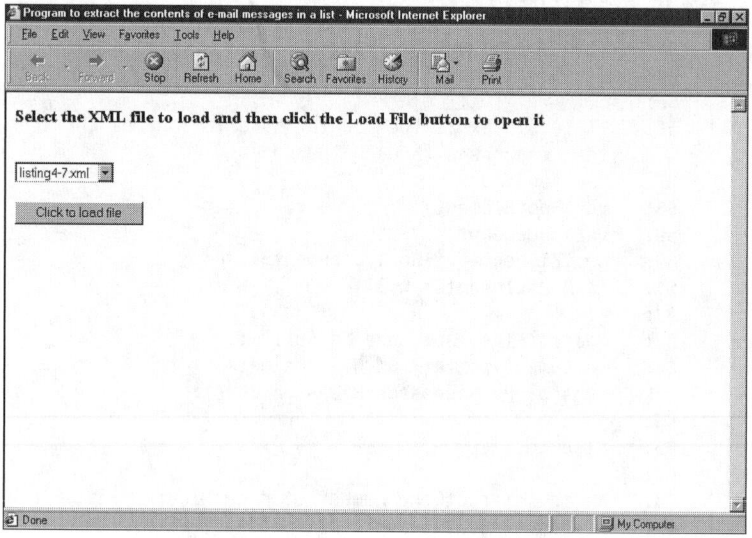

FIGURE 4.5

The SELECT box that will allow you to choose the archived message.

Click on the SELECT box to select a file, and then click the button. The contents of the selected file are displayed.

The XML data island on line 13 is the object that contains the list of messages. Lines 19 through 45 read through the messages in the list and dynamically create a SELECT box where the items are the filenames in the MESSAGELIST file. The LoadFile() function takes the value selected in the SELECT box and uses an ActiveX Object to open the file. The remainder of the function consists of code that you've previously examined.

Summary

This lesson exposed you to the placement of XML code inside your HTML code. Such code is known as inline code, and although it can be done, it is not the preferred way.

Examples of XML data islands illustrated how to modify the contents of the nodes, and you saw a simple real-world example of how to use XML files to display archived email messages.

Q&A

Q Are there other applications for the example where I displayed archived email messages?

A Absolutely. This basic structure can be used to display anything that's archived. Simply redefine the form of your data and change the names inside the XML file with the list of archived messages.

Q Why is it important to know the order in which files are loaded?

A Many files have relationships to other files, and the data from the first file that's read can be used to determine how the second is read.

Q Should inline XML code be avoided?

A Yes, your first thought should be to separate before you use inline code.

Workshop

Quiz

1. Is the text property of an XML node read-only?

    a. It's read-only by default

    b. It's not read-only by default

    c. It's read-only by default, but it can be reset so that it's not

    d. It's not read-only but can only be modified using special functions

2. Are the properties of an XML object created as a data island the same as those of an XML ActiveXControl object?

    a. Yes

    b. No, the data island has fewer and more restrictive properties

    c. No, the data island has more properties and they're less restrictive

3. Does modifying the value of a node's text property automatically update the file's data?

    a. Yes it does, although this can be disabled

    b. Yes, and it does it automatically

    c. No. The change is only in the node in working memory

Answers

1. b
2. a
3. d

Exercises

1. Modify xmlhour4-6.html so that it can handle the addition of <BCC> and <POSTSCRIPT> data components to the XML source file.

2. Create a series of files of the following form:

```
<CUSTOMER>
      <FIRSTNAME></FIRSTNAME>
      <LASTNAME></LASTNAME>
      <ADDRESS></ADDRESS>
      <CITY></CITY>
      <STATE></STATE>
      <PHONENUMBER></PHONENUMBER>
       <EMAIL></EMAIL>
      </CUSTOMER>
```

Write an XML file that defines the <CUSTOMERLIST> object that's similar to what was done in the example on reading the archived messages. Make any necessary modifications to the HTML file to view the data.

HOUR 5

Document Type Definitions

This hour will examine some of the basics of XML data. It will start with literal data and then move on to the Document Type Definition (DTD), which defines the structure of XML data and is the equivalent of the class template. To close the hour, some additional properties of the xmldom object will be presented.

In this hour, you'll learn the following:

- The syntax and usage of predefined entities
- The difference between parsed and unparsed entities
- The syntax and purpose of the DTD
- The syntax and reasons for separating the DTD into an external file
- The DTD-related properties of the xmldom object

Predefined Entities

As is the case in HTML, there are some characters that have special interpretations in XML. For example, the greater-than (>) and less-than (<) characters are used to delimit tags and therefore cannot be placed inside a data string directly. To insert them into a string, you need to use a special sequence of characters, or an *entity reference,* that's reserved for that purpose. An *entity* is a sequence of characters used to represent another sequence of characters, and those that the system provides are known as *predefined entities.* The notation of an entity reference is identical to that used in HTML. Table 5.1 contains the characters with their corresponding entity references.

TABLE 5.1   System-Provided Predefined Entities

Character	Meaning	Entity Reference
<	Less than	<
>	Greater than	>
&	Ampersand	&
'	Apostrophe	'
"	Quote	"

The file shown in Listing 5.1 demonstrates the use of predefined entities.

LISTING 5.1   Demonstration of System-Provided Predefined Entities

```
1: <?xml version="1.0" ?>
2: <!-- Demonstration of predefined entities. -->
3: <MESSAGE>
4: <TO>AUTHOR&amp;friend</TO>
5: <FROM>STUDENT</FROM>
6: <SUBJECT>RE: Introduction to XML</SUBJECT>
7: <BODY>Thank you, I&lt;really&gt; am &quot;excited&quot;
   about &apos;learning&apos; XML</BODY>
8: </MESSAGE>
```

When viewed in IE, the output will be

```
<?xml version="1.0" ?>
<!-- Demonstration of predefined entities.
 -->
<MESSAGE>
<TO>AUTHOR&friend</TO>
<FROM>STUDENT</FROM>
<SUBJECT>RE: Introduction to XML</SUBJECT>
<BODY>Thank you, I <really> am "excited" about 'learning' XML</BODY>
</MESSAGE>
```

As was the case in HTML, it's also possible to use numeric references to represent characters. The general form is

```
&#decimalnumber;
```

The numeric equivalents of the predefined entities are displayed in Table 5.2.

TABLE 5.2 Numeric References for Predefined Entities

Character	Meaning	Numeric Reference
<	Less than	<
>	Greater than	>
&	Ampersand	&
'	Apostrophe	'
"	Quote	"

Listing 5.2 provides a demonstration of how to use numeric references for predefined entities.

LISTING 5.2 Demonstration of Using Numeric References for Predefined Entities

```
1: <?xml version="1.0" ?>
2: <!-- Demonstration of predefined entities.
3: -->
4: <MESSAGE>
5: <TO>AUTHOR&#38;friend</TO>
6: <FROM>STUDENT</FROM>
7: <SUBJECT>RE: Introduction to XML</SUBJECT>
8: <BODY>Thank you, I&#60;really&#62; am &#34;excited&#34; about
   &#39;learning&#39; XML</BODY>
9: </MESSAGE>
```

5

Unicode

A quick examination of the numeric equivalents of the preceding characters will reveal that they're simply the ASCII code values. However, the "World Wide" part of "World Wide Web" is starting to become more significant, so we need a way to represent all languages. In order to represent the characters in languages that don't use the Roman alphabet, *Unicode* was developed. A Unicode character is given a 16-bit (or 2-byte) representation rather than the 8-bit ASCII value. Since the second byte can simply be assigned the value 0 for characters in the ASCII code, it's an extension rather than a replacement.

XML fully supports the Unicode character set. To represent the characters, you can use the numeric equivalents.

The body of Listing 5.3 is simply a listing of some of the characters in the Cyrillic alphabet.

LISTING 5.3 Using Numeric Equivalences to Display Unicode Characters

```
 1: <?xml version="1.0"?>
 2: <!-- This file demonstrates some of the Unicode characters.
 3: [-->
 4: <MESSAGE>
 5: <TO>Cyrillic readers</TO>
 6: <FROM>AUTHOR</FROM>
 7: <SUBJECT>Cyrillic Alphabet</SUBJECT>
 8: <BODY>
 9: &#1024;&#1025;&#1026;&#1027;&#1028;&#1029;&#1030;&#1031;
10: &#1032;&#1033;&#1034;&#1035;&#1036;&#1037;&#1038;&#1039;
11: &#1040;&#1041;&#1042;&#1043;&#1044;&#1045;&#1046;&#1047;
12: &#1048;&#1049;&#1050;&#1051;&#1052;&#1053;&#1054;&#1055;
13: &#1056;&#1057;&#1058;&#1059;&#1060;&#1061;&#1062;&#1063;
14: &#1064;&#1065;&#1066;&#1067;&#1068;&#1069;&#1070;&#1071;
15: &#1072;&#1073;&#1074;&#1075;&#1076;&#1077;&#1078;&#1079;
16: &#1080;&#1081;
17: </BODY>
18: </MESSAGE>
```

Figure 5.1 shows what this file looks like when read by the program from the previous hour.

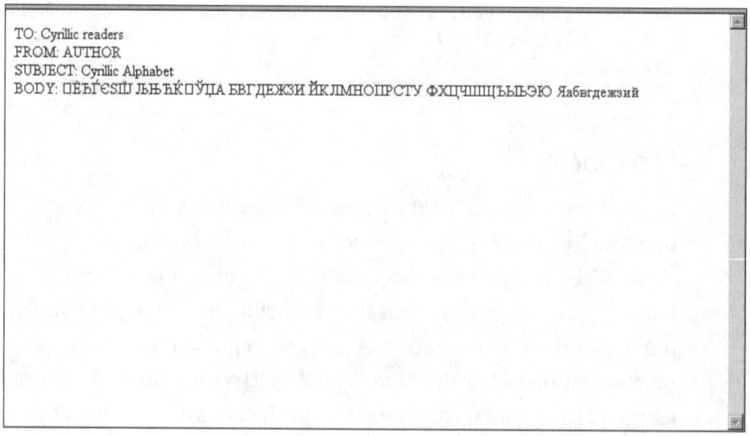

FIGURE 5.1

A demonstration of using the Cyrillic alphabet.

TO: Cyrillic readers
FROM: AUTHOR
SUBJECT: Cyrillic Alphabet
BODY: ЀЁЂЃЄЅ ЉЊЋЌ ЎЏАБВГДЕЖЗИ ЙКЛМНОПРСТУ ФХЦЧШЩЪЫЬЭЮ Яабвгдежзий

If you're interested in other aspects of Unicode, go to `http://www.unicode.org` or consult the excellent reference written by the Unicode consortium, *The Unicode Standard, Version 3.0* by Addison-Wesley.

Parsed and Unparsed Entities

In XML, entities are split into two distinct categories: parsed and unparsed. A *parsed* entity, sometimes referred to as a *text* entity, becomes part of the XML document after it's examined and processed. Examples of parsed entities include the predefined entities that you examined in the previous exercises. The text is first processed, and then the results are added to the XML document.

An *unparsed* entity may or may not be text, but even if it is, it isn't made part of the XML document. An example of such an entity is a binary image file. The file isn't parsed or interpreted by the XML processor, but is translated by the appropriate visualization tool.

> The default form for data in an XML file is parsed.

One commonly used type of parsed entity is essentially equivalent to the declaration of a constant and is inserted into the text using an assigned reference name. In XML, the definition of the "constant" is done using a command with the basic syntax

```
<!ENTITY ENTITYNAME "string to be assigned">
```

This will define a user-defined entity that can be inserted into the file much like the predefined entities in the previous exercises.

The Document Type Definition

Up to this point, all of the definitions of the structure of the data in your XML files have been implicit. While the organization was clear from the structure, that was due in large part to the simplicity of your files. That's not always the case, and it's always an advantage to explicitly define the order of the data. Therefore, it's possible to create a *Document Type Definition* or *DTD*, which is a description of how the data is to be organized.

The basic syntax of a DTD is as follows:

```
<!DOCTYPE DOCNAME [
 list of entities
 ]>
```

5

DOCTYPE is a reserved word, DOCNAME is the user-supplied name of the DTD, and the entries in the list are the components of the DTD.

Listing 5.4 demonstrates the use of text constants in XML files.

LISTING 5.4   Defining and Using User-Defined Entities

```
 1: <?xml version="1.0"?>
 2: <!-- This file demonstrates the use of text constants in
     XML files. -->
 3: <!DOCTYPE MESSAGE [
 4: <!ENTITY MYENTITYTO "Dear ">
 5: <!ENTITY MYENTITYFROM "Humble ">
 6: <!ENTITY MYENTITYSUBJECT "Books">
 7: <!ENTITY MYENTITYCYRILLIC
     "&#1025;&#1026;&#1027;&#1028;&#1029;">
 8: ]>
 9: <MESSAGE>
10: <TO>&MYENTITYTO;READER</TO>
11: <FROM>&MYENTITYFROM;AUTHOR</FROM>
12: <CC>&MYENTITYCYRILLIC;</CC>
13: <SUBJECT>My &MYENTITYSUBJECT;</SUBJECT>
14: <BODY>I am happy that you are reading my books.</BODY>
15: </MESSAGE>
```

Figure 5.2 shows what this file looks like when viewed in IE 5.

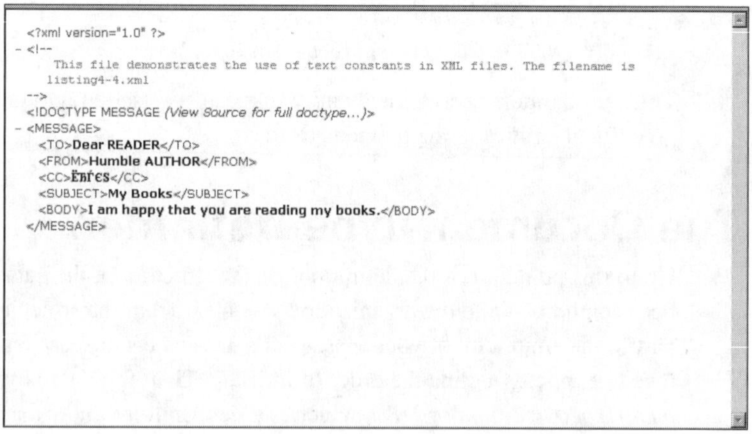

FIGURE 5.2

The appearance of user-defined entities.

It's clear that the entities are examined and interpreted by the XML processor before they're displayed. Also note that the DTD itself isn't displayed in the browser.

Comments can be placed in the DTD section of an XML file. The notation is the same as that for inserting comments in XML and HTML code.

Placing Parsed Entities in the DTD

The next step will be to introduce the notation to denote that an entry is a variable, rather than a literal character string. As you might have guessed, a parsed entity denotes that an entry is a variable. The notation to specify that an entry in the DTD is to be a parsed entity is

```
<!ELEMENT NameOfDataComponent (#PCDATA)>
```

There must be a blank space between the last character of the data component's name and the left parenthesis. Leaving it out will cause an error to be generated.

Since parsed entities describe the form of the data, rather than providing literal data, a list of the root data object's components must be included in the DTD. This has the following form:

```
<!ELEMENT RootName (List of data components separated by commas)>
```

The complete description of the MESSAGE object is demonstrated in Listing 5.5.

LISTING 5.5   Declaring Elements as Parsed Data

```
 1: <?xml version="1.0"?>
 2: <!-- This file demonstrates the use of parsed data
 3:      specifiers in a DTD. -->
 4:
 5: <!DOCTYPE MESSAGE [
 6: <!ELEMENT MESSAGE (TO,FROM,CC,SUBJECT,BODY)>
 7: <!ELEMENT TO (#PCDATA)>
 8: <!ELEMENT FROM (#PCDATA)>
 9: <!ELEMENT CC (#PCDATA)>
10: <!ELEMENT SUBJECT (#PCDATA)>
11: <!ELEMENT BODY (#PCDATA)>
12: <!ENTITY MYENTITYTO "Dear ">
13: <!ENTITY MYENTITYFROM "Humble ">
14: <!ENTITY MYENTITYSUBJECT " Books">
15: <!ENTITY MYENTITYCYRILLIC "&#1025;&#1026;&#1027;&#1028;&#1029;">
16: ]>
```

5

LISTING 5.5   continued

```
17: <MESSAGE>
18: <TO>&MYENTITYTO;READER</TO>
19: <FROM>&MYENTITYFROM;AUTHOR</FROM>
20: <CC>&MYENTITYCYRILLIC;</CC>
21: <SUBJECT>My &MYENTITYSUBJECT;</SUBJECT>
22: <BODY>I am happy that you are reading my books.</BODY>
23: </MESSAGE>
```

Figure 5.3 shows what this file looks like when viewed in IE.

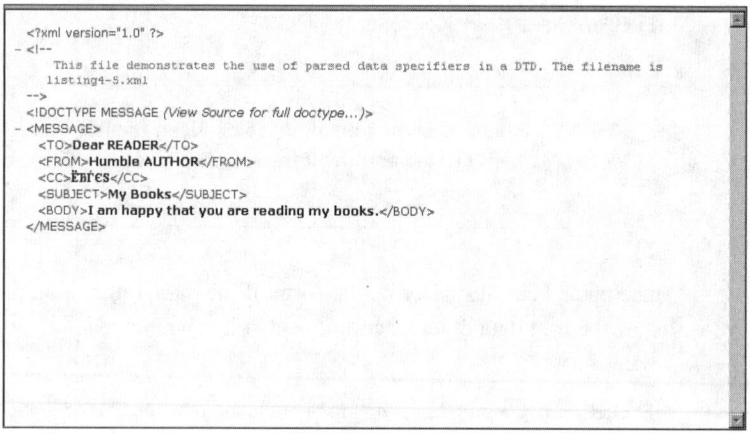

FIGURE 5.3

The appearance of parsed data.

```
<?xml version="1.0" ?>
- <!--
    This file demonstrates the use of parsed data specifiers in a DTD. The filename is
    listing4-5.xml
  -->
<!DOCTYPE MESSAGE (View Source for full doctype...)>
- <MESSAGE>
    <TO>Dear READER</TO>
    <FROM>Humble AUTHOR</FROM>
    <CC>Ënгés</CC>
    <SUBJECT>My Books</SUBJECT>
    <BODY>I am happy that you are reading my books.</BODY>
  </MESSAGE>
```

Placing Unparsed Entities in the DTD

The other form of data is *CDATA,* or *character data*, which is unparsed data. If the element is declared to be of this type, any markup characters found inside the string aren't processed but are treated as simple text. For example, you may not want to have the text parsed when you're using emoticons in an email message. Consider the message "How dare you say that to me <grin>." Clearly, this is meant as a joke. However, the XML processor would consider the <grin> to be an unmatched tag, and an HTML processor would leave it out. The first is an error, and the second dramatically changes the meaning of the message. The use of this type of data is demonstrated in the Listing 5.6.

LISTING 5.6   Using CDATA in an Element Definition

```
1: <?xml version="1.0" ?>
2: <!-- This file demonstrates the CDATA qualifier. -->
3: <BOOK>
4: <AUTHOR>Charles Ashbacher</AUTHOR>
5: <TITLE>
```

```
6: <![CDATA[<ELEMENT>
   <A HREF ="http://www.myfavoritebooks.htm">You are
   there</A></ELEMENT>]]>
7: </TITLE>
8: </BOOK>
```

View the file in IE and pay particular attention to the color coding of the anchor tag.

A modification of the previous listing will allow you to contrast the treatment of CDATA and PCDATA. The code is found in Listing 5.7.

LISTING 5.7   Contrasting PCDATA with CDATA

```
1: <?xml version="1.0" ?>
2: <!-- This file demonstrates how PCDATA compares to the CDATA qualifier.
3: -->
4: <BOOK>
5: <AUTHOR>Charles Ashbacher</AUTHOR>
6: <TITLE>
7: <ELEMENT><A HREF ="http://www.myfavoritebooks.htm">
   You are there</A></ELEMENT>
8: </TITLE>
9: </BOOK>
```

View it in IE. Again, pay particular attention to the color coding of the anchor tags.

Validating the DTD

An XML parser may or may not *validate* the data with respect to the DTD. If it does, it's said to be a *validating* parser. XML parsers can be either validating or nonvalidating.

Listing 5.8 is a modification of a previous program, and the changes are highlighted in bold.

LISTING 5.8   The Consequences of Adding an Entry Not in the ELEMENT List

```
 1: <?xml version="1.0"?>
 2: <!-- This file demonstrates the use of parsed data specifiers in a DTD. It
     also contains a data entry that does not match the DTD entries. -->
 3:
 4: <!DOCTYPE MESSAGE [
 5: <!ELEMENT MESSAGE (TO,FROM,CC,SUBJECT,BODY)>
 6: <!ELEMENT TO (#PCDATA)>
 7: <!ELEMENT FROM (#PCDATA)>
 8: <!ELEMENT CC (#PCDATA)>
 9: <!ELEMENT SUBJECT (#PCDATA)>
10: <!ELEMENT BODY (#PCDATA)>
11: <!ENTITY MYENTITYTO "Dear ">
```

5

LISTING 5.8   continued

```
12: <!ENTITY MYENTITYFROM "Humble ">
13: <!ENTITY MYENTITYSUBJECT " Books">
14: <!ENTITY MYENTITYCYRILLIC "&#1025;&#1026;&#1027;&#1028;&#1029;">
15: ]>
16: <MESSAGE>
17: <TO>&MYENTITYTO;READER</TO>
18: <FROM>&MYENTITYFROM;AUTHOR</FROM>
19: <CC>&MYENTITYCYRILLIC;</CC>
20: <BCC>My best friend</BCC>
21: <SUBJECT>My &MYENTITYSUBJECT;</SUBJECT>
22: <BODY>I am happy that you are reading my books.</BODY>
23: </MESSAGE>
```

Figure 5.4 shows what this file looks like in IE.

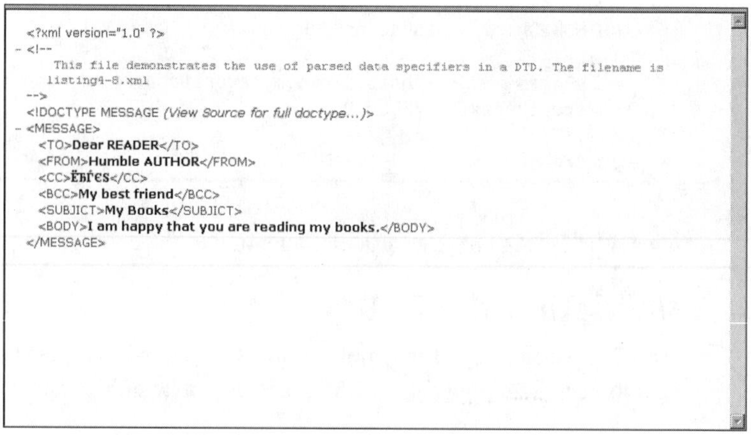

FIGURE 5.4

Checking the data versus the DTD.

To verify that the XML processor is indeed examining the data, you can reopen the file and modify the line

```
<!ELEMENT SUBJECT (#PCDATA)>
```

to

```
<!ELEMENT SUBJECT (#PCDTA)>
```

Qualifying the Data Components in the DTD

A list of data components is often more complex than the lists you've seen up to now. Some components can have more than one data value, some can be optional, and some are required and can appear only once. For example, Figure 5.5 defines the structure of an email message.

FIGURE 5.5

The structure of a standard, simple email.

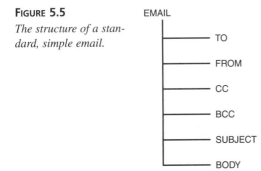

EMAIL

- TO
- FROM
- CC
- BCC
- SUBJECT
- BODY

The following are the qualifications commonly associated with the data components of this definition:

TO—At least one entry is required, and there can be more than one.

FROM—There can be only one entry and it is required.

CC—This entry is optional, and it can contain more than one entry.

BCC—This entry is optional, and it can contain more than one entry.

SUBJECT—While this is generally considered to be required, on some email systems a default will be inserted if none is present. For the purposes of this book, it can be absent, but if it's present, it can appear only once.

BODY—Once again, for the purposes of this book, this is optional and can appear only once.

It's possible to represent these qualifications in XML, and the ways to do this are summarized in Table 5.3.

5

TABLE 5.3 Symbols for Qualifying Data Components

Symbol(s)	Usage
()	Grouping of components.
,	Separator of items in a list.
|	Separator of options, one of which must be used.
?	Item can appear zero times or one time.
*	Item can appear zero or more times.
+	Item can appear one or more times.
No symbol	Item must appear once and only once.

Given the stated restrictions on the data components of an email message, the following would be a representation using the appropriate symbols:

```
<!ELEMENT E-MAIL (TO+,FROM,CC*,BCC*,SUBJECT?,BODY?)>
```

Listing 5.9 demonstrates the use of data qualifiers.

LISTING 5.9   Qualifying the Entries in the ELEMENT List

```
 1: <?xml version="1.0"?>
 2: <!-- This file demonstrates the use of data qualifiers.
 3:   -->
 4: <!DOCTYPE E-MAIL [
 5: <!ELEMENT E-MAIL (TO+,FROM,CC*,BCC*,SUBJECT?,BODY?)>
 6: <!ELEMENT TO (#PCDATA)>
 7: <!ELEMENT FROM (#PCDATA)>
 8: <!ELEMENT CC (#PCDATA)>
 9: <!ELEMENT BCC (#PCDATA)>
10: <!ELEMENT SUBJECT (#PCDATA)>
11: <!ELEMENT BODY (#PCDATA)>
12: ]>
13: <E-MAIL>
14: <TO>READER</TO>
15: <FROM>AUTHOR</FROM>
16: <CC></CC>
17: <BCC>Secret friend 1</BCC>
18: <BCC>Secret friend 2</BCC>
19: <BCC>Secret friend 3</BCC>
20: <BCC>Secret friend 4</BCC>
21: <SUBJECT>New book</SUBJECT>
22: <BODY>Announcing a new book being developed!</BODY>
23: </E-MAIL>
```

Figure 5.6 shows what this looks like when viewed in IE.

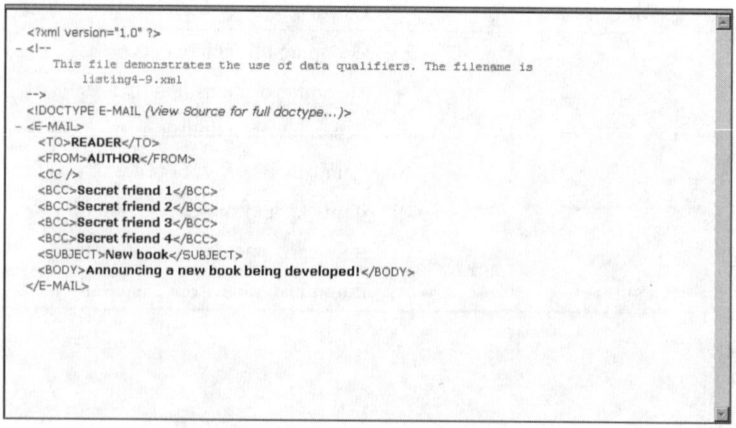

FIGURE 5.6

Illustration of a qualified DTD.

```
<?xml version="1.0" ?>
- <!--
        This file demonstrates the use of data qualifiers. The filename is
        listing4-9.xml
  -->
<!DOCTYPE E-MAIL (View Source for full doctype...)>
- <E-MAIL>
    <TO>READER</TO>
    <FROM>AUTHOR</FROM>
    <CC />
    <BCC>Secret friend 1</BCC>
    <BCC>Secret friend 2</BCC>
    <BCC>Secret friend 3</BCC>
    <BCC>Secret friend 4</BCC>
    <SUBJECT>New book</SUBJECT>
    <BODY>Announcing a new book being developed!</BODY>
  </E-MAIL>
```

If you use the HTML program from Hour 3 to display the data in Listing 5.9, the result is illustrated in Figure 5.7.

TO: READER
FROM: AUTHOR
CC:
BCC: Secret friend 1
BCC: Secret friend 2
BCC: Secret friend 3
BCC: Secret friend 4
SUBJECT: New book
BODY: Announcing a new book being developed!

Separating the DTD into an External File

In keeping with the general rule of moving things into separate files whenever possible, Listing 5.10 shows a separate file for the DTD.

LISTING 5.10   First Example of a Standalone DTD File

```
 1: <?xml version="1.0"?>
 2: <!-- This file is an external DTD that will be imported into
     another file. -->
 3: <!ELEMENT E-MAIL (TO+,FROM,CC*,BCC*,SUBJECT?,BODY?)>
 4: <!ELEMENT TO (#PCDATA)>
 5: <!ELEMENT FROM (#PCDATA)>
 6: <!ELEMENT CC (#PCDATA)>
 7: <!ELEMENT BCC (#PCDATA)>
 8: <!ELEMENT SUBJECT (#PCDATA)>
 9: <!ELEMENT BODY (#PCDATA)>
10:
11: <!ENTITY BCCPREFIX "A nice ">
```

Listing 5.11 imports the program from Listing 5.10.

LISTING 5.11   Importing a DTD File into an XML File

```
 1: <?xml version="1.0"?>
 2: <!-- This file demonstrates the importation of an external
 3:      DTD. -->
```

5

LISTING 5.11   continued

```
 4: <!DOCTYPE E-MAIL SYSTEM "listing4-10.dtd">
 5:
 6: <E-MAIL>
 7: <TO>READER</TO>
 8: <FROM>AUTHOR</FROM>
 9: <CC></CC>
10: <BCC>&BCCPREFIX;Secret friend 1</BCC>
11: <BCC>&BCCPREFIX;Secret friend 2</BCC>
12: <BCC>&BCCPREFIX;Secret friend 3</BCC>
13: <BCC>&BCCPREFIX;Secret friend 4</BCC>
14: <SUBJECT>New book</SUBJECT>
15: <BODY>Announcing a new book being developed!</BODY>
16: </E-MAIL>
```

Figure 5.8 shows what this file looks like when viewed in IE. Note the presence of the BCC prefix defined as an ENTITY.

FIGURE 5.8

The appearance of the data when the DTD is imported.

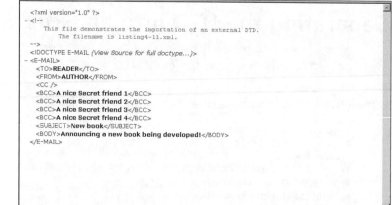

Overriding an External Entity Definition

The entity definitions imported via a DTD file can be overridden by local definitions, which is demonstrated in Listing 5.12.

Listing 5.12 is a modification of Listing 5.11. The line to be added is in bold.

LISTING 5.12   Locally Overriding an Entity Definition in a DTD

```
1: <?xml version="1.0"?>
2: <!-- This file demonstrates the importation of an external
3:     DTD. -->
4: <!DOCTYPE E-MAIL SYSTEM "listing4-10.dtd"[
```

```
 5: <!ENTITY BCCPREFIX "A mean ">]>
 6: <E-MAIL>
 7: <TO>READER</TO>
 8: <FROM>AUTHOR</FROM>
 9: <CC></CC>
10: <BCC>&BCCPREFIX;Secret friend 1</BCC>
11: <BCC>&BCCPREFIX;Secret friend 2</BCC>
12: <BCC>&BCCPREFIX;Secret friend 3</BCC>
13: <BCC>&BCCPREFIX;Secret friend 4</BCC>
14: <SUBJECT>New book</SUBJECT>
15: <BODY>Announcing a new book being developed!</BODY>
16: </E-MAIL>
```

View the file in IE. Note that the local definition of BCCPREFIX takes precedence over the one imported in via the external DTD file.

DTD-Related Properties of the xmldom Object

This hour will conclude by presenting some additional properties of the xmldom object.

TABLE 5.4   Additional Properties of the xmldom Object

Property	Data Type	Contains
url	String	The URL of the most recently loaded document
validateOnParse	Boolean	If true, document is validated when parsed; if false, it isn't
xml	Text	The XML representation of the node
nodeType	Number	A numeric code that specifies the DOM type for the node

The possible values for the nodeType and their meanings are summarized in Table 5.5.

TABLE 5.5   Possible Values of the nodeType Property

Value	Corresponding Node Type
1	ELEMENT
2	ATTRIBUTE
3	TEXT
4	CDATA

5

TABLE 5.5 continued

Value	Corresponding Node Type
5	ENTITY REFERENCE
6	ENTITY
7	PI (Processing instruction)
8	COMMENT
9	DOCUMENT
10	DOCUMENT TYPE (as found in the document declaration)
11	DOCUMENT FRAGMENT
12	NOTATION

Listing 5.13 is a modification of a listing in Hour 3. The modifications are marked in bold.

LISTING 5.13 Using the Array Properties of the nodeList Object to Step Through the Nodes

```
 1: <HTML>
 2: <HEAD>
 3: <TITLE>Using the Array Properties Of the nodeList to Read
    an XML File</TITLE>
 4: <SCRIPT LANGUAGE="JavaScript">
 5: <!--
 6:  var RootElement1;
 7: // nodecount will store the number of nodes containing data
 8: // in the XML file.
 9:  var nodecount;
10:  var xmlDoc1=new ActiveXObject("microsoft.xmldom");
11:
12:
13:    xmlDoc1.load("listing4-9.xml");
14:    function StartUp()
15:    {
16:
17: // Stores the URL of the last loaded file.
18:    var lastURL;
19: // Stores the Boolean as to whether the XML is validated.
20: var isValidate;
21: // Stores the xml code of the node
22: var xmlType;
23: // Stores the numeric code for the node type.
24:    var numNodeType;
25:    if(xmlDoc1.readyState=="4")
26:    {
27:
28:     lastURL=xmlDoc1.url;
```

```
29:     alert(lastURL);
30:     isValidate=xmlDoc1.validateOnParse;
31:     alert(isValidate);
32:     xmlType=xmlDoc1.xml;
33:     alert(xmlType);
34:     numNodeType=xmlDoc1.nodeType;
35:     alert(numNodeType);
36:     StartLoading();
37:     }
38:     else
39:     {
40:      alert("Process could not start");
41:     }
42:     }
43:     function StartLoading()
44:     {
45: // loopindex is the counter used to control the loop that
46: // traverses through the nodes
47:     var loopindex;
48:     RootElement1=xmlDoc1.documentElement;
49:     if(RootElement1==null)
50:     {
51:      alert("The root node is null");
52:      document.write("<B><BIG>The data of the XML file cannot
         be accessed</BIG></B><BR>");
53:     }
54:     else
55:     {
56: // We now extract the number of nodes in the list
57:     nodecount=RootElement1.childNodes.length;
58:     for(loopindex=0;loopindex<nodecount;loopindex++)
60:     {
61: // This line will write the name of the node to the body
62: // section of the HTML file
63:        document.write(RootElement1.childNodes.item(loopindex).
          nodeName+": ");
64: // This line will write out the contents of the node to the
65: // body section of the HTML file.
66:        document.write(RootElement1.childNodes.item(loopindex).text
       :  +"<BR>");
67:      }
68:     }
69:    }
70: //-->
71: </SCRIPT>
72: </HEAD>
73: <BODY onLoad="StartUp()">
74: <!-- Since all of the content is now being written from the
75:      JavaScript section, it is no longer
76:      necessary to put anything here. -->
77: </BODY>
78: </HTML>
```

View the file in IE. The values that came up when the author ran the file are sequentially captured in Figures 5.9 through 5.12. The value of 9 in Figure 5.13 reflects that the node you're examining is the root node of the file.

FIGURE 5.9
The display of the URL.

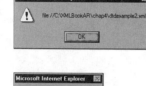

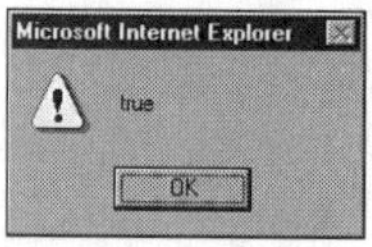

FIGURE 5.10
The display of the value of the validateOnParse property.

FIGURE 5.11
The XML form of the node.

FIGURE 5.12
The nodeType property.

Q&A

Q What's the difference between PCDATA and CDATA?

A PCDATA is parsed, and any tags or other key character sequences are given their XML interpretations. CDATA isn't interpreted in any way.

Q What criteria would cause you to write the DTD inside the xml file?

A The primary scenario is if the data isn't going to be used again and you need to isolate it for whatever reason. Otherwise, it should be placed in a distinct DTD file.

Q What are the two main categories of entities?

A There's the predefined entity, which can also be called the system-defined entity. The other category is the user-defined entity.

Q What operation is performed when entities are used?

A The operation can be considered a sophisticated substitution.

Workshop

Quiz

1. Unicode can represent every character used in every human language.

    True

    False

2. Which type of data is the default?

    a. Parsed data

    b. Unparsed data

    c. Neither is the default, the process is relative to the context

3. Once the value of an entity is set in the imported DTD file, it cannot be modified in the XML file.

    True

    False

4. Where can comments be placed in a DTD section?

    a. They cannot be placed in a DTD section

    b. Anywhere in the DTD section

    c. Anywhere, as long as they are on separate lines

Answers

1. True

2. a

3. False

4. The best answer is c, but technically b is true as well

Exercises

1. Go to a resource such as a book or a Web site and look up the Unicode representations for the lowercase letters of the Greek alphabet. Write a modification of the file that displays Cyrillic letters that will display them.

2. Given the following definition of a data type, write a DTD file for it:

    First Name—Required, and there can be only one.

    Middle Name—Optional, and there can be more than one.

    Last Name—Required, and there can be only one.

5

Address—Required, and there can be more than one.

City—Required, and there can be only one.

State—Required, and there can be only one.

Email address—Optional, and there can be more than one.

Phone number—Optional, and there can be at most one.

PART II
Beyond the Basics

Hour

Hour **6**

Attribute Lists and Writing Correct DTDs

In Hour 5, the basic features of a Document Type Definition (DTD) were examined. This hour will expand on that topic.

The elements in a DTD can be qualified by associating additional data items with them. These data items are known as *attributes*, and there can be more than one per element. Therefore, they'll be referred to as *attribute lists*. This hour starts with a large exercise on the inclusion of attribute lists associated with the elements of a DTD. The structure, organization, and types of attributes are all examined. The hour will close with brief remarks on processing instructions (PIs) and references to external resources. A *processing instruction* gives the XML processor information about how the file is to be interpreted. An *external resource* is a file or other data resource that is to be used but isn't necessarily XML.

In this hour, you'll learn the following:

- The basic syntax of the attribute list and how to create them with the proper qualification

- The syntax for referencing external entities or data that isn't in XML form
- The syntax for the processing instruction (PI) in XML and examples of what it does

The Attribute List

The previous qualification of the elements of a DTD deals solely with the number of times the element can appear in the data section. For example, an asterisk after the element name means that it can appear zero or more times, and a plus means it can appear one or more times. While this restricts the number of times the data element can appear, it doesn't restrict the contents of the data element to a data type. This type of restriction can be done by inserting an attribute list into the DTD and associating the attribute with the element.

The notation for an attribute list is

```
<!ATTLIST ElementName AttributeName Type Default>
```

where the entries have the following meanings:

ATTLIST—A reserved word that identifies the type of tag.

ElementName—The name of the element in the list that the attribute list is to be applied to.

AttributeName—The name assigned to the attribute.

Type—The specification of the type of data that the attribute is to contain.

Default—The default value that the attribute is to have.

Let's look at an example of an element for which you'd want to provide an attribute list. When a message is sent electronically, generally it's necessary to specify certain characteristics of that message. For example, if it's written in a language in the Western European group, you might be able to send it in a form where the characters are in one-byte extended ASCII rather than two-byte Unicode. This would reduce the message size by one-half. However, to do this, you would need to somehow note in the message that it's in that form.

Also, messages that may contain sensitive information are often encrypted. The type of encryption may vary depending on the sensitivity of the data. For example, if it's only mildly sensitive, you may use 64-bit encryption, which could also be designated as low priority. If the message is more sensitive, you could use 128-bit encryption, which is more difficult to break. This level of encryption could be designated as normal priority.

For the most secret of messages, you would use 256-bit encryption, which could be considered high priority.

Therefore, if the language possibilities for a <MESSAGE> tag are to be either Western or Extended, where the default is "Western", you would write the following attribute list:

```
<!ATTLIST MESSAGE LANGUAGE (Western|Extended) "Western" >
```

> Recall that the vertical bar is used to separate a list of options in which one must be used.

The following attribute list would list the options for ENCRYPTION and assign a default of 128:

```
<!ATTLIST MESSAGE ENCRYPTION (64|128|256) "128">
```

Finally, the following attribute list would list the options for PRIORITY and set the default to normal:

```
<!ATTLIST MESSAGE PRIORITY (low|normal|high) "normal">
```

Listing 6.1 is a modification of the <EMAIL> DTD from the previous hour, with attribute lists associated with some of the nodes. The lines to be added are marked in bold.

LISTING 6.1 Linking Attribute Lists to the Nodes of a DTD

```
 1: <?xml version="1.0"?>
 2: <!-- This file demonstrates the use of an attribute list
 3:      to qualify data. -->
 4: <!DOCTYPE E-MAIL [
 5: <!ELEMENT E-MAIL (TO+,FROM,CC*,BCC*,SUBJECT?,BODY?)>
 6: <!ATTLIST E-MAIL LANGUAGE (Western|Extended) "Western" >
 7: <!ATTLIST E-MAIL ENCRYPTION (64|128|256) "128">
 8: <!ATTLIST E-MAIL PRIORITY (low|normal|high) "normal">
 9: <!ELEMENT TO (#PCDATA)>
10: <!ELEMENT FROM (#PCDATA)>
11: <!ELEMENT CC (#PCDATA)>
12: <!ELEMENT BCC (#PCDATA)>
13: <!ELEMENT SUBJECT (#PCDATA)>
14: <!ELEMENT BODY (#PCDATA)>
15: ]>
16: <E-MAIL LANGUAGE="Western"
    ENCRYPTION="256" PRIORITY="normal">
17: <TO>READER</TO>
18: <FROM>AUTHOR</FROM>
19: <CC></CC>
```

6

LISTING 6.1   continued

```
20: <BCC>Secret friend 1</BCC>
21: <BCC>Secret friend 2</BCC>
22: <BCC>Secret friend 3</BCC>
23: <BCC>Secret friend 4</BCC>
24: <SUBJECT>New book</SUBJECT>
25: <BODY>Announcing a new book being developed!</BODY>
26: </E-MAIL>
```

View the file in IE 5 to verify that it's correct. Note how the inclusion of the attributes and their values is done by inserting the names and assigned values into the opening tag.

While separating the different attributes may be preferred by some, it's possible to combine them into a single list.

Go back to Listing 6.1 and combine the three attribute lists for E-MAIL into the following list:

```
<!ATTLIST E-MAIL LANGUAGE (Western|Extended) "Western"
         ENCRYPTION (64|128|256) "256"
         PRIORITY (low|normal|high) "normal">
```

View the updated file in IE to verify that it's correct.

Go back to Listing 3.7 and change the line that loads the file to

```
xmlDoc1.load("listing6-1.xml");
```

View the file in IE and note the correctness of the output.

Reopen listing6-1.xml and modify the line

```
<E-MAIL LANGUAGE="Western" ENCRYPTION="256"
PRIORITY="normal">
```

to

```
<E-MAIL LANGUAGE="Western" ENCRYPTION="512"
PRIORITY="normal">
```

Note that 512 is not one of the options for the value of ENCRYPTION.

When you run the HTML file again, an alert box with the following message appears:

```
The root node is null
```

As was the case before, when the XML processor detects a discrepancy between the DTD and the data, the root node cannot be assigned a value.

There's no syntax rule requiring the attribute list for a node to immediately follow that node. It can appear anywhere in the DTD. However, good form dictates that they appear together for clarity.

Assigning Attributes to the Data Nodes in the DTD

In the previous example, the only node that was assigned attributes was the root node of the data. The data nodes can also be qualified by the inclusion of attribute lists, as the following exercise demonstrates. It's rather extensive and requires some background preparation. The premise here is that you're creating the data components for a shipping company that accepts packages and hires other companies to actually move the goods. The name of the company is General Shippers, and it's the initial drop point for the movement of any package.

Your basic data component is SHIPORDER, and each package is assigned an element of the SHIPORDER data type. Here are the elements of an instance of this object type:

ShipNumber—The unique number assigned to each package that you accept for shipping. This is required, of course. Since General Shippers is a multinational shipper, some of the packages will require a customs declaration. Therefore, include the Customs attribute with the two possible values of yes or no.

To—The customer that the package is to be sent to. Each package must be sent to a unique entity. Also, each recipient is assigned a unique ID identifier as an attribute, and that attribute is required.

From—The customer that the package is from. Each package is from a unique entity. Also, each sender is assigned a unique ID identifier as an attribute, and that attribute is required.

Address—The location where the package is to be sent. Since many recipients can have alternate addresses, allow for the possibility of multiple addresses.

StateProvince—The state or province where the recipient resides. This is both required and unique.

Country—The country where the recipient resides. It's both required and unique. Since your company is based in the United States and most of your shipping is national, also declare the attribute with a value that can be either the USA or foreign.

6

Carrier—The company that you're hiring to deliver the package. Since you'll hire only one such company, it's both required and unique. Depending on the circumstances, the package may be sent by van, truck, or plane. Therefore, define an attribute called vehicle that must be one of those three values.

Insurance—Depending on the type of freight, the sender may wish to purchase insurance on the package. Several different insurance companies are available. This field stores the name of the company underwriting the policy. Since there's no requirement to purchase insurance, it's possible to leave this field blank. There are three levels of insurance available: none, fifty percent of value, or full value. Those options will be made available in an attribute list.

Security—Some of our clients ship very valuable merchandise, so there are times when a security company is hired to oversee the shipment. The name of that company is placed in this field. Since the product may not warrant such precautions, it's possible to leave this field empty. There are three levels of security: none, the vehicle is sealed upon departure and opened upon arrival, and armed guards accompany the shipment. This parameter is stored in an attribute.

GeneralCarrier—The company that oversees the shipment. This must always be your company, General Shippers.

Create the DTD file shown in Listing 6.2 and save it as listing6-2.dtd.

LISTING 6.2 A DTD with Attributes That Define an Order Processed by Your Shipping Company

```
1:<?xml version="1.0"?>
2:<!-- This file demonstrates the use of an attribute list
3:to qualify the data of our company, General
4:Shippers. The filename islisting6-2.dtd -->
5:<!ELEMENT SHIPORDER
 (ShipNumber,To,From,Address+,StateProvince,Country,
 Carrier,Insurance?,Security?,GeneralCarrier)>
6:<!ATTLIST SHIPORDER LANGUAGE (Western|Extended)
  "Western">
7:<!ATTLIST SHIPORDER PRIORITY (low|normal|high) "normal">
8:<!ELEMENT ShipNumber (#PCDATA)>
9:<!ATTLIST ShipNumber Customs (no|yes) "no">
10:<!ELEMENT To (#PCDATA)>
11:<!ATTLIST To idTo ID #REQUIRED>
12:<!ELEMENT From (#PCDATA)>
13:<!ATTLIST From idFrom ID #REQUIRED>
14:<!ELEMENT Address (#PCDATA)>
15:<!ELEMENT StateProvince (#PCDATA)>
16:<!ELEMENT Country (#PCDATA)>
```

```
17:<!ATTLIST Country  Destination (USA|Foreign) "USA">
18:<!ELEMENT Carrier (#PCDATA)>
19:<!ATTLIST Carrier Vehicle (van|truck|plane) "van">
20:<!ELEMENT Insurance (#PCDATA)>
21:<!ATTLIST Insurance Level (none|50percent|full) "none">
22:<!ELEMENT Security (#PCDATA)>
23:<!ATTLIST Security SLevel (none|ClosedVehicle|armed)
   "none">
24:<!ELEMENT GeneralCarrier (#PCDATA)>
25:<!ATTLIST GeneralCarrier Us CDATA #FIXED "General
   Shippers">
```

On lines 11 and 13, you see the new #REQUIRED keyword. When this is present, that data attribute must always be assigned a value.

The other new keyword is the #FIXED qualifier. When this is used, it means that the attribute must always be assigned the given value. Since you're the parent company, assign your company name to this.

The next step is to create an XML file in which this DTD is imported and the data format is implemented.

Create the file shown in Listing 6.3 and save it as listing6-3.xml.

LISTING 6.3 A Data File That Imports and Conforms to the DTD File in Listing 6.2

```
 1: <?xml version="1.0"?>
 2: <!-- This file imports in the DTD file that describes the
 3:      data form that  is a ship order for an international
 4:      shipping company. The filename islisting6-3.xml. -->
 5: <!DOCTYPE SHIPORDER SYSTEM "listing6-2.dtd">
 6: <SHIPORDER LANGUAGE="Extended" PRIORITY="high">
 7: <ShipNumber Customs="yes">B123456</ShipNumber>
 8: <To idTo="BH123">Valued Customer</To>
 9: <From idFrom="FG345">YourExpress Shippers</From>
10: <Address>100 South Street</Address>
11: <StateProvince>BigState</StateProvince>
12: <Country Destination="Foreign">Tropica</Country>
13: <Carrier Vehicle="plane">Air Freight</Carrier>
14: <Insurance Level="full">Perfect Safety Company</Insurance>
15: <Security SLevel="armed">Perfect Safety Company</Security>
16: <GeneralCarrier Us="General Shippers">General Shippers</GeneralCarrier>
17: </SHIPORDER>
```

6

Go back to Listing 3.7 and modify the line that loads the XML file so that it loads Listing 6.3.

Save and run the file in IE. The output is shown in Figure 6.1.

FIGURE **6.1**

The ShipOrder *data.*

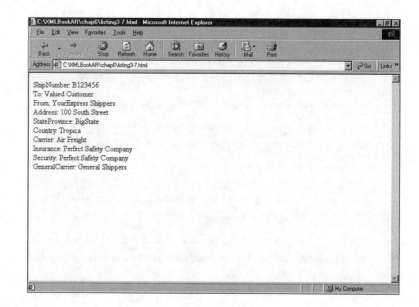

Each of the following changes will cause an error to be generated.

In listing6-3.xml, change this line

```
<GeneralCarrier Us="General Shippers">General
Shippers</GeneralCarrier>
```

to this:

```
<GeneralCarrier Us="General Shoppers">General
Shippers</GeneralCarrier>
```

This demonstrates the restrictions enforced by the #FIXED qualifier, because the value of the attribute is not that in the DTD. Change the line back to the original before continuing.

In listing6-3.xml, change this line

```
    <To idTo="BH123">Valued Customer</To>
```

to this:

```
    <To>Valued Customer</To>
```

This demonstrates the restrictions enforced by the #REQUIRED qualifier, because the attribute isn't assigned a value. Change the line back to the original before continuing.

In listing6-3.xml, change this line

```
<Country Destination="Foreign">Tropica</Country>
```

to this:

```
<Country Destination="foreign">Tropica</Country>
```

The only change is that "foreign" is now lowercase. This demonstrates the case requirements; the possible and assigned values must be an exact match. Change the file back to the original before continuing.

The previous exercise demonstrated qualifiers concerning the presence of an attribute that could be applied to the items in the attribute list. For example, if the #REQUIRED qualifier is included in the attribute in the DTD, that node must always have a value assigned to that attribute. The options for qualifiers concerning the presence are summarized in Table 6.1.

TABLE 6.1   The Qualifiers That Specify the Presence of the Attribute

Qualifier	Meaning
#REQUIRED	Every element of this type must have a value assigned to this attribute.
#IMPLIED	The attribute is optional.
#FIXED *fixedvalue*	The attribute is required and must be assigned the value *fixedvalue*.
default	Specifies the default value for the attribute.

There are also several different values for attribute types that can be used in XML, and they're summarized in Table 6.2.

TABLE 6.2   The List of Attribute Types Available in XML

Attribute type	Meaning
CDATA	Attribute must be character data.
ENTITY	Attribute value must refer to an external binary entity declared in the DTD.
ENTITIES	Same as ENTITY, but allows for multiple values separated by whitespace.
ID	Attribute value must be a unique identifier.
IDREF	Value must be a reference to an ID declared elsewhere in the document.
IDREFS	Same as ID, only now it's possible to have multiple values separated by whitespace.
NMTOKEN	Value is a mixture of name token characters. The valid characters are letters, numbers, periods, dashes, colons, or underscores.
NMTOKENS	Same as NMTOKEN, except multiple values separated by whitespace are allowed.

6

TABLE 6.2   continued

Attribute type	Meaning
NOTATION	Attribute value must refer to a notation declared elsewhere in the DTD.
Enumerated	A list of items in parentheses separated by vertical bars.

External Entities

Recall that when an entity is used, it's a substitution. The entity is essentially a place-holder, being replaced by the assigned value when the processing is done.

The ENTITY keyword can also be applied to an external binary item, such as an image file, and is still a type of substitution. However, it's no longer a simple one because the file cannot be placed directly into the reference location. The system needs to be told which program should be used to display the file's contents.

Suppose that the image file MyImage.gif is to be included in your DTD. Since it cannot be directly viewed, something else must be used to display it. In the following line, IMAGE1 is the name of the ENTITY, so you can use it in your files as a substitute for the image file:

```
<!ENTITY IMAGE1 SYSTEM "MyImage.gif" NDATA GIF>
```

The SYSTEM qualifier is used to denote that the processor needs to be outside the XML file to find the "MyImage.gif" resource. A URL could also be used to name the resource. The final segment of the declaration (NDATA GIF) is an example of a notation. This is a message to the processor about the type of object that's being processed.

If this line is used in isolation, the following error message appears:

```
Declaration 'IMAGE1' contains reference to undefined
notation 'GIF'
```

This is because you haven't included a second line explaining to the processor what the notation GIF means. This is done in the following companion line:

```
<NOTATION GIF SYSTEM "ie5.exe ">
```

The GIF notation tells the processor that the program ie5.exe should be used to process it. If the resource doesn't require a program to translate it, it can be referenced directly without a notation.

For example, suppose you create a simple text file with the name "import1.txt":

```
The contents of this external text file will be imported into the XML file. The
name of the file is import1.txt.
```

And create the additional file "import2.txt":

```
This is the text of the import2.txt file.
```

Listing 6.4 will establish two external references to these files. The references don't need any notations because the text can be inserted into the XML file directly.

LISTING 6.4   A Demonstration of the Importing of External Text Files into the XML File

```
 1: <?xml version="1.0"?>
 2: <!-- This file demonstrates the use of text constants in XML files. The
 3: filename is listing6-4.xml -->
 4: <!DOCTYPE MESSAGE [
 5: <!ENTITY FIRST1 SYSTEM "import1.txt">
 6: <!ENTITY FIRST2 SYSTEM "import2.txt">
 7: <!ENTITY MYENTITYSUBJECT " Books">
 8: <!ENTITY MYENTITYCYRILLIC "&#1025;&#1026;&#1027;&#1028;&#1029;">
 9: ]>
10: <MESSAGE>
11: <TO>&FIRST1;</TO>
12: <FROM>&FIRST2;</FROM>
13: <CC>&MYENTITYCYRILLIC;</CC>
14: <SUBJECT>My &MYENTITYSUBJECT;</SUBJECT>
15: <BODY>I am happy that you are reading my books.</BODY>
16: </MESSAGE>
```

Figure 6.2 shows what this looks like when viewed in IE.

FIGURE 6.2

The XML file after the external text files are imported.

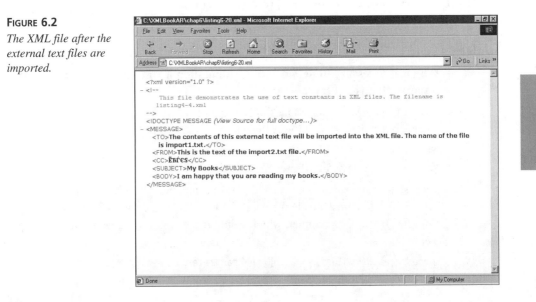

6

Processing Instructions

A *processing instruction (PI)* is an instruction for the application that's processing the XML document. So far, you've have seen only one:

```
<?xml version="1.0" ?>
```

This informs the processor that the file is to conform to xml version 1.0 standards.

The general syntax for a processing instruction is as follows:

```
<?PIname ValueOrInstruction ?>
```

Examples of other PIs include instructions on how to render image files. Very few are actually implemented, so if you're interested in additional PIs in the draft document, you should visit http://www.w3.org.

Summary

When constructing a DTD, it is possible to add additional information to the nodes by including variables known as attributes. These variables are linked to the name of the node and the values are assigned to them in the opening tag of that node. In this lesson, you learned the syntax of adding attributes as well as what the possible types are.

You also learned how to reference external resources, whether they be text or binary. When the resource is not text, it is necessary to define and use a NOTATION, an explanation to the XML processor that tells it what program to use to process it. We also briefly touched on the structure of a processing instruction.

Q&A

Q Why is it necessary to define and use a notation if you want to use an external resource that is not text?

A The XML processor understands only text and has no functionality built into it to process other files. A notation is the way that you call other programs including the input that they are to process.

Q Why would you use attributes in an XML file?

A Because in many cases, one word or phrase is not enough. While it's possible to use a complete phrase inside the data, a value such as the following would have to be parsed by the programmer, which would make your programs much more complex:

```
<NodeName>Node value is 12 and the parameter is Hello</NodeName>
```

With attributes, you can write this:

```
<NodeName parameter="Hello">12</NodeName>
```

Q What happens when you use an ENTITY reference in a DTD?

A An ENTITY reference is a substitution of one thing for another. If the replacement is text, it can be a direct substitution, but if it is not, it must first be converted by another program.

Workshop

Quiz

1. Are the entries in an attribute list case sensitive?

    a. Yes, they must always begin with an uppercase letter and the rest must be lowercase

    b. No

    c. Yes, but you can use any combination of upper- and lowercase as long as you use that combination everywhere it appears

2. Is the following processing instruction required?

    ```
    <?xml version="1.0"?>
    ```

    a. Yes, it is

    b. No, the system chooses the version automatically

    c. No, if it's not present the system uses the assigned default

    d. Yes, but only if you want the system to process it according to a specific version number

    e. c and d

3. The #REQUIRED qualifier is used to denote which characteristic about the attribute?

    a. It must have a specific value

    b. It must be listed, but it doesn't have to have an assigned value

    c. It must be present and must be assigned a value, and the value isn't fixed

4. The #IMPLIED qualifier is used to denote which characteristic of the attribute?

    a. It's optional

    b. It's optional, but if it isn't present, a default value is assigned

    c. It's used to imply that it has a specific form

6

Answers

1. c
2. e
3. c
4. a

Exercises

1. Go back to Listing 6.1. Make additional changes to the DTD file and determine if those changes generate an error.

2. Let's say you're in the business of publishing books. Your goal is to create a DTD that you can use to describe each book project. Construct the DTD according to the following parameters:

    - Each book will have an ISBN number as a data component and an internal ID number that will be an attribute. These values will be unique and required.

    - Each book will have one or more authors.

    - Each book will have one developmental editor. This element will have an attribute that's an ID for that editor. These values will be unique and required.

    - Each book will be assigned a title. An associated attribute chosen from a list of book types will also be used. The list is computers, mathematics, history. Both are unique and required.

HOUR 7

Data Typing in XML

The previous hour introduced the attribute list, which allows you to include additional criteria about a node. Your next step is to provide additional qualifiers that can be used on the data. A *qualifier* specifies a type that the data component must conform to.

The second major topic of this lesson is the parseError object, which contains easily accessible information concerning the reasons for and location of the last error that was generated. This object is an enormous aid in debugging your code.

In this hour, you'll learn the following:

- Data typing and the different data types supported by the dt namespace
- Using assignments to change the data type of an active node
- The parseError object and its role in error handling

An Introduction to Data Types in XML

When data is being defined in a programming language, there are two general strategies that can be employed. The difference between the two is the malleability of variables. In a *strongly typed* language, variables are declared to be of a certain type, and that type is maintained within fairly rigid rules. For example, take the following declaration in the Java programming language:

```
int myInt;
```

myInt is a signed integer type occupying 32 bits of storage. Other data types can be assigned to myInt, but only when the other data types can be converted into an int without loss of information. Furthermore, myInt itself is never altered from the declared type.

In a *weakly typed* language, there are no formal declarations of variable type. You've seen this in the JavaScript programs that you've used in previous hours. The keyword var is used to note that you have an variable, but no type specification follows the variable name:

```
var myInt;
```

As the JavaScript program is executed, the type of myInt can change, always corresponding to the value of the type of the last assignment. in the following code segment, the type of myInt is at times a string, a number, and a boolean:

```
var myInt;
// At this point, the type of myInt is undefined
. . .
myInt="String";
// At this point, the type of myInt is string.
. . .
myInt=(x>0);
// At this point, the type of myInt is boolean.
. . .
myInt=36;
// At this point, the type of myInt is numeric.
. . .
```

It's possible to place type restrictions on the data placed in XML files. However, to do that, you need to add the system specification qualifiers. In IE, this is done by including the following code in the tag that represents the root node:

```
xmlns:dt="urn:schemas-microsoft-com:datatypes"
```

The xmlns:dt acronym combination is an abbreviation of XML namespace and data types. The string surrounded by quotes is the uniform resource number qualifier followed by the resource that's to be used. This resource specifies the data types that can be used to qualify the data components. The types defined by this file are fairly typical of what's found in most programming environments and are summarized in Table 7.1.

TABLE 7.1   Data Types Allowed in the dt Dataspace

Data Type	Description
bin.base64	MIME-style Base64 binary data.
bin.hex	Base 16 binary data.
boolean	"0" (false) or "1" (true).
char	Single-character string
date	A date in the ISO 8601 format with no time.
dateTime	A date in the ISO 8601 format with a time but no optional zone.
dateTime.tz	A date in the ISO 8601 format with a time and a zone.
fixed.14.4	Uses the same format as number, but there can be no more than 14 digits to the left of the decimal point and 4 digits to the right.
i1	A number with optional sign, but it cannot be a fraction or contain an exponent.
i2	A number with optional sign, but it cannot be a fraction or contain an exponent.
i4	A number with optional sign, but it cannot be a fraction or contain an exponent.
i8	A number with optional sign, but it cannot be a fraction or contain an exponent.
int	A number with optional sign, but it cannot be a fraction or contain an exponent.
number	A number with no effective limit on the number of digits. It can contain an optional sign, fractional digits, and an exponent. The punctuation is that of American English.
r4	The same format as the number, but with an approximate minimum value of 1.17549435E-38 and an approximate maximum value of 3.40282347E+38.
r8	The same format as the number, but with an approximate minimum value of 2.2250738585072014E-308 and an approximate maximum value of 1.7976931348623157E+308.
string	A character string.
time	A time as a subset of the ISO 8601 format with no date or zone.
time.tz	A time as a subset of the ISO 8601 format with no date but including an optional zone.

7

TABLE 7.1   continued

Data Type	Description
ui1	An unsigned number with no decimal point or exponents.
ui2	An unsigned number with no decimal point or exponents.
ui4	An unsigned number with no decimal point or exponents.
ui8	An unsigned number with no decimal point or exponents.
uri	Uniform Resource Identifier, which can refer to a local resource or one on the Web.
user-defined type	VT_UNKNOWN, the system designation for a data type defined by the user and valid, but not in any system category.
uuid	Hexadecimal digits that make up a universal unique identifier. If hyphens are present, they're ignored.

Listing 7.1 demonstrates the use of the data types defined in the datatypes namespace. It's also found on the companion Web site.

LISTING 7.1   Examples of the Data Types in the XML datatypes Namespace

```
 1: <?xml version="1.0"?>
 2: <!-- This file is our first example of using the data type
 3:      qualifiers supported in XML to further refine the form
 4:      of our data. -->
 5: <Book xmlns:dt="urn:schemas-microsoft-com:datatypes">
 6: <Author dt:dt="string">Good Writer</Author>
 7: <Title dt:dt="string">Good Book</Title>
 8: <PriceHardBack dt:dt="number">12.95</PriceHardBack>
 9: <PricePaperBack dt:dt="float">2.95</PricePaperBack>
10: <Rank dt:dt="int">32</Rank>
11: <Grade dt:dt="char">A</Grade>
12: <InStock dt:dt="boolean">0</InStock>
13: <PublicationDate dt:dt="date">2000-03-30</PublicationDate>
14: <PreciseMoment dt:dt="dateTime.tz">
    2000-03-30T12:18</PreciseMoment>
15: <OneSignedInteger dt:dt="i1">12</OneSignedInteger>
16: <TwoSignedInteger dt:dt="i2">-12</TwoSignedInteger>
17: <OneUnsignedInteger dt:dt="ui1">12</OneUnsignedInteger>
18: <TwoUnsignedInteger dt:dt="ui2">12</TwoUnsignedInteger>
19: <OneRealNumber dt:dt="r4">12345.67891</OneRealNumber>
20: </Book>
```

This file is designed primarily to demonstrate how the data types are used. View the file in IE and note that the data type specifiers are in a different color than the other items in the display. This is shown in Figure 7.1.

FIGURE 7.1

The appearance of an XML file containing data type qualifiers.

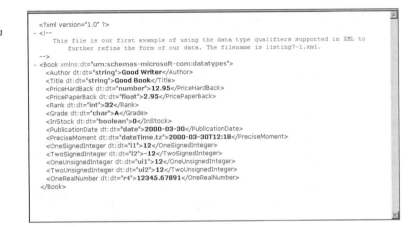

```
    <?xml version="1.0" ?>
-   <!--
        This file is our first example of using the data type qualifiers supported in XML to
        further refine the form of our data. The filename is listing7-1.xml.
    -->
-   <Book xmlns:dt="urn:schemas-microsoft-com:datatypes">
        <Author dt:dt="string">Good Writer</Author>
        <Title dt:dt="string">Good Book</Title>
        <PriceHardBack dt:dt="number">12.95</PriceHardBack>
        <PricePaperBack dt:dt="float">2.95</PricePaperBack>
        <Rank dt:dt="int">32</Rank>
        <Grade dt:dt="char">A</Grade>
        <InStock dt:dt="boolean">0</InStock>
        <PublicationDate dt:dt="date">2000-03-30</PublicationDate>
        <PreciseMoment dt:dt="dateTime.tz">2000-03-30T12:18</PreciseMoment>
        <OneSignedInteger dt:dt="i1">12</OneSignedInteger>
        <TwoSignedInteger dt:dt="i2">-12</TwoSignedInteger>
        <OneUnsignedInteger dt:dt="ui1">12</OneUnsignedInteger>
        <TwoUnsignedInteger dt:dt="ui2">12</TwoUnsignedInteger>
        <OneRealNumber dt:dt="r4">12345.67891</OneRealNumber>
    </Book>
```

Reopen the HTML file from Hour 6 and modify the line that loads the file to

```
xmlDoc1.load("listng7-1.xml");
```

Then save the file and run it in IE. The results are demonstrated in Figure 7.2.

FIGURE 7.2

A demonstration of the appearance of the types data.

```
Author: Good Writer
Title: Good Book
PriceHardBack: 12.95
PricePaperBack: 2.95
Rank: 32
Grade: A
InStock: 0
PublicationDate: 2000-03-30
PreciseMoment: 2000-03-30T12:18
OneSignedInteger: 12
TwoSignedInteger: -12
OneUnsignedInteger: 12
TwoUnsignedInteger: 12
OneRealNumber: 12345.67891
```

The purpose of the previous viewing of the data was to show you what happens when the data satisfies the data type qualifier.

The following is a list of changes to be made to Listing 7.1. Each modification will generate an error. In all cases, an alert box will pop up with the following message when the data is read from the file:

```
Root node is null
```

7

Each of the following changes will generate an error:

Change the following line of the xml file

```
<Rank dt:dt="int">32</Rank>
```

to

```
<Rank dt:dt="int">32.5</Rank>
```

When the HTML file is run in IE an error will be generated. This demonstrates that an integer cannot be assigned a floating point value.

Change the following line of the original xml file

```
<Grade dt:dt="char">A</Grade>
```

to

```
<Grade dt:dt="char">AB</Grade>
```

When you run the HTML file in IE, an error will be generated. This demonstrates that the char data type cannot be assigned a value that is more than one character in length.

Change the following line of the original xml file

```
<OneUnsignedInteger dt:dt="ui1">12</OneUnsignedInteger>
```

to

```
<OneUnsignedInteger dt:dt="ui1">-12</OneUnsignedInteger>
```

When you run the HTML file again, an error will be generated. This demonstrates that the ui1 data type is an unsigned integer and cannot have a negative value. Restore the XML file to the original form before continuing.

Change the following line of the original xml file

```
    <PreciseMoment dt:dt="dateTime.tz"> 2000-03-30T12:18</PreciseMoment>
```

to

```
    <PreciseMoment dt:dt="dateTime.tz"> 2000-03-3012:18</PreciseMoment>
```

The change is dropping the T from the dateTime string. When you run the HTML file again, an error is generated. This demonstrates that the form of the string must be precise.

Change the following line of the original xml file

```
<OneUnsignedInteger dt:dt="ui1">12</OneUnsignedInteger>
```

to

```
<OneUnsignedInteger dt:dt="ui1">255</OneUnsignedInteger>
```

When you run the HTML file again, there are no errors.

Reopen the XML file and change the line to

```
<OneUnsignedInteger dt:dt="ui1">256</OneUnsignedInteger>
```

Run the HTML file again, and an error will be generated. This demonstrates that the ui1 data type is an unsigned integer stored in one byte. The value of 256 is too large to fit in a single byte. If you've changed the file, restore it to its original form before continuing.

Similarly, i1 has a range of -128–127, i2 has a range of -32,768–32,767, and ui2 has a range of 0-65535. These are the standard ranges of integer data that's one, two, or three bytes in size.

Examining the Data Type of a Node

The node object contains the dataType and nodeTypedValue properties, which allow for the examination of the data type when read. The dataType property stores the current type assigned to the node, and nodeTypedValue returns the contents as a value having the assigned type.

Listing 7.2 is a modification of the HTML file that you've been using to read the XML file. The changes are marked in bold. This is also found on the companion Web site.

LISTING 7.2   Using the dataType and nodeTypedValue Properties of a Node

```
 1: <HTML>
 2:
 3: <HEAD>
 4: <TITLE>Using the Array Properties Of the nodeList to Read an XML
    File</TITLE>
 5: <SCRIPT LANGUAGE="JavaScript">
 6: <!--
 7:  var RootElement1;
 8: // nodecount will store the number of nodes containing data
 9: // in the XML file.
10:  var nodecount;
11:  var xmlDoc1=new ActiveXObject("microsoft.xmldom");
12: xmlDoc1.load("listing7-1.xml");
13: function StartUp()
14:  {
15:   if(xmlDoc1.readyState=="4")
16:   {
17:    StartLoading();
18:   }
```

7

LISTING 7.2   continued

```
19:    else
20:    {
21:     alert("Process could not start");
22:    }
23:    }
24:    function StartLoading()
25:    {
26: // loopindex is the counter used to control the loop that
27: // traverses through the nodes
28:     var loopindex;
29:     RootElement1=xmlDoc1.documentElement;
30:     if(RootElement1==null)
31:     {
32:      alert("The root node is null");
33:      document.write("<B><BIG>The data of the XML file cannot
           be accessed</BIG></B><BR>");
34:     }
35:     else
36:     {
37: // We now extract the number of nodes in the list
38:     nodecount=RootElement1.childNodes.length;
39:     for(loopindex=0;loopindex<nodecount;loopindex++)
40:     {
41: // This line will write the name of the node to the body
42: // section of the HTML file
43:         document.write(RootElement1.childNodes.item(loopindex).
           nodeName+": ");
44: // This line will write out the contents of the node to the
45: // body section of the HTML file.
46:         document.write(RootElement1.childNodes.item(loopindex).text
           +"<BR>");
47: // This line will write out the type of the node to the
48: // body section of the HTML file.
49:         document.write("The data type is "
           +RootElement1.childNodes.item(loopindex).dataType+
           "<BR>");
50: // This line will write out the nodeTypedValue property of
51: // the node to the body section of the HTML file.
52:         str1="The value of the nodeTypedValue property is ";
53:         document.write(str1+RootElement1.childNodes.item(loopindex).
           nodeTypedValue+"<BR><BR>");
54: }
55:     }
56:     }
57: //-->
58: </SCRIPT>
59: </HEAD>
60: <BODY onLoad="StartUp()">
61: <!-- Since all of the content is now being written from the
62:       JavaScript section, it is no longer necessary to put
```

```
63:     anything here. -->
64: </BODY>
65: </HTML>
```

The output of this HTML file in IE is shown in Figure 7.3.

Author: Good Writer
The data type is string
The value of the nodeTypedValue property is Good Writer

Title: Good Book
The data type is string
The value of the nodeTypedValue property is Good Book

PriceHardBack: 12.95
The data type is number
The value of the nodeTypedValue property is 12.95

PricePaperBack: 2.95
The data type is float
The value of the nodeTypedValue property is 2.95

Rank: 32
The data type is int
The value of the nodeTypedValue property is 32

Grade: A
The data type is char

Modifying the Data Type of a Node

It's possible to change the dataType property of a node during runtime. This is done by assigning the new type to the property. Once the new type is assigned, the allowable values that can be assigned to text will now match what that type allows. These simple modifications are the subject of the next example.

Listing 7.3 is an abbreviation of one used previously. It's also available on the companion Web site.

LISTING 7.3 A Simple File to Be Used in Dynamically Modifying the Data Type

```
 1: <?xml version="1.0"?>
 2: <!--This file is a shortened version of the XML data file used to
     demonstrate the assignment of specific data types to data
     components. It is used as the source code for the exercise
     on modifying the data types. -->
 3:
 4: <Book xmlns:dt="urn:schemas-microsoft-com:datatypes">
 5: <Grade dt:dt="char">A</Grade>
 6: <OneSignedInteger dt:dt="i1">12</OneSignedInteger>
 7: <TwoSignedInteger dt:dt="i2">-12</TwoSignedInteger>
 8: <OneUnsignedInteger dt:dt="ui1">12</OneUnsignedInteger>
 9: <TwoUnsignedInteger dt:dt="ui2">12</TwoUnsignedInteger>
10: </Book>
```

7

View this file in IE to verify its correctness before continuing.

Listing 7.4 is a modification of the HTML file previously used in this hour. The changes are marked in bold, and the file is found on the companion Web site.

LISTING 7.4 Modifying the Type of the Data in a Node

```
 1: <HTML>
 2: <HEAD>
 3: <TITLE>Using the Array Properties Of the nodeList to Read
 4:        an XML File</TITLE>
 5: <SCRIPT LANGUAGE="JavaScript">
 6: <!--
 7:  var RootElement1;
 8: // nodecount will store the number of nodes containing data
 9: // in the XML file.
10:  var nodecount;
11:  var xmlDoc1=new ActiveXObject("microsoft.xmldom");
12:  xmlDoc1.load("listing7-3.xml");
13: function StartUp()
14:  {
15:    if(xmlDoc1.readyState=="4")
16:    {
17:     StartLoading();
18:    }
19:    else
20:    {
21:     alert("Process could not start");
22:    }
23:  }
24:  function StartLoading()
25:   {
26: // loopindex is the counter used to control the loop that
27: // traverses through the nodes
28:     var loopindex;
29:     RootElement1=xmlDoc1.documentElement;
30:     if(RootElement1==null)
31:     {
32:      alert("The root node is null");
33:      document.write("<B><BIG>The data of the XML file cannot
          be accessed</BIG></B><BR>");
34:     }
35:     else
36:     {
37: // We now extract the number of nodes in the list
38:     nodecount=RootElement1.childNodes.length;
39:     for(loopindex=0;loopindex<nodecount;loopindex++)
40:     {
41: // This line will write the name of the node to the body
42: // section of the HTML file
43:       document.write(RootElement1.childNodes.item(loopindex).
          nodeName+": ");
```

```
44: // This line will write out the contents of the node to the
45: // body section of the HTML file.
46:     document.write(RootElement1.childNodes.item(loopindex).text
        +"<BR>");
47:     if(RootElement1.childNodes.item(loopindex).dataType=="i1")
48: {
49: // Modify the dataType and the value assigned to the node.
50: RootElement1.childNodes.item(loopindex).dataType="i2";
51: RootElement1.childNodes.item(loopindex).text="456";
52: // This line will write the name of the node to the body
53: // section of the HTML file
54:   document.write("The dataType is now "
        +RootElement1.childNodes.item(loopindex).dataType+
        "<BR>");
55: // This line will write the name of the node to the body
56: // section of the HTML file
57:     document.write(RootElement1.childNodes.item(loopindex).
        nodeName+": ");
58: // This line will write out the contents of the node to the
59: // body section of the HTML file.
60:     document.write(RootElement1.childNodes.item(loopindex).text
        +"<BR>");
61:     }
62:    }
63:   }
64:  }
65: //-->
66: </SCRIPT>
67: </HEAD>
68: <BODY onLoad="StartUp()">
69: <!-- Since all of the content is now being written from the
70:     JavaScript section, it is no longer necessary to put
71:     anything here. -->
72: </BODY>
73: </HTML>
```

The output when the previous xml file is displayed in this HTML file is shown in Figure 7.4.

FIGURE 7.4

Demonstrating the changing of the data type of a node.

```
<?xml version='1.0' ?>
- <!--
    This file is our first example of using the data typequalifiers supported in XML to
            further refine the form of our data. The filename is listing7-3.xml.
    -->
- <Book xmlns:dt="urn:schemas-microsoft-com-:datatypes">
    <Grade dt:dt="char">A</Grade>
    <OneSignedInteger dt:dt="i1">12</OneSignedInteger>
    <TwoSignedInteger dt:dt="i2">-12</TwoSignedInteger>
    <OneUnsignedInteger dt:dt="ui1">12</OneUnsignedInteger
    <TwoUnsignedInteger dt:dt="ui2">12</TwoUnsignedInteger>
  </Book>
```

Note that the data type of `OneSignedInteger` was changed to i2, and that the node can accept numbers within the range of -32,768 to 32,767.

Under what circumstances would you want to change the data type of the node? To understand this, you need to consider the role of XML in a complete database system. Because it's so flexible, it's being used to interface with many different databases. The interface that transfers the data from the XML form to the database could easily sample the type of the data in the node and perform a save based on the type. However, it may not be necessary to store all of the digits in the current number. To reduce the amount of space necessary to store the data, it could be converted into the data type with a smaller size.

This conversion to the smaller size could be done by the interface between XML and the database. The problem with this is that it breaks the general nature of that interface and leads to maintenance problems. The correct solution is to perform the conversion in the XML code, which can be done by modifying the data type of the nodes.

Error Handling

When an XML document is loaded, an instance of the parseError object is created. Since it's part of the XML object, it's accessed using the following notation:

```
xmlDoc1.parseError
```

A *parsing error* is an error that occurs when the `xmldom` object is processing the XML file and the structure doesn't satisfy the design parameters.

The `parseError` object contains several properties, all of which store characteristics of the last parsing error that was generated by the `xmldom` object running in your HTML program. Table 7.2 contains a list of properties of the `parseError` object.

TABLE 7.2 The Properties of the parseError Object

Property	Data Type	Explanation
errorCode	Long integer	Contains the error code of the last parsing error
filePos	Long integer	Contains the position in the file where the error occurred
line	Long integer	Contains the line number where the error occurred
linePos	Long integer	Contains the position in the line where the error occurred

Property	Data Type	Explanation
reason	String	Contains the reason for the last parsing error
srcText	String	Contains the text of the line generating the error

In XML the numbering of lines starts at 1, while the numbering of positions in a line starts at 0.

Of course, if you want to learn how to use these properties, you need a file that can be used to generate errors. Listing 7.5 is a simple XML file that you'll modify so that errors are generated.

LISTING 7.5   A Simple XML File That Will Be Used to Generate Errors

```
1: <?xml version="1.0"?>
2: <Book xmlns:dt="urn:schemas-microsoft-com:datatypes">
3: <Grade dt:dt="char">A</Grade>
4: <OneSignedInteger dt:dt="i1">12</OneSignedInteger>
5: <TwoSignedInteger dt:dt="i2">-12</TwoSignedInteger>
6: <OneUnsignedInteger dt:dt="ui1">12</OneUnsignedInteger>
7: <TwoUnsignedInteger dt:dt="ui2">12</TwoUnsignedInteger>
8: </Book>
```

To generate the errors, you need an HTML file to read the data. This will be served by Listing 7.2. However, to reduce the output clutter, remove these lines before you continue:

```
// This line will write out the type of the node to the
// body section of the HTML file.
    document.write("The data type is "
    +RootElement1.childNodes.item(loopindex).dataType+
    "<BR>");
// This line will write out the nodeTypedValue property of
// the node to the body section of the HTML file.
    str1="The value of the nodeTypedValue property is ";
    document.write(str1+RootElement1.childNodes.item(loopindex).
    nodeTypedValue+"<BR><BR>");
```

Modify the line that loads the file to

```
    xmlDoc1.load("xmlhour7-5.xml");
```

and run it in IE to verify that the XML file is correct.

In a previous example, you learned that the range of acceptable values for i1 was -128 through 127. Therefore, in Listing 7.5, if you change the line

```
<OneSignedInteger dt:dt="i1">12</OneSignedInteger>
```

7

to

```
<OneSignedInteger dt:dt="i1">128</OneSignedInteger>
```

an out-of-bounds error will be generated.

If Listing 7.2 is modified so that the StartLoading() function matches the following, the contents of the parseError object will be displayed. The lines to add are highlighted in bold:

```
function StartLoading()
   {
// loopindex is the counter used to control the loop that
// traverses through the nodes
   var loopindex;
   RootElement1=xmlDoc1.documentElement;
   alert(xmlDoc1.parseError.reason);
   alert(xmlDoc1.parseError.errorCode);
   alert(xmlDoc1.parseError.filePos);
   alert(xmlDoc1.parseError.line);
   alert(xmlDoc1.parseError.linePos);
   alert(xmlDoc1.parseError.srcText);
   if(RootElement1==null)
      {
      alert("The root node is null");
      document.write("<B><BIG>The data of the XML file cannot
      be accessed</BIG></B><BR>");
      }
      else
    {
// We now extract the number of nodes in the list
   nodecount=RootElement1.childNodes.length;
   for(loopindex=0;loopindex<nodecount;loopindex++)
      {
// This line will write the name of the node to the body
// section of the HTML file
      document.write(RootElement1.childNodes.item(loopindex).
      nodeName+": ");
// This line will write out the contents of the node to the
// body section of the HTML file.
      document.write(RootElement1.childNodes.item(loopindex).text
      +"<BR>");
      }
    }
   }
```

When the new file is saved and run in IE, the messages in the successive alert boxes displaying the contents of the parseError object are as follows:

```
Error parsing '128' as ui1 datatype

    -2147467259

    undefined

       6

    undefined
```

```
<OneSignedInteger dt:dt="i1">128</OneSignedInteger>
```

The first message is easy to understand. The contents of all nodes are stored as text, so when a data type is specified, the text must be converted. This action is called *parsing*, and the corresponding number is outside the bounds. The errorCode value of -2147467259 is of little use and the filePos and linePos parameters weren't assigned values, hence the values of undefined. The line parameter is also of little use because tracking the position down using that number is fruitless. However, the scrText parameter tells you quite clearly where the error occurred.

For the second example of error generation, use the DTD file defining a SHIPORDER that was used earlier. It's shown in Listing 7.6.

LISTING 7.6   The SHIPORDER DTD

```
 1: <?xml version="1.0"?>
 2: <!-- This file demonstrates the use of an attribute list
 3:      to qualify data. -->
 4: <!ELEMENT SHIPORDER (ShipNumber,To,From,Address+,StateProvince,
     Country,Carrier,Insurance?,Security?,GeneralCarrier)>
 5:
 6: <!ATTLIST SHIPORDER LANGUAGE (Western|Extended) "Western">
 7: <!ATTLIST SHIPORDER PRIORITY (low|normal|high) "normal">
 8: <!ELEMENT ShipNumber (#PCDATA)>
 9: <!ATTLIST ShipNumber Customs (no|yes) "no">
10: <!ELEMENT To (#PCDATA)>
11: <!ATTLIST To idTo ID #REQUIRED>
12: <!ELEMENT From (#PCDATA)>
13: <!ATTLIST From idFrom ID #REQUIRED>
14: <!ELEMENT Address (#PCDATA)>
15: <!ELEMENT StateProvince (#PCDATA)>
16: <!ELEMENT Country (#PCDATA)>
17: <!ATTLIST Country  Destination (USA|Foreign) "USA">
18: <!ELEMENT Carrier (#PCDATA)>
19: <!ATTLIST Carrier Vehicle (van|truck|plane) "van">
20: <!ELEMENT Insurance (#PCDATA)>
21: <!ATTLIST Insurance Level (none|50percent|full) "none">
22: <!ELEMENT Security (#PCDATA)>
```

7

LISTING 7.6 continued

```
23: <!ATTLIST Security SLevel (none|ClosedVehicle|armed)
    "none">
24: <!ELEMENT GeneralCarrier (#PCDATA)>
25: <!ATTLIST GeneralCarrier Us CDATA #FIXED "General Shippers">
```

You also need the corresponding data file that was created in the same lesson. See Listing 7.7.

LISTING 7.7 The Data in the SHIPORDER Example

```
 1: <?xml version="1.0"?>
 2: <!-- This file imports the DTD file that describes the
 3:      data form that is a shiporder for an international
 4:      company.-->
 5: <!DOCTYPE SHIPORDER SYSTEM "listing7-7.dtd">
 6: <SHIPORDER LANGUAGE="Extended" PRIORITY="high">
 7: <ShipNumber Customs="yes">B123456</ShipNumber>
 8: <To idTo="BH123">Valued Customer</To>
 9: <From idFrom="FG345">YourExpress Shippers</From>
10: <Address>100 South Street</Address>
11: <StateProvince>BigState</StateProvince>
12: <Country Destination="Foreign">Tropica</Country>
13: <Carrier Vehicle="plane">Air Freight</Carrier>
14: <Insurance Level="full">Perfect Safety Company</Insurance>
15: <Security SLevel="armed">Perfect Safety Company</Security>
16: <GeneralCarrier Us="General Shippers">General Shippers</GeneralCarrier>
17: </SHIPORDER>
```

Remove the line

```
<Carrier Vehicle="plane">Air Freight</Carrier>
```

and note that this entry is required by the parameters of the imported DTD file.

If you change the load line in Listing 7.6 to

```
xmlDoc1.load("listing7-5.xml");
```

and run the file in IE, the following sequence of messages is generated by the alert boxes displaying the contents of the parseError object:

```
Element content is invalid according to the DTD/Schema
                Expecting: Carrier

                 -1072898028

                  undefined

                     13

                  undefined
```

`<Insurance Level="full">Perfect Safety Company</Insurance>`

The first output that displays the reason for the error is very descriptive. The imported DTD requires the presence of the `<Carrier>` node, and you removed it. Once again, the errorCode, filePos, and linePos values are of little use. And once again, the line number is not accurate. The srcText parameter contains the line where the `<Carrier>` node is expected.

The advantage of using the components of the `parseError` object in debugging should be clear.

Recovering from Errors

Unfortunately, once parsing error has occurred in the reading of an XML file, there's little you can do to recover. As demonstrated by the alert box informing you that the root node is null, the error prevents any data from being loaded. Therefore, the only possible recovery would be to read the data from another file.

Summary

XML supports a substantial set of data types, and in this hour you learned about the standard types and how to use them. The dataType property is not read only and can be modified dynamically when necessary. The modification can be done by a simple assignment to the dataType property of the node. This operation may appear to be frivolous, but the value is obvious when XML is considered as just one part of a complete database package.

When an xmldom object is created, it contains an item known as the parseError object. This object will be filled with data describing the reasons for the error and where it took place.

7

Q&A

Q How do you make more than one comment node in an XML file?

A Each separate comment is a node, so all you have to do is make more than one comment.

Q The parseError object is part of which node type in the XML file?

A It's part of the xmldom object and therefore is not part of any node of the file.

Q What's the difference between a strongly typed and weakly typed language?

A In a strongly typed language, variables are declared to be a specific type and the type doesn't change throughout the scope of the variable. In a weakly typed language, the type of the variable changes as a consequence of the last assignment to that variable.

Workshop

Quiz

1. In a weakly typed language, the type of data stored by an identifier can be modified in which of the following ways?

   a. By assigning a type to the variable

   b. By assigning a value with the desired type

   c. You cannot alter the type of a variable in a weakly typed language

   d. By performing a recast

2. Is a comment in an XML file also considered a node?

   a. Yes

   b. No, because it cannot have child nodes

   c. No, because it cannot contain data

3. If the namespace line

   ```
   xmlns:dt="urn:schemas-microsoft-com:datatypes"
   ```

   is included, it's unnecessary to include the dt prefix when defining data types.

   True

   False

4. What are some nodes of an XML file that cannot have child nodes.

   a. Comment nodes

   b. Processing instructions

    c. Root nodes

    d. a and b

5. What are the main differences between the different types of available integers?

    a. Whether they're signed or unsigned

    b. The amount of storage allocated for the type

    c. a and b

    d. None of the above

6. The syntax of the allowed data types in XML is very specific.

    True

    False

Answers

1. b
2. a
3. False
4. d
5. c
6. True

Exercises

1. Go back to Listing 7.1 and modify the values of the int, float, and r4 data types to determine what the limits are.

2. Go back to the DTD file for the SHIPORDER, the associated XML file in Listing 7.7, and the HTML file that reads the data. Modify the DTD and XML files so that there are additional inconsistencies between them. Run the HTML file and note the errors.

7

HOUR **8**

Traversing the Node Tree and Adding and Replacing Nodes

In previous hours, you traversed the nodes of an XML tree by determining the number of nodes and then indexing on the array of nodes. While this method does allow you to move through the nodes, there's another way to do it. You can use the properties of firstChild, lastChild, nextSibling, and previousSibling. The first part of this hour will introduce these properties.

Although reading the nodes from a file is an important operation, performing updates is almost always an essential aspect of any work with databases. The insertion of additional nodes into the XML tree that's currently in active memory is the second item on the agenda for this hour.

In this hour, you'll learn the following:

- How to traverse a node tree using the firstChild, lastChild, nextSibling, and previousSibling properties
- How to add nodes to the XML tree currently in active memory

Traversing a Node Tree

In previous hours, you constructed hierarchical tree diagrams corresponding to XML files. In those diagrams, you concentrated only on the data portions of the XML files. However, every file entry that's surrounded by tags is considered a node, even the comments.

For example, consider Listing 8.1.

LISTING 8.1   A Small Example to Demonstrate a Node Tree

```
 1: <?xml version="1.0"?>
 2: <!-- This file is our first example of using the data type qualifiers
 3:     supported in XML to further refine the form of our data.  -->
 4: <Book xmlns:dt="urn:schemas-microsoft-com:datatypes">
 5: <Grade dt:dt="char">A</Grade>
 6: <OneSignedInteger dt:dt="i1">12</OneSignedInteger>
 7: <TwoSignedInteger dt:dt="i2">-12</TwoSignedInteger>
 8: <OneUnsignedInteger dt:dt="ui1">12</OneUnsignedInteger>
 9: <TwoUnsignedInteger dt:dt="ui2">12</TwoUnsignedInteger>
10: </Book>
```

When this is treated as a set of connected nodes, you obtain the node tree that appears in Figure 8.1.

FIGURE 8.1

The node tree for the entire XML file.

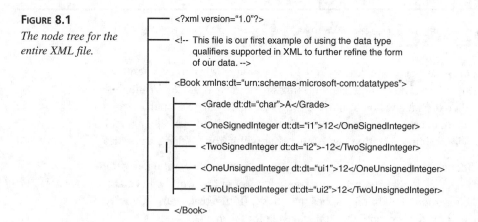

When such a tree of XML nodes is created, each node has a natural relationship to two of the other nodes, which are assigned to properties of the original node. These properties are the firstChild and lastChild properties. Therefore, if you consider the entire XML file as a node, the firstChild property would return the node that's the programming instruction:

```
<?xml version="1.0"?>
```

And the lastChild property would return the <Book> node:

```
<Book xmlns:dt="urn:schemas-microsoft-com:datatypes">
<Grade dt:dt="char">A</Grade>
<OneSignedInteger dt:dt="i1">12</OneSignedInteger>
<TwoSignedInteger dt:dt="i2">-12</TwoSignedInteger>
<OneUnsignedInteger dt:dt="ui1">12</OneUnsignedInteger>
<TwoUnsignedInteger dt:dt="ui2">12</TwoUnsignedInteger>
</Book>
```

The <Book> node in turn has a firstChild property of

```
<Grade dt:dt="char">A</Grade>
```

and a lastChild property of

```
<TwoUnsignedInteger dt:dt="ui2">12</TwoUnsignedInteger>
```

When a hierarchical tree is created, nodes that are at the same level and are attached to the same node are known as *siblings*. It's possible to traverse through the siblings using either the nextSibling or previousSibling properties.

Listing 8.2 is a modification of the HTML file that you used previously and is available on the companion Web site. The changes are marked in bold.

LISTING 8.2 Using the child and sibling Properties to Move Through a Tree of Nodes

```
 1: <HTML>
 2:
 3: <HEAD>
 4: <SCRIPT LANGUAGE="JavaScript">
 5: <!--
 6:  var RootElement1;
 7:  var xmlDoc1=new ActiveXObject("microsoft.xmldom");
 8:   xmlDoc1.load("listing8-1.xml");
 9: function StartUp()
10:  {
11:   if(xmlDoc1.readyState=="4")
12:   {
13:    StartLoading();
14:   }
15:   else
16:   {
17:    alert("Process could not start");
18:   }
19:  }
20:   function StartLoading()
21:   {
```

LISTING 8.2   continued

```
22: // This identifier is used to hold the first node of a tree
23: // of nodes.
24:    var holdNode;
25: // This is a working node used to traverse the subnodes.
26:    var newNode;
27:    RootElement1=xmlDoc1.documentElement;
28: // If the attempt to extract the document fails, we flag it
29: // with both an alert box and
30: // a message written to the web page. Once the messages are
31: // completed, the return is executed and the program
32: // terminates.
33:    if(RootElement1==null)
34:    {
35:     alert("The root node is null");
36:     document.write("<B><BIG>The data of the XML file cannot
           be accessed</BIG></B><BR>");
37:     return;
38:    }
39: // In this case, we are moving through the node tree by
40: // using the firstChild property to start the process
41: // and the nextSibling property to move forward through the
42: // tree. The nodes that we traverse all are on the first
43: // level.
44:
45:    treeNode=xmlDoc1.firstChild;
46:    alert("treeNode is "+treeNode.xml);
47:    while(treeNode!=xmlDoc1.lastChild)
48:    {
49:     treeNode=treeNode.nextSibling;
50:     alert("treeNode is "+treeNode.xml);
51:    }
52: // We have moved through the nodes of the tree and treeNode
53: // currently points to the <Book> node. We will now start
54: // at the last child node of the <Book> node and traverse
55: // upward using the previousSibling property.
56:
57:   holdNode=treeNode;
58:    treeNode=holdNode.lastChild;
59:    alert("treeNode is "+treeNode.xml);
60:    while(treeNode!=holdNode.firstChild)
61:    {
62:     treeNode=treeNode.previousSibling;
63:     alert("treeNode is "+treeNode.xml);
64:    }
65:   }
66: //-->
67: </SCRIPT>
68: </HEAD>
69: <BODY onLoad="StartUp()">
```

```
70: <!-- Since all of the content is now being written from the
71:      JavaScript section, it is no longer necessary to put
72:      anything here. -->
73: </BODY>
74: </HTML>
```

The output of the program is captured in Figures 8.2 through 8.9.

FIGURE 8.2

The display of the first node in the XML file.

Figure 8.2 is output by these lines:

```
treeNode=xmlDoc1.firstChild;
alert("treeNode is "+treeNode.xml);
```

The first line grabs the first node of the file, and the second line displays it. Since the first file is the processing instruction, that's what is displayed.

Figures 8.3 and 8.4 demonstrate the output from this loop:

```
while(treeNode!=xmlDoc1.lastChild)
    {
    treeNode=treeNode.nextSibling;
    alert("treeNode is "+treeNode.xml);
    }
```

The next sibling node at the upper level of the hierarchy is the comment node, and the last child node at the first level is the <Book> node. Therefore, that's what the alert calls from the loop display.

FIGURE 8.3

Displaying the comment node.

FIGURE 8.4

Displaying the <Book> node.

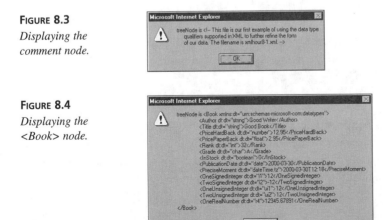

The next five figures are all a consequence of this loop:

```
treeNode=holdNode.lastChild;
   alert("treeNode is "+treeNode.xml);
   while(treeNode!=holdNode.firstChild)
   {
     treeNode=treeNode.previousSibling;
     alert("treeNode is "+treeNode.xml);
```

In this case, holdNode refers to the <Book> node, which has five child nodes. The assignment to treeNode will then be to the last of its child nodes. The loop then steps upward through the children of the <Book> node.

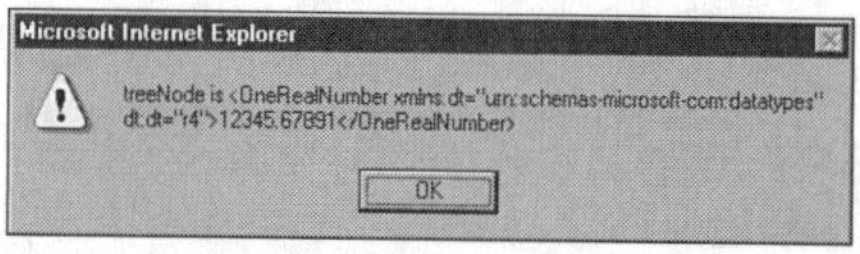

FIGURE 8.5

Displaying the last node of the <Book> node.

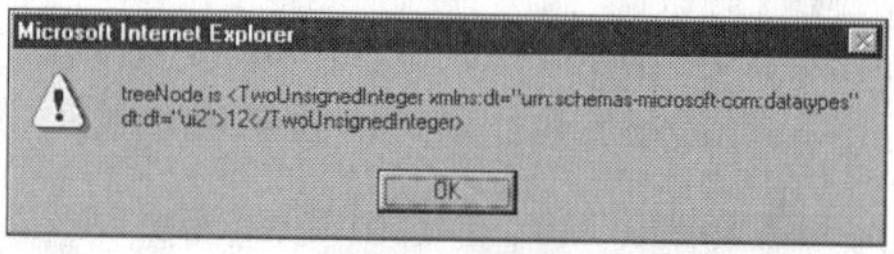

FIGURE 8.6

Displaying the second-to-last child node of the <Book> node.

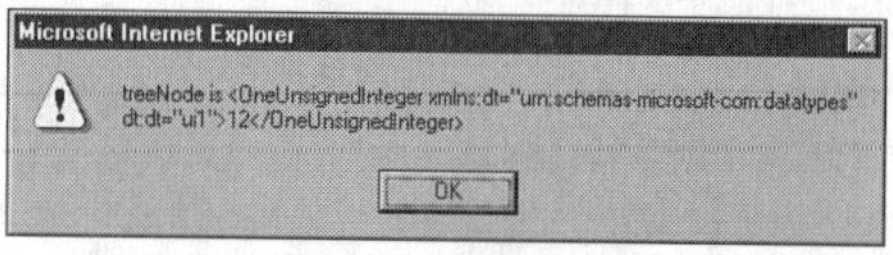

FIGURE 8.7

The node that's the third from the bottom.

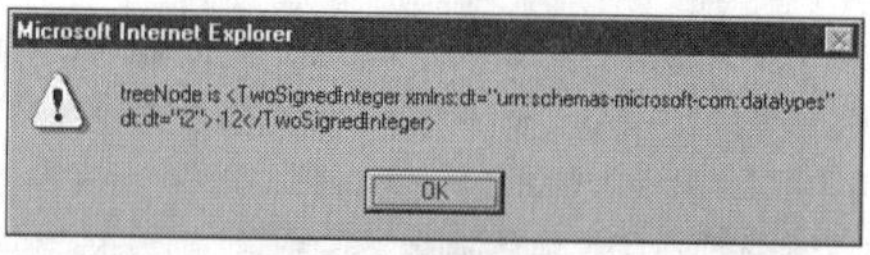

FIGURE 8.8

The node that's the fourth from the bottom.

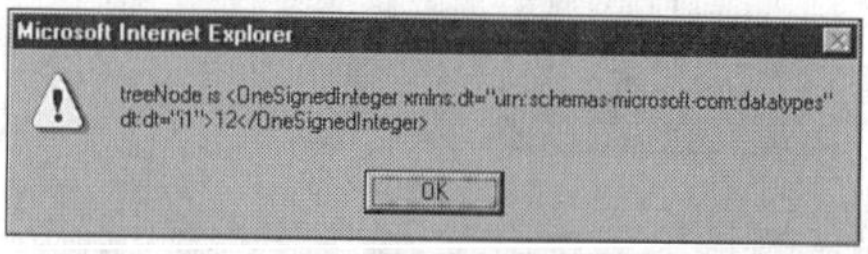

FIGURE 8.9

The node that's the fifth from the bottom, or the first child node.

The set of operations performed here should be clear from the sequence of figures. The first-level nodes are traversed from the first to the last by using the nextSibling property. Once you're at the last of the first-level nodes, the child nodes of that node are traversed from last to first using the previousSibling property.

Adding Nodes to a Tree

In this section, you'll load the data from an XML tree and then dynamically add additional nodes to that tree. This operation would be done when there's additional code that will write the modified tree back to a database file.

To add nodes to a tree, first you must *have* a tree. So let's start with Listing 8.3, which will be your imported XML file.

LISTING 8.3   An XML File That You'll Add Nodes To

```
 1: <?xml version="1.0"?>
 2: <!-- This file has a small number of nodes and is being
 3:      used as the basis for the addition of nodes to the
 4:      node tree. -->
 5: <Book xmlns:dt="urn:schemas-microsoft-com:datatypes">
 6: <Grade dt:dt="char">A</Grade>
 7: <OneSignedInteger dt:dt="i1">12</OneSignedInteger>
 8: <TwoSignedInteger dt:dt="i2">-12</TwoSignedInteger>
 9: <OneUnsignedInteger dt:dt="ui1">12</OneUnsignedInteger>
10: <TwoUnsignedInteger dt:dt="ui2">12</TwoUnsignedInteger>
11: </Book>
```

Obviously, if you're going to add nodes to the node tree, the first step is to create the node. The simplest way to do this is to use the cloneNode() method, which takes a single Boolean parameter. If the Boolean value is false, only the parent node is cloned. This is commonly referred to as a *shallow clone*. When the value is true, the entire node is cloned, including all descendants. The cloning of all nodes is known as a *deep clone*, so you'll sometimes see this parameter referred to as *deep*.

Once a new node is created, it must be added to the node tree. The first method that you'll use to do this is the appendChild() method, which takes the new node as a parameter. This method will take the node to be added and make it the last child of the node tree. These two methods are demonstrated in Listing 8.4.

LISTING 8.4   Code to Clone a Comment Node and Then Add It to the Node Tree

```
 1: <HTML>
 2:
 3: <HEAD>
 4: <SCRIPT LANGUAGE="JavaScript">
 5: <!--
 6:   var RootElement1;
 7:   var xmlDoc1=new ActiveXObject("microsoft.xmldom");
 8:   var newNode;
 9:   xmlDoc1.load("listing8-3.xml");
```

LISTING 8.4   continued

```
10:   function StartUp()
11:   {
12:   if(xmlDoc1.readyState=="4")
13:   {
14:    StartLoading();
15:   }
16:   else
17:   {
18:    alert("Process could not start");
19:   }
20:   }
21:   function StartLoading()
22:   {
23: // This identifier is used to hold the first node of a tree
24: // of nodes.
25:    var holdNode;
26:    RootElement1=xmlDoc1.documentElement;
27: // If the attempt to extract the document fails, we flag it
28: // with both an alert box and a message written to the web
29: // page. Once the messages are completed, the return is
30: // executed and the program terminates.
31:    if(RootElement1==null)
32:    {
33:     alert("The root node is null");
34:     document.write("<B><BIG>The data of the XML file cannot
          be accessed</BIG></B><BR>");
35:     return;
36:    }
37: // In this case, we are moving through the node tree by
38: // using the firstChild property to start the process
39: // and the nextSibling property to move through the tree.
40:
41: // Our first operation is to move to the second node, which
42: // is a comment line, and clone it.
43:
44:    treeNode=xmlDoc1.firstChild;
45:    treeNode=treeNode.nextSibling;
46:    newNode=treeNode.cloneNode(true);
47:
48: // We now move back to the first node of the main node
49: // tree.
50:    treeNode=xmlDoc1.firstChild;
51:    alert("treeNode is "+treeNode.xml);
52:    while(treeNode!=xmlDoc1.lastChild)
53:    {
54:     treeNode=treeNode.nextSibling;
55:     alert("treeNode is "+treeNode.xml);
56:    }
57:    holdNode=treeNode;
58: // holdNode is currently pointing to the last node of the
59: // main tree, which is the <Book> node, which also has
```

```
60: // child nodes. We now append the copy of the comment node
61: // to the end of those child nodes.
62:    holdNode.appendChild(newNode);
63:    treeNode=holdNode.lastChild;
64:    alert("lastNode of book is "+treeNode.xml);
65:    while(treeNode!=holdNode.firstChild)
66:      {
67:       treeNode=treeNode.previousSibling;
68:       alert("treeNode is "+treeNode.xml);
69:      }
70:    }
71: //-->
72: </SCRIPT>
73: </HEAD>
74: <BODY onLoad="StartUp()">
75: <!-- Since all of the content is now being written from the JavaScript
76: section, it is no longer necessary to put anything here. -->
77:
78: </BODY>
79: </HTML>
```

In the following lines, the treeNode pointer is moved to the comment node of the XML file:

```
treeNode=xmlDoc1.firstChild;
treeNode=treeNode.nextSibling;
newNode=treeNode.cloneNode(true);
```

A complete and distinct copy of the node is then made, and newNode is assigned as a reference to it.

The next operation is to reset to the start of the node list and step through it, displaying the contents of all the nodes:

```
treeNode=xmlDoc1.firstChild;
alert("treeNode is "+treeNode.xml);
while(treeNode!=xmlDoc1.lastChild)
  {
   treeNode=treeNode.nextSibling;
   alert("treeNode is "+treeNode.xml);
  }
```

When this loop terminates, treeNode is pointing to the last child node. At this point, append the copy of the comment node to the end of the list:

```
holdNode=treeNode;
// holdNode is currently pointing to the last node of the
// main tree, which is the <Book> node, which also has
// child nodes. We now append the copy of the comment node
// to the end of those child nodes.
   holdNode.appendChild(newNode);
```

Once the appendChild() function is done, the new last node of the tree will be the copy of the comment node.

The last step is a loop that starts at the end and steps upward, displaying the contents of the nodes:

```
treeNode=holdNode.lastChild;
   alert("lastNode of book is "+treeNode.xml);
   while(treeNode!=holdNode.firstChild)
    {
     treeNode=treeNode.previousSibling;
     alert("treeNode is "+treeNode.xml);
    }
```

When you run the HTML file, note that the comment node has indeed been appended to the end of the <Book> node's child nodes.

Go to the listing of the HTML file and modify this section:

```
// Our first step is to move to the second node, which is a
// comment line, and clone it.

   treeNode=xmlDoc1.firstChild;
   treeNode=treeNode.nextSibling;
   newNode=treeNode.cloneNode(true);
```

so that it matches the following:

```
// Our first step is to move to the book node, which
// contains child nodes, and clone it.

   treeNode=xmlDoc1.firstChild;
   treeNode=treeNode.nextSibling;
   treeNode=treeNode.nextSibling;
   newNode=treeNode.cloneNode(false);
```

In this case, you're cloning the <Book> node. However, because the input to the cloneNode method is false, none of the child nodes will be cloned. When you view the updated file in IE, pay particular attention to the node that is cloned. In this case, only the opening and closing <Book> tags are displayed. The appearance of that node is illustrated in Figure 8.10.

FIGURE 8.10

The appearance of the book node after a shallow cloning.

8

You've just learned how to add a node that contains data to a node tree. The processing instruction and comment nodes cannot contain data, so it should come as no surprise to you that they're treated differently than those that can contain data. It's possible to dynamically create such items and then add them to the node tree. The method to create a comment node is, appropriately, createComment. For example:

```
newNode=xmlDoc1.createComment("This is an inserted
comment");
```

Here, xmlDoc1 is an instance of the xmldom object. The node that's created will also have the proper comment delimiters added to the text. Therefore, when the node is examined, the complete contents will be

```
<!-- This is an inserted comment. -->
```

However, this doesn't add the node to the tree. There must be an explicit method call to place it in the tree. Besides the appendChild() method that you've already seen, another method that can be used to add a node to the tree is the insertBefore method. The syntax of the insertBefore method is shown here:

```
nodeName.insertBefore(InsertedNode,NodeToComeAfter);
```

As the name implies, this will insert the node pointed to by InsertedNode into a position immediately before the node pointed to by NodeToComeAfter.

Let's look at an example that uses the insertBefore method. When you were extracting the data from an XML file, you started by performing the initial operation:

```
RootElement1=xmlDoc1.documentElement;
```

The documentElement node of the XML document is in fact the section of the file that contains the data. For Listing 8.4, that corresponds to the <Book> element. In the following exercise, you'll create an instance of a comment node and then clone it twice. The three nodes will then be inserted into the node tree. The first location will be before the documentElement node, the second at the end of the <Book> node, and the third before the original last node of the file.

Listing 8.5 is a modification of Listing 8.4. The changes are marked in bold. Note that most of the calls of the alert method have been removed.

LISTING 8.5 Using the createComment and insertBefore Functions

```
1:<HTML>
2:<HEAD>
3:<SCRIPT LANGUAGE="JavaScript">
4:<!--
5: var RootElement1;
```

LISTING 8.5   continued

```
 6: var xmlDoc1=new ActiveXObject("microsoft.xmldom");
 7:// These are the nodes that will be created.
 8: var newNode3;
 9: var newNode1;
10: var newNode2;
11:  xmlDoc1.load("listing8-1.xml");
12:  function StartUp()
13: {
14:  if(xmlDoc1.readyState=="4")
15:  {
16:   StartLoading();
17:  }
18:  else
19:  {
20:   alert("Process could not start");
21:  }
22:  }
23:  function StartLoading()
24:  {
25:// This identifier is used to hold the first node of a tree
26:// of nodes.
27:   var holdNode;
28:   RootElement1=xmlDoc1.documentElement;
29:// If the attempt to extract the document fails, we flag it
30:// with both an alert box and a message written to the web
31:// page. Once the messages are completed, the return is
32:// executed and the program terminates.
33:   if(RootElement1==null)
34:   {
35:    alert("The root node is null");
36:    document.write("<B><BIG>The data of the XML file cannot
         be accessed</BIG></B><BR>");
37:    return;
38:   }
39:// In this case, we are moving through the node tree by
40:// using the firstChild property to start the process
41:// and the nextSibling property to move through the tree.
42:// Our first step is to create a comment node.
43:   newNode3=xmlDoc1.createComment("This is an inserted
         comment");
44:// Create two additional copies of the comment node.
45:   newNode1=newNode3.cloneNode(false);
46:   newNode2=newNode3.cloneNode(false);
47:// Output the node for viewing.
48:   alert(newNode3.xml);
49:// We now insert it before the documentElement part of the
50:// XML file.
51:   xmlDoc1.insertBefore(newNode3,xmlDoc1.documentElement);
```

```
52:    treeNode=xmlDoc1.firstChild;
53:      while(treeNode!=xmlDoc1.lastChild)
54:      {
55:       treeNode=treeNode.nextSibling;
56:      }
57:    holdNode=treeNode;
58://  holdNode is currently pointing to the last node of the
59://  main tree, which is the <Book> node, which also has
60://  child nodes. We now append the copy of the comment node
61://  to the end of those child nodes.
62:    holdNode.appendChild(newNode1);
63:    treeNode=holdNode.lastChild;
64:    treeNode=treeNode.previousSibling;
65:    xmlDoc1.documentElement.insertBefore(newNode2,treeNode);
66:    treeNode=holdNode.lastChild;
67:    while(treeNode!=holdNode.firstChild)
68:      {
69:       treeNode=treeNode.previousSibling;
70:      }
71://  The entire XML document is now output for viewing.
72:    alert(xmlDoc1.xml);
73:    }
74://-->
75:</SCRIPT>
76:</HEAD>
77:<BODY onLoad="StartUp()">
78:<!-- Since all of the content is now being written from the JavaScript
      section, it is no longer necessary to put anything here. -->
79:</BODY>
80:</HTML>
```

In lines 42 through 48, a new comment node is created and then duplicated twice before being displayed.

In line 72, the alert method is then called to display the contents of the XML tree, as illustrated in Figure 8.11.

FIGURE 8.11

The comment node that will be inserted.

Note that the proper comment tags have been placed around the text of the comment. The node is then inserted into the node tree immediately before the <Book> node.

Before lines 62-65 are executed, holdNode points to the <Book> tag.

Therefore, line 62 will cause newNode1 to be inserted as the new last child node of the
<Book> tag. The treeNode pointer is then moved to the position of the last node and then
up one node on the tree. At that point, newNode2 is inserted into the tree before the node:

```
<TwoUnsignedInteger dt:dt="ui2">12</TwoUnsignedInteger>
```

Finally, one more call of the alert method is done on line 72 to display the new contents
of the node tree.

The final appearance of the node tree is illustrated in Figure 8.12.

You can now append to the end of the tree or insert before any node in the tree, so it's
possible to add a node to any position on the tree. Go to Listing 8.5 and change the line

```
holdNode.appendChild(newNode1);
```

to

```
holdNode.appendChild(newNode3);
```

and the line

```
xmlDoc1.documentElement.insertBefore(newNode2,treeNode);
```

to

```
xmlDoc1.documentElement.insertBefore(newNode3,treeNode);
```

When you view the file in IE, note that only the last insertion of the new node appears.
In the first line, the node is placed at the end of the list. After that, the location is moved
one position up the list and then the node is inserted again. If the node was duplicated,
there would be two instances of that node in the list. Since the same node was inserted
every time, it's clear that the first instance was removed from the previous location when
reinserted. If you insert the same node into a tree twice without duplicating it, the previous entry is removed.

The method for dynamically creating a processing instruction is similar to the createComment method:

```
xmlDoc1.createProcessingInstruction(name,data);
```

Here, name is the name of the instruction and data is the value of the processing instruction. As was the case with the comment node, this simply creates the node. Inserting into the node tree requires a separate call to an insert method.

Replacing Nodes in a Tree

There are times when you want to replace a node rather than add a new one. To understand why this is important, recall that the XML code is only one part of the total package. In general, there will be application code that will write the data currently in XML form to a database. If the data is to be read and updated by removing an entry and then adding one, it makes more sense to perform a replacement rather than the two separate operations of deletion and insertion.

The replacement can be done by using the replaceChild(newChild,oldChild) method. As the names imply, the node pointed to by oldChild is replaced by the node pointed to by newChild.

In the following example, you'll first clone the documentElement node of the node tree. You'll then modify the contents of the clone and replace the original documentElement with the modified clone.

Listing 8.6 is a modification of Listing 8.5, and the key changes are marked in bold. This code will clone the <Book> node, which contains all the data in the XML file. Some of the data entries are updated, and then the updated copy is inserted back into the node tree in a destructive overwrite. In the real world, a node can be updated in many ways, only one of which involves the XML code performing the updates. A destructive overwrite would then be used to perform the update.

LISTING 8.6   Cloning a Node and Using the Clone as a Replacement

```
1:<HTML>
2:<HEAD>
3:<SCRIPT LANGUAGE="JavaScript">
4:<!--
5: var RootElement1;
6: var xmlDoc1=new ActiveXObject("microsoft.xmldom");
7:// This is the node that will be created.
8: var newNode;
9:   xmlDoc1.load("listing8-1.xml");
10:   function StartUp()
```

LISTING 8.6   continued

```
11: {
12:   if(xmlDoc1.readyState=="4")
13:   {
14:     StartLoading();
15:   }
16:   else
17:   {
18:     alert("Process could not start");
19:   }
20:   }
21:   function StartLoading()
22:   {
23:// This identifier is used to hold the first node of a tree
24:// of nodes.
25:     var holdNode;
26:     RootElement1=xmlDoc1.documentElement;
27:// If the attempt to extract the document fails, we flag it
28:// with both an alert box and a message written to the web
29:// page. Once the messages are completed, the return is
30:// executed and the program terminates.
31:   if(RootElement1==null)
32:   {
33:     alert("The root node is null");
34:     document.write("<B><BIG>The data of the XML file cannot
          be accessed</BIG></B><BR>");
35:     return;
36:   }
37:// We start by cloning the documentElement node.
38:   newNode=xmlDoc1.documentElement.cloneNode(true);
39:// We now update the data components of the clone.
40:   newNode.childNodes.item(0).text="B";
41:   newNode.childNodes.item(1).text="24";
42:   newNode.childNodes.item(2).text="-246";
43:   newNode.childNodes.item(3).text="128";
44:   newNode.childNodes.item(4).text="32768";
45:// Output the node for viewing.
46:   alert(newNode.xml);
47:// Perform the replacement.
48:   xmlDoc1.replaceChild(newNode,xmlDoc1.documentElement);
49:// The entire XML document is now output for viewing.
50:   alert(xmlDoc1.xml);
51:   }
52://-->
53:</SCRIPT>
54:</HEAD>
55:<BODY onLoad="StartUp()">
```

```
56:<!-- Since all of the content is now being written from the
    JavaScript section, it is no longer
    necessary to put anything here. -->
57:</BODY>
58:</HTML>
```

Your first step, which takes place on lines 38 through 46, is to perform a deep clone of the documentElement node, modify the contents of that node, and then use a call of the alert method to display the results.

The output from this call of the alert method is illustrated in Figure 8.13.

FIGURE 8.13

The contents of the cloned node after the updates.

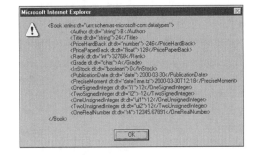

The next step is to perform the replacement and then output the contents of the entire node tree, which is done in line 48. The contents of the complete XML file are then output on line 50.

The consequences of the last call of the alert method are illustrated in Figure 8.14.

FIGURE 8.14

The contents of the complete XML file after the node is replaced.

Summary

At the beginning of this hour, you learned how to traverse a node tree by using the firstChild and lastChild properties to get started, and then using the nextSibling and previousSibling properties to move through the list. This technique considers the data as a node tree rather than as an array.

Then you created new nodes and inserted them into the node tree. After that, you cloned a new node and then updated it before inserting it into the node tree in a destructive overwrite.

Q&A

Q **If you have a node tree with three layers, how do you traverse the nodes at the third level?**

A Using either the firstChild or lastChild property will take you to the second level. A second use of the firstChild or lastChild property will take you to the third level. Using the nextSibling or previousSibling property will then allow you to traverse the siblings of that node.

Q **Under what circumstances would you extract the data from a node using the nodeTypedValue property rather than the text property?**

A If the data is typed, extracting it using the nodeTypedValue property will preserve the type information, whereas the text property is always just simple text.

Q **Under what circumstances would you perform a replaceChild() operation?**

A Updating a database entry by performing a destructive overwrite of it is a common operation, and it's more efficient that performing a deletion and insertion separately.

Workshop

Quiz

1. When you perform a deep clone, how many node levels are copied?

   a. Only the first level.

   b. Only the first and second levels.

   c. All levels of data; all comments and processing instructions are not copied.

   d. All nodes at all levels.

2. When a new comment node is created, what happens to that node?

   a. The node is inserted into the node tree at the top.

   b. The node is inserted into the node at the bottom.

   c. The node is inserted at the current working position in the tree.

   d. The node is not inserted; that operation must be done using another command.

3. If you have a reference to a node, what happens if that node is inserted into the node tree more than once?

   a. Only one entry is in the final form. All others are removed when a new insertion is performed.

b. Copies of the node are made for each insertion.

c. The node is inserted each time, but all references are to the single copy.

Answers

1. d.
2. d.
3. a.

Exercises

1. Given the hierarchical tree structure in Figure 8.15, write a program to traverse through all of the nodes using the firstChild, lastChild, nextSibling, and previousSibling properties. The items in parentheses are the data types of the entries. Create an instance of this data type to test your program.

FIGURE 8.15

The diagram of a book node.

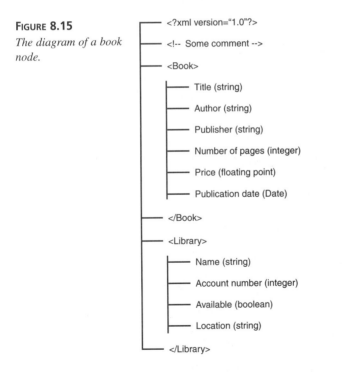

```
        <?xml version="1.0"?>

        <!-- Some comment -->

        <Book>

            Title (string)

            Author (string)

            Publisher (string)

            Number of pages (integer)

            Price (floating point)

            Publication date (Date)

        </Book>

        <Library>

            Name (string)

            Account number (integer)

            Available (boolean)

            Location (string)

        </Library>
```

2. Read in Listing 8.1 and add three different comment lines to the <Book> node so that a comment appears as the first, last, and fourth nodes of the <Book> node.

HOUR 9

Databases and XML

In the previous hours, you learned how the data in an XML file can be defined and how the contents of those files can be read. Such background material is always essential, but the important thing about XML is its capability to describe data and execute database operations. Accordingly, this hour will demonstrate how XML can be used to define, manipulate, and present the data in databases. This process will continue in many different forms all the way to Hour 22.

In this hour, you'll learn the following:

- The basic structure of the components of your simple database
- How to step through the <Book> nodes of your <Catalog> database
- How to construct a program that will allow you to display the contents of the <Catalog> database by clicking on buttons

The Definition of Your Basic Data Records

To perform any database operations, you first need a database, and before you have a database, you must have a definition of a record of that database. For the purposes of this hour, you'll be defining a catalog of books. Your basic <Book> data object will consist of a complex node describing the author, a complex node describing the publisher, and simple nodes with the title, ISBN, an ID number used by the publisher, the date of publication, and the price of the book. The <Book> nodes will satisfy the XML definition shown in Listing 9.1.

An entry in a database is known as a record, and all records must satisfy the definition of the record. Since your XML data files consist of nodes that satisfy the DTD, a node in the XML data file is equivalent to a record in a database.

LISTING 9.1   The <Book> Node

```
 1:   <Book>
 2:    <Title dt:dt="string"> </Title>
 3:    <Author>
 4:        <Name dt:dt="string" > </Name>
 5:        <Address dt:dt="string" > </Address>
 6:        <City dt:dt="string" > </City>
 7:        <State dt:dt="string"> </State>
 8:        <PostalCode dt:dt="string"> </PostalCode>
 9:        <Country dt:dt="string"> </Country>
10:        <Phone dt:dt="string"> </Phone>
11:        <Email dt:dt="string"> </Email>
12:        <URL dt:dt="string"> </URL>
13:     </Author>
14:    <Publisher>
15:      <Name dt:dt="string"> </Name>
16:      <Address dt:dt="string" > </Address>
17:      <City dt:dt="string" > </City>
18:      <State dt:dt="string"> </State>
19:      <PostalCode dt:dt="string"> </PostalCode>
20:      <Country dt:dt="string"> </Country>
21:      <Phone dt:dt="string"> </Phone>
22:      <Editor dt:dt="string"> </Editor>
23:      <EmailContact dt:dt="string"> </EmailContact>
24:      <URL dt:dt="string"> </URL>
25:     </Publisher>
26:    <ISBN dt:dt="string"> </ISBN>
27:    <PublisherBookID dt:dt="ui8"> </PublisherBookID>
```

```
28:    <PublicationDate dt:dt="date"> </PublicationDate>
29:    <Price dt:dt="fixed.14.4"> </Price>
30:    </Book>
```

Your database will consist of a list of <Book> nodes surrounded by a pair of <Catalog> tags. Therefore, Listing 9.2 is the initial form that the XML database file will have. Of course, you'll add additional <Book> entries to it as necessary.

LISTING 9.2   A Simple Catalog of Books with Type Information Included

```
 1: <?xml version="1.0"?>
 2: <!-- This file is the data component of an instance of the
 3:      Catalog object that contains a series of Book
 4:      objects. -->
 5: <Catalog xmlns:dt="urn:schemas-microsoft-com:datatypes">
 6: <Book>
 7: <Title dt:dt="string">Teach Yourself XML in 24 Hours</Title>
 8: <Author>
 9: <Name dt:dt="string">Charles Ashbacher</Name>
10: <Address dt:dt="string">119 Northwood Drive</Address>
11: <City dt:dt="string">Hiawatha</City>
12: <State dt:dt="string">Iowa</State>
13: <PostalCode dt:dt="string">52233</PostalCode>
14: <Country dt:dt="string">United States</Country>
15: <Phone dt:dt="string">(319) 378-4646</Phone>
16: <Email dt:dt="string">ashbacher@ashbacher.com</Email>
17: <URL dt:dt="string">http://www.ashbacher.com</URL>
18: </Author>
19: <Publisher>
20: <Name dt:dt="string">Sams Publishing</Name>
21: <Address dt:dt="string">201 West 103rd Street</Address>
22: <City dt:dt="string">Indianapolis</City>
23: <State dt:dt="string">Indiana</State>
24: <PostalCode dt:dt="string">46290</PostalCode>
25: <Country dt:dt="string">United States</Country>
26: <Phone dt:dt="string">(111) 123-4567</Phone>
27: <Editor dt:dt="string">Dummy Name</Editor>
28: <EmailContact dt:dt="string">Dummy.Name@samspublishing.com
    </EmailContact>
29: <URL dt:dt="string">http://www.samspublishing.com</URL>
30: </Publisher>
31: <ISBN dt:dt="string">0-672-31950-0</ISBN>
32: <PublisherBookID dt:dt="ui4">1234567</PublisherBookID>
33: <PublicationDate dt:dt="date">2000-04-01</PublicationDate>
34: <Price dt:dt="fixed.14.4">24.95</Price>
35: </Book>
36: </Catalog>
```

Listing 9.3 is a modification of a previous listing that will be used to read the nodes of your <Catalog> database.

LISTING 9.3 Reading the Nodes of Your <Catalog> Database

```
 1: <HTML>
 2: <HEAD>
 3: <SCRIPT LANGUAGE="JavaScript">
 4: <!--
 5:  var RootElement1;
 6: // nodecount will store the number of nodes containing data
 7: //in the XML file.
 8:  var nodecount;
 9:  var xmlDoc1=new ActiveXObject("microsoft.xmldom");
10:  var newNode;
11:   xmlDoc1.load("listing9-2.xml");
12: function StartUp()
13:  {
14:   if(xmlDoc1.readyState=="4")
15:   {
16:    StartLoading();
17:   }
18:   else
19:   {
20:    alert("Process could not start");
21:   }
22:  }
23:   function StartLoading()
24:   {
25:     RootElement1=xmlDoc1.documentElement;
26: // If the attempt to extract the document fails, we flag it
27: // with both an alert box and
28: // a message written to the web page. Once the messages are
29: // completed, the return is executed and the program
30: // terminates.
31:    if(RootElement1==null)
32:    {
33:     alert("The root node is null");
34:     document.write("<B><BIG>The data of the XML file cannot
         be accessed</BIG></B><BR>");
35:     return;
36:    }
37: // In this case, we are moving through the node tree by
38: // using the firstChild property to start the process
39: // and the nextSibling property to move through the tree.
40:    treeNode=xmlDoc1.firstChild;
41:    alert("treeNode is "+treeNode.xml);
42:   while(treeNode!=xmlDoc1.lastChild)
43:     {
44:      treeNode=treeNode.nextSibling;
45:      alert("treeNode is "+treeNode.xml);
```

```
46:    }
47: // We now extract and display the documentElement.
48:    treeNode=xmlDoc1.documentElement;
49:    alert(treeNode.xml);
50:    }
51: //-->
52: </SCRIPT>
53: </HEAD>
54: <BODY onLoad="StartUp()">
55: <!-- Since all of the content is now being written from the
56:      JavaScript section, it is no longer necessary to put
57:      anything here. -->
58: </BODY>
59: </HTML>
```

9

When this file is run in IE, only one node is displayed. The output from the third call of the alert method is illustrated in Figure 9.1. It's the same as the result of the fourth and last call.

FIGURE 9.1

The <Book> node in IE.

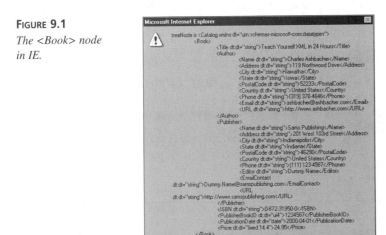

The output of the last two calls of the alert method demonstrates what you learned in the previous hour. The data portion of the node tree is documentElement and, in this case, is the third node. To extract the <Book> node from the <Catalog> node, you simply need to use the firstChild property of the <Catalog> node. Also understand that the loop to read the nodes will work for any number of <Book> nodes that may be found in the XML file.

Your next step is to make a slight modification to the StartLoading() function in the previous HTML listing. The changes to be made are highlighted in bold in Listing 9.4.

LISTING 9.4   Changing the StartLoading() Function

```
 1: function StartLoading()
 2:   {
 3:     // This node is for storing node for later use.
 4:     var holdNode;
 5:     RootElement1=xmlDoc1.documentElement;
 6: // If the attempt to extract the document fails, we flag it
 7: // with both an alert box and a message written to the web
 8: // page. Once the messages are completed, the return is
 9: // executed and the program terminates.
10:     if(RootElement1==null)
11:     {
12:       alert("The root node is null");
13:       document.write("<B><BIG>The data of the XML file cannot
          be accessed</BIG></B><BR>");
14:       return;
15:     }
16: // In this case, we are moving through the node tree by
17: // using the firstChild property to start the process
18: // and the nextSibling property to move through the tree.
19:     treeNode=xmlDoc1.firstChild;
20: while(treeNode!=xmlDoc1.lastChild)
21:       {
22:         treeNode=treeNode.nextSibling;
23:       }
24: // treeNode will now point to the last node of the file,
25: // which is the <Catalog> node.
26: // We store the <Catalog> node in case we need it later.
27:     holdNode=treeNode;
28: // This will set the treeNode pointer to the first of the
29: // <Book> nodes.
30:     treeNode=holdNode.firstChild;
31:     alert(treeNode.xml);
32:   }
```

The purpose of this modification is to set the holdNode pointer to the <Catalog> node of the XML file. Given the structure of the file, the child nodes of the <Catalog> node will be the <Book> nodes—the data you'll be working with.

The output of the alert will now be the <Book> node only. Because you're at the first child node of the <Catalog> node, you can now step through the <Book> nodes using the nextSibling property. Of course, you need to have more than one <Book> node, so the next step is to add two more instances of the <Book> node to your XML file so that it will contain three data nodes.

Listing 9.5 contains two additional <Book> nodes to add to Listing 9.2. The result will be a file with three <Book> nodes that you can use in the demonstrations of XML functionality

LISTING 9.5   Additional <Book> Nodes to Add to Listing 9.2

```
 1: <Book>
 2: <Title dt:dt="string">Teach Yourself Cool Stuff in 24 Hours</Title>
 3: <Author>
 4: <Name dt:dt="string">ReallySmart Person</Name>
 5: <Address dt:dt="string">110 Main Street</Address>
 6: <City dt:dt="string">Silicon City</City>
 7: <State dt:dt="string">California</State>
 8: <PostalCode dt:dt="string">10101</PostalCode>
 9: <Country dt:dt="string">United States</Country>
10: <Phone dt:dt="string">(101) 101-0101</Phone>
11: <Email dt:dt="string">RSmart@MyCompany.com</Email>
12: <URL dt:dt="string">http://www.MyCompany.com</URL>
13: </Author>
14: <Publisher>
15: <Name dt:dt="string">Sams Publishing</Name>
16: <Address dt:dt="string">201 West 103rd Street</Address>
17: <City dt:dt="string">Indianapolis</City>
18: <State dt:dt="string">Indiana</State>
19: <PostalCode dt:dt="string">46290</PostalCode>
20: <Country dt:dt="string">United States</Country>
21: <Phone dt:dt="string">(111) 123-4567</Phone>
22: <Editor dt:dt="string">Dummy Name</Editor>
23: <EmailContact dt:dt="string">Dummy.Name@samspublishing.com</EmailContact>
24: <URL dt:dt="string">http://www.samspublishing.com</URL>
25: </Publisher>
26: <ISBN dt:dt="string">0-672-1010-0</ISBN>
27: <PublisherBookID dt:dt="ui4">1234568</PublisherBookID>
28: <PublicationDate dt:dt="date">2000-06-01</PublicationDate>
29: <Price dt:dt="fixed.14.4">24.95</Price>
30: </Book>
31:
32: <Book>
33: <Title dt:dt="string">Teach Yourself Uses of Silicon in 24 Hours</Title>
34: <Author>
35: <Name dt:dt="string">Missy Fixit</Name>
36: <Address dt:dt="string">119 Hard Drive</Address>
37: <City dt:dt="string">Diskette City</City>
38: <State dt:dt="string">California</State>
39: <PostalCode dt:dt="string">10101</PostalCode>
40: <Country dt:dt="string">United States</Country>
41: <Phone dt:dt="string">(586) 212-3638</Phone>
42: <Email dt:dt="string">MFixit@Googol.com</Email>
43: <URL dt:dt="string">http://www.Googol.com</URL>
44: </Author>
45: <Publisher>
46: <Name dt:dt="string">Sams Publishing</Name>
47: <Address dt:dt="string">201 West 103rd Street</Address>
48: <City dt:dt="string">Indianapolis</City>
49: <State dt:dt="string">Indiana</State>
```

LISTING 9.5 continued

```
50: <PostalCode dt:dt="string">46290</PostalCode>
51: <Country dt:dt="string">United States</Country>
52: <Phone dt:dt="string">(111) 123-4567</Phone>
53: <Editor dt:dt="string">Dummy Name</Editor>
54: <EmailContact dt:dt="string">Dummy.Name@samspublishing.com</EmailContact>
55: <URL dt:dt="string">http://www.samspublishing.com</URL>
56: </Publisher>
57: <ISBN dt:dt="string">0-578-31950-0</ISBN>
58: <PublisherBookID dt:dt="ui4">1234569</PublisherBookID>
59: <PublicationDate dt:dt="date">2000-01-01</PublicationDate>
60: <Price dt:dt="fixed.14.4">26.95</Price>
61: </Book>
```

The file with three <Book> nodes will be used extensively as the example of data to be read. Refer to the complete file as listing9-5.xml. Therefore, you'll often see the following line in your HTML files:

```
xmlDoc1.load("listing9-5.xml");
```

Reading the <Book> Nodes of the Catalog Database

Change the StartLoading() function in Listing 9.3 as shown in Listing 9.6.

LISTING 9.6 Stepping Through the <Book> Nodes of the <Catalog> Database

```
 1: function StartLoading()
 2:   {
 3:    // This node is for storing node for later use.
 4:    var holdNode;
 5:    RootElement1=xmlDoc1.documentElement;
 6: // If the attempt to extract the document fails, we flag it
 7: // with both an alert box and a message written to the web
 8: // page. Once the messages are completed, the return is
 9: // executed and the program terminates.
10:    if(RootElement1==null)
11:    {
12:     alert("The root node is null");
13:     document.write("<B><BIG>The data of the XML file cannot
        be accessed</BIG></B><BR>");
14:     return;
15:    }
```

```
16: // In this case, we are moving through the node tree by
17: // using the firstChild property to start the process
18: // and the nextSibling property to move through the tree.
19:    treeNode=xmlDoc1.firstChild;
20:    while(treeNode!=xmlDoc1.lastChild)
21:      {
22:        treeNode=treeNode.nextSibling;
23:        }
24: // treeNode will now point to the last node of the file,
25: // which is the <Catalog> node.
26: // We store the <Catalog> node because we need it later.
27:    holdNode=treeNode;
28: // This will set the treeNode pointer to the first of the
29: // <Book> nodes.
30:    treeNode=holdNode.firstChild;
31:    alert(treeNode.xml);
32: // We then step through the book nodes.
33:    while(treeNode!=holdNode.lastChild)
34:    {
35:      treeNode=treeNode.nextSibling;
36:      alert(treeNode.xml);
37:    }
38:    }
```

You now have a program that will step through the <Book> nodes of the <Catalog> file. The output of the calls of the alert method are displayed in Figures 9.2 through 9.4.

FIGURE **9.2**

The first node of the
<Catalog> database.

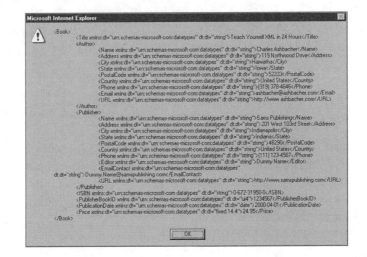

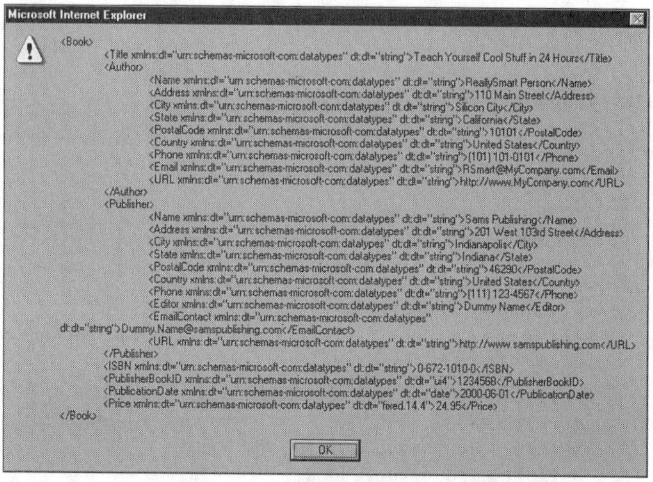

FIGURE 9.3

The second node of the
<Catalog> database.

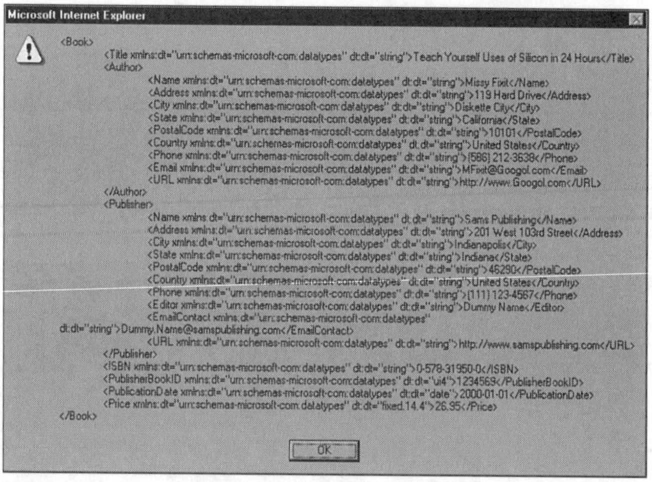

FIGURE 9.4

The third node of the
<Catalog> database.

Note that the output is the contents of the three <Book> nodes. Each of these nodes will
have seven child nodes: <Title>, <Author>, <Publisher>, <ISBN>, <PublisherBookID>,
<PublicationDate>, and <Price>. To obtain the contents of these nodes, you'll use the
Node.firstChild property to start at the beginning of the node list and the
Node.nextSibling property to move through the node tree.

Using Button Clicks to Move Through the <Catalog> Database

Listing 9.7 is a modification of the previous HTML listing. This program will read all of the child nodes of the <Book> nodes at all levels.

LISTING 9.7 Reading All Child Nodes of the <Book> Nodes

```
1:<HTML>
2:<HEAD>
3:<SCRIPT LANGUAGE="JavaScript">
4:<!--
5: // This identifier is used to force the XML processor to
6:// parse the file.
7: var RootElement1;
8:// This is the XML object.
9: var xmlDoc1=new ActiveXObject("microsoft.xmldom");
10:// This is the global pointer to a node that is used to
11:// move around the <Book> objects. It always stores the
12:// current <Book> object.
13: var globalHoldNode;
14:// This is a global pointer that points to the last
15:// <Book> node.
16: var globalLastBook;
17:// This is a global pointer that points to the first
18:// <Book> node.
19: var globalFirstBook;
20: xmlDoc1.load("listing9-5.xml");
21: function StartUp()
22: {
23:   if(xmlDoc1.readyState=="4")
24:   {
25:    StartLoading();
26:   }
27:   else
28:   {
29:    alert("Process could not start");
30:   }
31: }
32:  function StartLoading()
33:  {
34: // This node is used to move through the child nodes of
35: // the <Book> node.
36:    var moveNode;
37:    RootElement1=xmlDoc1.documentElement;
38:// If the attempt to extract the document fails, we flag
39:// it with both an alert box and a message written to
```

LISTING 9.7   continued

```
40:// the web page. Once the messages are completed, the
41: // return is executed and the program terminates.
42:    if(RootElement1==null)
43:    {
44:    alert("The root node is null");
45:    document.write("<B><BIG>The data of the XML file
       cannot be accessed</BIG></B><BR>");
46:    return;
47:    }
48:    treeNode=xmlDoc1.lastChild;
49:// This will set the pointer to the first child node of
50:// the current <Catalog> node.
51:    globalHoldNode=treeNode.firstChild;
52:// This global pointer stores the first of the <Book>
53:// objects.
54:    globalFirstBook=treeNode.firstChild;
55:// This global pointer stores the last of the <Book>
56:// objects.
57:    globalLastBook=treeNode.lastChild;
58:    DisplayNode();
59: }
60:// This function displays the contents of the node
61:// pointed to by globalHoldNode.
62: function DisplayNode()
63:{
64:// This pointer to a node will move through the nodes of
65:// the <Book> object.
66:  var moveNode;
67:// This pointer to a node will move through the subnodes
68:// if it is the <Author> or <Publisher> node.
69:  var inNode;
70:// This will hold the name of the node of the <Book>
71:// object.
72:  var nameNode;
73:// Since globalHoldNode points to an instance of a
74:// <Book> node, we need to first point to the first of
75:// the child nodes.
76:    moveNode=globalHoldNode.firstChild;
77:// This loop will cycle through the nodes of the <Book>
78:// node.
79:    while(moveNode!=null)
80:    {
81:     nameNode=moveNode.nodeName;
82:     switch(nameNode)
83:     {
84:      case "Title":
85:      Title.innerText=moveNode.text;
```

```
86:        break;
87:        case "Author":
88:// If we are at the author node, it is necessary to read
89:// the subnodes. We set inNode to the first child node
90:// and then use the nextChild property to step through
91:// the nodes.
92:        inNode=moveNode.firstChild;
93:        while(inNode!=null)
94:        {
95:          nameInNode=inNode.nodeName;
96:          switch(nameInNode)
97:          {
98:           case "Name":
99:           AuthorName.innerText=inNode.text;
100:           break;
101:           case "Address":
102:           AuthorAddress.innerText=inNode.text;
103:           break;
104:           case "City":
105:           AuthorCity.innerText=inNode.text;
106:           break;
107:           case "State":
108:           AuthorState.innerText=inNode.text;
109:           break;
110:           case "PostalCode":
112:           AuthorPostalCode.innerText=inNode.text;
112:           break;
113:           case "Country":
114:           AuthorCountry.innerText=inNode.text;
115:           break;
116:           case "Phone":
117:           AuthorPhone.innerText=inNode.text;
118:           break;
119:           case "Email":
120:           AuthorEmail.innerText=inNode.text;
121:           break;
122:           case "URL":
123:           AuthorURL.innerText=inNode.text;
124:           break;
125:          }
126:          inNode=inNode.nextSibling;
127:        }
128:        break;
129:        case"Publisher":
130:// If we are at the <Publisher> node, we need to read
131:// the subnodes. We do this by setting inNode to the
132:// first Child and then use the nextChild property to
133://step through the remaining nodes.
134:        inNode=moveNode.firstChild;
```

9

LISTING 9.7 continued

```
135:      while(inNode!=null)
136:      {
137:        nameInNode=inNode.nodeName;
138:        switch(nameInNode)
139:        {
140:         case "Name":
141:         PublisherName.innerText=inNode.text;
142:         break;
143:         case "Address":
144:         PublisherAddress.innerText=inNode.text;
145:         break;
146:         case "City":
147:         PublisherCity.innerText=inNode.text;
148:         break;
149:         case "State":
150:         PublisherState.innerText=inNode.text;
151:         break;
152:         case "PostalCode":
153:         PublisherPostalCode.innerText=inNode.text;
154:         break;
155:         case "Country":
156:         PublisherCountry.innerText=inNode.text;
157:         break;
158:         case "Phone":
159:         PublisherPhone.innerText=inNode.text;
160:         break;
161:         case "Editor":
162:         PublisherEditor.innerText=inNode.text;
163:         break;
164:         case "EmailContact":
165:         EmailContact. innerText=inNode.text;
166:         break;
167:         case "URL":
168:         PublisherURL.innerText=inNode.text;
169:         break;
170:        }
171:       inNode=inNode.nextSibling;
172:      }
173:      break;
174:      case "ISBN":
175:      ISBN.innerText=moveNode.text;
176:      break;
177:      case "PublisherBookID":
178:      PublisherBookID.innerText=moveNode.text;
179:      break;
180:      case "PublicationDate":
181:      PubDate.innerText=moveNode.text;
```

```
182:      break;
183:      case "Price":
184:      Price.innerText=moveNode.text;
185:      break;
186:      }
187:      moveNode=moveNode.nextSibling;
188:    }
189:}
190:function NextRecord()
191:{
192: if(globalHoldNode==globalLastBook)
193: {
194:  alert("You are attempting to go off the end of the
     database");
195: }
196: else
197: {
198:  globalHoldNode=globalHoldNode.nextSibling;
199:  DisplayNode();
200: }
201:}
202:function PrevRecord()
203:{
204: if(globalHoldNode==globalFirstBook)
205: {
206:  alert("You are attempting to go off the start end of
     the database");
207: }
208: else
209: {
210:  globalHoldNode=globalHoldNode.previousSibling;
211:  DisplayNode();
212: }
213:}
214: // This function moves to and displays the first
215: //record in the database.
216:function FirstRecord()
217:{
218: globalHoldNode=globalFirstBook;
219: DisplayNode();
220:}
221:// This function moves to and displays the last record
222:// in the database.
223:function LastRecord()
224:{
225: globalHoldNode=globalLastBook;
226: DisplayNode();
227:}
```

9

LISTING 9.7   continued

```
228://-->
229:</SCRIPT>
230:</HEAD>
231:<BODY onLoad="StartUp()">
232:<b>Title:</b> <SPAN ID=Title> </SPAN><br>
233:<big>Author:</big><br>
234:      Name: <SPAN
    ID=AuthorName></SPAN> 
235:      Address: <SPAN
    ID=AuthorAddress></SPAN><br>
236:      City: <SPAN
    ID=AuthorCity></SPAN> 
237:      State: <SPAN
    ID=AuthorState></SPAN><br>
238:      Postal
    Code: <SPAN ID=AuthorPostalCode></SPAN> 
239:      Country: <SPAN
    ID=AuthorCountry></SPAN><br>
240:      Phone: <SPAN
    ID=AuthorPhone></SPAN> 
241:      Email: <SPAN
    ID=AuthorEmail></SPAN><br>
242:      URL: <SPAN
    ID=AuthorURL></SPAN><br><br>
243:<big>Publisher:</big><br>
244:      Name: <SPAN
    ID=PublisherName></SPAN> 
245:      Address: <SPAN
    ID=PublisherAddress></SPAN><br>
246:      City: <SPAN
    ID=PublisherCity ></SPAN> 
247:      State: <SPAN
    ID=PublisherState ></SPAN><br>
248:      Postal
    Code: <SPAN
    ID=PublisherPostalCode></SPAN> 
249:      Country: <SPAN
    ID=PublisherCountry ></SPAN><br>
250:      Phone: <SPAN
    ID=PublisherPhone ></SPAN> 
251:       Editor: <SPAN
    ID=PublisherEditor ></SPAN><br>
252:      Email
    contact: <SPAN ID=EmailContact ></SPAN> 
253:      URL: <SPAN
    ID=PublisherURL ></SPAN><br><br>
254:<b>ISBN:</b> <SPAN ID=ISBN></SPAN>  
```

```
255:<b>Publisher Book ID:</b> <SPAN
    ID=PublisherBookID ></SPAN><br>
256:<b>Publication Date:</b> <SPAN
    ID=PubDate ></SPAN>  
257:<b>Price:</b> <SPAN ID=Price ></SPAN><br><br>
258:<form name=form1>
259:<Input type=button name=button1 value="Click for next
    record" onCLick="NextRecord()"> 
260:<Input type=button name=button1 value="Click for
    previous record" onClick="PrevRecord()">
261:<Input type=button name=button3 value="Click to go to
    first record" onClick="FirstRecord()"> 
262:<Input type=button name=button4 value="Click for last
    record" onClick="LastRecord()"><br>
263:</form>
264:</BODY>
265:</HTML>
```

The initial output of a run of this program is illustrated in Figure 9.5.

FIGURE 9.5

Using buttons to move through the data.

Title: Teach Yourself XML in 24 Hours
Author:
　Name: Charles Ashbacher　　Address: 119 Northwood Drive
　City: Hiawatha　　State: Iowa
　Postal Code: 52233　　Country: United States
　Phone: (319) 378-4646　　Email: ashbacher@ashbacher.com
　URL: http://www.ashbacher.com

Publisher:
　Name: Sams Publishing　　Address: 201 West 103rd Street
　City: Indianapolis　　State: Indiana
　Postal Code: 46290　　Country: United States
　Phone: (111) 123-4567　　Editor: Dummy Name
　Email contact: Dummy.Name@samspublishing.com　　URL: http://www.samspublishing.com

ISBN: 0-672-31950-0　Publisher Book ID: 1234567
Publication Date: 2000-04-01　Price: 24.95

Click for next record　　Click for previous record
Click to go to first record　　Click for last record

Lines 232-257 define a series of <SPAN> tags that receive the individual data components of an instance of the <Book> node. The individual ID tags are self-explanatory. For example, the PublisherEditor tag is the target for the Editor component of the Publisher tag.

Lines 258 to 263 define a form that contains four buttons. The one with the caption "Click for next record" will be used to move forward through the database. Conversely, the one with the caption "Click for previous record" will be used to move backward through the database. The one with the caption "Click to go to first record" will display the first record in the database. Conversely, the one with the caption "Click to go to last record" will move to and display the last record in the database.

In lines 10 through 19, three global pointers are defined. globalHoldNode stores the current instance of the <Book> node that you're working with. It will be modified as you move through the <Book> nodes. globalFirstBook will point to the first of the <Book> nodes, and globalLastBook will point to the last of the <Book> nodes. Neither of these values should be modified after the initial assignment:

```
10:// This is the global pointer to a node that is used to
11:// move around the <Book> objects. It always stores the
12:// current <Book> object.
13: var globalHoldNode;
14:// This is a global pointer that points to the last
15: <Book> node.
16: var globalLastBook;
17:// This is a global pointer that points to the first
18:// <Book> node.
19: var globalFirstBook;
```

The StartLoading() function defined in lines 32 through 59 has one major change from the one you used previously. On line 48, treeNode is assigned the value of the XML document's lastChild node. By construction of your XML files, this will always be the <Catalog> node. The globalHoldNode pointer is then set to the first <Book> node in <Catalog>. The globalFirstBook and globalLastBook pointers are then set to the first and last items in the list of <Book> nodes. This function is called from the StartUp() function, which is called as part of the onLoad() operations. On line 58, the DisplayNode() function is called. This function will read the data from the <Book> node currently pointed to by globalHodNode and place it into the <SPAN> containers in the <Body> portion.

```
48:    treeNode=xmlDoc1.lastChild;
49:// This will set the pointer to the first child node of
50:// the current <Catalog> node.
51:    globalHoldNode=treeNode.firstChild;
52:// This global pointer stores the first of the <Book>
53:// objects.
54:    globalFirstBook=treeNode.firstChild;
55:// This global pointer stores the last of the <Book>
56:// objects.
57:    globalLastBook=treeNode.lastChild;
58:    DisplayNode();
```

The DisplayNode() function extracts the data from the instance of the <Book> node currently pointed to by globalHoldNode and places it in the <SPAN> containers. Since both the <Author> and <Publisher> child nodes have child nodes, two identifiers are defined that will move through the nodes.

```
64://This pointer to a node will move through the nodes of
65://the <Book> object.
66:  var moveNode;
67://This pointer to a node will move through the subnodes
68://if it is the <Author> or <Publisher> node.
69:  var inNode;
```

The first step is to set the moveNode pointer to the first node of the <Book> node to display.

```
76:   moveNode=globalHoldNode.firstChild;
```

A loop structure is then constructed that will move through the nodes of the <Book> node. moveNode will be the entity that changes to step through the node. The name of the node is then extracted, and a switch construct is then used to determine where the data is to be sent.

```
77://This loop will cycle through the nodes of the <Book>
78://node.
79:    while(moveNode!=null)
80:    {
81:     nameNode=moveNode.nodeName;
82:     switch(nameNode)
```

With the exception of the <Author> and <Publisher> nodes, the process is clear. For the <Author> and <Publisher> nodes, it's necessary to construct additional loops, using the inNode pointer, that will read the data components of these child nodes. The first step is to set inNode to the first child node of the <Author> node. This is done on line 92. After that, the name of the node is extracted and a switch() construct is created that will send the data to the proper container.

```
87:      case "Author":
88://If we are at the author node, it is necessary to read
89://the subnodes. We set inNode to the first child node
90://and then use the nextChild property to step through
91://the nodes.
92:      inNode=moveNode.firstChild;
93:      while(inNode!=null)
94:      {
95:       nameInNode=inNode.nodeName;
96:       switch(nameInNode)
97:       {
98:        case "Name":
99:        AuthorName.innerText=inNode.text;
100:         break;
101:        case "Address":
102:        AuthorAddress.innerText=inNode.text;
103:         break;
104:        case "City":
```

```
105:            AuthorCity.innerText=inNode.text;
106:            break;
107:            case "State":
108:            AuthorState.innerText=inNode.text;
109:            break;
110:            case "PostalCode":
111:            AuthorPostalCode.innerText=inNode.text;
112:            break;
113:            case "Country":
114:            AuthorCountry.innerText=inNode.text;
115:            break;
116:            case "Phone":
117:            AuthorPhone.innerText=inNode.text;
118:            break;
119:            case "Email":
120:            AuthorEmail.innerText=inNode.text;
121:            break;
122:            case "URL":
123:            AuthorURL.innerText=inNode.text;
124:            break;
125:          }
126:         inNode=inNode.nextSibling;
127:        }
128:       break;
```

The code for the <Publisher> node is similar.

When the button with the caption "Click for next record" is clicked, the NextRecord()
function is called. At that time, either the globalHoldNode pointer is at the last record or
it's not. The first step is to test for that condition, which is done on line 192. If it's on the
last record, you cannot move another record, so the only action is to pop up an alert box
with a message to inform the user.

If globalHoldNode isn't currently on the last record, it's set to the next sibling and the
contents of that node are displayed.

```
190:function NextRecord()
191:{
192: if(globalHoldNode==globalLastBook)
193: {
194:  alert("You are attempting to go off the end of the
      database");
195: }
196: else
197: {
198:  globalHoldNode=globalHoldNode.nextSibling;
199:  DisplayNode();
200: }
201:}
```

When the button with the caption "Click for previous record" is clicked, the PrevRecord() function is called. At that time, either the globalHoldNode pointer is at the first record or it's not. The first step is to test for that condition, which is done on line 204. If it's on the first record, you cannot move another record, so the only action is to pop up an alert box with a message to inform the user.

If the pointer isn't on the first record, the pointer is moved to the previous sibling and the contents are displayed.

```
202:function PrevRecord()
203:{
204: if(globalHoldNode==globalFirstBook)
205: {
206:  alert("You are attempting to go off the start end of
      the database");
207: }
208: else
209: {
210:  globalHoldNode=globalHoldNode.previousSibling;
211:  DisplayNode();
212: }
213:}
```

When the button with the caption "Click to go to first record" is clicked, the FirstRecord() function is called. The operation here is simple, in that the value of globalHoldNode is assigned the value of globalFirstBook.

```
214: // This function moves to and displays the first
215: record in the database.
216:function FirstRecord()
217:{
218: globalHoldNode=globalFirstBook;
219: DisplayNode();
220:}
```

When the button with the caption "Click to go to last record" is clicked, the LastRecord() function is called. The operation here is also simple, in that the value of globalHoldNode is assigned the value of globalLastBook.

```
221:// This function moves to and displays the last record
222:// in the database.
223:function LastRecord()
224:{
225: globalHoldNode=globalLastBook;
226: DisplayNode();
227:}
```

You can read data from an XML file with several layers of nodes.

Summary

This hour started the process of making the connections between XML files and databases. The first part of the hour described an XML database and showed you how to create a simple one containing three nodes.

Once the database was created, you then examined a program that allows you to click on buttons to step through and examine the nodes in the database.

Q&A

Q What's the advantage of stepping through a database by clicking on buttons?

A If the database is small, clicking on a button to move to the next record allows the user to examine the records at leisure.

Q How are the buttons linked to the movement through the database?

A The buttons are the standard HTML buttons that can be placed on a form. Their onClick() events are mapped to JavaScript functions that will perform the proper movement.

Q Why were buttons placed on the form that will move to the first and last records of the database?

A In small databases, where movement a record at a time is practical, there are times when you want to start at the beginning and other times when you want to start at the end.

Q When I run the program to step through the database, what happens if I try to run off either end of the database?

A The program shows an alert box to inform you that you're trying to move off the end and sets the location pointer to the node on that end.

Workshop

Quiz

1. What's the limit on the number of nodes that the <Catalog> database can contain?

    a. The only limit is the memory limit of the hardware.

    b. Approximately 32,760.

    c. The three that you now have are all that it can contain.

2. What are the consequences of adding comment nodes to the data in the <Book> nodes?

   a. There are no consequences.

   b. Clicking on the buttons will no longer step from <Book> node to <Book> node.

   c. The order in which the child nodes of the <Book> nodes are read will be altered.

   d. Both b and c could occur.

3. What alterations are necessary if an additional layer is added to your database?

   a. No alterations are necessary.

   b. The child node of <Book> node that's the parent of the additional layer would have to be identified, and a loop on the children would have to be constructed.

   c. An additional button would have to be added to the display.

Answers

1. a

2. d (Depending on the location of the comments, either b or c could occur as well)

3. b

Exercises

1. Add an additional <Book> node to the <Catalog> database. Run the code to read the data from the database.

2. Draw the hierarchical node diagram that represents the <Catalog> database.

Hour **10**

Using the XML Data Source Object

One of the semi-cruelties that instructors are allowed to get away with is to first demonstrate the hard way to do something and then the easy way. The justification is that struggling enhances the learning process. That's also my excuse here.

In the previous hour, you read an XML database by using the properties that allow for the movement from node to node. That was the hard part. Now, the Data Source Object, or DSO, will be used to read an XML database. As you'll see, it's a much easier way to extract and process the data.

In this hour, you'll learn the following:

- The basic principles of the Data Source Object (DSO)
- How to use the DSO to extract and display the data in a multilevel database

The Data Source Object

In HTML files, you can insert instances of objects that can be used to perform various tasks. The two most common such components are Java applets and Microsoft ActiveX controls. These objects are inserted into the file by using the <OBJECT> tag. If the component is to be reused, a unique object identifier is assigned to it. This identifier is a 32-character hexadecimal string that's computed by an algorithm involving randomly generated digits based on the date, time, and other factors. This guarantees that no two object identifiers are alike.

> This guarantee isn't an absolute, but the odds of getting a duplicate are truly astronomical—on the order of 1 to the number of particles in the universe.

One such object is the *XML Data Source Object*, or *DSO*, which is supported by IE 4 or later. DSO performs much of the data extraction for you. The names of the nodes can be written as the data sources for the HTML entities.

Listing 10.1 contains a single instance of the <Book> node used in previous lessons, and it's saved as listing10-1.xml.

LISTING 10.1   A File Containing a Single <Book> Node Used to Introduce the DSO

```
 1: <?xml version="1.0"?>
 2: <!-- This file is a reduced form of the book catalog file
 3:      so that the Document Source Object or DSO can be
 4:      introduced. The filename is listing10-1.xml. -->
 5: <Book>
 6: <Title>Teach Yourself XML in 24 Hours</Title>
 7: <ISBN>0-672-31950-0</ISBN>
 8: <PublisherBookID>1234567</PublisherBookID>
 9: <PublicationDate>2000-04-01</PublicationDate>
10: <Price>24.95</Price>
11: </Book>
```

Listing 10.2 uses a DSO object to read the data in Listing 10.1.

LISTING 10.2 Using the DSO Object to Read Data from an XML File

```
1:<html>
2:<!-- This file is the first demonstration of how to use
        the Document Source Object to read the data from an
        XML file.. -->
3:<head>
4:<title>The first demonstration of the Document Source
  Object</title>
5:<SCRIPT LANGUAGE="JavaScript">
6:<!--
7: function StartUp()
8: {
9:  var xmlDso = xmldso.XMLDocument;
10:  xmlDso.load("listing10-1.xml");
11: }
12://-->
13:</SCRIPT>
14:</head>
15:<body onLoad="StartUp()">
16:    <OBJECT WIDTH="0" HEIGHT="0"
17:    CLASSID="clsid:550dda30-0541-11d2-9ca9-0060b0ec3d39"
18:      ID="xmldso">
19:    </OBJECT>
20: <DIV ID="Book">
21: <SPAN STYLE="font-weight:bold">Title:</SPAN>
22: <SPAN ID="title" DATASRC=#xmldso
23:        DATAFLD="Title" STYLE="color:red">
24:      </SPAN><br><br>
25:<SPAN STYLE="font-weight:bold">ISBN:</SPAN>
26:<SPAN ID="isbn" DATASRC=#xmldso
27:        DATAFLD="ISBN" STYLE="color:red">
28:        </SPAN><br><br>
29:<SPAN STYLE="font-weight:bold">Publisher Book ID:</SPAN>
30:<SPAN ID="pubbookid" DATASRC=#xmldso
31:        DATAFLD="PublisherBookID" STYLE="color:red">
32:        </SPAN><br><br>
33:<SPAN STYLE="font-weight:bold">Publication Date:</SPAN>
34:<SPAN ID="pubdate" DATASRC=#xmldso
35:        DATAFLD="PublicationDate" STYLE="color:red">
36:        </SPAN><br><br>
37:<SPAN STYLE="font-weight:bold">Price:</SPAN>
38:<SPAN ID="price" DATASRC=#xmldso
39:        DATAFLD="Price" STYLE="color:red">
40: </SPAN><br><br>
41:</DIV>
42:</body>
43:</html>
```

10

Figure 10.1 shows the output when Listing 10.2 is run in IE.

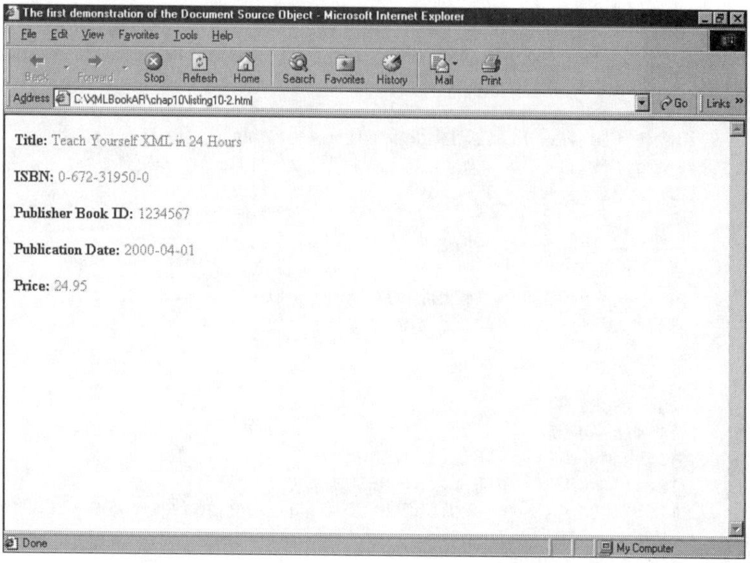

FIGURE 10.1

The output when using the DSO object to read the data from an XML file.

Lines 16 through 19 insert the XML DSO object into the Web page. Note that the WIDTH and HEIGHT of the <OBJECT> are both assigned the value 0 because it's intended to provide functionality only.

The StartUp() function is called when the page is loaded. In the two lines of that function, an object is created that can load the associated XML file and then that file is loaded. In line 9, the created object is assigned the value of the xmldso object's XML document property. Therefore, in line 10, the loaded file is assigned to the XML document component of the embedded xmldso object.

Once that connection is made, the DSO can examine the data in the XML file and understand what the nodes are. Therefore, to extract the data from the file, define <SPAN> tags and make the appropriate assignments to the options. The first assignment of the DATASRC, or datasource, property links it to the embedded DSO object. Once that's complete, assignments to the individual data components can be done. To label the output, also include <SPAN> tags that identify the data. Line 21 identifies the data, and lines 22 and 23 perform the appropriate data link.

Reading a single record from a file is generally suitable for demonstration purposes only. In general, your goal is to be able to read the data from a file one record at a time. The DSO provides a simple way to do that, but first it's necessary to create the appropriate source file.

Go back to listing10-1.xml and modify it to match Listing 10.3. It demonstrates the actions of the DSO object on a file containing multiple records. It should be saved as listing10-3.xml.

LISTING 10.3   A Reduced Form of the <Catalog> Database

```
 1: <?xml version="1.0"?>
 2: <!-- This file is a reduced form of the book catalog file
 3:      so that the Document Source Object or DSO can be
 4:      demonstrated. The filename is listing10-3.xml. -->
 5: <Catalog>
 6:
 7: <Book>
 8: <Title>Teach Yourself XML in 24 Hours</Title>
 9: <ISBN>0-672-31950-0</ISBN>
10: <PublisherBookID>1234567</PublisherBookID>
11: <PublicationDate>2000-04-01</PublicationDate>
12: <Price>24.95</Price>
13: </Book>
14: <Book>
15: <Title>Teach Yourself Cool Stuff in 24 Hours</Title>
16: <ISBN>0-672-1010-0</ISBN>
17: <PublisherBookID>1234568</PublisherBookID>
18: <PublicationDate>2000-06-01</PublicationDate>
19: <Price>24.95</Price>
20: </Book>
21: <Book>
22: <Title>Teach Yourself Uses of Silicon in 24 Hours</Title>
23: <ISBN>0-578-31950-0</ISBN>
24: <PublisherBookID>1234569</PublisherBookID>
25: <PublicationDate>2000-01-01</PublicationDate>
26: <Price>26.95</Price>
27: </Book>
28:
29: </Catalog>
```

This gives you a file that has multiple data nodes. The DSO object provides two functions that move from node to node. The `moveprevious()` method moves to the previous node in the list, and the `movenext()` method moves to the next node in the list. To trigger these events, link the methods to the clicking of buttons on a form.

Reopen xmlhour10-2.html and modify it to match Listing 10.4. Save the file as listing10-4.html. The changes are marked in bold.

LISTING 10.4   Using the DSO Object Methods to Move Between Records Linked
to Buttons on an HTML Form

```
 1: <html>
 2: <head>
 3: <title>The first demonstration of the Document Source
    Object</title>
 4: <SCRIPT LANGUAGE="JavaScript">
 5: <!--
 6:  function StartUp()
 7:  {
 8:   var xmlDso = xmldso.XMLDocument;
 9:   xmlDso.load("listing10-3.xml");
10:  }
11: //-->
12: </SCRIPT>
13: </head>
14: <body onLoad="StartUp()">
15:     <OBJECT WIDTH="0" HEIGHT="0"
16:      CLASSID="clsid:550dda30-0541-11d2-9ca9-0060b0ec3d39"
17:      ID="xmldso">
18:     </OBJECT>
19: <DIV ID="Book">
20: <SPAN STYLE="font-weight:bold">Title:</SPAN>
21:  <SPAN ID="title" DATASRC=#xmldso
22:        DATAFLD="Title" STYLE="color:red">
23:        </SPAN><br><br>
24: <SPAN STYLE="font-weight:bold">ISBN:</SPAN>
25: <SPAN ID="isbn" DATASRC=#xmldso
26:        DATAFLD="ISBN" STYLE="color:red">
27:        </SPAN><br><br>
28: <SPAN STYLE="font-weight:bold">Publisher Book ID:</SPAN>
29: <SPAN ID="pubbookid" DATASRC=#xmldso
30:        DATAFLD="PublisherBookID" STYLE="color:red">
31:        </SPAN><br><br>
32: <SPAN STYLE="font-weight:bold">Publication Date:</SPAN>
33: <SPAN ID="pubdate" DATASRC=#xmldso
34:        DATAFLD="PublicationDate" STYLE="color:red">
35:        </SPAN><br><br>
36: <SPAN STYLE="font-weight:bold">Price:</SPAN>
37: <SPAN ID="price" DATASRC=#xmldso
38:        DATAFLD="Price" STYLE="color:red">
39:        </SPAN><br><br>
40: <FORM>
41: <Input type=button name=button1 value="Click to go to
    previous record"
    onClick="xmldso.recordset.moveprevious()"> 
42: <Input type=button name=button2 value="Click to go to next
    record"
    onClick="xmldso. recordset.movenext()">
```

```
43: </FORM>
44: </DIV>
45: </body>
46: </html>
```

Run this file in IE and click on the buttons to move through the data. Note that if you run one record beyond either end, all of the fields are filled with blanks.

Another powerful technique you can use to visualize XML data is to link the data to a table. This is done in a manner similar to what you did with the <SPAN> tags. The initial linking is done as a DATASRC option to the TABLE tag, and then each of the columns is linked via a DATAFLD option to the specific node of the data.

Go back to Listing 10.4 and modify it to match Listing 10.5.

10

LISTING 10.5 Using the DSO to Insert Data into an HTML Table

```
 1: <html>
 2: <head>
 3: <SCRIPT LANGUAGE="JavaScript">
 4: <!--
 5:   function StartUp()
 6:   {
 7:     var xmlDso = xmldso.XMLDocument;
 8:     xmlDso.load("listing10-3.xml");
 9:   }
10: //-->
11: </SCRIPT>
12: </head>
13: <body onLoad="StartUp()">
14:     <OBJECT WIDTH="0" HEIGHT="0"
15:       CLASSID="clsid:550dda30-0541-11d2-9ca9-0060b0ec3d39"
16:       ID="xmldso">
17:     </OBJECT>
18: <TABLE DATASRC=#xmldso BORDER="1" CELLPADDING="2">
19: <THEAD>
20: <TH>Title</TH>
21: <TH>ISBN</TH>
22: <TH>Publisher Book ID</TH>
23: <TH>Publication Date</TH>
24: <TH>Price</TH>
25: </THEAD>
26: <TR align=center>
27: <TD><SPAN DATAFLD="Title"></SPAN></TD>
28: <TD><SPAN DATAFLD="ISBN"></SPAN></TD>
29: <TD><SPAN DATAFLD="PublisherBookID"></SPAN></TD>
30: <TD><SPAN DATAFLD="PublicationDate"></SPAN></TD>
31: <TD><SPAN DATAFLD="Price"></SPAN></TD>
```

LISTING 10.5   continued

```
32: </TR>
33:  </TABLE>
34: </body>
35: </html>
```

The output when this code is run in IE is illustrated in Figure 10.2.

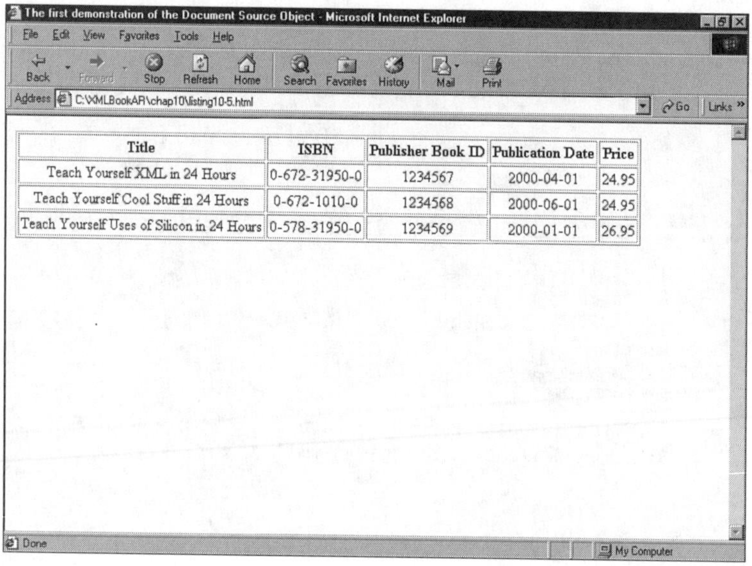

FIGURE 10.2

The table constructed by inserting the data from Listing 10.3.

While the results are easy to understand, they're somewhat remarkable when you consider them. When the row of the table is defined in the following segment of code, it's actually an implied loop:

```
<TR align=center>
<TD><SPAN DATAFLD="Title"></SPAN></TD>
<TD><SPAN DATAFLD="ISBN"></SPAN></TD>
<TD><SPAN DATAFLD="PublisherBookID"></SPAN></TD>
<TD><SPAN DATAFLD="PublicationDate"></SPAN></TD>
<TD><SPAN DATAFLD="Price"></SPAN></TD>
</TR>
```

The DSO object understands that there are multiple records in the XML file. Therefore, it uses the assignments to the <SPAN> tags inside the <TD> tags to cycle through all the records in the database. This creates the table with three rows of data.

Reading Data That Has Multiple Layers of Nodes

As you've probably determined from the previous exercise, the DSO object provides a great deal of functionality. When an XML file is linked to a DSO object, that object immediately understands the entire structure of the file. This can also be used to read the data from a file where there are multiple layers of nodes.

Listing 10.6 will be your data source, and it's saved as listing10-6.xml.

LISTING 10.6   A Data File That Contains Several Levels of Nodes

```
 1: <?xml version="1.0"?>
 2: <!-- This file is the data component of an instance of the
 3:      Book object. The name of the file is
 4:      xmlhour10-6.xml. -->
 5: <Book>
 6: <Title>Teach Yourself XML in 24 Hours</Title>
 7: <Author>
 8: <Name>Charles Ashbacher</Name>
 9: <Address>119 Northwood Drive</Address>
10: <City>Hiawatha</City>
11: <State>Iowa</State>
12: <PostalCode>52233</PostalCode>
13: <Country>United States</Country>
14: <Phone>(319) 378-4646</Phone>
15: <Email>ashbacher@ashbacher.com</Email>
16: <URL>http://www.ashbacher.com</URL>
17: </Author>
18: <Publisher>
19: <Name>Sams Publishing</Name>
20: <Address>201 West 103rd Street</Address>
21: <City>Indianapolis</City>
22: <State>Indiana</State>
23: <PostalCode>46290</PostalCode>
24: <Country>United States</Country>
25: <Phone>(111) 123-4567</Phone>
26: <Editor>Dummy Name</Editor>
27: <EmailContact>Dummy.Name@samspublishing.com</EmailContact>
28: <URL>http://www.samspublishing.com</URL>
29: </Publisher>
30: <ISBN>0-672-31950-0</ISBN>
31: <PublisherBookID>1234567</PublisherBookID>
32: <PublicationDate>2000-04-01</PublicationDate>
33: <Price>24.95</Price>
34: </Book>
```

10

Create the file shown in Listing 10.7 and save it as xmlhour10-7.html.

LISTING 10.7   Using Nested Tables to Display the Data in the XML File with Multiple Levels of Nodes

```
1:<html>
2:<!-- This file is another demonstration of how to use the
3:    Document Source Object to read the data from an XML
       file. In this case, the data is in multiple layers,
       so it is necessary to split it into the different
       subsections. This is easily done by using a series
       of nested tables. -->
4:<head>
5:<SCRIPT LANGUAGE="JavaScript">
6:<!--
7: function StartUp()
8: {
9:   var xmlDso = xmldso.XMLDocument;
10:   xmlDso.load("xmlhour11-6.xml");
11: }
12://-->
13:</SCRIPT>
14:</head>
15:<body onLoad="StartUp()">
16:     <OBJECT WIDTH="0" HEIGHT="0"
17:        CLASSID="clsid:550dda30-0541-11d2-9ca9-
           0060b0ec3d39"
18:        ID="xmldso">
19:     </OBJECT>
20:<TABLE ID="Catalog" BORDER="1" CELLSPACING="2"
  DATASRC=#xmldso>
21:<TR>
22:<TD>
23:<TABLE Border="2" DATASRC=#xmldso>
24:<TR>
25:<TD >
26:<SPAN STYLE="font-size:18;
  font-weight:bold">Title: </SPAN>
27:<SPAN DATAFLD="Title"></SPAN></TD>
28:</TR>
29:<TR>
30:<TD>
31:<TABLE DATASRC=#xmldso DATAFLD="Author">
32:<THEAD ALIGN="center">
33:  <TH>Name</TH>
34:  <TH>Address</TH>
35:  <TH>City</TH>
36:  <TH>State</TH>
37:  <TH>Postal Code</TH>
38:  <TH>Country</TH>
39:  <TH>Phone</TH>
40:  <TH>Email</TH>
41:  <TH>URL</TH>
42:</THEAD>
```

```
43:<TR>
44:<TD><SPAN DATAFLD="Name"></SPAN></TD>
45:<TD><SPAN DATAFLD="Address"></SPAN></TD>
46:<TD><SPAN DATAFLD="City"></SPAN></TD>
47:<TD><SPAN DATAFLD="State"></SPAN></TD>
48:<TD><SPAN DATAFLD="PostalCode"></SPAN></TD>
49:<TD><SPAN DATAFLD="Country"></SPAN></TD>
50:<TD><SPAN DATAFLD="Phone"></SPAN></TD>
51:<TD><SPAN DATAFLD="Email"></SPAN></TD>
52:<TD><SPAN DATAFLD="URL"></SPAN></TD>
53:</TR>
54:</TABLE>
55:</TD></TR>
56:<TR>
57:<TD>
58:<TABLE DATASRC=#xmldso DATAFLD="Publisher">
59:<THEAD ALIGN="center">
60:  <TH>Name</TH>
61:  <TH>Address</TH>
62:  <TH>City</TH>
63:  <TH>State</TH>
64:  <TH>Postal Code</TH>
65:  <TH>Country</TH>
66:  <TH>Phone</TH>
67:  <TH>Editor</TH>
68:  <TH>Email Contact</TH>
69:  <TH>URL</TH>
70:</THEAD>
71:<TR>
72:<TD><SPAN DATAFLD="Name"></SPAN></TD>
73:<TD><SPAN DATAFLD="Address"></SPAN></TD>
74:<TD><SPAN DATAFLD="City"></SPAN></TD>
75:<TD><SPAN DATAFLD="State"></SPAN></TD>
76:<TD><SPAN DATAFLD="PostalCode"></SPAN></TD>
77:<TD><SPAN DATAFLD="Country"></SPAN></TD>
78:<TD><SPAN DATAFLD="Phone"></SPAN></TD>
79:<TD><SPAN DATAFLD="Editor"></SPAN></TD>
80:<TD><SPAN DATAFLD="EmailContact"></SPAN></TD>
81:<TD><SPAN DATAFLD="URL"></SPAN></TD>
82:</TR>
83:</TABLE>
84:</TD></TR>
85:<TR><TD>
86:<SPAN STYLE="font-size:18; font-
  weight:bold">ISBN: </SPAN>
87:<SPAN DATAFLD="ISBN"></SPAN>
88:</TD></TR>
89:<TR><TD>
90:<SPAN STYLE="font-size:18;  font-weight:bold">
  Publisher Book ID: </SPAN>
91:<SPAN DATAFLD="PublisherBookID"></SPAN>
92:</TD></TR>
```

LISTING **10.7**   continued

```
93:<TR><TD>
94:<SPAN STYLE="font-size:18; font-weight:bold">
   Publication Date: </SPAN>
95:<SPAN DATAFLD="PublicationDate"></SPAN>
96:</TD></TR>
97:<TR><TD>
98:<SPAN STYLE="font-size:18;
   font-weight:bold">Price: </SPAN>
99:<SPAN DATAFLD="Price"></SPAN>
100:</TD></TR>
101:</TABLE>
102:</TABLE>
103:</body>
104: </html>
```

Run the file in IE. The output is demonstrated in Figure 10.3.

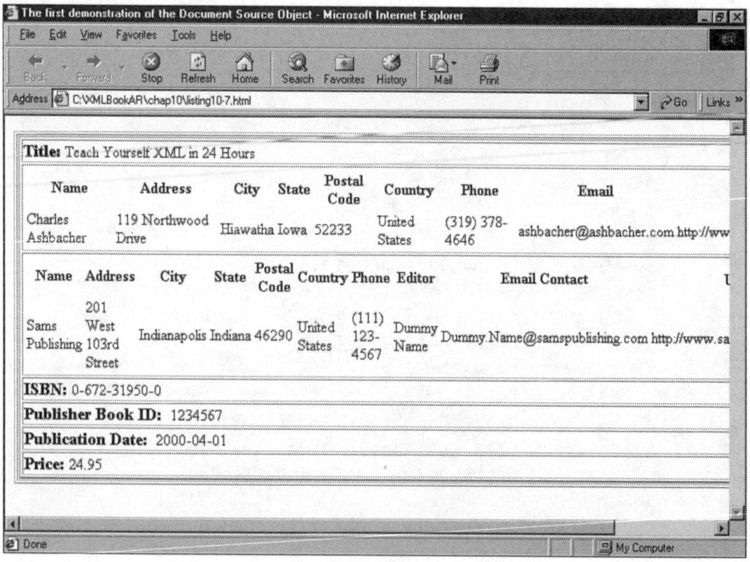

FIGURE **10.3**

*Nested tables used to
display the data of an
XML file with several
levels.*

Lines 25 and 107 are the opening and closing tags of the outer table that will be filled
with the data in the file. Some of the entries of this table will be tables as well.

Since the entries <Title>, <ISBN>, <PublisherBookID>, <PublicationDate>, and
<Price> are all singletons, the objects to extract and display the data are all single items.
A pair of <SPAN> tags is used, the first of which simply contains the label of the entry.
This is demonstrated in lines 29 through 35.

The <Author> and <Publisher> tags contain child nodes, so the objects that are to contain them need to be more complex. Therefore, use nested tables with "Author" and "Publisher" as the values assigned to the DATAFLD option. Lines 61, 62, and 89 are examples of the opening and closing tags of the row entry of the outermost of these nested tables. The entries are tables linked to a field of the xmldso object, so the next step is to make those links. The opening and closing tags of these tables are demonstrated in lines 63 and 88. The first entry after that is a series of table headers containing the names of the fields in the parent node. This is demonstrated in lines 64 through 75. Note that all the entries are in a single row of the table.

The final step in the process is to extract the data from the child nodes of the Author and Publisher nodes. Do this by creating a series of <SPAN> tags in which the DATAFLD property is set to the proper child node of the parent node. As was the case with the headers, all of the tags are placed on the same line. Lines 76 through 87 illustrate this process for the Publisher node.

Once again, reading one record is fine as a demonstration, but it's almost worthless in practice. The real power lies in the capability to read multiple records. Thanks to the power of the DSO object, you don't need to break a sweat to add this capability.

Reopen listing9-5.xml and modify it to match Listing 10.8. Save it as listing10-8.xml.

LISTING 10.8 An XML Database That Contains Several Nodes with Multiple Layers of Child Nodes

```
 1: <?xml version="1.0"?>
 2: <!-- This file is the <Catalog> database of Hour 9 with
 3:      all data typing information removed. -->
 4: <Catalog>
 5: <Book>
 6: <Title>Teach Yourself XML in 24 Hours</Title>
 7: <Author>
 8: <Name>Charles Ashbacher</Name>
 9: <Address>119 Northwood Drive</Address>
10: <City>Hiawatha</City>
11: <State>Iowa</State>
12: <PostalCode>52233</PostalCode>
13: <Country>United States</Country>
14: <Phone>(319) 378-4646</Phone>
15: <Email>ashbacher@ashbacher.com</Email>
16: <URL>http://www.ashbacher.com</URL>
17: </Author>
18: <Publisher>
19: <Name>Sams Publishing</Name>
20: <Address>201 West 103rd Street</Address>
21: <City>Indianapolis</City>
22: <State>Indiana</State>
```

LISTING 10.8 continued

```
23: <PostalCode>46290</PostalCode>
24: <Country>United States</Country>
25: <Phone>(111) 123-4567</Phone>
26: <Editor>Dummy Name</Editor>
27: <EmailContact>Dummy.Name@samspublishing.com</EmailContact>
28: <URL>http://www.samspublishing.com</URL>
29: </Publisher>
30: <ISBN>0-672-31950-0</ISBN>
31: <PublisherBookID>1234567</PublisherBookID>
32: <PublicationDate>2000-04-01</PublicationDate>
33: <Price>24.95</Price>
34: </Book>
35: <Book>
36: <Title>Teach Yourself Cool Stuff in 24 Hours</Title>
37: <Author>
38: <Name>ReallySmart Person</Name>
39: <Address>110 Main Street</Address>
40: <City>Silicon City</City>
41: <State>California</State>
42: <PostalCode>10101</PostalCode>
43: <Country>United States</Country>
44: <Phone>(101) 101-0101</Phone>
45: <Email>RSmart@MyCompany.com</Email>
46: <URL>http://www.MyCompany.com</URL>
47: </Author>
48: <Publisher>
49: <Name>Sams Publishing</Name>
50: <Address>201 West 103rd Street</Address>
51: <City>Indianapolis</City>
52: <State>Indiana</State>
53: <PostalCode>46290</PostalCode>
54: <Country>United States</Country>
55: <Phone>(111) 123-4567</Phone>
56: <Editor>Dummy Name</Editor>
57: <EmailContact>Dummy.Name@samspublishing.com</EmailContact>
58: <URL>http://www.samspublishing.com</URL>
59: </Publisher>
60: <ISBN>0-672-1010-0</ISBN>
61: <PublisherBookID>1234568</PublisherBookID>
62: <PublicationDate>2000-06-01</PublicationDate>
63: <Price>24.95</Price>
64: </Book>
65: <Book>
66: <Title>Teach Yourself Uses of Silicon in 24 Hours</Title>
67: <Author>
68: <Name>Missy Fixit</Name>
69: <Address>119 Hard Drive</Address>
70: <City>Diskette City</City>
71: <State>California</State>
72: <PostalCode>10101</PostalCode>
```

```
73: <Country>United States</Country>
74: <Phone>(586) 212-3638</Phone>
75: <Email>MFixit@Googol.com</Email>
76: <URL>http://www.Googol.com</URL>
77: </Author>
78: <Publisher>
79: <Name>Sams Publishing</Name>
80: <Address>201 West 103rd Street</Address>
81: <City>Indianapolis</City>
82: <State>Indiana</State>
83: <PostalCode>46290</PostalCode>
84: <Country>United States</Country>
85: <Phone>(111) 123-4567</Phone>
86: <Editor>Dummy Name</Editor>
87: <EmailContact>Dummy.Name@samspublishing.com</EmailContact>
88: <URL>http://www.samspublishing.com</URL>
89: </Publisher>
90: <ISBN>0-578-31950-0</ISBN>
91: <PublisherBookID>1234569</PublisherBookID>
92: <PublicationDate>2000-01-01</PublicationDate>
93: <Price>26.95</Price>
94: </Book>
95:
96: </Catalog>
```

Go back and modify Listing 10.7 so that it loads listing10-8.xml, and then run it in IE. The output is shown in Figure 10.4.

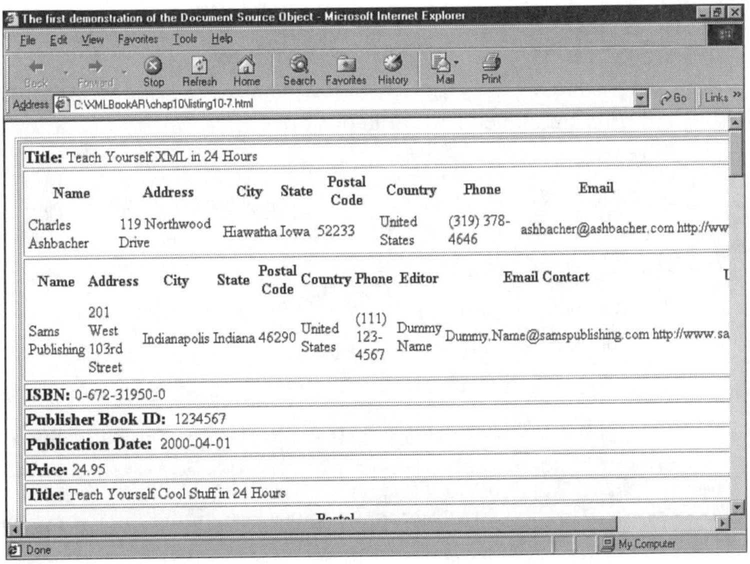

FIGURE 10.4

Using nested tables to output the data of an XML file with nodes at several levels.

Summary

In previous lessons, your data extractions involved creating custom code to read the data in your XML file. The Data Source Object can be used to read the data—once it's linked to an XML file, it understands the structure of that file.

In this lesson, the DSO object was used to read the data from XML files of increasing complexity. In all cases, the DATASRC and DATAFLD options were used in the HTML code to define the targets of the data assignments. In the more complex cases, HTML tables were defined as the containers for the data.

Workshop

Q&A

Q What's the purpose of an object's clsid property?

A *clsid* stands for *class ID*, and it's the globally unique identifier used by all programs. If the system has the object in its library, it uses the ID to get the information regarding the object's structure. The value of the ID is computed using an algorithm with random features that guarantee uniqueness.

Q Are there similarities between a Data Source Object and a database reader?

A Yes, there are. The Data Source Object understands the basic structure of an XML file and uses this knowledge to read its contents. The DSO methods to move forward and backward through the file are typical of database functions for getting the next and previous records.

Q When a DSO object is placed in the HTML file, why are the width and height both assigned the value of 0?

A The DSO object performs operations but is not to be displayed. No screen real estate should be reserved for it, so the width and height are set to 0.

Quiz

1. Once an XML file is assigned to a DSO object, what else must be done so that the object understands the structure of the XML file?

    a. The DSO must be initialized by a call to a startup function.

    b. A DTD file must be present to serve as a template.

    c. Nothing; the DSO object can determine the structure simply by reading it.

    d. The DSO needs to be told where in the file to begin the data extraction.

2. The DATASRC and DATAFLD properties are used to link what type of object to a DSO object?

   a. An HTML tag.

   b. A DTD element name.

   c. A DTD attribute name.

   d. An XML tag name.

3. How many levels of data can there be in an XML file read by a DSO?

   a. Two is the limit.

   b. Three is the limit.

   c. Five is the limit, which is the maximum that XML allows.

   d. There's no limit other than the practical one of being able to understand the data.

4. If you have an HTML with a DSO that reads an XML file, how difficult is it to change to reading another XML file?

   a. Always difficult.

   b. Always easy.

   c. Depends on how much you've hardcoded the display. If the HTML tags are specific to the data, it's hard.

   d. There's no way to know unless you know the form of the data.

10

Answers

1. c

2. a

3. d

4. c

Exercises

1. Modify listing10-7.html so that the output is more organized when it reads the file listing10-8.xml.

2. Given the following data definition, create an XML file containing at least three instances of this data type and an HTML file that will use a DSO to read and display the data:

```
<Customer>
 <FirstName>. . . </FirstName>
 <MiddleInitial> . . . </MiddleInitial>
```

```
        <LastName>. . . </LastName>
        <Address> . . . </Address>
        <City> . . . </City>
        <StateProvince> . . . </StateProvince>
        <PostalCode> . . . </PostalCode>
        <Country> . . . </Country>
        <DateOfLastPurchase> . . . </DateOfLastPurchase>
        <AmountOfPurchases> . . . </AmountOfPurchases>
        <CreditRating> . . . </CreditRating>
</Customer>
```

PART III

Extensible Stylesheet Language: The Way to Create Stylesheets and Access Databases

Hour

HOUR 11

Introduction to Extensible Stylesheet Language (XSL)

The focus of this hour is using style sheets to describe both the appearance and form of XML data. Not only does XSL allow you to do both, but it also contains commands that succinctly describe operations performed on the data.

In this hour, you'll learn the following:

- Some basic background on Cascading Style Sheets (CSS)
- The definition of namespaces and their role in XML
- The basic role of XSL
- The role of XSL templates and patterns in Web development

Cascading Style Sheets

Cascading Style Sheets, or CSS, is an extension of HTML in which the user can redefine the definition of a tag. This form then takes precedence over the default and is used to render the text.

Create the file shown in Listing 11.1 and save it as listing11-1.html.

LISTING 11.1   A Simple Example of Using Cascading Style Sheets

```
1: <html>
2: <!-- In this file, we define four different interpretations
3:     of the SPAN tag using style sheets. The name of the
4:     file is listing11-1.html. -->
5:
6: <head>
7: <title>First Style Sheet Example</title>
8: <STYLE TYPE="text/css">
9: <!--
10: SPAN.red
11: {
12:   color:red;
13:   font:14 pt;
14: }
15: SPAN.purple
16: {
17:   color:purple;
18:   font:16 pt;
19: }
20: SPAN.blue
21: {
22:   color:blue;
23:   font:18 pt;
24: }
25: SPAN.silver
26: {
27:   color:silver;
28:   font:18 pt;
29: }
30: //-->
31: </STYLE>
32: </head>
33: <body bgcolor="ffffff">
34: <SPAN CLASS="red">This text is rendered using the SPAN.red rule<
    /SPAN><br>
35: <SPAN CLASS="purple">This text is rendered using the SPAN.purple
    rule</SPAN><br>
36: <SPAN CLASS="blue">This text is rendered using the SPAN.blue rule
    </SPAN><br>
```

```
37: <SPAN CLASS="silver">This text is rendered using the SPAN.silver
    rule</SPAN>
38: </body>
39: </html>
```

The appearance of this file when viewed in IE is shown in Figure 11.1.

FIGURE 11.1

Demonstration of cascading style sheets.

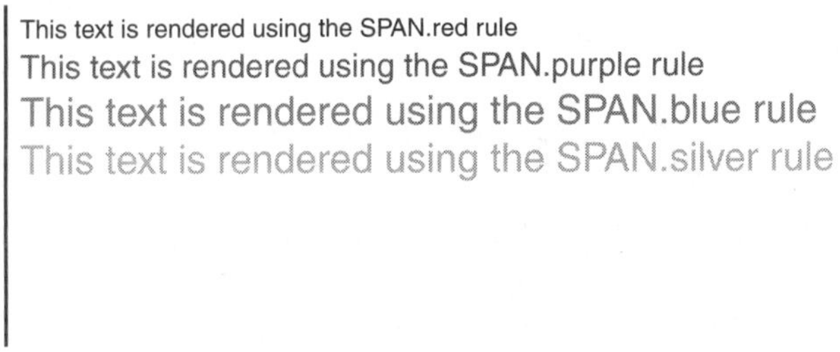

This text is rendered using the SPAN.red rule

This text is rendered using the SPAN.purple rule

This text is rendered using the SPAN.blue rule

This text is rendered using the SPAN.silver rule

The output of this file is easy to understand. Each rule of the following form defines a particular implementation of the <SPAN> tag:

```
SPAN.color
{

}
```

The CLASS qualifier of the tag specifies which one to use in rendering the text surrounded by the tag.

As was the case with the DTDs, it's also possible to create separate CSS files and import them. Create the file shown in Listing 11.2 and save it as listing11-2.css.

LISTING 11.2   Creating a Separate CSS File for Importing into an HTML File

```
 1: SPAN.red
 2: {
 3:  color:red;
 4:  font:14 pt;
 5: }
 6: SPAN.purple
 7: {
 8:  color:purple;
 9:  font:16 pt;
10: }
11: SPAN.blue
12: {
13:  color:blue;
14:  font:18 pt;
15: }
```

11

Listing 11.2   continued

```
16: SPAN.silver
17: {
18:  color:silver;
19:  font:18 pt;
20: }
```

Modify the HTML file Listing 11.1 to match Listing 11.3.

Listing 11.3   This HTML File Will Import the CSS File

```
 1: <html>
 2: <!-- In this file, we define four different interpretations
 3:      of the SPAN tag using style sheets in an external
 4:      file. That file is then imported into this one. -->
 5: <head>
 6: <title>First Style Sheet Example</title>
 7: <STYLE>
 8: @import_url(listing11-2.css);
 9: </STYLE>
10: </head>
11: <body bgcolor="ffffff">
12: <SPAN CLASS="red">This text is rendered using the SPAN.red rule<
    /SPAN><br>
13: <SPAN CLASS="purple">This text is rendered using the SPAN.purple
    rule</SPAN><br>
14: <SPAN CLASS="blue">This text is rendered using the SPAN.blue
    rule</SPAN><br>
15: <SPAN CLASS="silver">This text is rendered using the SPAN.silver
    rule</SPAN>
16:  </body>
17: </html>
```

When this file is viewed in IE, the appearance will be the same as that of Listing 11.1.

There's another way to import a CSS file into an HTML file. This uses the <LINK> tag, so it's more consistent with the notation of the other commands.

Modify Listing 11.1 to match Listing 11.4.

Listing 11.4   Using the LINK HREF Combination to Import the CSS File

```
 1: <html>
 2: <!-- In this file, we define four different interpretations
 3:      of the SPAN tag using style sheets in an external
 4:      file. That file is then imported into this one.  -->
 5: <head>
 6: <title>First Style Sheet Example</title>
```

```
 7: <LINK HREF="listing11-2.css"
    REL=STYLESHEET TYPE="text/css">
 8: </head>
 9: <body bgcolor="ffffff">
10: <SPAN CLASS="red">
11: This text is rendered using the SPAN.red rule</SPAN><br>
12: <SPAN CLASS="purple">
13: This text is rendered using the SPAN.purple rule</SPAN><br>
14: <SPAN CLASS="blue">
15: This text is rendered using the SPAN.blue rule</SPAN><br>
16: <SPAN CLASS="silver">
17: This text is rendered using the SPAN.silver rule</SPAN>
18: </body>
19: </html>
```

This file has the same appearance as Listing 11.1 and Listing 11.3 when viewed in IE. Note how the importation of the CSS file using this notation is more consistent with HTML syntax than the other notation.

There are several obvious advantages to using CSS in Web development. If a CSS file is created, it can then be imported into one or more files. This prevents the inherent problems that occur when code is duplicated several times, and it reduces file size.

If you're required to make a change, it's only necessary to change the contents of the CSS file and import the file again if necessary. Finally, if the coding is done for an organization with Web coding standards, those standards can be expressed in code rather than in one file at a time.

While CSS provides a valuable extension to HTML, it allows you to describe only the appearance of the text that's between the tags. There's no way to specify exactly what is to be placed between those tags. XSL is a further extension of this, allowing you to specify both the value of the innertext property and the way that it will appear.

There are currently two standards documents on Cascading Style Sheets. The first, the Cascading Style Sheet Level 1 Recommendations (CSS1), can be found at http://www.w3.org/TR/REC-CSS1.

The second and most recent document is the Cascading Style Sheet Level 2 Recommendations (CSS2), which can be found at http://www.w3.org/TR/REC-CSS2.

XML Namespaces

As you can see from the previous examples, when it's possible to define several different implementations of a tag, there's the potential for name collision. People have a tendency to use familiar names over and over again, relying on the context to remove any ambiguity. For example, consider the word *strike*. If the context is the sport of bowling, a strike is the act of knocking down all the pins with the first ball. In the context of organized labor, it's when the workers voluntarily stop working. And in the context of baseball, it's when the pitcher throws the baseball in a certain area.

A namespace can be considered the application of a context. In most cases, it's the application of a prefix, which can be either explicit or implicit.

With an explicit prefix, the namespace is attached to the front of the name. For example, if the name of the namespace is bowling, bowling:strike would mean a bowling ball knocking down all ten pins.

Using an implicit namespace requires some form of delimiters where a block of code is segmented. The segment is then marked in some manner to denote that items within the block are implicitly prefixed with the name of the namespace.

Suppose that the left and right curly braces ({}) are the delimiters and params is the name of your namespace. If par1 and par2 aren't locally defined in the following section of code, they will have the implicit params prefix:

```
namespace params
{
  par1

  par2
}
```

When evaluating, the system will treat them as if they were written in the form params:par1 and params:par2.

> When you're using namespaces, the section of code where the namespace is valid is known as the *scope* of the namespace.

In XML, it's possible to define a collection of names inside a namespace file. This file can be included in another file, and the tags in the file can be referenced by the assigned prefix.

Consider the multiple meanings of the word *quantity* when it comes to sales. Depending on the item, the quantity of that item can be measured in many different, and perhaps even contradictory, ways.

Suppose that you've defined two namespaces, "steel" and "flowers." Quantities of steel for transactions are measured by weight and flowers are measured by number, so any numeric quantity has different meanings for the two products. The following two lines will reference the namespaces and make them available in your code:

```
<?xml:namespace ns="file reference" prefix="steel"?>
<?xml:namespace ns="file reference" prefix="flowers"?>
```

> The "file reference" can be a URL. Since a URL is unique by definition, there's no problem with maintaining consistency.

By applying the appropriate prefixes to the tag names, you can then use the same basic tag names and maintain semantic uniqueness:

```
<steel:quantity>1000</steel:quantity>
<flowers:quantity>1000</flowers:quantity>
```

It's also possible to apply the namespace qualifier to a tag within the file itself. To understand this, you need to review the concept of a *Uniform Resource Name* or *URN*. A URN is a reference form that's complementary to a URL, and the basic idea is the same. It's a unique name assigned to the resource, but it can refer to more than one URL. The combination of URLs and URNs make up the *Uniform Resource Identifiers* or *URIs*.

The urn qualifier is used in a resource name reference to label the location of that resource. For example, the following would be an internal reference to the appropriate namespace file that describes an order of steel:

```
<steel:quantity
  xmlns:steel="urn:identification information of the file">
1000
</steel:quantity>
```

In this example, the scope of the namespace reference is within the tags only.

To make the namespace valid throughout the definition of an XML data object, simply include it within the opening tag of the object.

The following will implicitly consider all of the entries of the <PRODUCT> definition to have the steel prefix:

```
<PRODUCT xmlns:steel="urn:identification information of the file">
<NAME>Steel</NAME>
<QUANTITY>1000</QUANTITY>

  . . .
</PRODUCT>
```

The working document on XML namespaces can be found at
http://www.w3.org/TR/1998/WD-xml-names-19980327.

11

The XSL Namespace

The XML system provides a predefined namespace with the name *xsl*. It's a description of how the XML processor is to process the tags and display the data. This description can and most often does contain the references of the data to include. It's referenced by using this qualifier:

```
xmlns:xsl="uri:xsl"
```

Keep in mind that the rules of the xsl namespace are an extension of CSS and are used to specify the data and its appearance.

For example, suppose that you have the following generic <SPAN> tag:

```
<SPAN AppearanceQualifiers>
Data to be inserted here
</SPAN>
```

You can insert the appearance qualifiers explicitly, as in the following:

```
<SPAN STYLE="font-size:20pt;text-transform:uppercase">
This is another test
</SPAN>
```

Or you can write them as a style sheet, as was done in the first exercise of this hour.

In previous hours, you wrote JavaScript code that inserted the desired values of the data into the innerText property of the <SPAN> tag:

```
<SCRIPT LANGUAGE=JavaScript>

todata.innerText="Assigned data";

</SCRIPT>

<SPAN ID=todata></SPAN>
```

The output of the JavaScript code is HTML code with the data placed between the tags and then modified to display the proper appearance.

The rules of the XSL namespace perform the same operations, processing an HTML skeleton into HTML code for display. This example will use static HTML code to demonstrate how to use the xsl namespace.

Consider the code of Listing 11.5.

LISTING 11.5   The Importation of the xsl Namespace into an HTML File

```
1:<?xsl:template xmlns:xsl="uri:xsl">
2:<!-- This file is a simple demonstration of the inclusion
```

```
3:of the xsl namespace functionality into an HTML
4:file. -->
5:<html>
6:<head>
7:<title></title>
8:</head>
9:<body bgcolor="ffffff">
10:<SPAN >This is a test</SPAN><br>
11:<SPAN STYLE="font-size:20pt;text-transform:uppercase">
12:This is another test</SPAN>
13:</body>
14:</html>
15:</xsl: template>
```

The output of this file is rather dull, as shown in Figure 11.2.

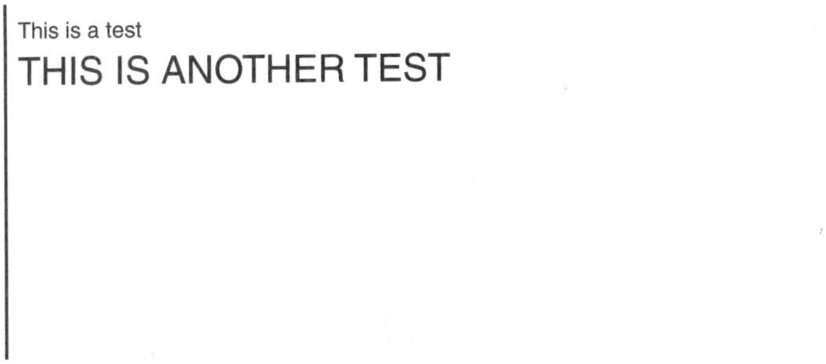

FIGURE 11.2

The output is all stati-cally generated.

This is a test

THIS IS ANOTHER TEST

In this case, the HTML file is all static, so there's nothing for the xsl processor to mod-ify. Also note the qualifications of the surrounding tags and the reference to the xsl namespace in the opening tag.

An xsl *template* is a map or description of the structure of the document. For example, lines 5 through 14 of Listing 11.5 would define a template for the file to be produced. Since it's nothing but static HTML code, the generated output is just the code directly translated without any intermediate processing.

The parts of the xsl template that perform the processing are known as *patterns*, and a template can contain zero or more patterns. There are many commands that can be placed inside a pattern, all of which are prefaced with the xsl namespace keyword. In fact, many of the commands will be familiar to you because they resemble those found in programming languages.

To demonstrate the use of xsl patterns, refer to the following XML file. Create the XML file shown in Listing 11.6 under the name listing11-6.xml and save it for future refer-ence.

LISTING 11.6   An XML Database That's a Catalog of Books

```
 1: <?xml version="1.0"?>
 2: <!-- This file is the data source for some examples of the
 3:     use of xsl patterns. The filename is listing11-6.xml. -->
 4: <CATALOG>
 5:   <BOOK>
 6:     <TITLE>Introduction to the Smarandache Function</TITLE>
 7:     <AUTHOR>Charles Ashbacher</AUTHOR>
 8:     <PRICE>12.44</PRICE>
 9:     <PUBLICATIONDATE>1995-09-15</PUBLICATIONDATE>
10:     <WRITEORDER>1</WRITEORDER>
11:     <PUBLISHER>Erhus University Press</PUBLISHER>
12:     <ISBN>1-879585-49-9</ISBN>
13:   </BOOK>
14:   <BOOK>
15:     <TITLE>Collection of Problems on
16:             Smarandache Notions</TITLE>
17:     <AUTHOR>Charles Ashbacher</AUTHOR>
18:     <PRICE>14.44</PRICE>
19:     <PUBLICATIONDATE>1996-11-15</PUBLICATIONDATE>
20:     <WRITEORDER>2</WRITEORDER>
21:     <PUBLISHER>Erhus University Press</PUBLISHER>
22:     <ISBN>1-879585-50-2</ISBN>
23:   </BOOK>
24:   <BOOK>
25:     <TITLE>Pluckings From the Tree of Smarandache
26:             Sequences and Functions</TITLE>
27:     <AUTHOR>Charles Ashbacher</AUTHOR>
28:     <PRICE>15.44</PRICE>
29:     <PUBLICATIONDATE>1998-06-15</PUBLICATIONDATE>
30:     <WRITEORDER>3</WRITEORDER>
31:     <PUBLISHER>American Research Press</PUBLISHER>
32:     <ISBN>1-879585-61-8</ISBN>
33:   </BOOK>
34: </CATALOG>
```

This is a list of <BOOK> objects under the root node <CATALOG>, where each instance of <BOOK> has a set of data properties.

Listing 11.7 is an xsl style sheet that can be used to output the values of the <TITLE> node for each of the entries. Create this file and save it as listing11-7.html. Note that it's an HTML file even though it contains an XSL stylesheet.

LISTING 11.7   An XSL Template That Will Dynamically Create HTML Code

```
1:<?xml version="1.0"?>
2:<xsl:template xmlns:xsl="uri:xsl">
3:<html>
4:<!-- This file is our first demonstration of the use of
```

```
5:      patterns in xsl templates. The filename is
6:listing11-7.html. -->
7:<head>
8:<title>First demonstration of XSL Patterns in a
  Template</title>
9:<LINK HREF="listing11-2.css" REL=STYLESHEET
  TYPE="text/css">
10:</head>
11:<body bgcolor=ffffff >
12:<xsl:repeat for="CATALOG/BOOK">
13: <DIV>
14:  <SPAN CLASS="blue">
15:   <xsl:get-value for="TITLE"/>
16:  </SPAN>
17: </DIV>
18:</xsl: repeat>
19:</body>
20:</html>
```

Line 9 is the importation of the same style sheet that you used in Listings 11.3 and 11.4. That style sheet will be applied to the <SPAN> tag after the text is inserted.

There are two xsl patterns in this program. The first is actually constructed from two lines:

```
12:<xsl:repeat for="CATALOG/BOOK">
```

```
18:</xsl:repeat>
```

This defines a loop that steps through the <BOOK> nodes of the <CATALOG> root node, of which there are three. This loop will act on the <DIV> node, the one that immediately follows it.

The second pattern is this single line:

```
15:   <xsl:get-value for=""TITLE"/>
```

This pattern will go to the current node, extract the value of the <TITLE> child node, and insert it into the innertext position of the <SPAN> tag.

When this file has made the proper connections to the XML data file, the xsl patterns will have generated the HTML file shown in Listing 11.8.

LISTING 11.8   This Is the HTML File Generated by the XSL Template Code

```
1: <html>
2: <!-- This file is our first demonstration of the use of
3:      patterns in xsl templates-->
4: <head>
```

11

LISTING 11.8   continued

```
 5: <title>First demonstration of XSL Patterns in a
    Template</title>
 6: <LINK HREF="listing11-2.css" REL=STYLESHEET
    TYPE="text/css">
 7: </head>
 8: <body bgcolor=ffffff >
 9:   <DIV>
10:    <SPAN CLASS="blue">
11:      Introduction to the Smarandache Function
12:    </SPAN>
13:   </DIV>
14:   <DIV>
15:    <SPAN CLASS="blue">
16:      Collection of Problems on Smarandache Notions
17:    </SPAN>
18:   </DIV>
19:   <DIV>
20:    <SPAN CLASS="blue">
21:      Pluckings From the Tree of Smarandache Sequences and
         Functions
22:    </SPAN>
23:   </DIV>
24:  </body>
25: </html>
```

Listing 11.7 by itself will not create this HTML file. A complete implementation of an xsl style sheet example will be shown in the next hour.

The Role of XSL Templates and Patterns in Web Development

Several years ago, when the Web was young and users' expectations were low, you could create a page with static content and it was accepted. Now, to attract and retain online customers, the content must be dynamic, both in appearance and creation. With xsl style sheets, you can write the code that will read the data from an XML file using only a few lines. This data can then be used to dynamically create the content of an HTML file that can be sent to the user.

To further appreciate how easy xsl style sheets are to use, go back to Listing 2.2 and examine the JavaScript code that reads the data from the XML file. What xsl can accomplish in only a few lines requires many more lines of JavaScript text.

Summary

This hour started with a brief overview of how cascading style sheets are used to modify text in HTML files. The style sheet code can be embedded in the HTML file or imported as a separate file.

XSL style sheets are templates that are constructed from segments of code called *patterns,* and they can be embedded in the file or imported as a separate file. These XSL style sheets create HTML code when executed. The XSL code can also read data from an XML file, which can be inserted into the HTML code.

Q&A

Q Why would I never embed the style sheet code inside the HTML file in commercial code?

A Because that effectively removes it from use by other programs. To use it, you'd need to duplicate it. Having separate CSS files also allows for the easy reuse and enforcement of companywide style sheet standards.

Q What's a namespace and how is it used?

A A namespace is something that applies a context to a phrase so it can be used to describe different operations. This is an advantage because programmers like to use the same names over and over again.

Q When XSL patterns and style sheets are used, what's the order of execution?

A The XSL pattern is performed first to embed the information into the region delimited by the tag. The style sheet is then performed to change the appearance of the inserted text.

11

Workshop

Quiz

1. Which of the following can be used to import a style sheet file into an HTML file?

    a. <LINK HREF="URLOfFile" . . . >

    b. <File="URLOfFile" . . . >

    c. @import url(URLOfFilename);

    d. a and c

2. What's an XSL pattern?

   a. The fundamental block of XSL code

   b. An executable segment of XSL code

   c. A block of code that can generate HTML code

   d. All of the above

3. Is it possible to nest one XSL pattern inside another?

   a. No; they generate HTML code, so one cannot be inside another

   b. Yes, provided that the actions they perform allow it

   c. Yes, but only if they're included in separate files

   d. Yes, but only if the XSL file is imported into the HTML file

4. Is an xsl pattern more difficult to implement than writing the equivalent JavaScript code?

   a. Yes, XSL patterns tend to be very complex

   b. No, XSL patterns are always simpler than the equivalent JavaScript code

   c. It depends on the circumstances; most of the time XSL patterns are simpler, but there are circumstances where the JavaScript could be easier

   d. It depends on the circumstances; most of the time the JavaScript is simpler, but there are situations where the XSL pattern is simpler

Answers

   1. d

   2. d

   3. b

   4. c

Exercises

1. Write an HTML file defining a set of four <DIV> tags that will cause the text to appear in the same style as the <SPAN> tags in Listing 11.1.

2. Write an HTML file defining a set of four <CENTER> tags that will cause the text to appear in the same style as the <SPAN> tags in Listing 11.1.

Hour **12**

Using an XSL Template to Read Data from an XML File

Hour 11 presented the basics of XSL templates. This hour will continue the demonstration of XSL, describing even more powerful techniques for the extraction and manipulation of XML data.

In this hour, you'll learn the following:

- The reasons for writing XSL template files that are distinct from the HTML
- How the XML data file, the XSL template file, and the HTML file for display interact in the reading of data from an XML file
- Four reasons why it's more efficient to use three different files in reading data from an XML file.

Separating the XSL Template from the HTML File

In Hour 11, you embedded the XSL template directly into the HTML file. That violates a general principle of computing—separate the different types of functionality into distinct files whenever possible. It's possible to write a separate XSL file and thereby have three files in the project: the XML data file, the XSL template, and the HTML file for the display. Of course, you need to understand that the XSL file will be used to dynamically change portions of the HTML file.

A Programming Example

In this example, you'll read the data from an XML file using an XSL template. That template will be contained in a file separate from the HTML file used for display in the browser. When the template acts on the XML data, it will create HTML code that will be dynamically inserted into the HTML file. Therefore, your project will be constructed from three files: the XML data file, the XSL template file, and an HTML file that will be updated dynamically.

The XML File

Of course, you need some data to read, so use the data in Listing 12.1, which is the catalog database from Hour 10.

LISTING 12.1   The Data to Be Read by the XSL Template File

```
 1: <?xml version="1.0"?>
 2: <Catalog>
 3:
 4: <Book>
 5: <Title>Teach Yourself XML in 24 Hours</Title>
 6: <Author>
 7:  <Name>Charles Ashbacher</Name>
 8:  <Address>119 Northwood Drive</Address>
 9:  <City>Hiawatha</City>
10:  <State>Iowa</State>
11:  <PostalCode>52233</PostalCode>
12:  <Country>United States</Country>
13:  <Phone>(319) 378-4646</Phone>
14:  <Email>ashbacher@ashbacher.com</Email>
15:  <URL>http://www.ashbacher.com</URL>
16: </Author>
17: <Publisher>
```

208

```
18:   <Name>Sams Publishing</Name>
19:   <Address>201 West 103rd Street</Addre
20:   <City>Indianapolis</City>
21:   <State>Indiana</State>
22:   <PostalCode>46290</PostalCode>
23:   <Country>United States</Country>
24:   <Phone>(111) 123-4567</Phone>
25:   <Editor>Dummy Name</Editor>
26:   <EmailContact>Dummy. Name@samspublish
27:   <URL>http://www.samspublishing.com</URL>
28:  </Publisher>
29:  <ISBN>0-672-31950-0</ISBN>
30:  <PublisherBookID>1234567</PublisherBookID>
31:  <PublicationDate>2000-04-01</PublicationDate>
32:  <Price>24.95</Price>
33: </Book>
34:
35: <Book>
36:  <Title>Teach Yourself Cool Stuff in 24 Hours</Title>
37:  <Author>
38:   <Name>ReallySmart Person</Name>
39:   <Address>110 Main Street</Address>
40:   <City>Silicon City</City>
41:   <State>California</State>
42:   <PostalCode>10101</PostalCode>
43:   <Country>United States</Country>
44:   <Phone>(101) 101-0101</Phone>
45:   <Email>RSmart@MyCompany.com</Email>
46:   <URL>http://www.MyCompany.com</URL>
47:  </Author>
48:  <Publisher>
49:   <Name>Sams Publishing</Name>
50:   <Address>201 West 103rd Street</Address>
51:   <City>Indianapolis</City>
52:   <State>Indiana</State>
53:   <PostalCode>46290</PostalCode>
54:   <Country>United States</Country>
55:   <Phone>(111) 123-4567</Phone>
56:   <Editor>Dummy Name</Editor>
57:   <EmailContact>Dummy.Name@samspublishing.com</EmailContact>
58:   <URL>http://www.samspublishing.com</URL>
59:  </Publisher>
60:  <ISBN>0-672-1010-0</ISBN>
61:  <PublisherBookID>1234568</PublisherBookID>
62:  <PublicationDate>2000-06-01</PublicationDate>
63:  <Price>24.95</Price>
64: </Book>
65:
66: <Book>
67:  <Title>Teach Yourself Uses of Silicon in 24 Hours</Title>
```

12

1   continued

```
     <Author>
 :    <Name>Missy Fixit</Name>
0:    <Address>119 Hard Drive</Address>
71:   <City>Diskette City</City>
72:   <State>California</State>
73:   <PostalCode>10101</PostalCode>
74:   <Country>United States</Country>
75:   <Phone>(586) 212-3638</Phone>
76:   <Email>MFixit@Googol.com</Email>
77:   <URL>http://www.Googol.com</URL>
78:  </Author>
79:  <Publisher>
80:   <Name>Sams Publishing</Name>
81:   <Address>201 West 103rd Street</Address>
82:   <City>Indianapolis</City>
83:   <State>Indiana</State>
84:   <PostalCode>46290</PostalCode>
85:   <Country>United States</Country>
86:   <Phone>(111) 123-4567</Phone>
87:   <Editor>Dummy Name</Editor>
88:   <EmailContact>Dummy.Name@samspublishing.com</EmailContact>
89:   <URL>http://www.samspublishing.com</URL>
90:  </Publisher>
91:  <ISBN>0-578-31950-0</ISBN>
92:  <PublisherBookID>1234569</PublisherBookID>
93:  <PublicationDate>2000-01-01</PublicationDate>
94:  <Price>26.95</Price>
95: </Book>
96:
97: </Catalog>
```

> Recall that this data file contains the child nodes Author and Publisher,
> which have child nodes themselves.

The XSL Template

You'll use an XSL template to read the data, only now it will be encapsulated in a separate file.

Create the file in Listing 12.2 and save it as listing 12-2.xsl. Once again, the line numbers are for reference purposes and are not part of the code.

LISTING 12.2 The XSL File to Read the XML File Containing the Catalog Database

```
1:<?xml version="1.0"?>
<!-- This file is an XSL style sheet file that is used to
     read the data from the simple book catalog database.
2:<xsl:stylesheet xmlns:xsl="uri:xsl">
3: <xsl:template match="/">
4: <html>
5:  <body>
6:  <table border="1">
7:   <tr style="font-weight:bold;color:blue">
8:    <td>Author Name</td>
9:    <td>Author Address</td>
10:   <td>Author City</td>
11:   <td>Author State</td>
12:   <td>Author e-mail</td>
13:   <td>Publisher Name</td>
14:   <td>Publisher Address</td>
15:   <td>Publisher Phone</td>
16:  </tr>
17:   <xsl:for-each select="Catalog/Book">
18:    <tr>
19:     <xsl:apply-templates/>
20:    </tr>
21:   </xsl:for-each>
22:  </table>
23:  </body>
24: </html>
25: </xsl:template>
26:<xsl:template match="Author">
27:   <td><xsl:value-of select="Name"/></td>
28:   <td><xsl:value-of select="Address"/></td>
29:   <td><xsl:value-of select="City"/></td>
30:   <td><xsl:value-of select="State"/></td>
31:   <td><xsl:value-of select="Email"/></td>
32:</xsl:template>
33:<xsl:template match="Publisher">
34:   <td><xsl:value-of select="Name"/></td>
35:   <td><xsl:value-of select="Address"/></td>
36:   <td><xsl:value-of select="Phone"/></td>
37:</xsl:template>
38:</xsl: stylesheet>
```

12

The HTML File

The third and final part of the example is the HTML file that will be the target of the XSL template acting on the XML data file.

Create the file in Listing 12.3 and save it as listing12-3.html.

LISTING 12.3   The HTML File That Receives the Data from the XSL Template and Displays the Output

```
1:<html>
<!-- This file is the HTML that will ultimately be
      displayed. Most of it will be created by the action of
      the template file of listing12-2 on the data file
      in listing 12-1.

-->
2:<head>
3:<title>This program demonstrates the use of an XSL 4)
  template to read XML data</title>
5:<script language="JavaScript">
6:<!--
7:function StartUp()
8:{
9: var DataSource=new ActiveXObject("microsoft.xmldom");
10: DataSource.load("xmlhour13-1.xml");
11: var XslStyle=new ActiveXObject("microsoft.xmldom");
12: XslStyle.load("xmlhour13-2.xsl");
13:document.all.item("xslcontainer").innerHTML=
    DataSource.transformNode(XslStyle.documentElement);
14:}
15://-->
16:</script>
17:</head>
18:<body onLoad="StartUp()">
19:<SPAN ID="xslcontainer"></Span>
20:</body>
21:</html>
```

The output of this file when run in IE is illustrated in Figure 12.1.

There are two steps to the display of this data. The first step is applying the XSL template to the XML data, thus creating HTML data to be displayed. The second step is connecting the data to the HTML file so the data can be displayed.

FIGURE 12.1

The data selected from the catalog database by the XSL file.

Author Name	Author Address	Author City	Author State	Author e-mail	Publisher Name	Publisher Address	Publisher Phone
Charles Ashbacher	119 Northwood Drive	Hiawatha	Iowa	ashbacher@ashbacher.com	Sams Publishing	201 West 103rd Street	(111) 123-4567
ReallySmart Person	110 Main Street	Silicon City	California	RSmart@MyCompany.com	Sams Publishing	201 West 103rd Street	(111) 123-4567
Missy Fixit	119 Hard Drive	Diskette City	California	MFixit@Googol.com	Sams Publishing	201 West 103rd Street	(111) 123-4567

Applying the XSL Template to the XML Data

Start with the XSL template shown in Listing 12.2. Lines 2 and 38 are the delimiting tags of the style sheet. There are three different templates defined in this file. Lines 3 and 25, 26 and 32, and 33 and 37 are the paired sets of delimiters for these templates.

The opening tag of each template contains an assignment to the MATCH option. In line 3, the assigned value is to the slash (/).

This assigns the template to the root of the XML document. In this case, the root is the <CATALOG> node, so this template is to be applied to that node.

In line 26, the template is linked to the <Author> child node of the <BOOK> node of the <Catalog> root node. Similarly, line 33 is where the template is linked to the <Publisher> child node of the <Book> node.

Lines 4, 5, 23, and 24 delimit the HTML section that will be constructed by applying the internal templates.

Lines 6 through 22 define an instance of a table that is used to organize the output's appearance.

Lines 7 through 16 are just routine headers for the columns of the table. These lines will only be executed once. Lines 17 and 21 define a loop. Because of the assignment to the select in the opening tag of line 17, the loop will step through the <Book> nodes of the <Catalog> tag. Lines 18 and 20 are the opening and closing delimiters of a single row of the table. Since this row delimiting occurs inside the loop, one row will be created for each instance of a <Book> node in the file.

The line of most interest is line 19, where data will be read and inserted into the table. As the name implies, apply-templates is where the template definitions (which appear on lines 26-32 and 33-37 at the end of the file) are implemented.

In line 26, the assignment of "Author" to the match parameter means that the data for any assignment to a select parameter will come from an <Author> node. Since the previous assignments have already taken you to the <Book> level of the hierarchical tree, no

12

further qualification is necessary. Lines 27 through 31 define a sequence of table data entries, where each one is an element in the <Author> node. The same thing is done in lines 33 through 37 for the <Publisher> node.

When the loop executes for the first time, the template mapped to the <Author> node is applied first. It will go to the first occurrence of the <Author> node in the XML file and extract the contents of the <Name>, <Address>, <City>, <State>, and <Email> fields. Those contents will then be placed within the appropriate <td>...</td> tag pairs in the template. The intermediate result will be as follows:

```
<td> Charles Ashbacher</td>
<td>119 Northwood Drive</td>
<td>Hiawatha</td><td>Iowa</td> <td>ashbacher@ashbacher.com</td>
```

The template mapped to the <Publisher> node will then be applied. It will go to the instance of the <Publisher> node contained in the current instance of the <Book> node and extract the relevant data values. The results, shown here, will be attached to those of the previous template:

```
<td>Sams Publishing</td>
<td>201 West 103rd Street</td>
<td>Indiana</td>
<td>(111) 123-4567</td>
```

Since there's no </tr> tag between these two segments, all of the data will be placed on a single line. Note that the order of the data items matches the order of the entries in the table header. The closing </tr> tag appears on line 20, after the <xsl:apply-templates/> line, causing the contents of the next read to appear on a new row of the table. Once the three iterations of the loop are complete, this file will have constructed an HTML table with the appropriate headers and three rows of selected data.

Connecting the Data to the HTML File

An HTML table has been constructed, but it's not connected to the HTML file being displayed. To create the connection, Listing 12.3 contains a startup sequence similar to what you've done in the past. The onLoad option of the body is mapped to a StartUp() function. However, on lines 9-12 of this StartUp() function, two instances of the xmldom object are created. One is linked to the XML data file and the other to the XSL template file.

Line 19, the single line of code in the <Body> section, does nothing more than define a target for the placement of the data for display.

The key line in this file, and the one that does most of the work, is Line 13. From your previous work with nodes, you should know that XslStyle.documentElement refers to the section of the XSL file that defines the style sheet. The transformNode() method is used to create a node by applying a style sheet, so the operations on the right side of the equality create an HTML node by applying the XSL template to the source file containing the

XML data. Once that node is created, it must be inserted into the HTML file. This is done by the left side of the expression as the target of the assignment. Previously, you have used the innerText property of HTML tags. Since you're going to be inserting HTML text in this case, use the innerHTML property instead.

The document object is the one that's assigned to the display window. Therefore, to insert the code into that window, you must start with it. When an HTML file is interpreted by a browser, several arrays of objects are created based on the tags that appear in the file. While most of the arrays store the instances of particular tags, such as images[], the all[] array stores every item in the file. Therefore, the following segment starts the process at the level of the document and refines it so that at the position of item, the reference is at the layer of the tags:

```
document.all.item("xslcontainer").
```

Since the <SPAN> tag has the ID "xslcontainer", the value in parentheses causes the final reference to be to the <SPAN> tag of the HTML file. Therefore, when it's all put together, the HTML document created by applying the XSL template file on the XML data file is inserted into the <SPAN> tag of the HTML file. All of which leads to the output that you saw in Figure 12.1.

Changing the Order in Which the Data Is Read

Go back to Listing 12.2 and change the order of the templates to match Listing 12.4.

LISTING 12.4   Reversing the Order of the Templates

```
 1: <xsl:template match="Publisher">
 2:   <td><xsl:value-of select="Name"/></td>
 3:   <td><xsl:value-of select="Address"/></td>
 4:   <td><xsl:value-of select="Phone"/></td>
 5: </xsl:template>
 6:
 7:
 8: <xsl:template match="Author">
 9:   <td><xsl:value-of select="Name"/></td>
10:   <td><xsl:value-of select="Address"/></td>
11:   <td><xsl:value-of select="City"/></td>
12:   <td><xsl:value-of select="State"/></td>
13:   <td><xsl:value-of select="Email"/></td>
14: </xsl:template>
```

12

Save the file as listing12-4.xsl.

Modify Listing 12.3 to read this file and then view it in a browser. The output is the same as that of the previous exercise and is illustrated in Figure 12.2.

FIGURE 12.2

The output after the order of the templates is modified.

Author Name	Author Address	Author City	Author State	Author e-mail	Publisher Name	Publisher Address	Publisher Phone
Charles Ashbacher	119 Northwood Drive	Hiawatha	Iowa	ashbacher@ashbacher.com	Sams Publishing	201 West 103rd Street	(111) 123-4567
ReallySmart Person	110 Main Street	Silicon City	California	R.Smart@MyCompany.com	Sams Publishing	201 West 103rd Street	(111) 123-4567
Missy Fixit	119 Hard Drive	Diskette City	California	MFixit@Googol.com	Sams Publishing	201 West 103rd Street	(111) 123-4567

This demonstrates that the order of the templates doesn't determine the order of the data in the table's rows. The templates are executed in the order in which their matched data is encountered in the XML file.

To verify this, reopen listing12-1.xml and reverse the order of the <Author> and <Publisher> nodes to match Listing 12.5. Save it as listing12-5.xml.

LISTING 12.5 Reversing the Order of the <Author> and <Publisher> Nodes

```
 1: <?xml version="1.0"?>
 2: <!-- This file is the <Catalog> database of Hour 10 with
 3:      all data typing information removed. In this case, the
 4:      order of the <Author> and <Publisher> nodes is
 5:      reversed. The name of the file is
 6: listing12-5.xml. -->
 7: <Catalog>
 8: <Book>
 9: <Title>Teach Yourself XML in 24 Hours</Title>
10: <Publisher>
11: <Name>Sams Publishing</Name>
12: <Address>201 West 103rd Street</Address>
13: <City>Indianapolis</City>
14: <State>Indiana</State>
15: <PostalCode>46290</PostalCode>
16: <Country>United States</Country>
17: <Phone>(111) 123-4567</Phone>
18: <Editor>Dummy Name</Editor>
19: <EmailContact>Dummy.Name@samspublishing.com</EmailContact>
20: <URL>http://www.samspublishing.com</URL>
21: </Publisher>
22: <Author>
23: <Name>Charles Ashbacher</Name>
24: <Address>119 Northwood Drive</Address>
25: <City>Hiawatha</City>
26: <State>Iowa</State>
27: <PostalCode>52233</PostalCode>
28: <Country>United States</Country>
29: <Phone>(319) 378-4646</Phone>
30: <Email>ashbacher@ashbacher.com</Email>
31: <URL>http://www.ashbacher.com</URL>
```

```
32: </Author>
33: <ISBN>0-672-31950-0</ISBN>
34: <PublisherBookID>1234567</PublisherBookID>
35: <PublicationDate>2000-04-01</PublicationDate>
36: <Price>24.95</Price>
37: </Book>
38: <Book>
39: <Title>Teach Yourself Cool Stuff in 24 Hours</Title>
40: <Publisher>
41: <Name>Sams Publishing</Name>
42: <Address>201 West 103rd Street</Address>
43: <City>Indianapolis</City>
44: <State>Indiana</State>
45: <PostalCode>46290</PostalCode>
46: <Country>United States</Country>
47: <Phone>(111) 123-4567</Phone>
48: <Editor>Dummy Name</Editor>
49: <EmailContact>Dummy.Name@samspublishing.com</EmailContact>
50: <URL>http://www.samspublishing.com</URL>
51: </Publisher>
52: <Author>
53: <Name>ReallySmart Person</Name>
54: <Address>110 Main Street</Address>
55: <City>Silicon City</City>
56: <State>California</State>
57: <PostalCode>10101</PostalCode>
58: <Country>United States</Country>
59: <Phone>(101) 101-0101</Phone>
60: <Email>RSmart@MyCompany.com</Email>
61: <URL>http://www.MyCompany.com</URL>
62: </Author>
63: <ISBN>0-672-1010-0</ISBN>
64: <PublisherBookID>1234568</PublisherBookID>
65: <PublicationDate>2000-06-01</PublicationDate>
66: <Price>24.95</Price>
67: </Book>
68: <Book>
69: <Title>Teach Yourself Uses of Silicon in 24 Hours</Title>
70: <Publisher>
71: <Name>Sams Publishing</Name>
72: <Address>201 West 103rd Street</Address>
73: <City>Indianapolis</City>
74: <State>Indiana</State>
75: <PostalCode>46290</PostalCode>
76: <Country>United States</Country>
77: <Phone>(111) 123-4567</Phone>
78: <Editor>Dummy Name</Editor>
79: <EmailContact>Dummy.Name@samspublishing.com</EmailContact>
80: <URL>http://www.samspublishing.com</URL>
81: </Publisher>
82: <Author>
```

12

LISTING 12.5   continued

```
83: <Name>Missy Fixit</Name>
84: <Address>119 Hard Drive</Address>
85: <City>Diskette City</City>
86: <State>California</State>
87: <PostalCode>10101</PostalCode>
88: <Country>United States</Country>
89: <Phone>(586) 212-3638</Phone>
90: <Email>MFixit@Googol.com</Email>
91: <URL>http://www.Googol.com</URL>
92: </Author>
93: <ISBN>0-578-31950-0</ISBN>
94: <PublisherBookID>1234569</PublisherBookID>
95: <PublicationDate>2000-01-01</PublicationDate>
96: <Price>26.95</Price>
97: </Book>
98:
99: </Catalog>
```

Reopen listing12-3.html and modify the line that loads the XML file so that it loads listing12-5.xml. When the updated file is viewed in the browser, the data will now be out of sequence with the table headers, as shown in Figure 12.3. This demonstrates quite clearly that the templates are executed in the order in which their matched data is encountered in the XML file.

FIGURE 12.3

The consequences of reversing the order of the data in the XML file.

Author Name	Author Address	Author City	Author State	Author e-mail	Publisher Name	Publisher Address	Publisher Phone
Sams Publishing	201 West 103rd Street	(111) 123-4567	Charles Ashbacher	119 Northwood Drive	Hiawatha	Iowa	ashbacher@ashbacher.com
Sams Publishing	201 West 103rd Street	(111) 123-4567	ReallySmart Person	110 Main Street	Silicon City	California	RSmart@MyCompany.com
Sams Publishing	201 West 103rd Street	(111) 123-4567	Missy Fixit	119 Hard Drive	Diskette City	California	MFixit@Googol.com

Adding Templates to Read the Data That Isn't in the <Author> or <Publisher> Nodes

In the previous example, the data that was extracted from the XML file by the template was from the <Author> and <Publisher> nodes, both of which have child nodes. In the next example, you'll see how the data from the nodes without child nodes is extracted. Reopen listing12-4.xsl and modify it to match Listing 12.6. Save it as listing12-5.xsl. The additional lines are marked in bold.

LISTING 12.6 Reading the Data That Isn't in the <Author> or <Publisher> Nodes

```
 1: <?xml version="1.0"?>
 2: <!-- This file is an XSL style sheet file that is used to
 3:      read the data from the simple book catalog database.
 4: -->
 5: <xsl:stylesheet xmlns:xsl="uri:xsl">
 6:  <xsl:template match="/">
 7:  <html>
 8:   <body>
 9:   <table border="1">
10:   <tr style="font-weight:bold;color:blue">
11:   <td>Author Name</td>
12:   <td>Author Address</td>
13:   <td>Author City</td>
14:   <td>Author State</td>
15:   <td>Author e-mail</td>
16:   <td>Publisher Name</td>
17:   <td>Publisher Address</td>
18:   <td>Publisher Phone</td>
19:   <td>ISBN</td>
20:   <td>Publisher Book ID</td>
21:   <td>Price</td>
22:   </tr>
23:    <xsl:for-each select="Catalog/Book">
24:     <tr>
25:     <xsl:apply-templates/>
26:     <td><xsl:value-of select="ISBN"/></td>
27:     <td><xsl:value-of select="PublisherBookID"/></td>
28:     <td><xsl:value-of select="Price"/></td>
29:     </tr>
30:    </xsl:for-each>
31:   </table>
32:   </body>
33:  </html>
34:  </xsl:template>
35:
36: <xsl:template match="Publisher">
37:    <td><xsl:value-of select="Name"/></td>
38:    <td><xsl:value-of select="Address"/></td>
39:    <td><xsl:value-of select="Phone"/></td>
40: </xsl:template>
41:
42: <xsl:template match="Author">
43:    <td><xsl:value-of select="Name"/></td>
44:    <td><xsl:value-of select="Address"/></td>
45:    <td><xsl:value-of select="City"/></td>
46:    <td><xsl:value-of select="State"/></td>
47:    <td><xsl:value-of select="Email"/></td>
48: </xsl:template>
49:
50: </xsl:stylesheet>
```

12

Modify the line to load the XSL template file in Listing 12.3 to read listing12-5.xsl and view it in IE. All of the data in the <Book> nodes will now be displayed, as illustrated in Figure 12.4.

FIGURE 12.4

Reading and display-ing all of the data in the Catalog database.

	Author Address	Author City	Author State	Author e-mail	Publisher Name	Publisher Address	Publisher Phone	ISBN	Publisher Book ID	Price
er	119 Northwood Drive	Hiawatha	Iowa	ashbacher@ashbacher.com	Sams Publishing	201 West 103rd Street	(111) 123-4567	0-672-31950-0	1234567	24.95
art	110 Main Street	Silicon City	California	RSmart@MyCompany.com	Sams Publishing	201 West 103rd Street	(111) 123-4567	0-672-1010-0	1234568	24.95
it	119 Hard Drive	Diskette City	California	MFixit@Googol.com	Sams Publishing	201 West 103rd Street	(111) 123-4567	0-578-31950-0	1234569	26.95

The Advantages of Using Separate Files

As I've mentioned many times throughout this book, separating functionality into differ-ent files is an efficient way to allow for code reuse. The example in this hour demon-strates four possibilities. First, if you want to apply the XSL template to a different XML file of the same structure, the only change is to the method in the HTML file that loads the XML file. Second, the HTML file is extremely generic and will work with any pro-ject containing an XSL and XML file, where only one data target is needed. Third, when more or less of the data is to be read from the XML file, it's only necessary to make changes to the XSL file. Finally, if additional data is to be added to the XML file, no changes need to be made to either the XSL or HTML files.

Summary

When you're using XSL templates to read the data from XML files, you need three things: the data, the XSL templates, and the HTML file to be displayed in the browser. In the long run, it's more efficient to create separate files for these three sections. In this hour, you learned how to create them and how they interact.

The order of the data in the XML file determines the order of execution of the templates, and two examples were presented that demonstrated this. Finally, four reasons for the separation into the three files were given.

Q&A

Q When there's more than one template in the XSL file, what determines the order of execution when the apply-templates command is encountered?

A The order of appearance of the templates is irrelevant. The determining factor is the order in which the data is encountered when the data is read from the XML file. Since this data is read sequentially, it's the order of the data in the file.

Q What's one argument for not splitting the project into three files?

A The most compelling argument involves security. Embedding the XSL template in some file where the source is hidden could protect trade secrets.

Q What does the transformNode() method do?

A It applies the XSL template to the XML data file. The operation generates HTML code, which is returned in the form of a node.

Workshop

Quiz

1. The match="/" assignment to the match qualifier will link the expression to which node of the XML file?

    a. The first node

    b. The last node

    c. The root node

    d. No node at all; the "/" is not a valid input

2. An XSL file can contain how many templates?

    a. One

    b. Two

    c. As many as ten

    d. The only limit is what is practical

3. What kind of code does an XSL template generate?

    a. XML

    b. XSL

    c. HTML

    d. JavaScript

12

Answers

1. c
2. d
3. c

Exercises

1. Remove the table header from the previous project and add a </tr> tag in the proper location so that the contents of the <Author> and <Publisher> tags are on separate rows. Make the first entries of the rows Author: and Publisher:, respectively.

2. Modify the XML data file so that the data entries ISBN, PublisherBookID, and Price are contained in a component of the following form:

```
<BookData>
  <ISBN> . . . </ISBN>
  <PublisherBookID> . . . </PublisherBookID>
  <Price> . . . </Price>
</BookData>
```

Add another template to the XSL file so that this data will be read properly.

Hour 13

Using Multiple XSL Templates to Read Data from Multiple XML Files

In the previous hour, you learned the basic principles of using XSL templates to extract the data from an XML file. The templates provide a great deal of functionality that supports data selection via queries. This functionality is similar to that found in database packages. Therefore, from this point on, the XML data file will be considered the database file. Although sometimes you'll work with a single database, many times you'll work with more than one at a time. Therefore, this hour will show you how to extract the data from more than one database at a time. The other main topic of this hour is the extraction of data by creating one XSL loop nested inside another. This is done to demonstrate that XSL templates are in fact a programming language, allowing for the construction of complex structures to extract the data.

In this hour, you'll learn the following:

- How to extract the data from more than one XML file using more than one XSL template
- That the nodes created by the actions of the XSL templates can be examined and processed using the methods available to act on nodes
- How to cross-reference data from two files and create a simple report

Working with Two Databases

In this and subsequent hours, you'll be using two different databases. For the first, you'll use the <Catalog> database that you used in the previous hour. The database is found in listing12-1.xml.

For the second database, you'll start with a root node named <Booksellers>. The records in the database are going to be <Seller> record(s) of the books. Each <Seller> record will consist of the following components:

- Name
- Address
- City
- State
- PostalCode
- Phone
- ContactPerson
- A list of Sams books the seller sells

Create the file shown in Listing 13.1 and save it as listing13-1.xml.

LISTING 13.1   Your Second Database to Be Processed with XSL Templates

```
 1: <?xml version="1.0"?>
 2: <!-- This file is the file that contains the information
 3:      concerning the sellers of books and internally a list
 4:      of Sams books that they sell. -->
 5:
 6: <Booksellers>
 7:
 8: <Seller>
 9: <Name>Old Books Made New</Name>
10: <Address>200 Third Street</Address>
11: <City>WannaReadOne</City>
```

```
12: <State>Iowa</State>
13: <PostalCode>52467</PostalCode>
14: <Phone>(319)356-0000</Phone>
15: <ContactPerson>Miss Manners</ContactPerson>
16: <SamsBooksSold>
17:  <Book>
18:    <Title>Teach Yourself XML in 24 Hours</Title>
19:    <ISBN>0-672-31950-0</ISBN>
20:  </Book>
21:  <Book>
22:   <Title>Teach Yourself Cool Stuff in 24 Hours</Title>
23:   <ISBN>0-672-1010-0</ISBN>
24:  </Book>
25:  <Book>
26:   <Title>Teach Yourself Uses of Silicon in 24 Hours</Title>
27:   <ISBN>0-578-31950-0</ISBN>
28:  </Book>
29: </SamsBooksSold>
30: </Seller>
31:
32: <Seller>
33: <Name>Read With Us</Name>
34: <Address>200 Chickadee Lane</Address>
35: <City>GoodTown</City>
36: <State>Iowa</State>
37: <PostalCode>52477</PostalCode>
38: <Phone>(319)356-0223</Phone>
39: <ContactPerson>Reed Lots</ContactPerson>
40: <SamsBooksSold>
41:  <Book>
42:    <Title>Teach Yourself XML in 24 Hours</Title>
43:    <ISBN>0-672-31950-0</ISBN>
44:  </Book>
45:  <Book>
46:   <Title>Teach Yourself Cool Stuff in 24 Hours</Title>
47:   <ISBN>0-672-1010-0</ISBN>
48:  </Book>
49: </SamsBooksSold>
50: </Seller>
51:
52: <Seller>
53: <Name>Books Are Good Business</Name>
54: <Address>121 Quail Drive</Address>
55: <City>Birdytown</City>
56: <State>Iowa</State>
57: <PostalCode>52299</PostalCode>
58: <Phone>(319)356-9999</Phone>
59: <ContactPerson>Bob White</ContactPerson>
60: <SamsBooksSold>
61:  <Book>
62:    <Title>Teach Yourself XML in 24 Hours</Title>
```

13

LISTING **13.1**   continued

```
63:    <ISBN>0-672-31950-0</ISBN>
64:    </Book>
65:  </SamsBooksSold>
66:  </Seller>
67:
68:  </Booksellers>
```

Since the data in Listing 12.1 and your operations on it are identical, use the same XSL file to process it. This file was used before as listing12-2.xsl, and that's the reference name you'll use here.

Since your goal is to read in the data from both files simultaneously, you need to modify the HTML file accordingly. Reopen listing12-3.html and modify it to match Listing 13.2. Save it as listing13-2.html. The changes are marked in bold.

LISTING 13.2   HTML File to Extract the Data from Two XML Database Files Simultaneously

```
1:<html>
<!-- This file is the HTML that will ultimately be
     displayed. Most of it will be created by the action
     of the template files listing12-2.xsl and
     listing13-2.xsl on the data files listing12-1.xml
     and listing13-1.xml. -->
2:<head>
3:<title>This program demonstrates the use of an XSL template
  to read XML data</title>
4:<script language="JavaScript">
5:<!--
6:function StartUp()
7:{
8:// This is the same as that for Hour 3, only the names
9:// of the variables are slightly changed.
10: var DataSource1=new ActiveXObject("microsoft.xmldom");
11: DataSource1.load("listing12-1.xml");
12: var XslStyle1=new ActiveXObject("microsoft.xmldom");
13: XslStyle1.load("listing12-2.xsl");
14: document.all.item("xslcontainer1").innerHTML=DataSource1.
    transformNode(XslStyle1.documentElement);
15:// Here we repeat the same set of operations to link
16:// a second pair of XSL and XML files.
17: var DataSource2=new ActiveXObject("microsoft.xmldom");
18: DataSource2.load("listing13-1-1.xml");
19: var XslStyle2=new ActiveXObject("microsoft.xmldom");
20: XslStyle2.load("listing13-3.xsl");
21: document.all.item("xslcontainer2").innerHTML=DataSource2.
    transformNode(XslStyle2.documentElement);
22:}
```

```
23://-->
24:</script>
25: </head>
26:<body onLoad="StartUp()">
27:<Span ID="xslcontainer1"></Span>
28:<br><br>
29:<!--We add a second target container to the <BODY>
30:    section. -->
31:<Span ID="xslcontainer2"></Span>
32: </body>
33:</html>
```

The changes should be rather easy to understand. You're going to display the data from a second file, so a second container is needed. That's done in lines 30 and 31.

Creating the combination of the ActiveX object and loading and linking the XSL and XML files are very similar to what was done for the first file. Finally, as was the case before, you need to call the transformNode() method with the appropriate XSL file as input.

Which brings us to the creation of the XSL file that will read the data from the <Booksellers> database. This template will have to be more complex, in that it will require a set of nested loops to read the data.

Create the file in Listing 13.3 and save it as listing13-3.xsl.

LISTING 13.3   The XSL File That Extracts the Data from the Booksellers Database

```
1:<?xml version="1.0"?>
2:<!-- This file is an XSL style sheet file that is used to
3:    read the data from the Booksellers database. The
4:    filename is listing13-3.xsl. -->
5:<xsl:stylesheet xmlns:xsl="uri:xsl">
6: <xsl:template match="/">
7: <html>
8:  <body>
9:  <table border="1">
10:    <xsl:for-each select="Booksellers/Seller">
11:    <tr style="font-weight:bold;color:blue">
12:    <td>Seller Name</td>
13:    <td>Seller Address</td>
14:    <td>SellerCity</td>
15:    <td>Seller State</td>
16:    <td>Seller Postal Code</td>
17:    <td>Seller Phone</td>
18:    <td>Seller Contact Person</td>
19:    </tr>
20:    <tr>
21:    <td><xsl:value-of select="Name"/></td>
```

13

LISTING 13.3   continued

```
22:    <td><xsl:value-of select="Address"/></td>
23:    <td><xsl:value-of select="City"/></td>
24:    <td><xsl:value-of select="State"/></td>
25:    <td><xsl:value-of select="PostalCode"/></td>
26:    <td><xsl:value-of select="Phone"/></td>
27:    <td><xsl:value-of select="ContactPerson"/></td>
28:   </tr>
29:   <tr style="font-weight:bold;color:red">
30:   <td>Titles sold by this company</td>
31:   </tr>
32:   <tr style="font-weight:bold;color:blue">
33:   <td>Title</td>
34:   <td>ISBN</td>
35:   </tr>
36:       <xsl:apply-templates/>
37:   <tr><td></td></tr>
38:    </xsl:for-each>
39:  </table>
40:  </body>
41:</html>
42:</xsl:template>
43:<xsl:template match="Booksellers/Seller/SamsBooksSold">
44:   <xsl:for-each select="Book">
45:     <tr>
46:      <td><xsl:value-of select="Title"/></td>
47:      <td><xsl:value-of select="ISBN"/></td>
48:     </tr>
49:   </xsl:for-each>
50:  </xsl:template>
51:</xsl: stylesheet>
```

Run listing13-2.html in IE. The first portion of the output is illustrated in Figure 13.1.

FIGURE 13.1

The output of the data from the two XML files.

Author Name	Author Address	Author City	Author State	Author e-mail	Publisher Name	Publisher Address	Publisher Phone
Charles Ashbacher	119 Northwood Drive	Hiawatha	Iowa	ashbacher@ashbacher.com	Sams Publishing	201 West 103rd Street	(111) 123-4567
ReallySmart Person	110 Main Street	Silicon City	California	RSmart@MyCompany.com	Sams Publishing	201 West 103rd Street	(111) 123-4567
Missy Fixit	119 Hard Drive	Diskette City	California	MFixit@Googol.com	Sams Publishing	201 West 103rd Street	(111) 123-4567

Seller Name	Seller Address	Seller City	Seller State	Seller Postal Code	Seller Phone	Seller Contact Person
Old Books Made New	200 Third Street	WannaReadOne	Iowa	52467	(319)356-0000	Miss Manners
Titles sold by this company						
Title	ISBN					
Teach Yourself XML in 24 Hours	0-672-31950-0					

Once again, lines 6 and 42 delimit the main style sheet of the file, and the value assigned to the match option sets it to the root node of the XML data file. As was the case in the previous hour, you'll construct a table using the data, so lines 9 and 39 delimit that table.

Lines 10 and 38 delimit the section that will be a loop on the <Seller> nodes of the file. Since there's going to be an inner loop, the column headers are inserted each time a <Seller> entry is constructed and lines 11 through 19 create the line of headers.

Each <Seller> node is made up of a set of nodes with no children and one node with zero or more child nodes. The set of nodes with no children is then output into a row of the table, which is done in lines 20 through 28.

The next portion of the table will be the listing of Sams books that this instance of a <Seller> sells, so place two header labels in the next two rows. The first is a single entry in the row and is done by lines 29 through 31.

The second header lists the type of data that will appear in the listing of books, which is done in lines 32 through 35.

Once all the headers are placed in the table, the data in the <SamsBooksSold> element's child nodes is inserted into the table. This is done in line 36.

Line 37 inserts a blank row into the table, separating the records.

There's only one template, and it's linked to the Booksellers/Seller/SamsBooksSold node. Since this is the parent node of one or more instances of the <Book> node, a for-each loop on the <Book> node is constructed. The two data components are then extracted and placed in a row of the table. This is accomplished in lines 43 through 50.

> Once again, this section is concentrating on displaying the data instead of making the table's appearance truly presentable. Feel free to make any changes to the display that you wish.

13

Working with the Nodes Created by the XSL Template

Once the XSL template has operated on the XML file's data and created a node, it's possible to perform operations on the node similar to what you've done in previous hours. These operations include viewing the node's contents, updating the values of the data components, or performing comparisons to select the data to be viewed. Later in this hour, you'll perform comparisons to select out the data common to the two different XML databases.

Modify Listing 13.2 to match Listing 13.4. The changes are marked in bold.

LISTING 13.4   Modification of Listing 13.2

```
1: <html>
2: <!-- This file is the HTML that will ultimately be
3:      displayed. It differs from the previous HTML
4:      file in that we are now going to perform operations
5:      on the generated nodes. -->
6: <head>
7: <title>This program demonstrates the use of an XSL template
   to read XML data</title>
8: <script language="JavaScript">
9: <!--
10: function StartUp()
11: {
12:   var DataSource1=new ActiveXObject("microsoft.xmldom");
13:   DataSource1.load("listing12-1.xml");
14:   var XslStyle1=new ActiveXObject("microsoft.xmldom");
15:   XslStyle1.load("listing12-2.xsl");
16:   DataSource1.transformNode(XslStyle1.documentElement);
17:   alert(DataSource1.xml);
18:   var DataSource2=new ActiveXObject("microsoft.xmldom");
19:   DataSource2.load("listing13-1.xml");
20:   var XslStyle2=new ActiveXObject("microsoft.xmldom");
21:   XslStyle2.load("listing13-3.xsl");
22:   DataSource2.transformNode(XslStyle2.documentElement);
23:   alert(DataSource2.xml);
24: }
25: //-->
26: </script>
27: </head>
28: <body onLoad="StartUp()">
29: <SPAN ID="xslcontainer1"></Span>
30: <br>
31: <SPAN ID="xslcontainer2"></Span>
32: </body>
33: </html>
```

Run the file in IE. In this case, the result will be the appearance of each of the generated nodes as the text of an alert box. The partial appearance of the first node is illustrated in Figure 13.2.

FIGURE 13.2

The XML version of the first node generated by the actions of the XSL templates.

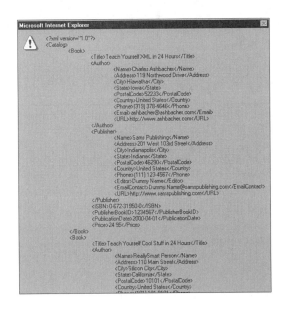

While you did nothing more than output the contents of the generated nodes, this exercise demonstrates a very important point. Once the XSL template generates the node, it's a node object with all of the properties and methods of the nodes. Therefore, you can process the nodes. In the next section, you'll perform a query by cross-referencing the data from two different XML databases.

Cross-Referencing the Two Databases

Now that you're reading two data files and creating the corresponding nodes, it's possible to perform operations that cross-reference the data from the two files. This is a very common operation in database work. If you were to place all of your data in a single database file, it would become large and ungainly. This would make it difficult to understand and could lead to slow access times. Furthermore, putting the data into a common database would often mean combining data forms unnecessarily. The solution is to have multiple database files and perform cross-references based on common components. In the next exercise, you'll perform what can be considered a simple query of the databases.

The premise here is simple. Listing 12.1 contains a list of books, each with an ISBN number. The second database, Listing 13.1, contains a list of booksellers. Inside each <Seller> entry, there's a list of books that the seller sells. The ISBN of each of those books is a field of the entries in that list. Therefore, your query will search through both databases and report all books in the <Catalog> database that are sold by the <Seller>(s) in the <Booksellers> database.

13

Reopen listing13-4.html and change it to match Listing 13.5. Save it as listing13-5.html. All changes are in bold.

LISTING 13.5 Performing a Cross-Reference of the Data in the Two XML Database Files

```
1:<html>
2:<!-- This file will demonstrate the reading of two
        different XML data files and the
        examination of the data to extract all of the
        booksellers that sell each individual Sams selection.
    -->
3:<head>
4:<title>This program demonstrates the use of an XSL
    template to read XML data</title>
5:<script language="JavaScript">
6:<!--
7: var BooksNode;
8: var GetISBN;
9: var SellersNode;
10: var ISBN;
11: var SearchBooks;
12:function StartUp()
13:{
// Attach the data and XSL files to the objects as before.
14: var DataSource1=new ActiveXObject("microsoft.xmldom");
15: DataSource1.load("listing12-1.xml");
16: var XslStyle1=new ActiveXObject("microsoft.xmldom");
17:XslStyle1.load("listing12-2.xsl");
// Create the <Catalog> by applying the XSL file to the XML
// file.
18: DataSource1.transformNode(XslStyle1.documentElement);
// Assign an identifier to the data part of the node.
19: BooksNode=DataSource1.documentElement;
// This assignment will be to the first instance of a
// <Book> node in the XML data file.
20: BooksNode=BooksNode.firstChild;
// Assign the data and XSL files to the objects as before
21: var DataSource2=new ActiveXObject("microsoft.xmldom");
22: DataSource2.load("listing13-1.xml");
23: var XslStyle2=new ActiveXObject("microsoft.xmldom");
24: XslStyle2.load("listing13-3.xsl");
// Create the <Booksellers> node by applying the XSL file
// to the XML file.
25: DataSource2.transformNode(XslStyle2.documentElement);
// This loop will step through the <Book> nodes of the
// <Catalog> database.
26: while(BooksNode!=null)
```

```
27: {
// We now move to the proper node of the current <Book>
// node in order to extract the ISBN of the current
// book.
28:  GetISBN=BooksNode.lastChild;
29:  GetISBN=GetISBN.previousSibling;
30:  GetISBN=GetISBN.previousSibling;
31:  GetISBN=GetISBN.previousSibling;
// This is the ISBN of the current <Book> node.
32:  ISBN=GetISBN.text;
// SellersNode is now assigned to the first of the <Seller>
// nodes in the <BookSellers>  database.
33:  SellersNode=DataSource2.documentElement.firstChild;
// This loop will step through the <Seller> nodes of the
// <BookSellers> database.
34:   while(SellersNode!=null)
35:   {
// The last child of each <Seller> node is the list of
// books sold, so we set the pointer to that list.
36:    SearchBooks=SellersNode.lastChild;
// We are going to search through the list of books sold,
// so we need to set the pointer to the first entry in the
// list.
37:    SearchBooks=SearchBooks.firstChild;
// This loop will step through the list of books sold.
38:    while(SearchBooks!=null)
39:    {
// Extract the ISBN of this book that the <Seller> sells.
40:     SellerISBN=SearchBooks.lastChild;
41:     SellISBN=SellerISBN.text;
// Test to see if it is the same as that of the current
// <Book> node.
42:     if(SellISBN==ISBN)
43:     {
// If this <Seller> sells the current <Book> simply write
// that fact to the document window.
44:      str1=SellersNode.firstChild.text;
45:      str1="The bookseller "+str1+" sells the book
         "+ISBN;
46:      document.write(str1+"<BR>");
47:     }
48:    SearchBooks=SearchBooks.nextSibling;
49:   } // End of SearchBooks!=null loop
50:   SellersNode=SellersNode.nextSibling;
51: } // end of the SellersNode!=null loop
52:  BooksNode=BooksNode.nextSibling;
53: } // end of the BooksNode!=null loop
54:}
55://-->
56:</script>
```

13

LISTING 13.5 continued

```
57:</head>
58:<body onLoad="StartUp()">
<!-- We will now be writing the text from the StartUp()
     function, so there is no need to have targets for the
     data. -->
59:</body>
60:</html>
```

The output when this file is run in IE is shown in Figure 13.3.

FIGURE 13.3

The display of the cross-referenced data.

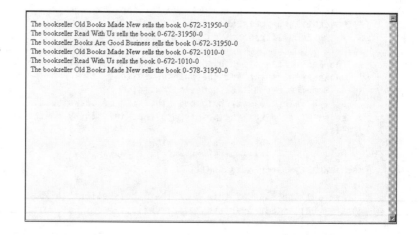

The bookseller Old Books Made New sells the book 0-672-31950-0
The bookseller Read With Us sells the book 0-672-31950-0
The bookseller Books Are Good Business sells the book 0-672-31950-0
The bookseller Old Books Made New sells the book 0-672-1010-0
The bookseller Read With Us sells the book 0-672-1010-0
The bookseller Old Books Made New sells the book 0-578-31950-0

Although this code may appear complicated at first glance, it's easy to understand when it's split into its component parts.

Once the links are made to the XML and XSL files for the <Catalog> database, the node for the <Catalog> database is created in line 18.

You're interested in the data portion of the node, so line 19 assigns BooksNode to the data component.

The search will go through all of the <Book> nodes, so line 20 sets a pointer to the first node in the list.

At this point, BooksNode will point to the first of the <Book> nodes. Lines 26 and 53 delimit a loop that will step through each of the <Book> nodes. The nextSibling property is used in line 52 to move to the next node.

Once you're at an instance of the <Book> node, the next step is to extract the ISBN number of that book. A glance at the records of the database will remind you that the <ISBN> node is the fourth from the last node in the <Book> node. Therefore, to get the data you want, go to the last child node and move up three locations. This is done in lines 28 through 31.

Once you're at the node containing the ISBN number, extract that value by capturing the text property of the node. This is done on line 32.

Now that you have the ISBN of the current book, the next step is to search through the <BookSellers> database looking for <Seller>(s) of this book. The first step, which is accomplished by line 33, is to set a pointer to the first data node of the file. This node is used to step through the file, so the next step is to construct a loop where this pointer moves through the <Seller> nodes. Lines 38 and 51 delimit this loop.

Once you have a pointer to an instance of the <Seller> node, you need to go to the node that's the list of books that this <Seller> sells. Since this is the last node of the current <Seller> node, you only need to apply the lastChild property, which is done on line 36. This pointer is now assigned to the <SamsBooksSold> node of the <Seller> node. You need to search through this entire list, so line 37 sets a pointer to the first node. Lines 38-49 then loop through the child nodes that make up the list.

The ISBN is the last node of the <Book> node, so lines 40-41 move to that node and extract the value of the ISBN. If this value matches that of the <Book> extracted from the database of books, lines 42-47 write a message to the document window.

Summary

This hour demonstrated that it's possible to perform collective searches and data extractions on one or more databases. However, what you just did has an unclean feel to it, in the sense that every step in the extraction was hard-coded to this specific data file. Although this shows that the nodes generated by an XSL template are no different from the others, it's not a general solution. The XSL templates provide a great deal of functionality that can be used to query databases, and that will be the topic of the next several hours.

13

Q&A

Q What are the differences between a node that's generated by the XML dom object acting on an entry delimited by a pair of opening and closing tags and a node that's generated by an XSL template?

A Since both are node objects, they contain the same properties and methods. The only differences are the values of the data assigned to those properties.

Q **Why do I need to be able to read the data from more than one XML data file at a time?**

A Placing too much data in a single database can lead to awkward situations where the files contain data that's only distantly related, if at all. Placing the data in more than one database prevents this problem. However, this requires methods whereby the data from more than one database can be read and cross-referenced.

Q **Why are you now using the term *database* to refer to the XML files containing data?**

A In general, any file that contains data that will be processed is referred to as a database. Such processing includes selecting or cross-referencing multiple files, and that's what you're now doing to the data in your XML files, so the term is being used properly.

Workshop

Quiz

1. Which of the following best describes the nodes created by the transformNode() method?

    a. It's a node that contains more methods than the nodes that are generated in other ways.

    b. It's not a node object.

    c. It's a node object just like those generated in other ways.

    d. It's a node that contains fewer methods than the nodes generated in other ways.

2. What are the limits on the number of XML files that can be processed simultaneously?

    a. Two.

    b. Ten.

    c. There are no limits; the number is infinite.

    d. The limits are the practical ones: understanding and the amount of available memory.

3. How many XSL templates can be nested inside each other?

    a. Two.

    b. The limits are the practical ones: understanding and the form of the data.

    c. There are no limits.

    d. The maximum depth is five levels.

4. Is it possible to create data reports using JavaScript code?

    a. Yes, it's possible and very easy.

    b. Yes, it's possible, but it's somewhat awkward because there are no JavaScript methods to do it directly.

    c. Yes, but it's extremely difficult and should be avoided.

    d. No, it's not possible.

Answers

1. c
2. d
3. b
4. b

Exercises

1. Add an additional <Seller> node to the <Booksellers> database. Although this <Seller> will sell books, none of them are to be published by Sams. Run Listing 13.2 again.

2. Modify Listing 13.5 so that the match is done based on book title rather than ISBN.

13

HOUR 14

Using XSL Templates to Perform Basic Database Queries

The last exercise in Hour 13 demonstrated that it's possible to perform selective data extractions from one or more XML files. However, the method used was rather lengthy and inefficient. This hour will introduce options that qualify the actions of the XSL templates that will perform queries and other data extractions with a minimum of programming effort. Furthermore, if the data is stored in an XML format, the code that performs the queries is easily embedded in the HTML Web pages. You don't need to write helper functions in other languages, such as C or C++, to perform the operations. This makes the inclusion of the queries seamless, reducing the overall effort needed to build a powerful Web site. This makes it easier to incorporate e-commerce into your site, since e-commerce is driven by the rapid and accurate creation, storage, and display of data.

In this hour, you'll learn the following:

- What qualifying options are and what they're used for
- How to perform an extraction using an XSL template in which the data is sorted in both ascending and descending order
- How to filter the data based on the values of parameters and attributes

Using Options in the XSL Templates to Create Selective Data Extractions

The data extractions in the previous hour are the simplest ones to perform. When the template acts on the data in the XML file, it simply goes through the data sequentially and displays the data values of all the nodes whose names are in the selection criteria. In practice, this is rarely done. The power of database operations is that you can examine the data set and select only those values that fit some precise set of criteria.

XSL templates allow for the inclusion of *qualifying options* that can be included in the commands. These options either change the order of the output or filter out all data values except for the ones matching the criteria defined by the qualifiers.

These expressions are options that may or may not be present. When included, they qualify the data that is extracted. Therefore, the best way to describe them is as qualifying options. Either of the shorthand representations of qualifier or option is also acceptable.

The options that are available in the XSL templates are very powerful and generally easy to use, having been built from operators that are used in other contexts.

The standard language used for conducting database queries is *Structured Query Language* or *SQL*. SQL contains many operators, and most of them were created with natural language equivalents in mind. When the options for XSL were being designed, the SQL equivalents were always taken into consideration.

Sorting the Data

The human mind naturally prefers to have information organized in some sequential order. Even short lists confuse us when they're unorganized. Therefore, sorting functions are the most widely used functions in the selection and presentation of data. Since this applies to XML data as well, there's an option in XSL that will sort the data for presentation.

In this first exercise, you'll use the order-by option to extract the data from the <Catalog> database and sort it in both ascending and descending order.

The XML database file that you'll use in this example is the <Catalog> database from Listing 12.1.

Listing 14.1 is a modification of Listing 12.2. Save it as listing14-1.xsl. The changes are marked in bold.

LISTING 14.1   An XSL File That Will Present the Sorted Data in Ascending Order

```
 1: <?xml version="1.0"?>
 2: <!-- This file is an XSL style sheet file that is used to
 3:      read the data from the  simple book catalog database.
 4:      In this case, the data will be sorted when read.
 5: -->
 6: <xsl:stylesheet xmlns:xsl="uri:xsl">
 7:  <xsl:template match="/">
 8:   <html>
 9:    <body>
10:    <table border="1">
11:    <tr style="font-weight:bold;color:blue">
12:    <td>Author Name</td>
13:    <td>Author Address</td>
14:    <td>Author City</td>
15:    <td>Author State</td>
16:    <td>Author e-mail</td>
17:    <td>Publisher Name</td>
18:    <td>Publisher Address</td>
19:    <td>Publisher Phone</td>
20:    </tr>
21:     <xsl:for-each select="Catalog/Book"
        order-by="+Author/City">
22:      <tr>
23:       <xsl:apply-templates/>
24:      </tr>
25:     </xsl:for-each>
26:    </table>
27:    </body>
28:   </html>
```

14

LISTING 14.1   continued

```
29:  </xsl:template>
30:
31:  <xsl:template match="Author">
32:    <td><xsl:value-of select="Name"/></td>
33:    <td><xsl:value-of select="Address"/></td>
34:    <td><xsl:value-of select="City"/></td>
35:    <td><xsl:value-of select="State"/></td>
36:    <td><xsl:value-of select="Email"/></td>
37:  </xsl:template>
38:
39:  <xsl:template match="Publisher">
40:    <td><xsl:value-of select="Name"/></td>
41:    <td><xsl:value-of select="Address"/></td>
42:    <td><xsl:value-of select="Phone"/></td>
43:  </xsl:template>
44:
45:  </xsl: stylesheet>
```

The order-by qualifier does what its name implies—it orders the data based on the node assigned to it. The plus (+) prefix causes the data to be sorted in ascending order. If the plus sign (+) is replaced by a minus sign (-), the sorting is in descending order.

Listing 14.2 is a modification of Listing 13.4.

LISTING 14.2   Displaying the Sorted Data in Ascending Order

```
 1:  <html>
 2:  <!-- This file is the HTML that will ultimately be
 3:       displayed. In this case the <Catalog> database will be
 4:       read in and sorted in ascending order.
 5:  -->
 6:  <head>
 7:  <script language="JavaScript">
 8:  <!--
 9:  function StartUp()
10:  {
11:    var DataSource1=new ActiveXObject("microsoft.xmldom");
12:    DataSource1.load("xmlhour14-1.xml");
13:    var XslStyle1=new ActiveXObject ("microsoft.xmldom");
14:    XslStyle1.load("xmlhour14-2.xsl");
15:    document.all.item("xslcontainer1").innerHTML=DataSource1.
       transformNode(XslStyle1.documentElement);
16:
17:  }
18:  //-->
19:  </script>
20:  </head>
```

```
21: <body onLoad="StartUp()">
22: <SPAN ID="xslcontainer1"></Span>
23: </body>
24: </html>
```

Run the file in IE. The output is illustrated in Figure 14.1. Note the entries in the Author-City column.

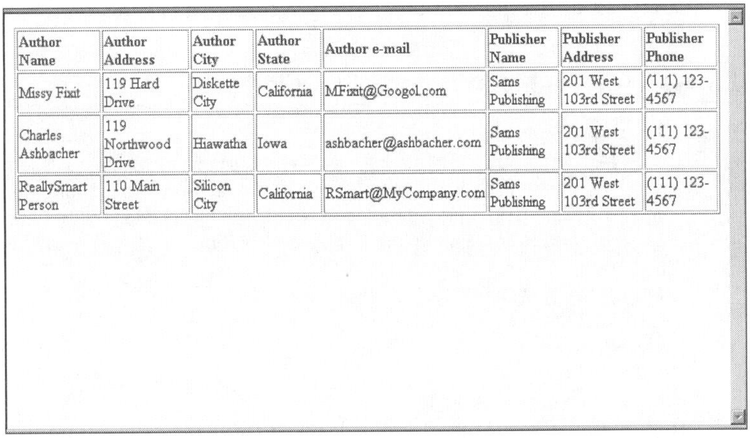

FIGURE 14.1

Extracting and sorting the data before presentation.

Author Name	Author Address	Author City	Author State	Author e-mail	Publisher Name	Publisher Address	Publisher Phone
Missy Fixit	119 Hard Drive	Diskette City	California	MFixit@Googol.com	Sams Publishing	201 West 103rd Street	(111) 123-4567
Charles Ashbacher	119 Northwood Drive	Hiawatha	Iowa	ashbacher@ashbacher.com	Sams Publishing	201 West 103rd Street	(111) 123-4567
ReallySmart Person	110 Main Street	Silicon City	California	RSmart@MyCompany.com	Sams Publishing	201 West 103rd Street	(111) 123-4567

Go back to Listing 14.1 and change the line

```
<xsl:for-each select="Catalog/Book" order-by="+Author/City">
```

to

```
<xsl:for-each select="Catalog/Book" order-by="+ISBN">
```

When you view Listing 14.2 in IE, the data will be selected and sorted in ascending order on the basis of the ISBN number. Recall that the default data type is text, so the sorting is in alphabetical order rather than numerical order.

Filtering the Data

In all but the most trivial of cases, your database files will be so large that you won't even be able to comprehend the entire contents. Your interest will be in only those items that satisfy some specific criteria. Therefore, you must write a program that will examine all the data and *filter* out and display only those values that satisfy your requirements.

You can filter the data in many different ways. The two that you'll look at now are using comparison operators and examining XML attributes.

14

Filtering by Using Comparison Operators

When you're performing queries, it's possible to select only those records in which the values of a field satisfy a specific criteria. You do this by inserting the correct operator inside the assignment to the MATCH qualifier. The simplest way is to select all records where a field is equal to a specific value, and this is demonstrated in the following exercise.

A Filtering Example That Uses a Comparison Operator

Go back to Listing 14.1 and modify it to match Listing 14.3. Save it as listing14-3.xsl.

LISTING 14.3   A Modification of Listing 14.1

```
 1: <?xml version="1.0"?>
 2: <!-- This file is an XSL style sheet file that is used to
 3:      read the data from the simple book catalog database.
 4:      In this case, the data will be sorted when read and
 5:      selected based on specific values.
 6: -->
 7: <xsl:stylesheet xmlns:xsl="uri:xsl">
 8:  <xsl:template match="/">
 9:  <html>
10:   <body>
11:   <table border="1">
12:   <tr style="font-weight:bold;color:blue">
13:   <td>Author Name</td>
14:   <td>Author Address</td>
15:   <td>Author City</td>
16:   <td>Author State</td>
17:   <td>Author e-mail</td>
18: </tr>
19:    <xsl:for-each select="Catalog/Book"
       order-by="+Author/City">
20:     <tr>
21:      <xsl:apply-templates/>
22:     </tr>
23:    </xsl:for-each>
24:   </table>
25:   </body>
26:  </html>
27:  </xsl:template>
28:
29: <xsl:template match="Author[Name='Charles Ashbacher']">
30:    <td><xsl:value-of select="Name"/></td>
31:    <td><xsl:value-of select="Address"/></td>
32:    <td><xsl:value-of select="City"/></td>
33:    <td><xsl:value-of select="State"/></td>
34:    <td><xsl:value-of select="Email"/></td>
35: </xsl:template>
36:
37: </xsl: stylesheet>
```

The only line that is modified from the original is

```
<xsl:template match="Author[Name='Charles Ashbacher']">
```

The qualification [Name='Charles Ashbacher'] causes the data select to extract only those records where the name of the <Author> is 'Charles Ashbacher'. The single quotes are necessary because the string is embedded within double quotes.

Also note that the XSL listing contains more than one selection/display qualifier. The data will be listed in ascending order based on Author/City, and only those records where the Author is 'Charles Ashbacher' will be displayed.

Go back to Listing 14.2 and modify the XSL file so that it reads Listing 14.3. Make no other changes to the file.

Run the file in IE. The output will be the single <Author> record where the <Name> is 'Charles Ashbacher'. This is illustrated in Figure 14.2.

FIGURE 14.2

Filtering by using the equality operator.

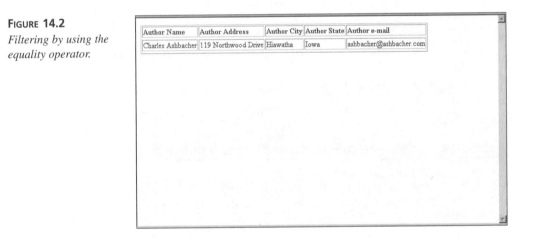

Author Name	Author Address	Author City	Author State	Author e-mail
Charles Ashbacher	119 Northwood Drive	Hiawatha	Iowa	ashbacher@ashbacher.com

The opposite of the equals sign is the not equals sign (!=). It extracts all the data where there's not equality. For example, if the comparison is changed to the following, the output will be all the records not selected in the previous run:

```
<xsl:template match="Author[Name!='Charles Ashbacher']">
```

The greater-than and less-than operators (>, <) cannot appear in the code because they're the delimiters of tags. Recall from your knowledge of HTML that this forces you to use the predefined entities > and < instead. For example, the following qualifier would select out all records where the name of the author follows 'Charles Ashbacher' in alphabetical order:

```
<xsl:template match="Author[Name&gt;'Charles Ashbacher']">
```

14

Filtering Based on XML Attributes

Defining and using attributes were covered in Hour 6. It's also possible to select records based on the values or existence of attributes.

A Filtering Example Based on Attribute Values

To illustrate the selection of records based on the values of attributes, you need to modify your XML data files so that they contain attributes. Reopen listing12-1.xml and modify the opening <Book> tags to match Listing 14.4. Only the <Book> and <Title> tags are shown for brevity.

LISTING 14.4   Modifying the <Book> Tags

```
1: <Book BestSeller="yes">
2: <Title>Teach Yourself XML in 24 Hours</Title>. . .
3: <Book BestSeller="no">
4: <Title>Teach Yourself Cool Stuff in 24 Hours</Title>
5: . . .
6: <Book BestSeller="yes">
7: <Title>Teach Yourself Uses of Silicon in 24 Hours</Title>
```

Save the file as listing14-4.xml.

Reopen listing14-3.xsl and modify it to match Listing 14.5. Save it as listing14-5.xsl.

LISTING 14.5   Selecting the Data Based on the Value of an Attribute

```
 1: <?xml version="1.0"?>
 2: <!-- The purpose of this file is to demonstrate the use of
 3:      the attributes when filtering data from an XML file.
 4: -->
 5: <xsl:stylesheet xmlns:xsl="uri:xsl">
 6:   <xsl:template match="/">
 7:     <html>
 8:       <body>
 9:         <h1>Bestseller Books</h1>
10:         <table cellspacing="4" cellpadding="2">
11:           <tr style="font-weight:bold; font-size:18">
12:             <td>Name </td>
13:           </tr>
14:     <xsl:for-each select="Catalog/Book[@BestSeller='yes']"
          order-by="+ Author/Name">
15:             <TR>
16:               <xsl:apply-templates/>
17:             </TR>
18:         </xsl:for-each>
19:       </table>
```

```
20:        </body>
21:      </html>
22:    </xsl:template>
23:    <xsl:template match="Author">
24:      <td STYLE="font-style:italic; font-size:20">
25:    <td><xsl:value-of select="Name"/></td>
26:    <td><xsl:value-of select="Address"/></td>
27:    <td><xsl:value-of select="City"/></td>
28:    <td><xsl:value-of select="State"/></td>
29:    <td><xsl:value-of select="Email"/></td>
30:    </td>
31:      </xsl:template>
32: </xsl: stylesheet>
```

The line that differs from what you've seen before is

```
<xsl:for-each select="Catalog/Book[@BestSeller='yes']"
order-by="+ Author/Name">
```

The appearance of [@BestSeller='yes'] in that context informs the system that only the <Book> nodes in which the BestSeller attribute is 'yes' are to be selected. The at symbol (@) must be present because that's how the system determines that the selection is based on the value of an attribute rather than the value of the text. Also recall that the 'yes' must be surrounded by single quotes, since it's embedded within double quotes.

Go back to Listing 14.2 and modify the lines that link the files to match the following:

```
DataSource1.load("listing14-4.xml");
var XslStyle1=new ActiveXObject("microsoft.xmldom");
XslStyle1.load("listing14-5.xsl");
```

When the modified file is run, only the entries where the BestSeller attribute is assigned the value 'yes' will be output. This is illustrated in Figure 14.3.

FIGURE 14.3

Selecting all records where the BestSeller attribute of the <Book> node is yes.

Bestseller Books

Name

Charles Ashbacher 119 Northwood Drive Hiawatha Iowa ashbacher@ashbacher.com

14

A Filtering Example Based on Attribute Existence

For your second exercise in filtering by using attribute data, you're interested in whether the attribute exists at all.

Reopen listing14-4.xml and modify the line

```
<Book BestSeller="yes">
<Title>Teach Yourself Uses of Silicon in 24 Hours</Title>
```

to

```
<Book>
<Title>Teach Yourself Uses of Silicon in 24 Hours</Title>
```

You've simply removed the assignment to the BestSeller attribute. Save the file.

Reopen listing14-5.xsl and modify the line

```
<xsl:for-each select="Catalog/Book[@BestSeller='yes']"
```

to

```
<xsl:for-each select="Catalog/Book[@BestSeller]"
```

Save the file and then run listing14-2.html again. In this case, the two entries where the BestSeller attribute exists are output. The notation [@BestSeller] is the command to select all entries where the BestSeller attribute exists.

Summary

The real power of databases lies not in the fact that the data can be displayed, but that you can select or filter out only those records that are of interest. While it's possible to write JavaScript code to perform the selection, XSL templates provide a much more efficient approach.

In this hour, you learned how to output the data sorted by the variable of your choice. You also learned how to filter out the data based on either the value of the text or an attribute of the node. The final example demonstrated how to filter out the records where the attribute was assigned a value.

Efficient processing of databases on the Web is essential for all but the most trivial of e-commerce operations. XML is rapidly becoming the method of choice for such operations because it can be incorporated directly into the HTML code. The ease of use of the XSL templates should also convince you of the value of learning XML.

Q&A

Q I'm a very fast and efficient programmer. Why should I use XML templates when I can code the solutions myself?

A Unless you have a great deal of time on your hands (which is unlikely if you're a good programmer), there's no reason to build what the XSL templates provide for free. The templates can also be directly embedded inside the HTML code, making them as easy to incorporate as a scripting language.

Q Why is the sorting done by the order-by command based on alphabetical order rather than numerical order?

A The default data type for all data is text. Without some additional processing to convert the data into a number, the ordering must be alphabetical.

Q When a filtering qualifier is encountered, how can you look at it and determine whether it's an attribute or a text value?

A If the value has the @ symbol prefix, it's an attribute of the node.

Workshop

Quiz

1. Which of the following are options of the order-by command to control the type of sort?

   a. a+

   b. a-

   c. +

   d. -

   e. a and b

   f. c and d

2. Which of the following commands will select out all the nodes with a Height attribute?

   a. @Height==null

   b. @Height=null

   c. @Height

   d. @Height==""

   e. @Height=""

14

3. Which of the following is a syntactically correct expression for testing the value of a node?

    a. select="Catalog/Book[@BestSeller="yes"]"

    b. select="Catalog/Book[@BestSeller=='yes']"

    c. select="Catalog/Book[@BestSeller='yes']"

    d. select="Catalog/Book[@BestSeller=="yes"]"

Answers

1. f
2. c
3. c

Exercises

1. Create an XSL file that will select the data in listing12-1.xml and sort it based on descending order of the PublisherBookID.

2. Reopen listing12-1.xml and add the attribute Type to all instances of the <Book> tag. This attribute can have three possible values, {Fiction, Nonfiction, Reference}. Assign suitable values for all three nodes, and then perform a query to select on the basis of the type of the book.

HOUR 15

Using Conditional XSL Statements and Embedding Scripting Code to Perform Database Queries

In your work with XSL templates so far, you've used statements such as xsl:apply-templates and xsl:value-of select="NodeName". These are examples from the list of available *XSL elements*, which are statements that can be used to extract data and insert nodes into the node tree, among other operations. This hour will use some *conditional* XSL elements and will list all those that are currently supported.

Conditional elements are those that allow for the selective processing of segments of code. The selection can be based on the value of a *boolean*, or logical, expression, or the value of a variable or expression. Conditional expressions are very powerful tools, allowing decisions to be made as the program is running.

It seems to be a law of programming that no matter what a system provides, there's always some bit of functionality that's lacking. Although XSL is powerful, it's no exception. Therefore, this hour will examine an XSL element that allows segments of scripting code to be embedded inside the XSL template.

In this hour, you'll learn the following:

- The complete set of XSL elements that can be used in templates
- How to use the conditional elements to selectively extract data from an XSL file
- How to embed segments of scripting code in an XSL template

The XSL Elements

So far, you've used only a few of the XSL elements that are supported. See Table 15.1 for more of them.

TABLE 15.1   XSL Elements

Element	Function
xsl:apply-templates	Commands the XSL processor to find and execute the appropriate template(s).
xsl:attribute	Creates an attribute node and applies it to the output node structure.
xsl:cdata	Inserts a CDATA section into the output.
xsl:choose	Used for conditional testing and processing. Generally used in combination with the xsl:otherwise and xsl:when elements.
xsl:comment	Inserts a comment into the output node structure.
xsl:copy	Makes a copy of a source node.
xsl:define-template-set	Defines a set of templates.
xsl:element	Inserts an element into the output with the specified name.
xsl:entity-ref	Inserts an entity reference with the specified name into the output.
xsl:eval	Evaluates a string of text; more specifically, used to insert sections of scripting code into the file.
xsl:for-each	Applies the template(s) to each child node of the specified parent node.
xsl:if	Used to apply a true/false test and perform conditional processing.
xsl:node-name	Inserts the name of the current node into the output structure.
xsl:otherwise	Used to specify an alternative when conditional processing is performed.

Element	Function
xsl:pi	Inserts a processing instruction into the output structure.
xsl:script	Used to define global variables.
xsl:stylesheet	Delimits an XSL style sheet.
xsl:template:	Delimits a template for generating output based on a pattern or patterns.
xsl:value-of	Extracts the current value of the item specified in the SELECT attribute and returns it as text.
xsl:when	Used to test an attribute in conditional processing.

The xsl:if Element

All programming languages contain a construct to test for an item that can be only either true or false. If the value is true, a section of code is executed. If it's false, the first section is skipped, and another section may or may not be executed. In JavaScript, the construct is an if-else statement. The else part is optional. If your goal is to execute a segment of code when the value is true and do nothing otherwise, the else is not included.

In XSL, you can use the xsl:if command to construct an expression that will control the conditional execution of a block of XSL code. The delimiters of the block of code are the opening and closing <xsl:if> tags. There's no companion xsl:else command, although it can be mimicked in an awkward manner. For example, consider the following if construct:

```
<xsl:if match="Author[Name='Charles Ashbacher']">
</xsl:if>
```

The if equivalent for the else would be as follows:

```
<xsl:if match="Author[Name!='Charles Ashbacher']">
</xsl:if>
```

An xsl:if Example That Will Read the Catalog Database and Extract the Book Records with a BestSeller Attribute

The first example demonstrates how to use xsl:if to selectively extract and display information from an XML file. The data file that you'll use is listing14-4.xml. Note that this is the <Catalog> database with the BestSeller attribute added to the <Book> tag.

Go back to Listing 14.3 and modify it to match Listing 15.1. Save it as listing15-1.xsl.

LISTING 15.1   An xsl:if Conditional That's True If the Book Record Has a BestSeller Attribute

```
 1: <?xml version="1.0"?>
 2: <!-- This file is an XSL style sheet file that is used to
 3:      read the data from the simple book catalog database.
 4:      In this case, the data will be sorted when read and
 5:      we are using conditional xsl elements to filter the
 6:      data.
 7: -->
 8: <xsl:stylesheet xmlns:xsl="uri:xsl">
 9:  <xsl:template match="/">
10:  <html>
11:   <body>
12:   <table border="1">
13:   <tr style="font-weight:bold;color:blue">
14:   <td>Author Name</td>
15:   <td>Author Address</td>
16:   <td>Author City</td>
17:   <td>Author State</td>
18:   <td>Author e-mail</td>
19:   <td>Publisher Name</td>
20:   <td>Publisher Address</td>
21:   <td>Publisher Phone</td>
22:   </tr>
23:    <xsl:for-each select="Catalog/Book"
          order-by="+Author/City">
24:     <xsl:if match=".[@BestSeller]">
25:     <tr>
26:      <xsl:apply-templates/>
27:     </tr>
28:    </xsl:if>
29:    </xsl:for-each>
30:   </table>
31:   </body>
32:  </html>
33:  </xsl: template>
34: <xsl:template match="Author">
35:   <td><xsl:value-of select="Name"/></td>
36:   <td><xsl:value-of select="Address"/></td>
37:   <td><xsl:value-of select="City"/></td>
38:   <td><xsl:value-of select="State"/></td>
39:   <td><xsl:value-of select="Email"/></td>
40: </xsl:template>
41: <xsl:template match="Publisher">
42:   <td><xsl:value-of select="Name"/></td>
43:   <td><xsl:value-of select="Address"/></td>
44:   <td><xsl:value-of select="Phone"/></td>
45: </xsl:template>
46: </xsl: stylesheet>
```

Run the file in IE and note that only the entries where the BestSeller attribute is assigned a value are displayed. The output is illustrated in Figure 15.1.

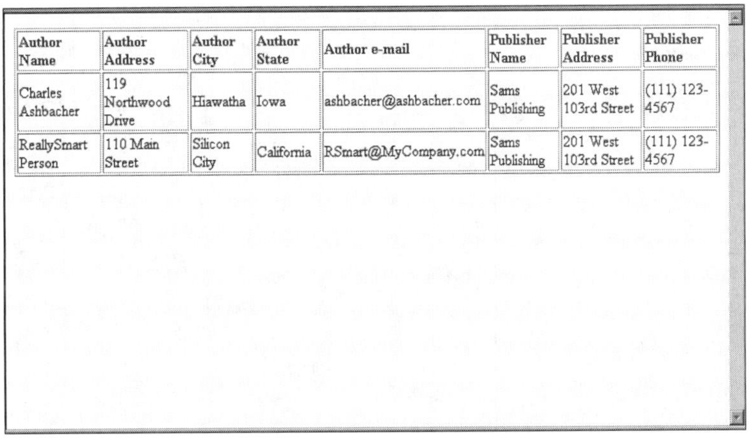

FIGURE **15.1**

The output.

Author Name	Author Address	Author City	Author State	Author e-mail	Publisher Name	Publisher Address	Publisher Phone
Charles Ashbacher	119 Northwood Drive	Hiawatha	Iowa	ashbacher@ashbacher.com	Sams Publishing	201 West 103rd Street	(111) 123-4567
ReallySmart Person	110 Main Street	Silicon City	California	RSmart@MyCompany.com	Sams Publishing	201 West 103rd Street	(111) 123-4567

This result is the consequence of the xsl:if, where the code guarded by the if is executed only when the following is true:

```
match=".[@BestSeller]"
```

This is the syntax for the presence of the BestSeller attribute. Of course, if the attribute is present, the following line is executed and the data is extracted:

```
<xsl:apply-templates/>
```

Since there's no alternative, nothing is done when there's no BestSeller attribute.

Note that the code guarded by the if is delimited by the following tags:

```
<xsl:if . . . >
```

```
</xsl:if>
```

An xsl:if Example That Selects Only the Records Where the BestSeller Attribute Has a Specific Value

Go back to Listing 15.1 and change the line

```
<xsl:if match=".[@BestSeller]">
```

to

```
<xsl:if match=".[@BestSeller='yes']">
```

This is the notation for selecting only those cases where the BestSeller attribute is assigned the value 'yes'. Save the file before continuing.

View `listing 14-4.html` in IE 5. The output will be the only entry where BestSeller is assigned a value of 'yes'. This is illustrated in Figure 15.2.

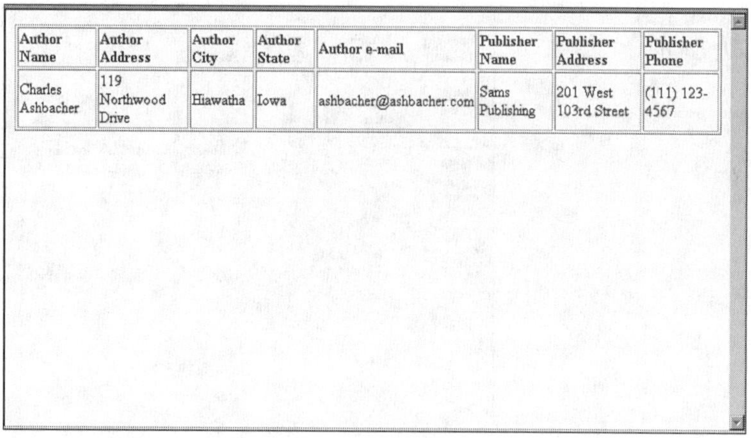

FIGURE 15.2

Extracting only the bestsellers.

Author Name	Author Address	Author City	Author State	Author e-mail	Publisher Name	Publisher Address	Publisher Phone
Charles Ashbacher	119 Northwood Drive	Hiawatha	Iowa	ashbacher@ashbacher.com	Sams Publishing	201 West 103rd Street	(111) 123-4567

Using Multiple xsl:if elements in an XSL File

If you're dealing with an attribute with more than one possible value, you can handle each of the possibilities by using an additional <xsl:if>. Listing 15.2 demonstrates the use of more than one xsl:if inside an XSL file.

LISTING 15.2   Using Multiple xsl:if Elements in an XSL File

```
 1: <?xml version="1.0"?>
 2: <!-- This file is an XSL stylesheet file that is used to read the data from
 3: the simple book catalog database. In this case, the data will be sorted
 4: when read and we are using conditional xsl elements to filter the data.
 5: The filename is listing15-2.xsl. -->
 6: <xsl:stylesheet xmlns:xsl="uri:xsl">
 7:  <xsl:template match="/">
 8:  <html>
 9:  <body>
10:  <table border="1">
11:  <tr style="font-weight:bold;color:blue">
12:  <td>Author Name</td>
13:  <td>Author Address</td>
14:  <td>Author City</td>
15:  <td>Author State</td>
16:  <td>Author e-mail</td>
17:  <td>Publisher Name</td>
18:  <td>Publisher Address</td>
19:  <td>Publisher Phone</td>
```

```
20:   </tr>
21:     <xsl:for-each select="Catalog/Book" order-by="+Author/City">
22:      <xsl:if match=".[@BestSeller='yes']">
23:      <tr>
24:       <xsl:apply-templates/>
25:      </tr>
26:     </xsl:if>
27:      <xsl:if match=".[@BestSeller='no']">
28:      <tr style="font-weight:bold;color:red">
29:     <td>Not a bestseller</td>
30:      </tr>
31:     </xsl:if>
32:     </xsl:for-each>
33:    </table>
34:    </body>
35:   </html>
36:   </xsl: template>
37: <xsl:template match="Author">
38:    <td><xsl:value-of select="Name"/></td>
39:    <td><xsl:value-of select="Address"/></td>
40:    <td><xsl:value-of select="City"/></td>
41:    <td><xsl:value-of select="State"/></td>
42:    <td><xsl:value-of select="Email"/></td>
43: </xsl:template>
44: <xsl:template match="Publisher">
45:    <td><xsl:value-of select="Name"/></td>
46:    <td><xsl:value-of select="Address"/></td>
47:    <td><xsl:value-of select="Phone"/></td>
48: </xsl:template>
49: </xsl: stylesheet>
```

Modify listing14-2.html so that listing15-2.xsl is the XSL file opened. The output when the file is viewed in IE is illustrated in Figure 15.3.

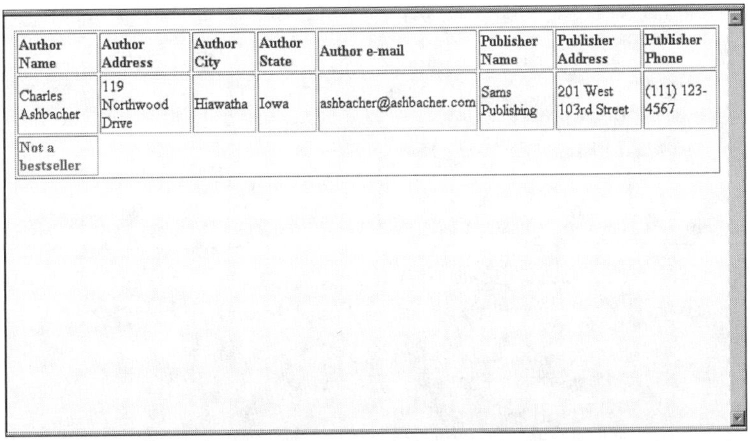

FIGURE 15.3

Outputting a simple message when the BestSeller attribute is 'no'.

Author Name	Author Address	Author City	Author State	Author e-mail	Publisher Name	Publisher Address	Publisher Phone
Charles Ashbacher	119 Northwood Drive	Hiawatha	Iowa	ashbacher@ashbacher.com	Sams Publishing	201 West 103rd Street	(111) 123-4567
Not a bestseller							

The XML data file has two different values assigned to the BestSeller attribute, 'yes' and 'no'. This example includes two different xsl:if elements, one for each possible value of the BestSeller. The output when it was 'no' was rather crude, consisting of a message in red. Since the only point was to demonstrate the difference, this was acceptable.

If an attribute can have several values, it's possible to include an xsl:if element for every one. However, this rapidly becomes awkward and difficult to understand. The solution is to create a multiple alternative construct using a combination of xsl:choose, xsl:when, and xsl:otherwise elements.

The xsl:choose, xsl:when, and xsl:otherwise Elements

The previous example showed you how to use multiple <xsl:if> elements in situations where there are alternatives. Although this works, it's ungainly when there are several possible values. In that case, it's better to use a combination of the <xsl:choose>, <xsl:when>, and <xsl:otherwise> elements. The following two sections illustrate how these elements are used.

An xsl:choose and xsl:when Example

Reopen listing14-4.xml and change

```
<Book>
<Title>Teach Yourself Uses of Silicon in 24 Hours</Title>
<Author>
<Name>Missy Fixit</Name>
```

to

```
<Book BestSeller="impossible">
<Title>Teach Yourself Uses of Silicon in 24 Hours</Title>
<Author>
<Name>Missy Fixit</Name>
```

Add the two additional records that appear in Listing 15.3 to the end of the file. Save the updated file as listing15-3.xml.

LISTING 15.3   Two Records with Additional Values for the BestSeller Attribute

```
1: <Book BestSeller="guaranteed">
2: <Title>101 Unusual Uses for Hairspray</Title>
3: <Author>
4: <Name>Harpo Hair</Name>
5: <Address>101 Furrball</Address>
6: <City>Clipper City</City>
7: <State>California</State>
```

```
 8:  <PostalCode>10102</PostalCode>
 9:  <Country>United States</Country>
10:  <Phone>(586) 212-3498</Phone>
11:  <Email>HairX@HairClip.com</Email>
12:  <URL>http://www.HairClip.com</URL>
13:  </Author>
14:  <Publisher>
15:  <Name>Sams Publishing</Name>
16:  <Address>201 West 103rd Street</Address>
17:  <City>Indianapolis</City>
18:  <State>Indiana</State>
19:  <PostalCode>46290</PostalCode>
20:  <Country>United States</Country>
21:  <Phone>(111) 123-4567</Phone>
22:  <Editor>Dummy Name</Editor>
23:  <EmailContact>Dummy.Name@samspublishing.com</EmailContact>
24:  <URL>http://www.samspublishing.com</URL>
25:  </Publisher>
26:  <ISBN>0-578-3411-0</ISBN>
27:  <PublisherBookID>1234576</PublisherBookID>
28:  <PublicationDate>2000-03-01</PublicationDate>
29:  <Price>36.95</Price>
30:  </Book>
31:  <Book BestSeller="dud">
32:  <Title>Celebrity Toenail Clippings</Title>
33:  <Author>
34:  <Name>Foot Lover</Name>
35:  <Address>101 Podiatrist Center</Address>
36:  <City>Clipper City</City>
37:  <State>California</State>
38:  <PostalCode>10102</PostalCode>
39:  <Country>United States</Country>
40:  <Phone>(586) 212-2112</Phone>
41:  <Email>Exotic@CToesClip.com</Email>
42:  <URL>http://www.CToesClip.com</URL>
43:  </Author>
44:  <Publisher>
45:  <Name>Sams Publishing</Name>
46:  <Address>201 West 103rd Street</Address>
47:  <City>Indianapolis</City>
48:  <State>Indiana</State>
49:  <PostalCode>46290</PostalCode>
50:  <Country>United States</Country>
51:  <Phone>(111) 123-4567</Phone>
52:  <Editor>Dummy Name</Editor>
53:  <EmailContact>Dummy.Name@samspublishing.com</EmailContact>
54:  <URL>http://www.samspublishing.com</URL>
55:  </Publisher>
56:  <ISBN>0-578-3001-0</ISBN>
57:  <PublisherBookID>1234476</PublisherBookID>
58:  <PublicationDate>2000-06-01</PublicationDate>
59:  <Price>46. 95</Price>
60:  </Book>
```

Before you continue, understand that there are now five different values assigned to the BestSeller option: { yes, no, impossible, guaranteed, dud }.

Reopen listing15-2.xsl and modify the <xsl:for-each> loop to match Listing 15.4. Save the updated file as listing15-4.xsl.

LISTING 15.4 Using the XSL Elements to Create a Multiple Alternative Construct

```
 1: <xsl:for-each select="Catalog/Book"
    order-by="+Author/City">
 2:    <xsl:choose>
 3:     <xsl:when match=".[@BestSeller='yes']">
 4:     <tr>
 5:      <xsl:apply-templates/>
 6:     </tr>
 7:     </xsl:when>
 8:     <xsl:when match=".[@BestSeller='no']">
 9:     <tr style="font-weight:bold;color:red">
10:     <td>Not a bestseller</td>
11:     </tr>
12:    </xsl:when>
13:     <xsl:when match=".[@BestSeller='impossible']">
14:     <tr style="font-weight:bold;color:red">
15:     <td>It is impossible for this to be a
        bestseller</td>
16:     </tr>
17:    </xsl:when>
18:     <xsl:when match=".[@BestSeller='guaranteed']">
19:     <tr style="font-weight:bold;color:red">
20:     <td>Guaranteed to be a bestseller</td>
21:     </tr>
22:    </xsl:when>
23:     <xsl:when match=".[@BestSeller='dud']">
24:     <tr style="font-weight:bold;color:red">
25:     <td>Definitely a dud</td>
26:     </tr>
27:    </xsl:when>
28:    </xsl:choose>
29:    </xsl: for-each>
```

Note that there's an xsl:when element for each of the possible values that the BestSeller attribute can have.

Reopen listing14-2.html and modify the lines that load the files so that listing15-3.xml is the XML file and listing15-4.xsl is the XSL file. The output when it's viewed in IE is shown in Figure 15.4.

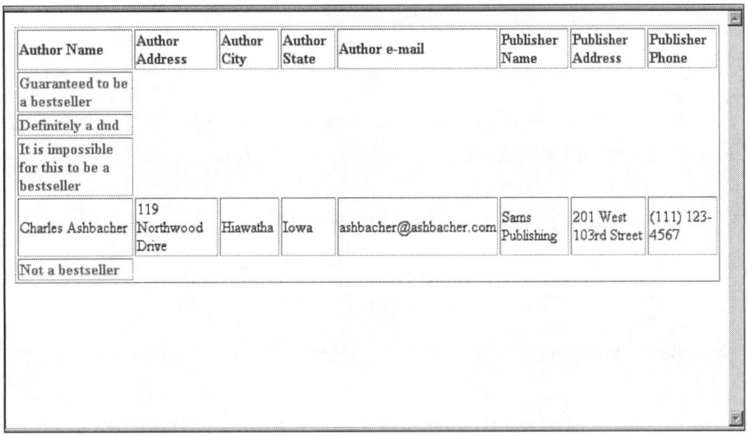

FIGURE 15.4

A different output for each possible value of the BestSeller attribute.

15

The following XSL element pair delimits a set of multiple alternatives written using the <xsl:when> and <xsl:otherwise> elements:

```
<xsl:choose>

</xsl:choose>
```

There are five <xsl:when> elements in the construct, one for each of the possible values of the attribute:

```
<xsl:when match=".[@BestSeller='yes']">
    <tr>
     <xsl:apply-templates/>
    </tr>
    </xsl:when>
    <xsl:when match=".[@BestSeller='no']">
    <tr style="font-weight:bold;color:red">
    <td>Not a bestseller</td>
    </tr>
</xsl:when>
    <xsl:when match=".[@BestSeller='impossible']">
    <tr style="font-weight:bold;color:red">
    <td>It is impossible for this to be a bestseller</td>
    </tr>
</xsl:when>
    <xsl:when match=".[@BestSeller='guaranteed']">
    <tr style="font-weight:bold;color:red">
    <td>Guaranteed to be a bestseller</td>
    </tr>
</xsl:when>
    <xsl:when match=".[@BestSeller='dud']">
     <tr style="font-weight:bold;color:red">
```

```
<td>Definitely a dud</td>
</tr>
</xsl: when>
```

In this case, the data is extracted only when the value of BestSeller is 'yes'. For all other cases, a simple message is written to that row of the table.

An xsl:otherwise Example

As has already been mentioned, the other element used in association with <xsl:choose> is the <xsl:otherwise> element. It can be considered as the "none of the above" option.

Reopen listing15-4.xsl and modify it to match Listing 15.5. Save it as listing15-5.xsl.

LISTING 15.5   Using the xsl:otherwise Element to Catch All Remaining Options

```
 1: <xsl:for-each select="Catalog/Book" order-by="+Author/City">
 2:     <xsl:choose>
 3:      <xsl:when match=".[@BestSeller='yes']">
 4:      <tr>
 5:       <xsl:apply-templates/>
 6:      </tr>
 7:      </xsl:when>
 8:      <xsl:when match=".[@BestSeller='no']">
 9:      <tr style="font-weight:bold;color:red">
10:      <td>Not a bestseller</td>
11:      </tr>
12:      </xsl:when>
13:      <xsl:when match=".[@BestSeller='impossible']">
14:      <tr style="font-weight:bold;color:red">
15:      <td>It is impossible for this to be a bestseller</td>
16:      </tr>
17:      </xsl:when>
18:      <xsl:otherwise>
19:      <tr style="font-weight:bold;color:red">
20:      <td>Guaranteed to be a bestseller or a dud</td>
21:      </tr>
22:      </xsl:otherwise>
23:     </xsl:choose>
24:    </xsl: for-each>
```

Reopen listing14-2.html and modify the lines that load the files so that listing15-3.xml is the XML file and listing15-5.xsl is the XSL file. The output when it's viewed in IE is shown in Figure 15.5.

15

FIGURE 15.5

Illustrating the xsl:otherwise element.

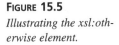

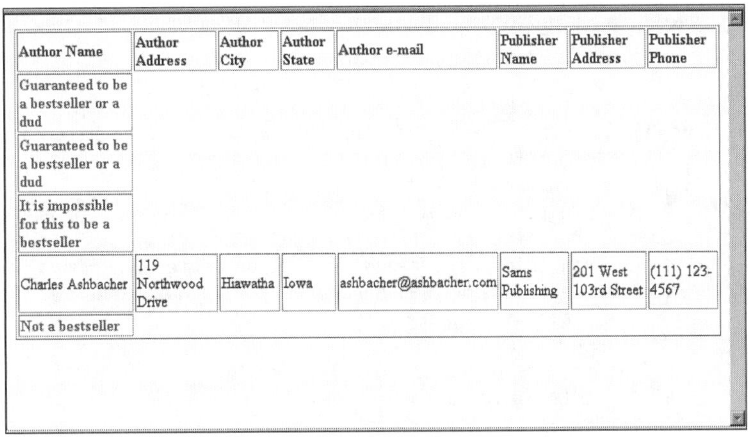

Author Name	Author Address	Author City	Author State	Author e-mail	Publisher Name	Publisher Address	Publisher Phone
Guaranteed to be a bestseller or a dud							
Guaranteed to be a bestseller or a dud							
It is impossible for this to be a bestseller							
Charles Ashbacher	119 Northwood Drive	Hiawatha	Iowa	ashbacher@ashbacher.com	Sams Publishing	201 West 103rd Street	(111) 123-4567
Not a bestseller							

For the three values of yes, no, and impossible, there's an xsl:if element that will lead to specific actions. If the value of the BestSeller attribute is 'dud' or guaranteed, the message in the xsl:otherwise option is displayed.

The xsl:eval Element

In previous hours, you used JavaScript to perform the data-reading operations. The sections of JavaScript code were delimited by the opening and closing <SCRIPT> tags where the scripting language was specified by assignment. The XSL equivalent of this is the <xsl:eval> tag.

An xsl:eval Example

To demonstrate how to embed a section of JavaScript code in an XSL file, you'll need to recall a function present in the JavaScript library. This function is the random number generator, which can be used to generate an arbitrary number within any desired range. It's a member of the Math library, so the notation to call it is as follows:

```
Math.random();
```

It will return a floating point number between 0 and 1.

Since your goal is to return an integer between 0 and 50, you'd perform the following sequence of operations:

```
Math.round(Math.random()*50)
```

For this demonstration of embedded JavaScript, assume that the random number that's generated is the percentage discount that's offered to the current visitor. In other words, if the random number is 37, the user can buy a book for 37% off the regular price.

Reopen listing15-5.xsl and modify the <xsl:for-each . . . > loop to match Listing 15.6.
Save the file as listing15-6.xsl.

LISTING 15.6   Embedding and Using JavaScript Code in an xsl File

```
 1: <?xml version="1.0"?>
 2: <!-- This file is an XSL style sheet file that is used to
 3:       read the data from the simple book catalog database.
 4:       In this case, the data will be sorted when read and
 5:       we are using embedded JavaScript inside the XSL
 6:       template.
 7: -->
 8: <xsl:stylesheet xmlns:xsl="uri:xsl">
 9: <xsl:template match="/">
10: <html>
11:   <body>
12:   <table border="1">
13:   <tr style="font-weight:bold;color:blue">
14:   <td>Author Name</td>
15:   <td>Author Address</td>
16:   <td>Author City</td>
17:   <td>Author State</td>
18:   <td>Author e-mail</td>
19:   <td>Publisher Name</td>
20:   <td>Publisher Address</td>
21:   <td>Publisher Phone</td>
22:   <td>Current discount percentage</td>
23:   </tr>
24:     <xsl:for-each select="Catalog/Book" order-by="+Author/City">
25:       <tr>
26:       <xsl:apply-templates/>
27:       <td>
28:       discount:
29:       <xsl:eval language="JavaScript">
30:       pvalue=Math.round (50*Math.random());
31:       </xsl:eval>
32:       </td>
33:       </tr>
34:     </xsl:for-each>
35:   </table>
36:   </body>
37: </html>
38: </xsl:template>
39: <xsl:template match="Author">
40:   <td><xsl:value-of select="Name"/></td>
41:   <td><xsl:value-of select="Address"/></td>
42:   <td><xsl:value-of select="City"/></td>
43:   <td><xsl:value-of select="State"/></td>
44:   <td><xsl:value-of select="Email"/></td>
```

```
45: </xsl:template>
46: <xsl:template match="Publisher">
47:    <td><xsl:value-of select="Name"/></td>
48:    <td><xsl:value-of select="Address"/></td>
49:    <td><xsl:value-of select="Phone"/></td>
50: </xsl:template>
51: </xsl: stylesheet>
```

Reopen `listing14-2.html` and modify the lines that load the files so that `listing15-3.xml` is the XML file and `listing15-6.xsl` is the XSL file. The output when it's viewed in IE is shown in Figure 15.6.

FIGURE 15.6

Using JavaScript code to generate content for display.

Author Name	Author Address	Author City	Author State	Author e-mail	Publisher Name	Publisher Address	Publisher Phone	Current discount percentage
Harpo Hair	101 Furrball	Clipper City	California	HairX@HairClip.com	Sams Publishing	201 West 103rd Street	(111) 123-4567	discount: 47
Foot Lover	101 Podiatrist Center	Clipper City	California	Exotic@CToesClip.com	Sams Publishing	201 West 103rd Street	(111) 123-4567	discount: 37
Missy Fixit	119 Hard Drive	Diskette City	California	MFixit@Googol.com	Sams Publishing	201 West 103rd Street	(111) 123-4567	discount: 28
Charles Ashbacher	119 Northwood Drive	Hiawatha	Iowa	ashbacher@ashbacher.com	Sams Publishing	201 West 103rd Street	(111) 123-4567	discount: 22
ReallySmart Person	110 Main Street	Silicon City	California	RSmart@MyCompany.com	Sams Publishing	201 West 103rd Street	(111) 123-4567	discount: 11

Since the numbers are randomly generated, the values you get in the Current Discount Percentage column will be different than those shown here.

The key to understanding the output is to realize that the following line creates a row of entries for the table from the <Author> and <Publisher> data:

```
<xsls:apply-templates/>
```

However, the </tr> is not encountered, so the <td>, </td> tag pair that surrounds the <xsl:eval . . . > pair will create another entry in that row of the table. The assignment of language="JavaScript" inside the xsl:eval element does the same thing that it does inside a <Script> tag. The discount: identifier assigns a name to the entry, and the value for that identifier is generated inside the single line of JavaScript code. This line uses the random number generator to compute an integer from 0 to 50, and that value is then used as the row entry:

```
<tr>
 <xsl:apply-templates/>
 <td>
 discount:
 <xsl:eval language="JavaScript">
 pvalue=Math.round(50*Math.random());
 </xsl: eval>
 </td>
 </tr>
```

An xsl:eval Example That Uses a JavaScript Function

JavaScript functions created by the user can also be written and called from within an <xsl:eval . . . > element, and that's the subject of this exercise.

Reopen listing15-6.xsl and modify it to match Listing 15.7. Save the file as listing15-7.xml.

LISTING 15.7   Creating and Calling JavaScript Functions Inside an XSL File

```
 1: <?xml version="1.0"?>
 2: <!-- This file is an XSL style sheet file that is used to
 3:      read the data from the simple book catalog database.
 4:      In this case, the data will be sorted when read and
 5:      we are using embedded JavaScript inside the XSL
 6:      template.
 7:   -->
 8: <xsl:stylesheet xmlns:xsl="uri:xsl">
 9:  <xsl:template match="/">
10:  <html>
11:    <body>
12:    <table border="1">
13:    <tr style="font-weight:bold;color:blue">
14:    <td>Author Name</td>
15:    <td>Author Address</td>
16:    <td>Author City</td>
17:    <td>Author State</td>
18:    <td>Author e-mail</td>
19:    <td>Publisher Name</td>
20:    <td>Publisher Address</td>
21:    <td>Publisher Phone</td>
22:    <td>Current discount percentage</td>
23:    </tr>
24:    <xsl:for-each select="Catalog/Book" order-by="+Author/City">
```

15

```
25:     <tr>
26:     <xsl:apply-templates/>
27:     <td>
28:     discount:
29:     <xsl:eval language="JavaScript">
30:      DiscountCalc();
31:    </xsl:eval>
32:    </td>
33:    </tr>
34:    </xsl:for-each>
35:   </table>
36:   </body>
37:  </html>
38:  </xsl:template>
39: <xsl:script language="JavaScript">
40:    function DiscountCalc()
41:    {
42:    discount=Math. round(50*Math.random());
43:    return discount;
44:    }
45:  </xsl:script>
46: <xsl:template match="Author">
47:    <td><xsl:value-of select="Name"/></td>
48:    <td><xsl:value-of select="Address"/></td>
49:    <td><xsl:value-of select="City"/></td>
50:    <td><xsl:value-of select="State"/></td>
51:    <td><xsl:value-of select="Email"/></td>
52: </xsl:template>
53: <xsl:template match="Publisher">
54:    <td><xsl:value-of select="Name"/></td>
55:    <td><xsl:value-of select="Address"/></td>
56:    <td><xsl:value-of select="Phone"/></td>
57: </xsl:template>
58: </xsl: stylesheet>
```

> The <xsl:script . . . > element is used to define global entities, which are functions or data that will be referenced from other places in the file. Therefore, it must be placed outside the templates if it's to be accessible by all templates.

Reopen listing14-2.html and modify the lines that load the files so that listing15-3.xml is the XML file and listing15-7.xsl is the XSL file. With the exception of the values of the randomly generated numbers, the output is the same as in the previous example.

The code does essentially the same thing as the code from the previous exercise. The only difference is that there's a function call to perform the computation, rather than it being done at that position in the code. Since that function was placed within <xsl:script> tags and outside any templates, it's available for reference anywhere within the file.

Summary

This hour gave you the complete list of supported XSL elements. Although there wasn't enough time to cover all of the elements, the most significant ones were demonstrated. Conditional processing is an important component of all computing, and the xsl:if, xsl:choose, xsl:when, and xsl:otherwise elements were all used in situations where alternatives were available.

Despite all the power of the XSL elements, there are still some things they cannot do. Therefore, the syntax for the inclusion of JavaScript code in XSL files was demonstrated. There are two ways to do this: either inline or as a globally defined function.

Q&A

Q Is it possible to use the <xsl:otherwise> element as the false alternative to an <xsl:if> element?

A No, the <xsl:otherwise> element is used inside an <xsl:choose> wrapper in conjunction with one or more <xls:when> elements.

Q If a JavaScript function is written using the <xls:script> tag, can it be placed inside a template if it's to be called from other templates?

A No. The <xls:script> tag is used to define global entities, so if you want the function to be globally accessible, it cannot be defined locally.

Q What's the main advantage of using a set of <xls:when> elements rather than a set of <xls:if> elements?

A The <xls:when> elements allow for the <xsl:otherwise> or "none of the above" option. Since the available options may expand or be combined, there's greater flexibility when you use the <xls:when>.

Workshop

Quiz

1. Which of the following XSL elements will insert a node into the output structure?

    a. <xsl:otherwise>

    b. <xsl:comment>

    c. <xsl:choose>

    d. All of the above

2. Which of the following XSL elements is used to insert segments of JavaScript code into the XSL file?

    a. <xsl:choose>

    b. <xsl:eval>

    c. <xsl:script>

    d. <xsl:pi>

    e. b and c

3. The complete JavaScript library of functions is available for use in XSL files.

    True

    False

Answers

1. b

2. e

3. True

Exercises

1. Modify listing15-3.xml by adding two additional data entries. Give the BestSeller attribute of one entry the value "possibly" and give the other one the value "probably". Modify listing15-4.xsl to handle the additional options. Test your code.

2. Modify listing15-3.xml by including a "Temperament" attribute to the <Author> tag. Assign it values from the list { impulsive, sanguine, sedate, unavailable}. Write corresponding XSL and HTML files to selectively output the data based on the values of the Temperament attribute.

Hour **16**

Using XSL Selection and Boolean Operators to Perform Database Queries

Regarding XSL, so far this book has concentrated on the XSL elements and how they're used in the extraction of data. XSL also contains a rich set of operators that are similar to those found in database programs. The primary operation performed on databases is to query out a subset based on specific criteria, and that's what these operators are used for.

In this hour, you'll learn the following:

- The syntax of the xsl:comment element that's used to insert a comment into the generated HTML file

- The syntax of the basic selection operators with the selectNodes() method and the results of their use

- The ALL operator and how it's used to select all nodes with a given name
- The syntax of the Boolean operators and how they operate on their inputs

The xsl:comment Element

Amidst all the syntactic clutter of XML, XSL, and HTML files, it's easy to lose track of the fact that an XSL file generates an HTML file. The xsl:comment element is used to insert an HTML style comment into the HTML file that's created by the execution of the XSL file. Before you look at the XSL operators, this hour will illustrate how the xsl:comment element will insert a comment into the HTML code generated by the XSL template. As a data source, use Listing 15.3.

Reopen listing15-8.xsl and insert the following boldfaced lines into the code:

```
<html>
<xsl:comment>
This comment was inserted using the xsl:comment element
</xsl:comment>
<body>
```

Reopen listing14-2.html and modify it to match Listing 16.1.

LISTING 16.1   Examining the Contents of the Generated Node After Insertion of the Comment

```
 1: <html>
 2: <!-- This file is the HTML that will ultimately be
 3:      displayed. In this case the <Catalog> database will be
 4:      read in and an xsl:comment element will be used to
 5:      insert an HTML comment inserted into the output.
 6:      The name of the file is listing16-1.html. -->
 7: <head>
 8: <title>This program demonstrates the use of an XSL template
 9: to read XML data</title>
10: <script language="JavaScript">
11: <!--
12: function StartUp()
13: {
14:   var DataSource1=new ActiveXObject("microsoft.xmldom");
15:   DataSource1.load("listing15-3.xml");
16:   var XslStyle1=new ActiveXObject("microsoft.xmldom");
17:   XslStyle1.load("listing15-8.xsl");
18:   testNode=DataSource1.transformNode(XslStyle1.
        documentElement);
19:   document.all.item("xslcontainer1").innerHTML=DataSource1.
```

```
        transformNode(XslStyle1. documentElement);
20:   alert(testNode);
21: }
22: //-->
23: </script>
24: </head>
25: <body onLoad="StartUp()">
26: <SPAN ID="xslcontainer1"></Span>
27: </body>
28: </html>
```

16

The key here is that in the following line, the results of the node transformation are captured in the testNode identifier:

```
testNode=DataSource1.transformNode(XslStyle1.
documentElement);
```

Once captured, they can then be output using an alert box:

```
 alert(testNode);
```

The output is illustrated in Figure 16.1.

Figure 16.1

Displaying the generated node that includes an inserted comment.

Note the appearance of the HTML comment in the location where the xsl:comment line appeared.

The XSL Selection Operators

When a query is performed in a database operation, the result is a set of objects that's a subset of the data in the database. In the XML/XSL world, this set will be a set of nodes. The simplest way to create a result set is to apply the selectNodes() method with a suitable input in the parentheses. As the name implies, the selectNodes() method will simply select out all of the nodes that satisfy the given criteria.

The selection operators are used to move to a specific level in the node tree. You've already used one of them, the forward slash (/). Used in isolation, as in the following, it takes you to the root node of the XML file:

```
<xsl:template match="/">
```

It has also been used to separate node levels in the tree:

```
<xsl:for-each select="Catalog/Book"
order-by="+Author/City">
```

For the next example, use Listing 13.1. Recall that this is the <BookSellers> database with the <SamsBooksSold> child node, which also has child nodes. One of the nodes in that file is reproduced in Listing 16.2 for reference.

LISTING 16.2   A Node of the <BookSellers> Database

```
 1: <Seller>
 2: <Name>Old Books Made New</Name>
 3: <Address>200 Third Street</Address>
 4: <City>WannaReadOne</City>
 5: <State>Iowa</State>
 6: <PostalCode>52467</PostalCode>
 7: <Phone>(319)356-0000</Phone>
 8: <ContactPerson>Miss Manners</ContactPerson>
 9: <SamsBooksSold>
10:   <Book>
11:     <Title>Teach Yourself XML in 24 Hours</Title>
12:     <ISBN>0-672-31950-0</ISBN>
13:   </Book>
14:   <Book>
15:   <Title>Teach Yourself Cool Stuff in 24 Hours</Title>
16:   <ISBN>0-672-1010-0</ISBN>
17:   </Book>
18:   <Book>
19:   <Title>Teach Yourself Uses of Silicon in 24 Hours</Title>
20:   <ISBN>0-578-31950-0</ISBN>
21:   </Book>
22: </SamsBooksSold>
23:   </Seller>
```

Go back to Listing 16.1 and modify it to match Listing 16.3.

LISTING 16.3   Demonstrating the Selection of Nodes Using the "/" Operator

```
 1: <html>
 2: <!-- This file is the HTML that will ultimately be
 3:     displayed. In this case, the <BookSellers> database is
 4:     being queried.
 5:     The name of the file is listing16-3.html. -->
 6: <head>
 7: <title>This program demonstrates the use of an XSL template to
 8: read XML data</title>
 9: <script language="JavaScript">
10: <!--
11:  var DataSource1=new ActiveXObject("microsoft.xmldom");
12:  DataSource1.load("listing13-1.xml");
13: function StartUp()
14: {
15:  if(DataSource1.readyState==4)
16:  {
17:   GrabNodes();
18:  }
19:  else
20:  {
21:   alert("The data source file is unavailable");
22:  }
23: }
24:
25: function GrabNodes()
26: {
27:  var NodeData=DataSource1.selectNodes("/");
28:  moveNode=NodeData.nextNode();
29:  alert(moveNode.nodeType);
30:  alert(moveNode.nodeName);
31:  moveNode=moveNode.firstChild;
32:  alert(moveNode.nodeType);
33:  alert(moveNode.nodeName);
34:  moveNode=moveNode.nextSibling;
35:  alert(moveNode.nodeType);
36:  alert(moveNode.nodeName);
37:  moveNode=moveNode.nextSibling;
38:  alert(moveNode.nodeType);
39:  alert(moveNode.nodeName);
40: }
41: //-->
42: </script>
43: </head>
44: <body onLoad="StartUp()">
45: </body>
46: </html>
```

Run the file in IE. The text in the sequence of alert boxes is

```
9
#document
7
xml
8
#comment
1
Booksellers
```

The first one is the reference to the entire document. Then, because the pointer is set to the first child node, the next three are to the first three child nodes of the document.

Go back to Listing 16.3 and modify the GrabNodes() function to match Listing 16.4.

LISTING 16.4 A Selection That Will Return the Booksellers Node Before the Alert Operations Are Performed

```
 1: function GrabNodes()
 2: {
 3:   var NodeData=DataSource1.selectNodes("Booksellers");
 4:   moveNode=NodeData.nextNode();
 5:   alert(moveNode.nodeType);
 6:   alert(moveNode.nodeName);
 7:   moveNode=moveNode.firstChild;
 8:   alert(moveNode.nodeType);
 9:   alert(moveNode.nodeName);
10:   moveNode=moveNode.nextSibling;
11:   alert(moveNode.nodeType);
12:   alert(moveNode.nodeName);
13:   moveNode=moveNode.nextSibling;
14:   alert(moveNode.nodeType);
15:   alert(moveNode. nodeName);
16: }
```

Run the file in IE. Now the sequence of values in the alert boxes is as follows:

```
1
Booksellers
1
Seller
1
Seller
1
Seller
```

This clearly illustrates that the structure of the selected nodes now begins at the <Booksellers> level.

Go back to Listing 16.3 and modify the `GrabNodes()` function to match Listing 16.5.

LISTING 16.5 A Selection That Will Return the List of Seller Nodes

```
 1: function GrabNodes()
 2: {
 3:   var NodeData =
      DataSource1.selectNodes("Booksellers/Seller");
 4:   moveNode=NodeData.nextNode();
 5:   alert(moveNode.nodeType);
 6:   alert(moveNode.nodeName);
 7:   moveNode=NodeData.nextNode();
 8:   alert(moveNode.nodeType);
 9:   alert(moveNode.nodeName);
10:   moveNode=NodeData.nextNode();
11:   alert(moveNode.nodeType);
12:   alert(moveNode.nodeName);
13:   moveNode=moveNode.firstChild;
14:   alert(moveNode.nodeType);
15: alert(moveNode.nodeName);
16: }
```

When the file is run in IE, the contents of the sequence of alert boxes are as follows:

```
1
Seller
1
Seller
1
Seller
1
Name
```

This illustrates that the basic structure of the selected nodes is now a list of `<Seller>` nodes whose child nodes can be accessed.

Go back to Listing 16.3 and modify the `GrabNodes()` function to match Listing 16.6.

LISTING 16.6 A Selection That Will Return the List of SamsBooksSold Nodes

```
 1: function GrabNodes()
 2: {
 3:   var NodeData = DataSource1.
      selectNodes("Booksellers/Seller/SamsBooksSold");
 4:   moveNode=NodeData.nextNode();
 5:   alert(moveNode.nodeType);
 6:   alert(moveNode.nodeName);
 7:   alert(moveNode.text);
```

LISTING 16.6 continued

```
 8:   moveNode=NodeData.nextNode();
 9:   alert(moveNode.nodeType);
10:   alert(moveNode.nodeName);
11:   alert(moveNode.text);
12:   moveNode=NodeData.nextNode();
13:   alert(moveNode.nodeType);
14:   alert(moveNode.nodeName);
15:   alert(moveNode.text);
16:   moveNode=moveNode.firstChild;
17:   alert(moveNode.nodeType);
18:   alert(moveNode.nodeName);
19: alert(moveNode.text);
20: }
```

Run the file in IE. Pay very close attention to the contents of the sequence of alert boxes:

```
1
SamsBooksSold
{Complete text of the node}
1
SamsBooksSold
{Complete text of the node}
1
SamsBooksSold
{Complete text of the node}
1
Book
{Complete text of the node}
```

Here, {Complete text of the node} is an abbreviation for the contents of the current node.

Notice what has happened here. A selected set of nodes has been extracted, and that set is the list of all SamsBooksSold nodes. The data making up those nodes is also fully accessible.

Go back to Listing 16.3 and modify the GrabNodes() function to match Listing 16.7.

LISTING 16.7 A Selection That Will Return the List of Book Nodes

```
1: function GrabNodes()
2: {
3:   var NodeData=DataSource1.selectNodes("Booksellers/
     Seller/SamsBooksSold/Book");
4:   moveNode=NodeData.nextNode();
5:   while(moveNode!=null)
```

```
 6:  {
 7:    alert(moveNode.nodeType);
 8:    alert(moveNode.nodeName);
 9:    alert(moveNode.text);
10:    moveNode=NodeData.nextNode();
11:  }
12: }
```

16

Run the file in IE and note that all the <Book> nodes at the Booksellers/Seller/SamsBooksSold/Book level were extracted.

At this point, it's a good idea to stop and review what happens when the selectNodes() method is used. All nodes in the XML file that satisfy the input criteria of the method are extracted and placed in a structure. To move to the first node of the structure, you need to perform a nextNode() operation on it. This also creates a pointer inside the structure that will point to the current node being accessed from inside the structure. When the nextNode() method is called for that structure, the pointer is iterated to the next item in the list.

The Double-Slash Selection Operator

While the slash operator is very specific as a separator of levels, the double-slash operator can be used to conduct recursive searches throughout all levels. To demonstrate how this works, you need to modify the XML source data file.

Reopen listing13-1.xml and modify it by inserting the lines in bold in Listing 16.8. Save the file as listing16-8.xml.

LISTING 16.8   Adding an Additional <ContactPerson> Node to the XML Data File

```
 1: <ContactPerson>Miss Manners</ContactPerson>
 2: <Book>Bestseller 1</Book>
 3: <SamsBooksSold>
 4:  . . .
 5: <ContactPerson>Reed Lots</ContactPerson>
 6: <Book>Bestseller2</Book>
 7: <SamsBooksSold>
 8: . . .
 9: <ContactPerson>Bob White</ContactPerson>
10: <Book>Bestseller 3</Book>
11: <SamsBooksSold>
```

You've just created two levels of <Book> nodes in the file.

Go back to Listing 16.3 and modify the GrabNodes() function to match Listing 16.9.

LISTING 16.9   Extracting the Book Nodes at All Levels

```
 1: function GrabNodes()
 2: {
 3:   var NodeData=DataSource1.selectNodes("//Book");
 4:   moveNode=NodeData.nextNode();
 5:   while(moveNode!=null)
 6:   {
 7:    document.write(moveNode.text+"<BR>");
 8:    moveNode=NodeData.nextNode();
 9:   }
10:  }
```

In this case, you're simply writing the contents of the nodes to the document window. The output is as follows:

```
Bestseller 1
        Teach Yourself XML in 24 Hours 0-672-31950-0
        Teach Yourself Cool Stuff in 24 Hours 0-672-1010-0
        Teach Yourself Uses of Silicon in 24 Hours 0-578-31950-0
Bestseller2
        Teach Yourself XML in 24 Hours 0-672-31950-0
        Teach Yourself Cool Stuff in 24 Hours 0-672-1010-0
Bestseller 3
        Teach Yourself XML in 24 Hours 0-672-31950-0
```

It's clear that all of the <Book> nodes in the data file were extracted by the operation of the selectNodes() method.

> There are two other selection operators you can use, the dot slash (./) and the dot slash slash (.//). The ./ means that the pattern to the right of the operator should be followed in the location specified on the left of the operator. The .// is similar, except that the pattern is to be followed recursively down the tree from the specified location.

The ALL Operator

In some ways, the ALL operator (*) is the least useful of the set extraction operators. As the name implies, it does no filtering, simply returning every node in the given location. Used as the last item in the list, it simply makes explicit what the default operation would be.

Go back to Listing 16.3 and modify the `GrabNodes()` function to match Listing 16.10. Change the line that loads the XML file so that it now loads listing 14-4.xml, the `<Catalog>` database.

LISTING 16.10   Using the Default for Node Selection

```
 1: function GrabNodes()
 2: {
 3:   var NodeData=DataSource1.selectNodes("Catalog/Book");
 4:   moveNode=NodeData.nextNode();
 5:   while(moveNode!=null)
 6:   {
 7:    document.write(moveNode.text+"<BR>");
 8:    moveNode=NodeData.nextNode();
 9:   }
10: }
```

Save and run the file in IE and note that all `<Book>` nodes are selected.

Go back to Listing 16.3 and modify the selection line to match the following:

```
var NodeData=DataSource1.selectNodes("Catalog/Book/*");
```

Save and run the file. Note that once again, all the `<Book>` nodes are selected.

The ALL operator can also be used as a wildcard character inside the node selection list to indicate that all nodes of a specific name are to be selected.

You go back to Listing 16.3 and modify the selection line to match the following:

```
var NodeData=
DataSource1.selectNodes("Catalog/Book/*/Name");
```

Then run it in IE the output is the contents of all `<Name>` nodes in the file. In this context, the ALL operator means to select all `<Name>` nodes that are grandchildren of the `<Book>` nodes. This is illustrated in Figure 16.2.

The ALL operator can appear at more than one level in the input to the `selectNodes()` method.

Go back to Listing 16.3 and modify the selection line to match the following:

```
var NodeData=DataSource1.selectNodes("Catalog/*/*/Name");
```

Save the file and run it in IE. In this case, you're selecting all nodes with the name `<Name>` that are found at the third level down from the `<Catalog>` node. Since these would be the `<Name>` nodes in both the `<Author>` and `<Publisher>` nodes, the result set is the same as the previous run.

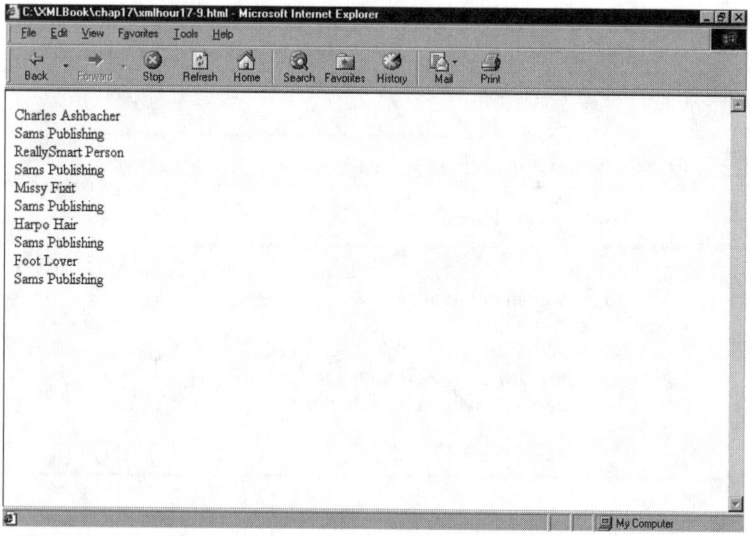

FIGURE 16.2

Extracting all Name nodes that are grand-children of the Book nodes.

The XSL Boolean Operators

By definition, Boolean operators are operators that accept one or more values of true or false and return a single value of either true or false. The three primary Boolean operators in any language are AND, OR, and NOT. While you may be aware of additional Boolean operators in other languages, it's well known that these three can be used to create all possible Boolean expressions. Therefore, the presence of other operators adds no additional power to the language.

Since AND, OR, and NOT can appear in normal use, there needs to be something to differentiate them from English syntax. The notation for the Boolean operators relies on the dollar sign ($) character to differentiate the operators from the corresponding English words. The Boolean operators are summarized in the following table.

TABLE 16.1 The Boolean Operators That Are Available in XML

Operator	Usage	Meaning
not	unary	Returns false if input is true and true if input is false.
and	binary	Returns true if both inputs are true and false otherwise.
or	binary	Returns true if at least one of the inputs is true.

For the next example, use Listing 15.3. Recall that this file is the `<Catalog>` database, in which each book has a value assigned to the BestSeller attribute:

```
<Book BestSeller="yes">
<Title>Teach Yourself XML in 24 Hours</Title>
```

There are five records in the database, and each BestSeller attribute is assigned a different value. The values assigned to the BestSeller attributes in the file are { yes, no, impossible, guaranteed, dud }.

Go back to Listing 16.3 and modify the GrabNodes() function to match Listing 16.11.

LISTING 16.11 Extracting Nodes by Performing a Boolean Test on the BestSeller Attribute

```
 1: function GrabNodes()
 2: {
 3:  var NodeData= DataSource1.selectNodes
     ("Catalog/Book[$not$@BestSeller='yes']");
 4:  moveNode=NodeData.nextNode();
 5:  while(moveNode!=null)
 6:  {
 7:   document.write(moveNode.text+"<BR>");
 8:   moveNode=NodeData.nextNode();
 9:  }
10: }
```

Change the command to load the file so that it loads listing15-3.xml, and then run the file in IE. The output will be all the nodes in which the attribute isn't 'yes', as illustrated in Figure 16.3.

FIGURE 16.3

The data in all nodes where the BestSeller attribute is not "yes".

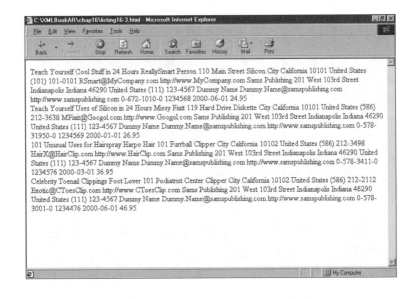

Go back to Listing 16.3 and modify the `GrabNodes()` function to match Listing 16.12.

LISTING 16.12   Extracting All Nodes Where the BestSeller Attribute Is Either 'yes' or 'no'

```
 1: function GrabNodes()
 2: {
 3:  var NodeData=DataSource1.selectNodes("Catalog/Book
     [@BestSeller='yes'$or$@BestSeller='no']");
 4:  moveNode=NodeData.nextNode();
 5:  while(moveNode!=null)
 6:  {
 7:   document.write(moveNode.text+"<BR>");
 8:   moveNode=NodeData.nextNode();
 9:  }
10: }
```

Save the file and run it in IE. The output will be the two nodes in which BestSeller is either 'yes' or 'no', as illustrated in Figure 16.4.

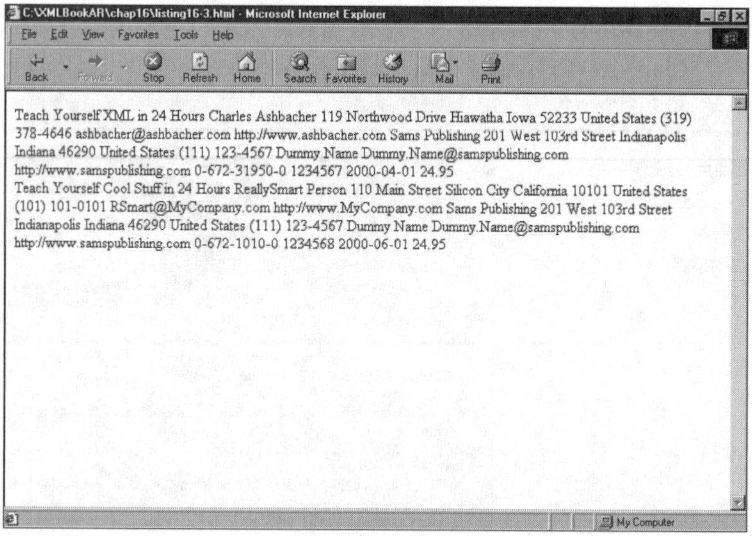

FIGURE 16.4

The nodes where the BestSeller attribute is either 'yes' or 'no'.

Go back to Listing 16.3 and modify the `GrabNodes()` function to match Listing 16.13.

LISTING 16.13 Applying the not Operator to Extract All Nodes Where the BestSeller Attribute Is Not 'yes' or 'no'

```
 1: function GrabNodes()
 2: {
 3:  var NodeData=DataSource1.selectNodes("Catalog/Book
     [$not$(@BestSeller='yes'$or$@BestSeller='no')]");
 4:  moveNode=NodeData.nextNode();
 5:  while(moveNode!=null)
 6:  {
 8:   document.write(moveNode.text+"<BR>");
 8:   moveNode=NodeData.nextNode();
 9:  }
10: }
```

Save the file and run it in IE. The output is all nodes in which the value of the BestSeller attribute isn't 'yes' or 'no'. This is illustrated in Figure 16.5.

FIGURE 16.5

All nodes where the value of the BestSeller attribute is not 'yes' or 'no'.

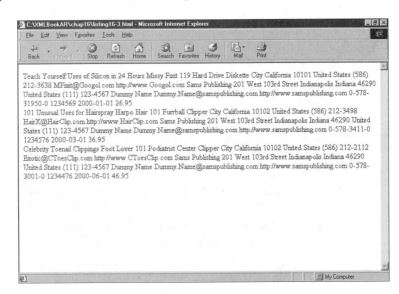

Summary

Comments are an integral part of programming in all languages and at all levels. Inserting a comment into a file that's being generated is an important operation, so that was the point of the first part of this hour.

Database queries return a subset of the data file's contents, and XSL queries are no exception. The selection operators allow for the selective extraction of all nodes with specific names at various levels. With the capability to recursively extract all nodes at all sublevels of the hierarchical tree, these operators significantly reduce the amount of programming that's necessary.

The Boolean operators allow for data to be selected based on whether they satisfy one or more criteria. That way the selections can be made more precise.

Finally, the ALL operator can be used to extract all nodes that match a current location or all nodes that reside at particular level in the hierarchical tree.

Q&A

Q Are there restrictions on where the xsl:comment element can appear in the XSL file that's generating the HTML code?

A An HTML comment can be placed anywhere in an HTML file where the code is HTML. However, it cannot be placed inside SCRIPT code. Therefore, it can appear anywhere in the HTML code, but not necessarily everywhere in the HTML file.

Q What's the precise result of the selectNodes() method?

A Like all database queries, the result is a subset of the nodes in the XML file. It's possible for that set to be empty (although this was never demonstrated in any of the examples). However, the method doesn't return a pointer to the first element of the set. That operation must be done explicitly.

Q As a programmer, I've used other languages that have additional Boolean operators, such as the exclusive or (XOR) and the logical equality. Why aren't they part of the set of XSL Boolean operators?

A A thorough explanation would take us into logical theory, so suffice it to say that every operation using these and all other logical operators can be done using and, or, and not. Therefore, the presence of any additional operators is more a matter of convenience than of any additional computing power.

Workshop

Quiz

1. Which of the following will return only the nodes with the name <Seller> that are three levels down in the hierarchical tree?

    a. ("//Seller")

    b. ("Catalog/*/Seller")

    c. ("Catalog/*/*/Seller")

    d. a and c

2. Which of the following will extract only the nodes in which the WebCompany attribute is 'yes'?

    a. @WebCompany='yes'

    b. not@WebCompany='no'

    c. @WebCompany='no'or@WebCompany='yes'

    d. a and b

3. Recursive searches for all nodes with a given name can be done easily in XSL.

    a. True

    b. False

Answers

1. The answer is c. If a is used, it will return all nodes in the tree with the name <Seller>.

2. Strictly speaking, the answer is a. Although b may appear to be true, there's no guarantee that 'yes' and 'no' are the only options for the WebCompany attribute.

3. True, simply use the slash slash (//) operator.

Exercises

The following operation is a precondition for the exercises in this hour.

Reopen listing15-7.xml and change the <Phone> node of each of the <Publisher> nodes to <Phonelist>. This entry will now be a list of phone numbers rather than a single number. There will be four such entries for each <Publisher> node, and each one will also contain an attribute. As an example, consider the following list:

```
<Phonelist>
 <Phone Contact="DE"> (111) 345-5675</Phone>
```

```
<Phone Contact="AE"> (111) 345-5789</Phone>
<Phone Contact="Production"> (111) 345-4578</Phone>
</Phonelist>
```

Save this file as listing16-9.xml.

1. Go back to Listing 16.3 and change the selectNodes() method call so that all <Phone> nodes in the file are selected.

2. Go back to Listing 16.3 and change the selectNodes() method call so that all <Phone> nodes in a <Phonelist> are selected.

3. Go back to Listing 16.3 and change the selectNodes() method call so that all phone numbers of either a DE or AE are selected. Use Boolean operators to do this.

Hour **17**

Using XSL Comparison and Collection Operators and XSL Methods to Perform Database Queries

Many times you're concerned about the relative size of two data items. Most data types support some form of relative size comparison, and XSL supports a set of operators for doing this.

In this hour, you'll learn the following:

- The set of equality operators and how they're used in queries
- The set of size comparison operators and how they're used in queries
- How to use the any and all operators and what they return

- The syntax to access the contents of a node using the `value()` method
- How to use the `selectSingleNode()` method to extract the data from one node of interest
- How to use the `end()` method to extract the data from the last node of the current list
- How to use the `index()` method to extract the data from a node using the number of that node in the sequential list

The Equality Operators

As you would expect, this set of operators is used to determine whether two items are equal or not. The complete set of these operators is summed up in Table 17.1.

TABLE 17.1 The Operators That Test for Equality

Operator(s)	Meaning
eq or =	Equality
ieq	Equality (not case sensitive)
ne or !=	Not equal
ine	Inequality (not case sensitive)

To demonstrate these operators, you'll continue to use the files from the previous hour.

For the source of your data, use the <Catalog> database that was used in the previous hour. The HTML files used to demonstrate the operators will be modifications of those used in the previous hour. In general, the only change will be in the line that performs the node selection.

Go back to the HTML file in the previous hour and modify the line that performs the node selection to the following:

```
var NodeData=DataSource1.selectNodes("Catalog/Book
[@BestSeller$eq$'yes'$or$@BestSeller$eq$'no']");
```

When the updated file is viewed in IE, the output will be the two nodes where the BestSeller attribute is either 'yes' or 'no'.

Go back to the HTML file and modify the line that performs the node selection to match the following:

```
var NodeData=DataSource1.selectNodes("Catalog/Book
[@BestSeller$ieq$'Yes'$or$@BestSeller$ieq$'NO']");
```

Note that the equality tests are no longer case sensitive and that the constants now contain uppercase characters. When the updated file is saved and viewed in IE, the output is the same as that of the previous run.

Go back to the HTML file and modify the node selection line to match the following:

```
var NodeData=DataSource1.selectNodes
 ("Catalog/Book[@BestSeller$ne$'yes']");
```

The output is all four nodes where the BestSeller attribute is not 'yes'.

Go back to the HTML file and modify the line that selects the nodes to match the following:

```
var NodeData=DataSource1.selectNodes
 ("Catalog/Book[@BestSeller$ine$'Yes']");
```

The output matches that of the previous run. In this instance, the case differences between 'Yes' and the values of the attributes are ignored.

The Comparison Operators

Strictly speaking, the equal and not equal operators are also comparison operators. However, they don't involve relative evaluations of values, so they're often considered distinct from the set of inequality operators. Although all data types support equal and not equal examinations, there are some data types where inequality isn't easily defined.

XSL supports a complete set of inequality operators, as summarized in Table 17.2.

TABLE 17.2 The Inequality Comparison Operators

Operator(s)	Meaning
lt or <	Less than
ilt	Less than (not case sensitive)
le or <=	Less than or equal to
ile	Less than or equal to (not case sensitive)
gt or >	Greater than
igt	Greater than (not case sensitive)
ge or >=	Greater than or equal to
ige	Greater than or equal to (not case sensitive)

Recall that all of the data components of XML files are extracted as character strings. Since strings are constructed from characters whose numeric equivalents preserve alphabetical order, the comparison operators can be used on strings.

Go back to the HTML file and modify the line that performs the node selection to the following:

```
var NodeData=DataSource1.selectNodes
 ("Catalog/Book[@BestSeller>'m']");
```

The output is the two nodes in which the values of the BestSeller attributes are after m in alphabetical order.

Go back to the HTML file and modify the line that performs the node selection to the following:

```
var NodeData=DataSource1.selectNodes
 ("Catalog/Book[@BestSeller$ige$'IMPOSSIBLE']");
```

The entry where the BestSeller attribute is 'impossible' is now included.

However, not all data is character-based. Many things are best described by numbers, and often you want to extract data as numbers that can be used in arithmetic computations. Since all data is extracted from an XML file in the form of text, you need to convert it into the equivalent number by using the value method. The syntax for calling it is something that you haven't seen yet.

Before you proceed with the reading of the data, you need to modify your XML data file. In this case, you're going to add an attribute to the <Author> node of each entry in the <Catalog> file. This attribute is given the name 'Priority' and is designed to be an integer.

Reopen the <Catalog> database file and add the segments highlighted in bold in Listing 17.1.

LISTING 17.1 The <Catalog> Database with a Numeric Attribute Assigned to the Author Node

```
 1: <Title>Teach Yourself XML in 24 Hours</Title>
 2: <Author Priority="1">
 3: <Name>Charles Ashbacher</Name>
 4: . . .
 5: <Title>Teach Yourself Cool Stuff in 24 Hours</Title>
 6: <Author Priority="2">
 7: <Name>ReallySmart Person</Name>
 8: . . .
 9: <Title>Teach Yourself Uses of Silicon in 24 Hours</Title>
10: <Author Priority="3">
11: <Name>Missy Fixit</Name>
12: . . .
13: <Title>101 Unusual Uses for Hairspray</Title>
```

```
14: <Author Priority="4">
15: <Name>Harpo Hair</Name>
16: .  .  .
17: <Title>Celebrity Toenail Clippings</Title>
18: <Author Priority="5">
19: <Name>Foot Lover</Name>
```

The file should be saved as listing17-1.xml.

Go back to the HTML file and make sure that the line that loads the file is modified to match the following:

```
DataSource1.load("listing17-1.xml");
```

Also modify the line that selects the nodes to match the following:

```
var NodeData=DataSource1.selectNodes
  ("Catalog/Book/Author[@Priority!value()>1]");
```

Note the syntax of the call to the value() method. The exclamation point is the separator between the attribute name and the method call. Also note that the 1 in the comparison isn't surrounded by quotes.

When the file is viewed in IE, the output is the data for all authors where the priority is greater than 1.

Go back to the HTML file and modify the line that selects the nodes to match the following:

```
var NodeData=DataSource1.selectNodes
  ("Catalog/Book/Author[@Priority!value()>1
  $and$@Priority!value()<5]");
```

The output is the data for all authors where the priority is between 1 and 5.

The data comparisons can be done in one of three ways: integer, real, or string. The form is determined largely by context. If the item to be compared against is surrounded by quotation marks, the comparison is string-to-string. If there are no quotes and the item is in numeric form, it's interpreted as either a long integer or a double precision real number. The particular type of the number is determined by the presence or absence of a decimal point.

Go back to the HTML file and modify the line that selects the nodes to the following:

```
var NodeData=DataSource1.selectNodes("Catalog/Book/Author
  [@Priority!value()>1.5$and$
  @Priority!value()<5.1]");
```

When the program is viewed, the entries where the priorities are 2 and 5 are included in the output. This verifies that the literal numbers are kept in their floating point form for comparison and are not truncated or rounded to integers.

Since the data value is always in text form in the XML file, the value() method has performed an implicit type conversion. The type of the number it's converted into is determined by the characters in the text. If it contains a decimal point, it's converted into a floating point number.

Go back to the <Catalog> database in Listing 17.1 and make the following changes marked in bold:

```
<Title>Teach Yourself XML in 24 Hours</Title>
<Author Priority="1.5">
<Name>Charles Ashbacher</Name>
. . .
<Title>Celebrity Toenail Clippings</Title>
<Author Priority="5.1">
<Name>Foot Lover</Name>
```

Save the file and run the HTML file again. The middle three nodes are output. This demonstrates that the values of Priority are converted into floating point numbers so that the comparisons can take place.

The all and any Operators

The all and any operators have very specific behaviors. The all operator examines every node at the specified level and returns the result only if all of the nodes satisfy the stated criteria. The any operator is in many ways the opposite, in that it returns the result if any of the nodes satisfy the given criteria.

Go back to the HTML file and modify the line that selects the nodes to match the following:

```
var NodeData=DataSource1.selectNodes("//Catalog[$any$
Book/Title='101 Unusual Uses for Hairspray']");
```

The output will be all five nodes of the <Catalog> file because there's one node where the book title is the one listed.

Go back to the HTML file and modify the line that selects the nodes to match the following:

```
var NodeData=DataSource1.selectNodes("//Catalog[$all$
Book/Title='101 Unusual Uses for Hairspray']");
```

Since not all entries have this book title, no items will be listed.

Reopen Listing 17.1 and change the <Title> property of all the books so that they're as follows:

```
101 Unusual Uses for Hairspray
```

When the HTML file is viewed in IE, the output will be all of the nodes.

Accessing the Contents of a Node Using the value() Method

There are several library functions or methods that can be used to construct queries. You've already used one of these, the value() method. It was used to extract the value assigned to the attributes. While attributes are certainly important, the significant data is most often placed inside the tags. The value() method can also be used to extract this data, and that's the subject of the next example.

Go back to the HTML file and modify the line that selects the nodes so that it matches the following:

```
var NodeData=DataSource1.selectNodes("Catalog/Book/
Author[Name!value()='Charles Ashbacher']");
```

As expected, the only information that will appear in the output is the <Author> data for 'Charles Ashbacher'.

These results can be used in combination with the Boolean operators to create more complex queries.

Go back to the HTML file and modify the line that selects the nodes to match the following:

```
var NodeData=DataSource1.selectNodes("Catalog/Book/Author
[Name!value()='Charles Ashbacher'$or$
City!value()='Clipper City']");
```

In this case, the output will be the <Author> data for 'Charles Ashbacher', 'Harpo Hair', and 'Foot Lover'.

The statements made earlier regarding the type of data that's returned from this method call also hold true when the data is extracted from the node. If the number contains a decimal point, the result is a floating point number.

17

Go back to the HTML file and modify the line that selects the nodes to match the following:

```
var NodeData=DataSource1.selectNodes
("Catalog/Book[Price!value()>=36.95]");
```

Now, the data returned is the <Book> data for all books whose price is greater than or equal to $36.95.

Queries can also be performed in which the selection criteria are a combination of node and attribute data. Go back to the HTML file and modify the line that selects the nodes to match the following:

```
var NodeData=DataSource1.selectNodes
("Catalog/Book[Price!value()>=36.95$and$
@BestSeller='guaranteed']");
```

The output is the contents of the single node representing the book with the title *101 Unusual Uses for Hairspray*.

The `selectSingleNode()` Method

In all of your queries so far, you've used the `selectNodes()` method to perform the extraction. There is another method that can be used, and it's known as the `selectSingleNode()` method. The only difference between it and the selectNodes() method is that it only returns the first node that satisfies the selection criteria. Of course, if no nodes satisfy the criteria, the result is the empty set.

Go back to the HTML file and modify the `GrabNodes()` function to match the following:

```
function GrabNodes()
{
var NodeData=DataSource1.selectSingleNode("Catalog/Book");
document.write(NodeData.text);
/* moveNode=NodeData.nextNode();
 while(moveNode!=null)
  {
   document.write(moveNode.text+"<BR>");
   moveNode=NodeData.nextNode();
  } */
}
```

Note that you comment out the code that's no longer needed rather than deleting it.

When the updated file is viewed in IE, the only output is the first <Book> node. Note that the code to move through the node list is now commented out. Since this selection method returns only one node and not a list, these methods aren't supported by the result.

The end() Method

Like the selectSingleNode() method, the end() method will also return a single node. However, in this case, the only selection criterion is that the node must be the last one in the list at the given level. Once again, since the method returns a single node, the methods used to traverse a node list cannot be used on it.

Go back to the HTML file used in the previous example and modify the line that selects the nodes to match the following:

```
var NodeData=
DataSource1.selectSingleNode("Catalog[end()]");
```

The output is all of the data in the <Catalog> database.

Go back to the HTML file and modify the line that selects the nodes to match the following:

```
var NodeData=DataSource1.selectSingleNode
("Catalog/Book[end()]");
```

The output is the contents of the last <Book> node.

The index() Method

As you've seen many times s in your study of XML, the child nodes of XML are automatically numbered or indexed starting at 0. The index() method allows for the selection of a single node by extracting the node with a specific index.

Go back to the HTML file and modify the GrabNodes() function to match Listing 17.2.

LISTING 17.2 Selecting Nodes Based on Their Index Values

```
 1: function GrabNodes()
 2: {
 3:  var NodeData=DataSource1.selectNodes("//Book/*[index()=2]");
 4:  moveNode=NodeData.nextNode();
 5:  while(moveNode!=null)
 6:  {
 7:   document.write(moveNode.text+"<BR>");
 8:   moveNode=NodeData.nextNode ();
 9:  }
10: }
```

17

When you view the file in IE, the output is the contents of the <Publisher> nodes. Since you're using the `selectNodes()` method, all child nodes in index position 2 of the <Book> nodes are selected.

Summary

When you're performing database queries, the criteria are often constructed based on tests for equality and relative size. In this hour, the complete set of equality and inequality operators was presented.

The any and `all` operators differ from the others in that they either return all of the set or none of it. When all nodes have a property, the `all` operator returns the set. When any node has the property, the any operator returns the set.

To access the value of either an attribute or a node, you can use the `value()` method. Once extracted, the value can be used as a data point in the construction of queries. Two additional, somewhat specialized methods are the `selectSingleNode()` and `end()` methods. Both return a single node. In the case of `selectSingleNode()`, the first node satisfying the search criteria is returned, and `end()` returns the last node in the list.

As you learned in the very first hour, the nodes of an XML file are indexed at all levels. The `index()` method is used to extract all nodes with a specific index for the specified level.

Q&A

Q What is the default type of data, and why is it used?

A The default type of data is the text or character string. It's used because all data can be stored as a string.

Q What property differentiates the any and `all` operators from the others?

A These operators return either the entire set or nothing.

Q What single property differentiates an integer from a real number?

A When a decimal point is present, the number is real.

Q How do you perform typecasting in XSL?

A Correct typecasts are done automatically when values are extracted and used.

Workshop

Quiz

1. Which of the following methods returns, at most, one node?

    a. `index()`

    b. `selectSingleNode()`

    c. `end()`

    d. b and c

    e. a, b, and c

2. Which of the following operators have symbolic representations?

    a. Only the case sensitive ones

    b. Only the equals and not equals

    c. The case sensitive inequalities

    d. All case sensitive operators and the non-case sensitive equality.

3. The primary differences between the `selectNodes()` and `selectSingleNode()` methods are:

    a. The `selectSingleNode()` method returns, at most, one node

    b. The `selectNodes()` method returns a list of nodes and the selectSingleNode() does not

    c. The syntax of the query criteria is different

    d. a and b

Answers

1. d

2. a

3. d

Exercises

1. Write a query that will return all <Author> nodes in the <Catalog> database in which the <Name> of the author begins with a 'B', the <PostalCode> begins with a '5', and the author lives in Iowa.

2. Write a query that will return all <Author> nodes in which either the author does not live in California or is a Priority 2 author living in California.

PART IV

XML in e-Commerce and Other Advanced Topics

Hour

HOUR 18

The Document Object Model

As has been mentioned many times in this book, XSL provides a very rich set of functionality that can be used to manipulate XML data. So far, this book's approach has been to give you the background material needed to construct a dynamic, data-driven Web site. This, the last hour devoted to the essentials before you begin building the site, will present a complete list of the methods available.

It will also spend some time recapitulating the Document Object Model, or DOM, as it's applied to XML. After presenting the model, lists of the available properties and methods for each level of the model will be given. Some of the properties and methods that weren't illustrated in earlier hours will be demonstrated here. In many ways, this hour is a potpourri of available components that weren't covered in previous hours, for whatever reason.

In this hour, you'll learn the following:

- The complete list of XSL methods that extract data from the nodes of an XML file

- The complete list of XSL methods that create collections of nodes
- The four main objects of the Document Object Model and its organizational structure
- The complete list of methods for the document object
- The complete list of properties and methods for the node object
- The complete list of properties and methods for the nodelist object

The Data Extraction and Node Collection Methods

Previous hours have demonstrated several of the XSL methods available for node selection, but there are others that haven't been mentioned. There are two different categories that these methods can be placed in. One group is used to extract information from the nodes, and the other group creates a collection of nodes. The data extraction methods are shown in Table 18.1, and the node collection methods are shown in Table 18.2.

TABLE 18.1 XSL Data Extraction Methods

Method	Purpose
absoluteChildNumber	Returns the number of the node relative to its siblings.
ancestorChildNumber	Returns the number of the nearest ancestor of a node.
childNumber	Returns the number of the node relative to siblings with the same name.
depth	Returns the depth of the node in the hierarchical tree.
elementIndexList	Returns an array of child numbers, starting at the node and moving recursively up the tree to the root.
formatDate	Formats a date using specified formatting options.
formatIndex	Formats an integer using the specified formatting options.
formatNumber	Formats the number using the specified formatting options.
formatTime	Formats the time using the specified formatting options.
uniqueID	Returns the unique ID assigned to the node.
date	Casts the value to a date format.
end	Returns true for the last element in the collection, false otherwise.
index	Returns the index of the node relative to the parent.
nodeName	Returns the tag name of the node, including any namespace qualifications.
nodeType	Returns a number that corresponds to the type of the node.
text	Returns the text within an element.
value	Returns the typecast equivalent of the value of an item.

TABLE 18.2 XSL Node Collection Methods

Method	Purpose
ancestor	Finds the ancestor nearest the node that satisfies the pattern.
attribute	Returns the collection of all attributes. If the optional text parameter is included, it returns only those that match it.
comment	Returns the collection of comment nodes.
element	Returns the collection of element nodes.
node	Returns the collection of all nonattribute nodes.
pi	Returns the collection of all processing instruction nodes for the document.
textnode	Returns the collection of all text nodes for the current document.

The Document Object Model

You've used the Document Object Model throughout this book, but we've never really stopped to formally examine it. This section will consider the various parts of the DOM and how they're put together.

There are four basic components of the DOM:

- The document object—This is the overall container of the data and all other components, such as the comment and processing instruction nodes.
- The node object—This is each individual component of the document. Nodes are defined by pairs of opening and closing tags.
- The nodelist object—This is a list of nodes that are all at the same level. The nodes of the list all have the relative relationship of sibling.
- The parseError object —This is a singleton object created for each document that does not contain content. The properties of the object are assigned values based on the results of the document's processing. As the name implies, the properties are filled primarily when errors occur.

The general relationship of these objects is illustrated in Figure 18.1.

You've used many of the properties of the document object, but not all of them. Table 18.3 is a complete list of all document properties.

18

FIGURE 18.1

The relationship of the four components of the DOM: document, parseError, node, and nodelist.

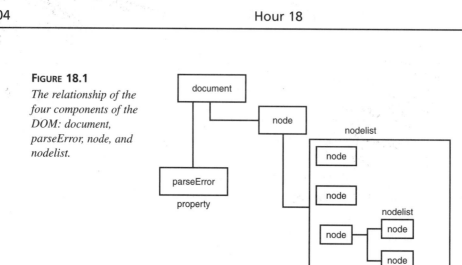

TABLE 18.3   The Properties of the Document Object

Property	Usage
async	Specifies whether asynchronous download of the file is allowed. Returns a boolean value.
attributes	Returns a list of the attributes for the current node.
childNodes	Returns a nodeList containing all child nodes of the current node.
doctype	Returns the document type node that contains the DTD of the current document.
documentElement	Contains the root node of the document.
firstChild	Returns the first child node of the document.
implementation	Returns the implementation object for the current document.
lastChild	Returns the last child node for the current document.
nextSibling	Returns the next sibling in the list of child nodes of the given document.
nodeName	Returns the name of the current node.
nodeType	Returns a number corresponding to the DOM type of the given node.
nodeValue	Returns the text of the given node.
ondataavailable	Specifies an event handler for the ondataavailable event.
onreadystatechange	Specifies an event handler for the onreadystatechange event.
ownerDocument	Returns the root node of the document that contains the current node.
parentNode	Returns the parent node of the current node.
parseError	An error object that will be filled with the data generated by errors.
previousSibling	Returns the sibling node immediately before the current node.

Property	Usage
readyState	Returns a numeric code reflecting the current status of the document.
url	Returns the URL of the most recently loaded XML document.
validateOnParse	Tells the parser whether the document should be validated.
xml	Returns the XML representation of the specified node.

Many of these properties have been used in previous exercises. The focus here is on the properties that you can use to better manage the loading process.

Let's say you want to download an XML file for use. In general, you want your processing to begin as soon as possible. This corresponds to the readyState property having a value of 3. However, if an asynchronous download isn't allowed, you need to wait until the readyState property is 4 before you proceed with your processing. Therefore, your initial check on startup should be modified to match Listing 18.1.

LISTING 18.1   Start Processing If Asynchronous Download Is Allowed

```
 1: isasync=xmlDoc1.async;
 2: function StartUp()
 3: {
 4:  if((xmlDoc1.readyState=="4")||
 5: (xmlDoc1.readyState=="3"&&isasync=="true"))
 6:  {
 7:   StartLoading();
 8:  }
 9:  else
10:  {
11:   alert("Process could not start");
12:  }
13: }
```

In this case, you proceed with the processing as soon as possible only if the data can be downloaded in an asynchronous manner.

Another situation that can arise is the downloading of XML data files in which the data is constrained by a DTD. It's possible that the data can satisfy more than one DTD, one of which may be outdated. The structure of the data may satisfy the older DTD, but not the newer, correct one. In that case, you could perform selective processing on the file based on the DTD specifications that the data satisfies. To do that, you need a way to extract and examine the DTD. The doctype property allows you to determine which DTD file is being used for data verification.

18

Consider the DTD file shown in Listing 18.2, which you used in a previous hour. For reference purposes, name it listing18-2-.dtd.

LISTING 18.2   Checking Which DTD Is Being Used

```
 1: <?xml version="1.0"?>
 2: <!--For reference purposes, the filename is listing18-2.dtd.
 3: <!ELEMENT SHIPORDER
    (ShipNumber,To,From,Address+,StateProvince,Country,
    Carrier,Insurance?,Security?,GeneralCarrier)>
 4: <!ATTLIST SHIPORDER LANGUAGE (Western|Extended) "Western">
 5: <!ATTLIST SHIPORDER PRIORITY (low|normal|high) "normal">
 6: <!ELEMENT ShipNumber (#PCDATA)>
 7: <!ATTLIST ShipNumber Customs (no|yes) "no">
 8: <!ELEMENT To (#PCDATA)>
 9: <!ATTLIST To idTo ID #REQUIRED>
10: <!ELEMENT From (#PCDATA)>
11: <!ATTLIST From idFrom ID #REQUIRED>
12: <!ELEMENT Address (#PCDATA)>
13: <!ELEMENT StateProvince (#PCDATA)>
14: <!ELEMENT Country (#PCDATA)>
15: <!ATTLIST Country  Destination (USA|Foreign) "USA">
16: <!ELEMENT Carrier (#PCDATA)>
17: <!ATTLIST Carrier Vehicle (van|truck|plane) "van">
18: <!ELEMENT Insurance (#PCDATA)>
19: <!ATTLIST Insurance Level (none|50percent|full) "none">
20: <!ELEMENT Security (#PCDATA)>
21: <!ATTLIST Security SLevel (none|ClosedVehicle|armed)"none">
22: <!ELEMENT GeneralCarrier (#PCDATA)>
23: <!ATTLIST GeneralCarrier Us CDATA #FIXED
    "General Shippers">
```

This file is then imported into the XML file shown in Listing 18.3. For reference purposes, name it listing18-3.xml.

LISTING 18.3   The XML File That Imports the Previous DTD File

```
 1: <?xml version="1.0"?>
 2: <!-- This file imports in the DTD file that describes the
 3:      data form that is a shiporder for an international
 4:      company. The filename is listing18-3.xml.xml. -->
 5: <!DOCTYPE SHIPORDER SYSTEM "listing18-3-.dtd">
 6: <SHIPORDER LANGUAGE="Extended" PRIORITY="high">
 7: <ShipNumber Customs="yes">B123456</ShipNumber>
 8: <To idTo="BH123">Valued Customer</To>
 9: <From idFrom="FG345">YourExpress Shippers</From>
10: <Address>100 South Street</Address>
```

```
11: <StateProvince>BigState</StateProvince>
12: <Country Destination="Foreign">Tropica</Country>
13: <Carrier Vehicle="plane">Air Freight</Carrier>
14: <Insurance Level="full">Perfect Safety Company</Insurance>
15: <Security SLevel="armed">Perfect Safety Company</Security>
16: <GeneralCarrier Us="General Shippers">General Shippers</GeneralCarrier>
17: </SHIPORDER>
```

If this file is then used as the input into an HTML file, you can obtain the necessary information concerning which DTD file was imported by performing the operations shown in Listing 18.4.

LISTING 18.4 Determining the DTD File Imported into the XML File in the HTML Code

```
1: theDoctype=xmlDoc1.doctype;
2:   alert(theDoctype.nodeType);
3:   str1=theDoctype.xml;
4:   alert(str1);
```

The nodeType will be 10, which corresponds to a DOCUMENT TYPE node. The value of str1 will be

```
<!DOCTYPE SHIPORDER SYSTEM "xmlhour18-1.dtd">
```

and will be an instance of the string data type. Since it's an instance of a string, you can then use the JavaScript string methods to take it apart and examine which DTD file is being used.

The following code will extract the name of the DTD file used to validate the data from the doctype property:

```
theDoctype=xmlDoc1.doctype;
str1=theDoctype.xml;
firstquote=str1.indexOf('\"');
lastquote=str1.lastIndexOf('\"');
fname=str1.substring(firstquote+1,lastquote);
alert(fname);
```

Given the value of str1 in the previous example, the value of fname here would be "xmlhour18-1.dtd".

The method of extraction is easy to understand. The indexOf method returns the first position in the string where the double quote appears, and lastIndexOf returns the last position. Since the pair delimits the filename in the string, the characters between them will be the filename. The method substring(m,n) returns the string that starts at character position m and goes up to, but does not include, the character at position n.

18

For the purposes of illustration, assume that there are two different *.dtd files that could be used, and their names are "listing18-1.dtd" and "listing18-2.dtd". Given that you now have the filename, you can perform selective processing based on which one was used to validate the data:

```
if(fname=="listing18-1.dtd")
{
 // process according to the first DTD
}
else
{
 // process according to the second DTD
}
```

The ondataavailable and onreadystatechange properties can be assigned executable commands that will be fired when the current state is changed.

For example, add the following two lines to an HTML file that reads data from an XML file:

```
xmlDoc1.ondataavailable=alert("Data is now available");
xmlDoc1.onreadystatechange=alert("Readystate property has
just changed");
```

These alert boxes with messages will then be executed when the data from the file becomes available and when the readyState property is changed.

> The following sections describe the methods and properties of the document, node, and nodeList objects. The parseError object was covered in detail in Hour 7, so it won't be examined further.

Document Object Methods

Many of the methods found in the document object have also been used in previous exercises. There are others available that haven't been used yet, and the complete list is given in Table 18.4.

TABLE 18.4　The Methods of the Document Object

Method	Purpose
abort()	Cancels a download in progress.
appendChild(newChild)	Adds a node to the end of the current list of nodes.
cloneNode(boolvalue)	Creates a duplicate of the given node. The clone will be shallow or deep depending on the value of the input.

Method	Purpose
createAttribute(name)	Creates an attribute with the given name.
createCDATASection(name)	Creates a CDATA section containing the input.
createComment(name)	Creates a comment node containing name.
createDocumentFragment()	Creates an empty document fragment.
createElement(tagname)	Creates an element with a tag name matching the input.
createEntityReference(name)	Creates an entity reference with a name matching the input.
createNode (Type,Name,namespaceURI)	Creates a node with the type Type and name Name, and that uses namespaceURI as the namespace URI.
createProcessingInstruction (Name,Data)	Creates a new processing instruction with the name Name and value Data.
createTextNode(data)	Creates a new text node where the text of the node is data.
getElementsByTagName (tagname)	Creates a collection of elements matching the tagname. A value of "*" will return all elements.
hasChildNodes()	Returns true or false depending on whether the current node has children.
insertBefore (newNode,RefNode)	Inserts the node referenced by newNode into the list before RefNode.
load(pathname)	Loads a file into the document.
loadXML(string)	Loads an XML document or fragment.
nodeFromID(string)	Returns a node whose ID matches string.
parsed()	Returns true if the document has been parsed and false otherwise.
removeChild(node)	Removes node from the list of child nodes.
replaceChild (newNode,oldNode)	Replaces the old node with the new node.
selectNodes(pattern)	Makes a list of all nodes satisfying the pattern.
selectSingleNode(pattern)	Returns the first node that matches the pattern.
transformNode(Stylesheet)	Creates a node by using the XSL style sheet input as Stylesheet.

The hasChildNodes() method can be used to perform a test on a node before the properties that sample child nodes are examined. For example, if testNode doesn't have any children, testNode.firstChild will return a null. Any attempt to use a component of the child node will then generate an error.

If the XML file that is read is the one in Listing 18.3, these lines of code:

```
alert(xmlDoc1.hasChildNodes());
alert(xmlDoc1.documentElement.hasChildNodes());
alert(xmlDoc1.firstChild.hasChildNodes());
```

will generate this output:

```
true
true
false
```

Of course, it's possible to create a processing instruction node. As was the case with the createComment method, the creation of such a node doesn't automatically cause the node to be inserted into the node tree. The construction of PI nodes is demonstrated in the following code segment:

```
pinode=xmlDoc1.createProcessingInstruction
                        ('xml', 'version="1.0"');
alert(pinode.xml);
```

When these lines are executed, the string in the alert box is

```
            <?xml version="1.0"?>
```

The creation of a node of CDATA text is just as straightforward:

```
cdnode=xmlDoc1.createCDATASection("This is a <CDATA> section of text");
alert(cdnode.xml);
```

When these lines are executed, the string in the alert box is

```
<![CDATA[This is a <CDATA>section of text]]>
```

The creation of attributes and entity references is done in a similar manner. If the following code segment is executed

```
attnode=xmlDoc1.createAttribute("EncryptionLevel");
alert(attnode.xml);

erefnode=xmlDoc1.createEntityReference("Eref");
alert(erefnode.xml);
```

the text output in the two alert boxes will be

```
EncryptionLevel=""
```

and

```
&Eref;
```

The final two methods of the form createXXX() are the createDocumentFragment() and createTextNode(string) methods. If the following code segment is executed, the text caption of the first alert box will be empty:

```
fragNode=xmlDoc1.createDocumentFragment();
 alert(fragNode.xml);

tnode=xmlDoc1.createTextNode("A new text node");
alert(tnode.xml);
```

The text caption of the second alert box will contain the following string:

```
"A new text node"
```

The Properties and Methods of the Node Object

Given that the document is a node in its own right, it shouldn't come as a surprise that many of the properties and methods of the node object are the same as those for the document object. The complete list of the node properties is summarized in Table 18.5.

TABLE 18.5 The Properties of the Node Object

Property	Purpose
attributes	Same as for the document.
baseName	Returns the basename of a name qualified by a namespace. For example, if the name is dt:date, the value of baseName would be date.
childNodes	Same as for the document.
dataType	Used to set or get the data type for a node.
definition	Returns the definition of the node as specified in the DTD or schema.
firstChild	Same as for the document.
lastChild	Same as for the document.
nameSpace	Returns the URI for a namespace.
nextSibling	Same as for the document.
nodeName	Same as for the document.
nodeStringType	Returns the node type as a string.
nodeType	Same as for the document.
nodeTypedValue	Returns the node value using the defined data type.
nodeValue	Same as for the document.

TABLE 18.5   continued

Property	Purpose
ownerDocument	Same as for the document.
parentNode	Same as for the document.
prefix	Returns the prefix of the namespace.
previousSibling	Same as for the document.
specified	Used to denote whether the node value is explicitly specified or derived from a DTD or schema.
text	Sets or gets the text of a node.
xml	Same as for the document.

Since so many of these properties are similar to what you've seen in previous hours, examples of their use are left as an exercise for you.

The methods of the node object have all been encountered in earlier hours:

- appendChild
- cloneNode
- hasChildNodes
- insertBefore
- parsed
- removeChild
- replaceChild
- selectNodes
- selectSingleNode
- transformNode

Properties and Methods of the nodeList Object

Since the nodeList object is a list and not a node, there are none of the properties that the document and node objects use to work with their data. In fact, there's only one property, the length, which is one that you've used many times in this book.

There are only three member methods in the nodeList, and you've encountered all of them in previous hours:

- `item(index)`
- `nextNode()`
- `reset()`

Given your previous experience, there's no need to demonstrate them further.

Summary

There are many methods you can use to extract the data from XML files and create collections of nodes based on selection criteria. This hour collected them into tables.

The Document Object Model splits the XML data into four objects: the `document`, `node`, `nodeList`, and `parseError` objects. The complete list of all properties and methods of the document, node, and nodeList objects were presented in this hour. The methods that are used to create nodes were all demonstrated. Since the `parseError` object was covered in detail in an earlier hour, the methods and properties weren't examined.

18

Q&A

Q When a node is to be added to a nodelist, what are the advantages and disadvantages to performing the two-step process of creating the node and then inserting it?

A The disadvantage is obvious—it takes two steps to do what could be done in one step. The advantage is the standard one in computing, where a complex task is broken up into several simpler ones. This makes it more difficult to make accidental insertions and deletions.

Q Why are the methods of the document and node objects so similar?

A The document object is in fact a node with certain specific components that make it the document. Therefore, whenever you treat it as just another instance of a node, you're using the same properties that the node object has.

Q What's the relationship between the document and `parseError` objects?

A The `parseError` object is a property of the document object, specifically reserved as a target for generated errors.

Workshop

Quiz

1. Which of the following is a node collection method?

   a. The `selectNodes` method

   b. The `element` method

   c. The `selectSingleNode` method

   d. All of the above

2. Once the value of a property is returned, it's possible to take it apart and examine the pieces.

   a. True

   b. False

3. Are there nodes in XML that aren't delimited by tags?

   a. Yes

   b. No

4. What's an event handler?

   a. A method name

   b. A function that allows for access to data inside an XML file

   c. A function mapped to an event

   d. A placeholder function that does nothing

Answers

1. c

2. True

3. Yes

4. c

Exercises

1. Modify the HTML program so that it will create instances of processing instructions and CDATA nodes, and attempt to insert them into the data from the file listing17-1.xml.

2. Modify the HTML code so that you're testing the results of the implementation property.

3. Modify the HTML file to test the ondataavailable and onreadystatechange event handlers.

HOUR 19

The XML Schema Language

If you've ever done any work with databases, you understand the value of precise, understandable prototypes of the data. In previous hours, you've used DTDs to write a description of the form that the data is to take.

Although DTDs are valuable and effective, they're deficient in several areas. Therefore, a movement has developed to create a different system of writing the prototypes of XML data. This new system is a specific XML application called XML-Data. It's a language used to create *schemas*, which are descriptions of the data in an XML file. The neat thing about schemas is that the description of the data can be written in XML.

In this hour, you'll learn the following:

- The basic structure and purpose of schemas
- How to use the ElementType declaration to construct XML data types
- Defining a range using the combination of minOccurs and maxOccurs
- How to use the AttributeType declaration to qualify the elements of a data type
- The list of types supported for attributes

The Basics of Schemas

When you're working with databases, there are two primary perspectives to use when working with the data. The first is the syntactic approach, which is a description of the data's structure. A schema used to describe the structure of the data is known as a *syntactic schema*. The other approach is to examine the concepts and relationships between the data. The schema to describe this is known as a *conceptual schema*, and XML-Data can be used to describe schemas of both types.

Since you're using XML to construct the schemas, the basic structure of a schema is that of an XML file. This is demonstrated in the following code:

```
<? xml version="1.0" ?>
<Schema name="NameOfSchema"
 xmlns="urn:schemas-microsoft-com:xml-data">
<!--body of schema -->
</Schema>
```

In this example, the name assigned to the schema is a placeholder. To be consistent with what you did earlier, give it the name "Catalog".

To view the complete XML-Data specification, visit
http://www.w3.org/TR/1998/NOTE-XML-data/.

A subset of the XML-Data specification is implemented in IE 5. Therefore, although this hour will refer to the complete XML-Data specification, it will focus on what's implemented in IE.

Consider the skeleton of a schema file shown in Listing 19.1.

LISTING 19.1   The Skeleton of a XML Schema File

```
1: <?xml version="1.0"?>
2: <!-- This is a simple demo file of an XML schema. The name
3:      of the file is xmlhour19-1.xml. -->
4: <Schema name="Catalog"
5: xmlns="urn:schemas-microsoft-com:xml-data">
6: <!-- Body of schema -->
7: </Schema>
```

When you run the file in IE, you'll see that it's syntactically correct.

The qualifier xmlns="urn:schemas-microsoft-com:xml-data" should be very familiar to you by now. This is an assignment to the XML-Data namespace that is provided in IE 5. If this notation is used, it's not necessary to include a prefix in the declarations that appear in the body of the schema. The XML processor will use the default from the XML-Data namespace.

The ElementType Declaration

The schema entry that defines the nodes of the XML data files is the ElementType declaration. A list of ElementType declarations inside the schema corresponds to the elements of the data file. For example, if the object you're prototyping contains an <Author> node, you'll have an entry of the following form:

```
<ElementType name="Author"/>
```

It's also possible to specify the content type by assigning a value to the content qualifier in the ElementType declaration. The possible values that can be assigned to content and their meanings are listed in Table 19.1.

TABLE 19.1   The Possible Content Types That Can Be Assigned to Nodes

Value	Meaning
empty	The element cannot contain any content.
textOnly	The element can contain only text.
eltOnly	The element can contain only subelements.
mixed	The element can contain a mixture of text and subelements.

If an object is being built by instances of various defined ElementTypes, each of the specific types are defined first. The instances of the data components are then placed inside the object using tags of the following form:

```
<element type="TypeName"/>
```

Let's start with the very first XML data file that you used, which is shown in Listing 19.2.

LISTING 19.2   A Simple XML File Used to Demonstrate an XML Schema

```
1:  <MESSAGE>
2:  <TO>STUDENT</TO>
3:  <FROM>AUTHOR</FROM>
4:  <SUBJECT>Introduction to XML</SUBJECT>
5:  <BODY>Welcome to XML!</BODY>
6:  </MESSAGE>
```

19

Assuming that each of the interior nodes can only contain text, an XML schema that describes the data in this file would be something like Listing 19.3.

LISTING 19.3   The XML Schema That Defines the MESSAGE Data Type

```
 1: <?xml version="1.0"?>
 2: <!-- This is a simple XML schema that corresponds to the
 3:     Message data object.
 4:     The name of the file is listing19-3.xml. -->
 5: <Schema name="MessageDef" xmlns="urn:schemas-microsoft-com:xml-data">
 6: <!-- These are the definitions of the individual components of
     the MESSAGE object -->
 7: <ElementType name="TO" content="textOnly"/>
 8: <ElementType name="FROM" content="textOnly"/>
 9: <ElementType name="SUBJECT" content="textOnly"/>
10: <ElementType name="BODY" content="textOnly"/>
11:
12: <!-- Now that the components are defined, we can use them to
     build the MESSAGE object -->
13: <ElementType name="MESSAGE" content="eltOnly">
14: <element type="TO"/>
15: <element type="FROM"/>
16: <element type="SUBJECT"/>
17: <element type="BODY"/>
18: </ElementType>
19: </Schema>
```

Create this file, save it as listing19-3.xml and run it in IE. The output is demonstrated in Figure 19.1.

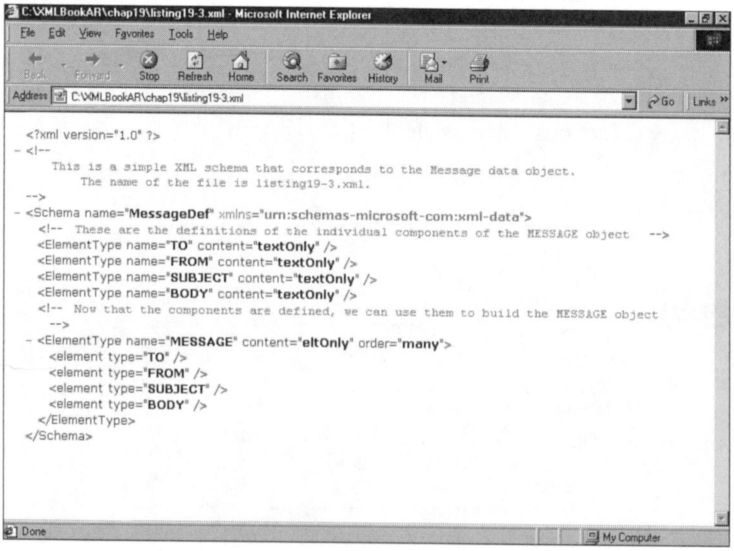

FIGURE 19.1

The appearance of the schema file in IE.

The notation to include this file in an XML data file is similar to what's done for DTD files and is demonstrated in Listing 19.4.

LISTING 19.4 The Importation of an XML Schema File into a File Containing Data

```
 1: <?xml version="1.0"?>
 2: <!-- This file demonstrates the process of importing an XML
 3:      schema file into an XML data file. The verification of
 4:      the data organization is then done in a manner similar
 5:      to what you've seen with DTDs. The name of the file
 6:      is listing19-4.xml. -->
 7: <mm:MESSAGE xmlns:mm="x-schema:listing19-3.xml">
 8: <mm:TO>Honorable readers</mm:TO>
 9: <mm:FROM>Humble Author</mm:FROM>
10: <mm:SUBJECT>XML Schema construction</mm:SUBJECT>
11: <mm:BODY>Demonstration of an XML schema in action</mm:BODY>
12: </mm: MESSAGE>
```

Run the file in IE. The output is demonstrated in Figure 19.2.

FIGURE 19.2

The data file that imports the XML schema file.

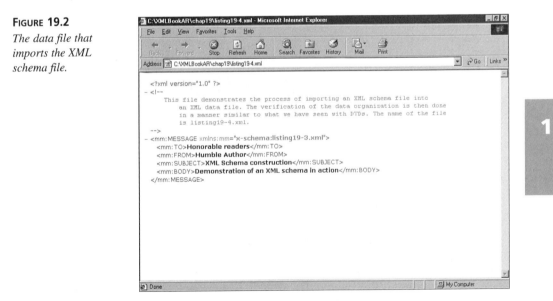

You can verify that the schema file is imported and that the XML processor actually pays attention to it by reopening listing19-3.xml and modifying the line

```
<ElementType name="TO" content="textOnly"/>
```

to

```
<ElementType Name="TO" content="textOnly"/>
```

When the file is displayed again, an error will be generated because 'Name' isn't supported in the XML-Data language. Reopen the file and change it back to its original form before continuing.

The final step in all of this is to display the data in the XML file. To do that, you'll use a program that has been used many times before.

Reopen listing3-5.html and modify the line that loads the file to xmlDoc1.load("listing19-4.xml"); and run it in IE. The output is illustrated in Figure 19.3.

FIGURE 19.3

The appearance of the imported XML file using the XML schema.

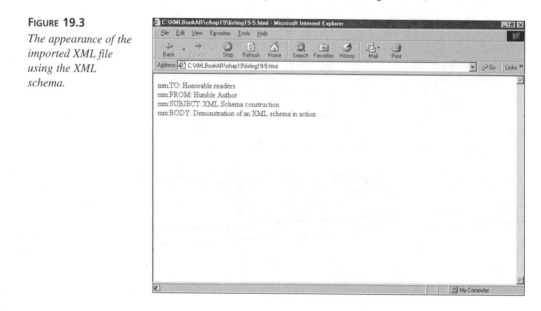

To demonstrate the consequences of the node definition, reopen listing19-4.xml and modify it to match Listing 19.5. The code to add is marked in bold.

LISTING 19.5   Violating the Node Definition of the Schema File by Putting Text in the <MESSAGE> Node

```
 1: <?xml version="1.0"?>
 2: <!-- This file demonstrates the process of importing an XML
 3:      schema file into an XML data file. The verification of
 4:      the data organization is then done in a manner similar
 5:      to what you've seen with DTDs. -->
 6: <mm:MESSAGE xmlns:mm="x-schema:listing19-4.xml">
 7: This would be text allowed in the message node
 8: <mm:TO>Honorable readers</mm:TO>
 9: <mm:FROM>Humble Author</mm:FROM>
10: <mm:SUBJECT>XML Schema construction</mm:SUBJECT>
11: <mm:BODY>Demonstration of an XML schema in action</mm:BODY>
12: </mm: MESSAGE>
```

In this case, the text in bold is added to the <MESSAGE> node. However, since the schema has the <MESSAGE> node as 'eltOnly' for content, this is not allowed. When you view the HTML file, the violation of the data definition will generate an error.

Go back to Listing 19.3 and modify the line

```
<ElementType name="MESSAGE" content="eltOnly">
```

to

```
<ElementType name="MESSAGE" content="mixed">
```

Now that the <MESSAGE> node can contain both text and elements, the data definition is not violated by the change in Listing 19.4. The output when the HTML file is run is illustrated in Figure 19.4.

FIGURE 19.4

The appearance of the data when a node is of mixed type.

```
#text: This would be text allowed in the message node
mm:TO: Honorable readers
mm:FROM: Humble Author
mm:SUBJECT: XML Schema construction
mm:BODY: Demonstration of an XML schema in action
```

The ElementType declaration also has an option to constrain the order of the elements that define it. This attribute is called 'order', and the list of possible values is summarized in Table 19.2.

TABLE 19.2   The Allowed Values for the Order Option

Value	Meaning
seq	The elements must appear in the same order as they're listed. This is the default for the eltOnly content type.
one	One subelement of the type must appear in the parent element.
all	An element of each declared type must appear as a subelement. However, they can be in any order.
many	Any of the subelements can appear in the element type declaration, and they can be in any order. This is the default for mixed content.

It should be clear that these options generally are placed in a parent node where the content element has a value of 'eltOnly'.

Go back to Listing 19.3 and change the opening tag for the <MESSAGE> type to

```
<ElementType name="MESSAGE" content="eltOnly" order="seq">
```

Reopen Listing 19.4 and modify it to match Listing 19.6. The two lines that are interchanged are highlighted in bold.

LISTING 19.6   Interchanging Two of the Values Will Violate the Schema, Which Now Requires the Elements to Be in the Specified Order

```
 1: <?xml version="1.0"?>
 2: <!-- This file demonstrates the process of importing an XML
 3:      schema file into an XML data file. The verification of
 4:      the data organization is then done in a manner similar
 5:      to what you've seen with DTDs
-->
 6: <mm:MESSAGE xmlns:mm="x-schema:listing19-3.xml">
 7: <mm:TO>Honorable readers</mm:TO>
 8: <mm:FROM>Humble Author</mm:FROM>
 9: <mm:BODY>Demonstration of an XML schema in action</mm:BODY>
10: <mm:SUBJECT>XML Schema construction</mm: SUBJECT>
11: </mm:MESSAGE>
```

Note that the order of the elements doesn't match the order in the schema file.

When you run the HTML file in IE, an error is now generated because the schema has been violated.

Go back to Listing 19.3 and modify the opening MESSAGE to match the following: <ElementType name="MESSAGE" content="eltOnly" order="many">

When the HTML file is run, the file is displayed with the order of <SUBJECT> and <BODY> reversed to match what's in the data file.

Go back to Listing 19.4 and modify it to match Listing 19.7.

LISTING 19.7   Adding Duplicate Nodes When the order Property Is Set to "many"

```
 1: <?xml version="1.0"?>
 2: <!-- This file demonstrates the process of importing an XML
 3:      schema file into an XML data file. The verification of
 4:      the data organization is then done in a manner similar
 5:      to what you've seen with DTDs. The name of the file
 6:      is xmlhour19-7.xml. -->
 7: <mm:MESSAGE xmlns:mm="x-schema:xmlhour22-2.xml">
 8: <mm:TO>Honorable readers</mm:TO>
 9: <mm:TO>Honorable editors</mm:TO>
10: <mm:TO>Children</mm:TO>
11: <mm:FROM>Humble Author</mm:FROM>
12: <mm:BODY>Demonstration of an XML schema in action</mm:BODY>
13: <mm:SUBJECT>XML Schema construction</mm:SUBJECT>
14: </mm:MESSAGE>
```

When you run the HTML file again, you'll see that all of the nodes are output.

Assigning Values to `minOccurs` and `maxOccurs`

Recall that in a previous hour you constructed a DTD using the character qualifiers. The object you were describing was an EMAIL object, and the list of elements was as follows:

```
<!ELEMENT E-MAIL (TO+,FROM,CC*,BCC*,SUBJECT?,BODY?)>
```

Although the qualification symbols (+, *, ?) do specify the multiplicity of the entries, they're very imprecise. For example, the plus sign (+) simply notes that there can be one or more instances. This imprecision is the primary reason why the `minOccurs` and `maxOccurs` parameters were introduced. Used in tandem, they allow you to specify a range of times that an element can appear. The combinations of values have varying interpretations, which are summarized in Table 19.3.

TABLE 19.3 The Different Ways to Define a Range of Possible Values

minOccurs	maxOccurs	*Number of times element can appear*
1 or unspecified	1 or unspecified	Precisely 1
0	1 or unspecified	0 or 1
Greater than 1	Greater than 1	At least the value of minOccurs, but not more than the value of maxOccurs
0	*	Zero or more times
1	*	One or more times
Greater than 0	*	At least minOccurs times
Any number	0	0

Create the file shown in Listing 19.8 and save it as listing19-8.xml. This code will be the schema that describes the email message that was used in earlier lessons.

LISTING 19.8 A Schema to Define an Email Message

```
1: <?xml version="1.0"?>
2: <!-- This is a simple XML schema that corresponds to the
3:      E-MAIL data object. The name of the file is
4:      Listing19-8.xml. -->
5: <Schema name="EmailDef"
   xmlns="urn:schemas-microsoft-com:xml-data">
6: <!-- These are the definitions of the individual components of the
   Email object -->
7: <ElementType name="TO" content="textOnly"/>
```

19

LISTING 19.8 continued

```
 8: <ElementType name="FROM" content="textOnly"/>
 9: <ElementType name="CC" content="textOnly"/>
10: <ElementType name="BCC" content="textOnly"/>
11: <ElementType name="SUBJECT" content="textOnly"/>
12: <ElementType name="BODY" content="textOnly"/>
13: <!-- Now that the components are defined, we can use them to build the
    Email object -->
14: <ElementType name="Email" content="eltOnly" order="seq">
15: <element type="TO" minOccurs="1" maxOccurs="*"/>
16: <element type="FROM" minOccurs="1" maxOccurs="1"/>
17: <element type="CC" minOccurs="0" maxOccurs="*"/>
18: <element type="BCC" minOccurs="0" maxOccurs="*"/>
19: <element type="SUBJECT" minOccurs="0" maxOccurs="1"/>
20: <element type="BODY" minOccurs="0" maxOccurs="1"/>
21: </ElementType>
22: </Schema>
```

Note the range specified for the nodes. It matches the definition you used in earlier lessons.

Create the file shown in Listing 19.9 and save it as listing19-9.xml. This file is an instance of the email message and imports the schema file that defines it.

LISTING 19.9 An Instance of the Email Message Object That Imports the Schema File

```
 1: <?xml version="1.0"?>
 2: <!-- This file demonstrates the process of importing an XML
 3:      schema file into an XML data file. The verification of
 4:      the data organization is then done in a manner similar
 5:      to what you've seen with DTDs. The name of the file
 6:      is listing19-9.xml. -->
 7: <em:Email xmlns:em="x-schema:listing19-8.xml">
 8: <em:TO>Honorable readers</em:TO>
 9: <em:FROM>Humble Author</em:FROM>
10: <em:SUBJECT>XML Schema construction</em:SUBJECT>
11: <em:BODY>Demonstration of an XML schema in action</em:BODY>
12: </em:Email>
```

Reopen HTML file and modify the line that loads the file so that it uses Listing 19.9. Run it in IE and note that the nodes are listed.

Reopen the listing and modify it to match Listing 19.10.

LISTING **19.10**   Adding Multiple Values for the Nodes

```
 1: <?xml version="1.0"?>
 2: <!-- This file demonstrates the process of importing an XML
 3:      schema file into an XML data file. The verification of
 4:      the data organization is then done in a manner similar
 5:      to what you've seen with DTDs. The name of the file
 6:      is listing19-10.xml. -->
 7: <em:Email xmlns:em="x-schema:listing19-8.xml">
 8: <em:TO>Honorable readers</em:TO>
 9: <em:TO>Honorable editors</em:TO>
10: <em:FROM>Humble Author</em:FROM>
11: <em:CC>Avid reader 1</em:CC>
12: <em:CC>Avid reader 1</em:CC>
13: <em:CC>Avid reader 1</em:CC>
14: <em:BCC>Anonymous reader 1</em:BCC>
15: <em:BCC>Anonymous reader 2</em:BCC>
16: <em:BCC>Anonymous reader 3</em:BCC>
17: <em:BCC>Anonymous reader 4</em:BCC>
18: <em:SUBJECT>XML Schema construction</em:SUBJECT>
19: <em:BODY>Demonstration of an XML schema in action</em:BODY>
20: </em:Email>
```

Run the HTML file with this XML file as input. Note that all of the nodes are displayed with no errors.

The data types supported for elements in schemas are the same as those for DTD attributes. To see the complete list, consult Table 7.1 in Hour 7.

Attribute Type Declarations

The XML-Data package also supports attribute type declarations, and the types are the same as those for the XML DTD package. As was the case with ElementType declarations, the attribute is defined before the element definition and then an instance is included. It's possible to use the attribute in more than one element.

Recall the first XML file that you created, which included attributes. The listing was first used in Hour 6.

LISTING **19.11**   The DTD File That Defines the Email Message and Includes Qualifying Attributes

```
 1: <?xml version="1.0"?>
 2: <!-- This file demonstrates the use of an attribute list to
 3:      qualify data. The filename is xmlhour7-5.xml -->
 4: <!DOCTYPE E-MAIL [
```

19

LISTING 19.11   continued

```
 5: <!ELEMENT E-MAIL (TO+,FROM,CC*,BCC*,SUBJECT?,BODY?)>
 6: <!ATTLIST MESSAGE LANGUAGE (Western|Extended) "Western" >
 7: <!ATTLIST MESSAGE ENCRYPTION (64|128|256) "256">
 8: <!ATTLIST MESSAGE PRIORITY (low|normal|high) "normal">
 9: <!ELEMENT TO (#PCDATA)>
10: <!ELEMENT FROM (#PCDATA)>
11: <!ELEMENT CC (#PCDATA)>
12: <!ELEMENT BCC (#PCDATA)>
13: <!ELEMENT SUBJECT (#PCDATA)>
14: <!ELEMENT BODY (#PCDATA)>
15: ]>
16: <E-MAIL LANGUAGE="Western" ENCRYPTION="256"
    PRIORITY="normal" >
17: <TO>READER</TO>
18: <FROM>AUTHOR</FROM>
19: <CC></CC>
20: <BCC>Secret friend 1</BCC>
21: <BCC>Secret friend 2</BCC>
22: <BCC>Secret friend 3</BCC>
23: <BCC>Secret friend 4</BCC>
24: <SUBJECT>New book</SUBJECT>
25: <BODY>Announcing a new book being developed!</BODY>
26: </E-MAIL>
```

The next step is to write an XML schema that corresponds to the DTD and the data file. To use the attributes, you need to make the datatypes namespace available. One of the supported data types is the enumeration type, which is the one that you'll use in this exercise.

Create the file shown in Listing 19.12 and save it as listing19-12.xml.

LISTING 19.12   The XML Schema That Corresponds to the Definition of the Email Object

```
1: <?xml version="1.0"?>
2: <!-- This is a simple XML schema that corresponds to the
3:      E-MAIL data object. The name of the file is
4:      Listing19-12.xml. -->
5: <!--Note the inclusion of the datatypes file and that we
6:    will be using the dt prefix. This is not a mandatory
7:    prefix, just the one that best combines accuracy with
8:    brevity. -->
9: <Schema name="EmailDef"
   xmlns="urn:schemas-microsoft-com:xml-data"
   xmlns:dt="urn:schemas-microsoft-com:datatypes">
```

```
10: <!-- These are the definitions of the individual components of the Email
11:     object -->
12: <ElementType name="TO" content="textOnly"/>
13: <ElementType name="FROM" content="textOnly"/>
14: <ElementType name="CC" content="textOnly"/>
15: <ElementType name="BCC" content="textOnly"/>
16: <ElementType name="SUBJECT" content="textOnly"/>
17: <ElementType name="BODY" content="textOnly"/>
18: <AttributeType name="LANGUAGE" dt:type="enumeration"
    dt:values="Western Extended" default="Western"/>
19: <AttributeType name="ENCRYPTION" dt:type="enumeration"
    dt:values="64 128 256" default="128"/>
20: <AttributeType name="PRIORITY" dt:type="enumeration"
    dt:values="low normal high" default="normal"/>
21: <!-- Now that the components are defined, we can use them to build
    the Email object -->
22: <ElementType name="Email" content="eltOnly" order="seq">
23: <attribute type="LANGUAGE"/>
24: <attribute type="ENCRYPTION"/>
25: <attribute type="PRIORITY"/>
26: <element type="TO" minOccurs="1" maxOccurs="*"/>
27: <element type="FROM" minOccurs="1" maxOccurs="1"/>
28: <element type="CC" minOccurs="0" maxOccurs="*"/>
29: <element type="BCC" minOccurs="0" maxOccurs="*"/>
30: <element type="SUBJECT" minOccurs="0" maxOccurs="1"/>
31: <element type="BODY" minOccurs="0" maxOccurs="1"/>
32: </ElementType>
33: </Schema>
```

Note that it's necessary to use the namespace prefix to specify both the type as enumeration and the list of values.

Create the following file and save it as listing19-13.xml:

LISTING 19.13   An Instance of the Email Data Object That Imports the Schema File

```
 1: <?xml version="1.0"?>
 2: <!-- This file demonstrates the process of importing an XML
 3:     schema file into an XML data file. The verification of
 4:     the data organization is then done in a manner similar
 5:     to what you've seen with DTDs. The name of the file
 6:     is listing19-13.xml. -->
 7: <em:Email xmlns:em="x-schema:xmlhour22-8.xml" LANGUAGE="Western"
    ENCRYPTION="256" PRIORITY="normal" >
 8: <em:TO>READER</em:TO>
 9: <em:FROM>AUTHOR</em:FROM>
10: <em:CC></em:CC>
```

19

LISTING 19.13   continued

```
11: <em:BCC>Secret friend 1</em:BCC>
12: <em:BCC>Secret friend 2</em:BCC>
13: <em:BCC>Secret friend 3</em:BCC>
14: <em:BCC>Secret friend 4</em:BCC>
15: <em:SUBJECT>New book</em:SUBJECT>
16: <em:BODY>Announcing a new book being developed!</em:BODY>
17: </em:Email>
```

This file imports the schema file, and appropriate assignments are made to the attributes of the Email object.

Reopen the HTML and modify the line that loads the file so that it opens Listing 19.13.

Run the file in IE and note that the nodes are displayed with no errors.

Attribute Types Supported in IE

Given the attributes that were used in Listing 19.12, the only data type that you needed was the enumeration type. There are several types that are supported, as summarized in Table 19.4.

TABLE 19.4   The Valid Types That Can Be Assigned to an Attribute

Data Type	XML Equivalent	Meaning
id	ID	Attribute value must be a unique identifier.
string	PCDATA	Only character data can be used.
entity	ENTITY	Attribute value must refer to an entity.
entities	ENTITIES	Same as entity, but allows for multiple values separated by whitespace.
idref	IDREF	Value must be a reference to an id attribute.
idrefs	IDREFS	Same as idref, but allows for multiple values separated by whitespace.
nmtoken	NMTOKEN	Attribute is a mixture of name token characters, which can include letters, numbers, periods, dashes, colons, or underscores.
nmtokens	NMTOKENS	Same as nmtoken, but allows for multiple values separated by whitespace.
enumeration	ENUMERATION	Attribute must be one of the values in the list.
notation	NOTATION	Attributevalue e must refer to a notation.

Summary

The XML data schema language was created because of weaknesses in the DTD model. In many ways, it's cleaner than the DTD language and provides greater expressive powers. There's the added advantage that schemas are written in XML, providing a consistency of expression not found when DTDs are used.

To demonstrate how XML schemas are written, this hour revisited data files that were used to demonstrate the construction of DTDs, and you rewrote them into the schema equivalents.

Q&A

Q Which form should you use to prototype your XML data, a DTD or a schema?

A Like most questions of this type, the answer is relative. When you're programming, your goal is to create correct, understandable code. If you're better at writing DTDs than you are at writing schemas, your chances of writing correct code are better if you use a DTD. However, schemas are easy to learn and you should migrate to that mode as soon as possible.

Q Should a value always be assigned to the content option of a node?

A Absolutely! Relying on defaults in programming is always a questionable practice. The more precision and description that you can impose on your data, the less likely an error is.

Q Given any DTD, is it possible to write a schema that corresponds to it?

A Yes, it is. If you examine the table of attribute types, there's a schema version for every type in the DTD. In terms of supported datatypes, the same file is used for both the DTD and schema constructions.

19

Workshop

Quiz

1. Which of the following options for the content qualifier of a schema will cause the order of appearance to be enforced?

    a. The default (no entry)

    b. Seq

    c. All

    d. Many

    e. a and b

    f. a, b, and c

2. Which of the following assignments to the minOccurs and maxOccurs pair corresponds to the * qualifier of a DTD?

   a. minOccurs="1" maxOccurs="*"

   b. minOccurs="0" maxOccurs="*"

   c. minOccurs="*" maxOccurs="1"

   d. minOccurs="0" maxOccurs="1"

3. It's impossible to construct a node that contains text and subnodes.

   a. True

   b. False

Answers

1. e

2. b

3. b

Exercise

1. Given the following DTD, construct an equivalent schema:

```
<?xml version="1.0"?>
<!-- This file demonstrates the use of an attribute list
     to qualify data. The filename is xmlhour7-8.dtd -->
<!ELEMENT SHIPORDER
(ShipNumber,To,From,Address+,StateProvince,Country,Carrier,
Insurance?,Security?,GeneralCarrier)>
<!ATTLIST SHIPORDER LANGUAGE (Western|Extended) "Western">
<!ATTLIST SHIPORDER PRIORITY (low|normal|high) "normal">
<!ELEMENT ShipNumber (#PCDATA)>
<!ATTLIST ShipNumber Customs (no|yes) "no">
<!ELEMENT To (#PCDATA)>
<!ATTLIST To idTo ID #REQUIRED>
<!ELEMENT From (#PCDATA)>
<!ATTLIST From idFrom ID #REQUIRED>
<!ELEMENT Address (#PCDATA)>
<!ELEMENT StateProvince (#PCDATA)>
<!ELEMENT Country (#PCDATA)>
<!ATTLIST Country  Destination (USA|Foreign) "USA">
<!ELEMENT Carrier (#PCDATA)>
<!ATTLIST Carrier Vehicle (van|truck|plane) "van">
<!ELEMENT Insurance (#PCDATA)>
<!ATTLIST Insurance Level (none|50percent|full) "none">
<!ELEMENT Security (#PCDATA)>
<!ATTLIST Security SLevel (none|ClosedVehicle|armed)
<!ELEMENT GeneralCarrier (#PCDATA)>
<!ATTLIST GeneralCarrier Us CDATA #FIXED "General Shippers">
```

Hour **20**

Creating an Online Bookstore

So far, this book has focused on demonstrating principles rather than the real-world applications of those principles. In this and the following two hours, you're going to put all of that background knowledge to use.

The scenario is a simple one: Your business sells books online, and you're going to use XML to build a basic retail site on the Web. Although not every possible feature will be constructed, the site will be functional.

In this hour, you'll learn the following:

- The structure of the data entries in your catalog of books
- The structure of the data object containing additional information about the books in your catalog
- The structure of the data object used to store the information about a purchased item
- How to create the HTML file for the opening page of your online store

The Structure of the `<Catalog>` Database

You've used a database of books under the `<Catalog>` XML tag in previous hours. That same tag will be used again, but now the data will be of a slightly different form and a schema will be used to describe it.

The entries in the `<Catalog>` database will all be books, and the `<Book>` entries will have the components shown in Table 20.1.

TABLE 20.1   The Data Components of the Online `<Catalog>` Database

Tag name	What it contains	Data type
`<Title>`	The title of the book	Text
`<Subject>`	A list of keywords about the topics covered in the book	Text
`<Author>`		
`<Name>`	The name of the author	Text
`<Address>`	The address of the author	Text
`<City>`	The city of residence	Text
`<State>`	The state of residence	Text
`<PostalCode>`	The postal code of residence	Text
`<Country>`	The country of residence	Text
`<Email>`	The email address of the author	Text
`<URL>`	The URL of the author	Text
`</Author>`		
`<Publisher>`		
`<Name>`	The name of the publisher	Text
`<Address>`	The address of the publisher	Text
`<City>`	The city of the publisher	Text
`<State>`	The state of the publisher	Text
`<PostalCode>`	The postal code of the publisher	Text
`<Country>`	The country of the publisher	Text
`<URL>`	The URL of the publisher	Text
`</Publisher>`		

Tag name	What it contains	Data type
`<PublicationDate>`	The date the book was published	Date
`<GivenPrice>`	The basic price of the book	Real
`<DiscountPrice>`	The discount price that you'll sell the book for	Real
`<Availability>`	One of three values: available, unavailable, and out of print	Enumerated

Since the author may not want personal information to be published, it's possible for all personal address information fields to be empty.

Listing 20.1 is the schema for the <Book> data object that you'll be using to build your online bookstore. The project will reference it under the filename listing20-1.xml.

LISTING 20.1 The Definition of a <Book> Object for the Online <Catalog> Database

```
 1: <?xml version="1.0"?>
 2: <!-- This is an XML schema that corresponds to the Book
 3:      data object which will be used in the online bookstore
 4:      project.
 5:      The name of the file is listing20-1.xml. -->
 6: <Schema name="BookDef"
 7: xmlns="urn:schemas-microsoft-com:xml-data"
 8:   xmlns:dt="urn:schemas-microsoft-com:datatypes">
 9: <!-- These are the definitions of the base components of
10:      the Book object -->
11: <ElementType name="Title" content="textOnly"/>
12: <ElementType name="Name" content="textOnly"/>
13: <ElementType name="Address" content="textOnly"/>
14: <ElementType name="City" content="textOnly"/>
15: <ElementType name="State" content="textOnly"/>
16: <ElementType name="PostalCode" content="textOnly"/>
17: <ElementType name="Country" content="textOnly"/>
18: <ElementType name="Email" content="textOnly"/>
19: <ElementType name="URL" content="textOnly"/>
20: <ElementType name="PublicationDate" dt:type="date"/>
21: <ElementType name="GivenPrice" dt:type="float"/>
22: <ElementType name="DiscountPrice" dt:type="float"/>
23: <ElementType name="Availability" content="textOnly"/>
24: <ElementType name="ISBN" content="textOnly"/>
25: <ElementType name="Subject" content="textOnly"/>
26: <!-- Now that all of our primitive components are defined,
27:      we can use them to build our complex components. These
28:      two are our complex subcomponents. -->
29: <ElementType name="Author" content="eltOnly" order="seq">
```

20

LISTING 20.1   continued

```
30:   <element type="Name"/>
31:   <element type="Address"/>
32:   <element type="City"/>
33:   <element type="State"/>
34:   <element type="PostalCode"/>
35:   <element type="Country"/>
36:   <element type="Email"/>
37:   <element type="URL"/>
38: </ElementType>
39: <ElementType name="Publisher" content="eltOnly" order="seq">
40:   <element type="Name"/>
41:   <element type="Address"/>
42:   <element type="City"/>
43:   <element type="State"/>
44:   <element type="PostalCode"/>
45:   <element type="Country"/>
46:   <element type="URL"/>
47: </ElementType>
48: <!-- Now that all of the components have been defined, we can construct
     the <Book> data type. -->
49: <ElementType name="Book" content="eltOnly" order="seq">
50:   <element type="Title"/>
51:   <element type="Subject"/>
52:   <element type="Author"/>
53:   <element type="Publisher"/>
54:   <element type="ISBN"/>
55:   <element type="PublicationDate"/>
56:   <element type="GivenPrice"/>
57:   <element type="DiscountPrice"/>
58:   <element type="Availability"/>
59: </ElementType>
60: </Schema>
```

This file will be imported into the <Catalog> database that will be your online catalog. The following is a simple database with three <Book> entries that you'll use to test your online bookstore. Listing 20.2 will be saved as listing20-2.xml.

LISTING 20.2   A Small Database of <Book> Objects for Testing the Bookstore

```
1: <?xml version="1.0"?>
2: <!-- This file is a demonstration of the online book
3:      catalog database. The name of the file is
4:      listing20-2.xml. -->
5: <Catalog xmlns:mm="x-schema:listing20-1.xml">
6: <mm:Book>
7: <mm:Title>Teach Yourself XML in 24 Hours</mm:Title>
```

```
 8: <mm:Subject>computers,XML</mm:Subject>
 9: <mm:Author>
10: <mm:Name>Charles Ashbacher</mm:Name>
11: <mm:Address>118 Chaffee Drive</mm:Address>
12: <mm:City>Hiawatha</mm:City>
13: <mm:State>Iowa</mm:State>
14: <mm:PostalCode>52233</mm:PostalCode>
15: <mm:Country>United States</mm:Country>
16: <mm:Email>ashbacher@ashbacher.com</mm:Email>
17: <mm:URL>http://www.ashbacher.com</mm:URL>
18: </mm:Author>
19: <mm:Publisher>
20: <mm:Name>Sams Publishing</mm:Name>
21: <mm:Address>201 West 103rd Street</mm:Address>
22: <mm:City>Indianapolis</mm:City>
23: <mm:State>Indiana</mm:State>
24: <mm:PostalCode>46290</mm:PostalCode>
25: <mm:Country>United States</mm:Country>
26: <mm:URL>http://www.samspublishing.com</mm:URL>
27: </mm:Publisher>
28: <mm:ISBN>0-672-31950-0</mm: ISBN>
29: <mm:PublicationDate>2000-04-01</mm:PublicationDate>
30: <mm:GivenPrice>24.95</mm:GivenPrice>
31: <mm:DiscountPrice>18.95</mm:DiscountPrice>
32: <mm:Availability>In stock</mm:Availability>
33: </mm:Book>
34: <mm:Book >
35: <mm:Title>Teach Yourself Cool Stuff in 24 Hours</mm:Title>
36: <mm:Subject>computers</mm:Subject>
37: <Author>
38: <mm:Name>ReallySmart Person</mm:Name>
39: <mm:Address>110 Main Street</mm:Address>
40: <mm:City>Silicon City</mm:City>
41: <mm:State>California</mm:State>
42: <mm:PostalCode>10101</mm:PostalCode>
43: <mm:Country>United States</mm:Country>
44: <mm:Email>RSmart@MyCompany.com</mm:Email>
45: <mm:URL>http://www.MyCompany.com</mm:URL>
46: </Author>
47: <Publisher>
48: <mm:Name>Sams Publishing</mm:Name>
49: <mm:Address>201 West 103rd Street</mm:Address>
50: <mm:City>Indianapolis</mm:City>
51: <mm:State>Indiana</mm:State>
52: <mm:PostalCode>46290</mm:PostalCode>
53: <mm:Country>United States</mm:Country>
54: <mm:URL>http://www.samspublishing.com</mm:URL>
55: </Publisher>
56: <mm:ISBN>0-672-1010-0</mm:ISBN>
57: <mm:PublicationDate>2000-06-01</mm:PublicationDate>
```

20

LISTING 20.2   continued

```
58: <mm:GivenPrice>24.95</mm:GivenPrice>
59: <mm:DiscountPrice>17.95</mm:DiscountPrice>
60: <mm:Availability>Out of print</mm:Availability>
61: </mm:Book>
62: <mm:Book>
63: <mm:Title>Teach Yourself Uses of Silicon in 24 Hours</mm:Title>
64: <mm:Subject>computers,silicon</mm:Subject>
65: <mm:Author>
66: <mm:Name>Missy Fixit</mm:Name>
67: <mm:Address>119 Hard Drive</mm:Address>
68: <mm:City>Diskette City</mm:City>
69: <mm:State>California</mm:State>
70: <mm:PostalCode>10101</mm:PostalCode>
71: <mm:Country>United States</mm:Country>
72: <mm:Email>MFixit@Googol.com</mm:Email>
73: <mm:URL>http://www.Googol.com</mm:URL>
74: </mm:Author>
75: <mm:Publisher>
76: <mm:Name>Sams Publishing</mm:Name>
77: <mm:Address>201 West 103rd Street</mm:Address>
78: <mm:City>Indianapolis</mm:City>
79: <mm:State>Indiana</mm:State>
80: <mm:PostalCode>46290</mm:PostalCode>
81: <mm:Country>United States</mm:Country>
82: <mm:URL>http://www.samspublishing.com</mm:URL>
83: </mm:Publisher>
84: <mm:ISBN>0-578-31950-0</mm:ISBN>
85: <mm:PublicationDate>2000-01-01</mm:PublicationDate>
86: <mm:GivenPrice>26.95</mm:GivenPrice>
87: <mm:DiscountPrice>26.95</mm:DiscountPrice>
88: <mm:Availability>Out of stock</mm:Availability>
89: </mm:Book>
90: </Catalog>
```

Once again, for the sake of brevity, only a few entries have been placed in the file. Feel free to add additional entries to the database. View the file in IE to verify that it's correct.

The Database of Additional Information

Book lovers are ravenous for information about books. Reviews of books are a very popular feature, and many people read them before deciding to purchase a book. Your main <Catalog> database is going to be supplemented by a file of additional information, and your next step is to describe the structure of that data.

The entries in this database will have the following form, and all of them will contain text:

ISBN—The international reference code for the book. This will be the field that's common to the database of books and will be used for cross-referencing.

Publisher's description—A description of the book written by the publisher.

Author's description—A description of the book written by the author.

The table of contents—Self-explanatory.

Sample chapter—Either a portion or an entire chapter from the book.

Listing 20.3 is the schema file for this data type. It's saved as xmlhour20-3.xml.

LISTING 20.3 The Definition of the Additional Information Data Object

```
 1: <?xml version="1.0"?>
 2: <!-- This is an XML schema that corresponds to the
 3:      Additional Information data object which will be used
 4:      in the online bookstore project. The name of the file
 5:      is xmlhour20-3.xml. -->
 6: <Schema name="InformationDef"
 7:  xmlns="urn:schemas-microsoft-com:xml-data"
 8:  xmlns:dt="urn:schemas-microsoft-com:datatypes">
 9: <!-- These are the definitions of the base components of the
     BookInformation object -->
10: <ElementType name="ISBN" content="textOnly"/>
11: <ElementType name="PubDescription" content="textOnly"/>
12: <ElementType name="AuthorDescription" content="textOnly"/>
13: <ElementType name="TOC" content="textOnly"/>
14: <ElementType name="SampleChapter" content="textOnly"/>
15: <!-- Now that all of the components have been defined, we can construct
     the <BookInformation> data type. -->
16: <ElementType name="BookInformation" content="eltOnly"
17:   order="seq">
18:  <element type="ISBN"/>
19:  <element type="PubDescription"/>
20:  <element type="AuthorDescription"/>
21:  <element type="TOC"/>
22:  <element type="SampleChapter"/>
23: </ElementType>
24: </Schema>
```

20

Your simple database of entries corresponding to the books in your <Catalog> is listed in Listing 20.4 and saved as listing20-4.xml. In the interest of brevity, the entries are nothing more than brief placeholders.

LISTING 20.4   Sample Database of Additional Information Objects Corresponding
to Listing 20.2

```
 1: <?xml version="1.0"?>
 2: <!-- This file is a demonstration of the online book
 3:      catalog database. The name of the file is
 4:      listing20-4.xml. -->
 5: <CatalogInformation xmlns:mm="x-schema:listing20-3.xml">
 6: <mm:BookInformation>
 7: <mm:ISBN>0-672-31950-0</mm:ISBN>
 8: <mm:PubDescription>The book Teach Yourself XML in 24 hours
    is a good book</mm:PubDescription>
 9: <mm:AuthorDescription>This book is a very good
    book.</mm:AuthorDescription>
10: <mm:TOC>Table of contents for Teach Yourself XML in 24
    hours</mm:TOC>
11: <mm:SampleChapter>Chapter from Teach Yourself XML in 24
    hours</mm:SampleChapter>
12: </mm:BookInformation>
13: <mm:BookInformation>
14: <mm:ISBN>0-672-1010-0</mm:ISBN>
15: <mm:PubDescription>The book Teach Yourself Really Cool
    Stuff in 24 hours is a good book
    </mm:PubDescription>
16: <mm:AuthorDescription>This book is a book you will find of
    value.</mm:AuthorDescription>
17: <mm:TOC>Table of contents for Teach Yourself Really Cool
    Stuff in 24 hours</mm:TOC>
18: <mm:SampleChapter>Chapter from Teach Yourself Really Cool
    Stuff in 24 hours</mm:SampleChapter>
19: </mm:BookInformation>
20: <mm:BookInformation>
21: <mm:ISBN>0-578-31950-0</mm:ISBN>
22: <mm:PubDescription>The book Teach Yourself Uses of Silicon
    in 24 hours is a good book</mm:PubDescription>
23: <mm:AuthorDescription>This book is a book you will find
    very helpful.</mm:AuthorDescription>
24: <mm:TOC>Table of contents for Teach Yourself Uses of
    Silicon in 24 hours</mm:TOC>
25: <mm:SampleChapter>Chapter from Teach Yourself Uses of
    Silicon in 24 hours</mm:SampleChapter>
26: </mm:BookInformation>
27: </CatalogInformation>
```

View this file in IE to verify the correctness of the schema and the data.

The Data Form of a Purchased Item

When an item is marked for purchase, it will be entered into an XML file that's updated dynamically in response to the user's actions. The entries will be abbreviated versions of the book object and are described by the XML schema in Listing 20.5.

LISTING 20.5   The Form of the Data Used to Represent a Purchased Item

```
 1: <?xml version="1.0"?>
 2: <!-- This is an XML schema that corresponds to the
 3:      PurchasedBook data object which will be used
 4:      in the online bookstore project. The name of the file
 5:      is listing20-5.xml. -->
 6: <Schema name="PurchasedBookDef"
 7: xmlns="urn:schemas-microsoft-com:xml-data"
 8: xmlns:dt="urn:schemas-microsoft-com:datatypes">
 9: <!-- These are the definitions of the base components of the
     PurchasedBook object -->
10: <ElementType name="AuthorName" content="textOnly"/>
11: <ElementType name="GivenPrice" dt:type="float"/>
12: <ElementType name="DiscountPrice" dt:type="float"/>
13: <ElementType name="Availability" content="textOnly"/>
14: <ElementType name="ISBN" content="textOnly"/>
15: <ElementType name="Subject" content="textOnly"/>
16: <!-- Now that all of the components have been defined, we can construct
     the <PurchasedBook> data type. -->
17: <ElementType name="PurchasedBook" content="eltOnly" order="seq">
18:  <element type="Title"/>
19:  <element type="AuthorName"/>
20:  <element type="GivenPrice"/>
21:  <element type="DiscountPrice"/>
22:  <element type="Availability"/>
23:  <element type="ISBN"/>
24:  <element type="Subject"/>
25: </ElementType>
26: </Schema>
```

20

The Bookstore's Opening Page

Your online bookstore is going to present an opening page to the user. This page will be little more than a welcome and an overview. The key functionality will be embedded in the linked pages. Generally, online stores have simple opening displays. This leads to faster downloads and less confusion for the user.

In keeping with this book's policy of minimal prettiness, very little has been done to make these pages aesthetically pleasing.

Create the file shown in Listing 20.6 and save it as listing20-6.html.

LISTING 20.6   The Opening Page of the Online Bookstore

```
 1: <html>
 2: <!-- This is the opening page of the online bookstore that
 3:      has been created to demonstrate the practical uses of
 4:      XML. The name of the file is listing20-6.html. -->
 5: <head>
 6: <title>Opening Page of the XML Online Bookstore</title>
 7: </head>
 8: <body>
 9: <h2 align=center>Welcome to the Teach Yourself XML in 24 Hours
    Online Bookstore!</h2>
10: <hr>
11: <h3>This page is a simple implementation of an online bookstore, where the
    user can scan the list of available books and order them online.
    There are two databases available. One is a list of the books
12: available
    for purchase, and the other is a companion containing
    additional information about them.
    If you have found a book and are interested in learning more
    about it, you will be able to
    access the database of additional information.</h3>
13: <h2 align=center>Available options</h2>
14: <UL>
15: <LI><A href="Searchdata.html">Search the available books database</A></LI>
16: <LI><A href="Yourbooks.html">View your purchases</A></LI>
17: <LI><U>Contact us</U></LI>
18: </UL>
19: <br><br>
20: <table align=center>
21: <tr><td><u> Privacy
    Policy</u></td><td>      </td>
    <td><u>About our company</u></td>
22: <td>       
    <u>Security issues</u></td></tr>
23: </table>
24: </body>
25: </html>
```

The appearance of this page when viewed in IE is shown in Figure 20.1.

FIGURE 20.1

The opening page of your online bookstore.

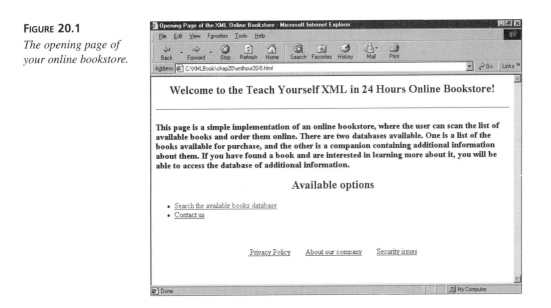

In a functional page, the underlined entries at the bottom would be links to the relevant files. Since you have no interest in devoting time and space to those files, the links aren't implemented. The same holds for the "Contact us" entry in the list of options.

The functionality to search, browse, and purchase the books will all be found in the "SearchData.html" file. This page will contain a method for searching the database of available books by author name, title of book, subject, or ISBN.

Since you're a valued customer and eligible for the frequent purchaser program, you also have the option to view all of the books that you've purchased through the site. The functionality to do this is all in the file "YourBooks.html". This file will provide access to a data file that will be updated dynamically as you make additional purchases.

Summary

This chapter was the primer for the online bookstore that you're constructing. You created data types for three items: a description of a book that's available in your online catalog, a further description of the book, and a purchased book (a subset of the description of the book). The HTML file for the opening page of the online bookstore was also presented.

20

Q&A

Q **Why have two separate files to describe the books?**

A Although book buyers are interested in information, they're not interested in *all* the information about *all* the books. In the interest of speed, the additional information isn't loaded until the user requests it.

Q **Why should I define an additional data type for the books purchased?**

A If a book has been purchased, you can assume that the seller wants to retain some information about that book. Therefore, rather than reuse the larger data type for a <Book>, use a subset that contains all the information that's needed.

Workshop

Quiz

1. Why is the ISBN number used to cross-reference book entries across files?

   a. It's easier to process numbers than titles

   b. The ISBN number is always unique; titles are not

   c. The author is a mathematician and likes numbers

   d. Titles can be of any length, whereas ISBN numbers are all of the same length

2. Why should I make my opening page as simple as possible?

   a. It will download faster

   b. It's easier to read; your goal is to sell books, not to make money by plastering the screen with flashy ads

   c. The purpose of this book is to teach XML, and unnecessary HTML code will detract from that

   d. You know HTML and can modify it to suit your tastes

   e. All of the above

Answers

1. b (although c and d are also true)

2. e

Exercises

1. Modify the schema that defines a `<Book>` to reflect the possibility that a book was edited rather than authored.

2. Modify the schema that defines a book to reflect the possibility that a book has multiple authors.

3. Use cascading style sheets to modify the HTML file for the opening page and give it more color.

20

Hour 21

Accessing the Databases for an Online Bookstore

In the previous hour, the three forms of data that you'll be using in your online bookstore were presented. This hour will present the HTML page that will allow the customer to conduct a search for books.

In this hour, you'll learn the following:

- The general appearance of the page for searching the XML database, and the design features to use
- The search mechanism used to find the books of interest to the user
- How the list of purchased books is displayed

Constructing the Page Used to Search the Database

A basic HTML form is used to construct the interface that allows the user to enter the search criteria. The HTML that does this is displayed in Listing 21.1.

LISTING 21.1   The HTML Code That Creates the Interface for Inputting Search
Criteria

```
 1: <h3 align=center>Use This Page To Search for the Book of
 2: Interest</h3>
 3:  This page presents four boxes where information can be entered and
 4: a search button clicked. The boxes are labeled: <B>Search by title:
 5: </B>, <b>Search by Author Name:</b>, <b>Search by ISBN</b> and
 6: <b>Search by Keywords</b>. <br><br>
 7: The search algorithm is rather simple. If there is any information
 8: in the <b>Search by Title:</b> editbox, the search is done by title
 9: using the information in the box. If the <b>Title</b> box is
10: empty, it then checks the Search by <b>Author Name:</b> editbox.
11: If the <b>Author Name</b> box is not empty, the search is done
12: based on the author name. If it is empty, the test moves on to
13: the <b>ISBN</b> box. <br><br>
14:  The keyword search is a little different in that more than one
15: word can be used. To use more than one word, separate them by
16: commas, which are interpreted as an OR. Therefore, is you enter
17: the phrase, &quot;computer,HTML&quot;, the search will return
18: all entries containing the keyword &quot;computer&quot; or
19: &quot;HTML&quot;. The search is also case sensitive.<br><br>
20: <form name=form1>
21: <b>Enter the title to search for:</b>   
22: <input type=text name=titlesearch value="" size=50><br><br>
23: <b>Enter the author name to search for:</b>   
24: <input type=text name=authorsearch value=""  size=50><br><br>
25: <b>Enter the ISBN to search for:</b>   
26: <input type=text name=isbnsearch value=""  size=50><br><br>
27: <b>Enter the keyword(s) to search for:</b>   
28: <input type=text name=keywordsearch value=""  size=50><br><br>
29: <input type=button name=button1 value="Click to begin the search"
onClick="SearchTheData()">  
30: <DIV align=right><A href="xmlhour20-6.html">Go back to opening
page</a></DIV><br>
31: </form>
```

The output of this code is displayed in Figure 21.1.

The search algorithm is explained in the figure. If the text box with the label Enter the
title to search for: contains text, the search will be for a title match of that text
box's contents. If it's empty, the code will then examine the text box with the label Enter
the author name to search for: If that text box isn't empty, the search will be for an
author name that's an exact match with the contents of the text box. This continues down
through all of the text boxes. If no text box contains text, a message pops up notifying
the user that no search was performed.

FIGURE 21.1

The page used to conduct searches for books of interest.

This page is used to search for the books of interest - Microsoft Internet Explorer

File Edit View Favorites Tools Help

Back   Forward   Stop   Refresh   Home   Search   Favorites   History   Mail   Print

Address C:\XMLBook\chap21\SearchData.html

Use This Page To Search for the Book of Interest

This page presents four boxes where information can be entered and a search button clicked. The boxes are labeled: **Search by title:**, **Search by Author Name:**, **Search by ISBN** aand **Search by Keywords**.

The search algorithm is rather simple. If there is any information in the **Search by Title:** editbox, the search is done by title using the information in the box. If the **Title** box is empty, it then checks the **Search by Author Name:** editbox. If the **Author Name** box is not empty, the search is done based on the author name. If it is empty, the test moves on to the ISBN box.

The keyword search is a little different in that more than one word can be used. To use more than one word, separate them by commas, which are interpreted as an OR. Therefore, is you enter the phrase, "computer,HTML", the search will return all entries containing the keyword "computer" or "HTML". The search is also case sensitive.

Enter the title to search for:

Enter the author name to search for:

Enter the ISBN to search for:

Enter the keyword(s) to search for:

Click to begin the search

Done   My Computer

The search based on keywords is more complex. Multiple keywords are allowed, provided that they're separated by commas. A comma is interpreted as a logical OR, so the search will return all entries in which the `<Subject>` text contains one or more of the entered keywords.

Searching the Online Book Database

The main page contains a link to the mechanism that searches the book database, which is to Searchdata.html. That file appears in Listing 21.2.

The search mechanism uses JScript code to perform the search, rather than XSL templates. JScript is the Microsoft equivalent of the JavaScript language, which was created by Netscape. While there are some differences between the two, they're essentially the same. If you know JavaScript, you know JScript.

LISTING 21.2 Using the Criteria Input by the User to Search the Book Database

21

```
1:<html>
<!-- This file is used to perform the search of the online
    book database based on criteria input by the user.
    The name of the file is Searchdata.html. -->
2:<head>
```

LISTING 21.2   continued

```
3:<title>This page is used to search for the books of interest</title>
4:<SCRIPT LANGUAGE="JScript">
<!--
5: var xmlDoc1=new ActiveXObject("microsoft.xmldom");
6: var RootElement1;
7: xmlDoc1.load("xmlhour20-2.xml");
/* The purpose of this function is to filter out the situations where
the data loading fails for whatever reason. If the XML data file does
not conform to the schema or there is any other parsing problem,
RootElement1 will have the value of null. */
8: function StartUp()
9: {
10:  RootElement1=xmlDoc1.documentElement;
11:  if(RootElement1==null)
12:  {
13:   document.write("<h2 align=center>Data load unsuccessful,
     terminating the search process</h2>");
14:   document.write("<A href='xmlhour20-6.html'>Go back to
     main page</A><BR>");
15:  }
16:}
/* This is the function that is called to perform the search when
the command button of the form is clicked. Only one of the criteria
are used per search. The choice is a simple one, based on a simple
movement down the list until a textbox is found that contains
information. When one is found, it is used in the search. */
17: function SearchTheData()
18: {
// A simple list of the variables
19:  var str1;
20:  var str2;
21:  var BookTitle;
22:  var AuthName;
23:  var available;
24:  var subject;
25:  var fullprice;
26:  var disprice;
27:  var pubDate;
28:  var isbn;
29:  var informationstring;
30:  var BuyString;
31:  var moveNode;
32:  var keyarray;
33:  var counter;
34:  var lastposition;
35:  var slength;
36:  var arrayindex;
37:  var bookkeywords;
```

```
38:  var bookindex;
// Extract the contents of the textbox reserved for
// entering the title.
39:  str1=form1.titlesearch.value;
40: if(str1!="")
41: {
// We will be searching for a match of titles. The
// algorithm is simple, we move through the entries
// in the database looking for a book with a title
// that is an exact match of the data input by the user. The
// algorithm and the writing of the data is the same for
// all except the keyword search.
42:  document.write("<h2>Results for search on book
     title</h2>");
43:  moveNode=RootElement1.firstChild;
44:  while(moveNode!=null)
45: {
46:  str2=moveNode.firstChild.text;
47:  if(str1==str2)
48: {
// There is a match, so we extract all of the relevant data
// and dynamically write it to the HTML page.
49:   BookTitle=str1;
50:   document.write("Title: "+BookTitle+"<br>");
51:   AuthName=moveNode.firstChild.nextSibling.
      nextSibling.firstChild.text;
52:   document.write("Author: "+AuthName+"<br>");
53:   available=moveNode.lastChild.text;
54:   subject=moveNode.firstChild.nextSibling.text;
55:   disprice=moveNode.lastChild.previousSibling.text;
56:   fullprice=moveNode.lastChild.previousSibling.
      previousSibling.text;
57:   pubDate=moveNode.lastChild.previousSibling.previousSibling.
      previousSibling.text;
58:   isbn=moveNode.lastChild.previousSibling.previousSibling.
      previousSibling.previousSibling.text;
59:   document.write("ISBN: "+isbn+"<br>");
60:   document.write("Publisher Price: "+fullprice+"<br>");
61:   document.write("Our price: "+disprice+"<br>");
62:   document.write("Availability:  "+available+"<br><br>");
// In the following lines, reference is made to active
// server page (*.asp) files. An explanation of these files
// is deferred to the next lesson.
63:   informationstring="<A href=AdditionalInformation.asp?isbn="
      +isbn+">Click here to view additional information
      about this book</A><br>";
64:   document.write(informationstring);
65:   BuyString="<A href='BookBuy.asp?BookTitle="+BookTitle+
      "&AuthName="+AuthName+"&fullprice=$"+fullprice+
      "&disprice=$"+disprice+"&available="+available+
      "&isbn="+isbn+"&subject="+subject+"'>Click here to buy
      this book</A><br><br><hr>";
```

21

LISTING 21.2   continued

```
66:   document.write(BuyString);
67:   }
68:  moveNode=moveNode.nextSibling;
69: }
70: }
71: else
72: {
// We extract the data from the author textbox and perform a search
//using that string.
73:   str1=form1.authorsearch.value;
74: if(str1!="")
75: {
// We will be searching for a match on the authorname
76:   moveNode=RootElement1.firstChild;
77:   while(moveNode!=null)
78: {
79:   AuthName=moveNode.firstChild.nextSibling.nextSibling.firstChild.text;
80:   if(str1==AuthName)
81:   {
82:    BookTitle=moveNode.firstChild.text;
83:    document.write("Title: "+BookTitle+"<br>");
84:    document.write("Author: "+AuthName+"<br>");
85:    subject=moveNode.firstChild.nextSibling.text;
86:    available=moveNode.lastChild.text;
87:    disprice=moveNode.lastChild.previousSibling.text;
88:    fullprice=moveNode.lastChild.previousSibling.
       previousSibling.text;
89:    pubDate=moveNode.lastChild.previousSibling.
       previousSibling.previousSibling.text;
90:    isbn=moveNode.lastChild.previousSibling.
       previousSibling.previousSibling.
       previousSibling.text;
91:    document.write("ISBN:   "+isbn+"<br>");
92:    document.write("Publisher Price: "+fullprice+"<br>");
93:    document.write("Our price: "+disprice+"<br>");
94:    document.write("Availability: "+available+"<br><br>");
// In the following lines, reference is made to active
// server page (*.asp)files. An explanation of these files
// is deferred to the next lesson.
95:    informationstring=
       "<A href=AdditionalInformation.asp?isbn="+isbn+">Click here to
       view additional information about this book</A><br>";
96:    document.write(informationstring);
97:    BuyString="<A href='BookBuy.asp?BookTitle="+
       BookTitle+"&AuthName="+AuthName+"&fullprice=$"+
       fullprice+"&disprice=$"+disprice+"&available="+
       available+"&isbn="+isbn+"&subject="+subject+"'>
       Click here to buy this book</A><br><br><hr>";
98:    document.write(BuyString);
```

```
99:    }
100:   moveNode=moveNode.nextSibling;
101:   }
102: }
103: else
104: {
// We extract the contents of the ISBN textbox so that we
// can perform the search. The algorithm is the
// same as that used for the previous cases.
105:   str1=form1.isbnsearch.value;
106:   if(str1!="")
107:   {
// We will be searching for a match of the ISBN number
108:   moveNode=RootElement1.firstChild;
109:   while(moveNode!=null)
110:   {
111:   isbn=moveNode.lastChild.previousSibling.
       previousSibling.previousSibling.
       previousSibling.text;
112:   if(str1==isbn)
113:   {
114:     BookTitle=moveNode.firstChild.text;
115:     document.write("Title: "+BookTitle+"<br>");
116:     AuthName=moveNode.firstChild.nextSibling.nextSibling.
         firstChild.text;
117:     document.write("Author: "+AuthName+"<br>");
118:     subject=moveNode.firstChild.nextSibling.text;
119:     available=moveNode.lastChild.text;
120:     disprice=moveNode.lastChild.previousSibling.text;
121:     fullprice=moveNode.lastChild.previousSibling.
         previousSibling.text;
122:     pubDate=moveNode.lastChild.previousSibling.
         previousSibling.previousSibling.text;
123:     document.write("ISBN: "+isbn+"<br>");
124:     document.write("Publisher Price: "+fullprice+"<br>");
125:     document.write("Our price: "+disprice+"<br>");
126:     document.write("Availability: "+available+"<br><br>");
// In the following lines, reference is made to active
// server page (*.asp)files. An explanation of these files
// is deferred to the next lesson.
127:     informationstring="<A href=
         AdditionalInformation.asp?isbn="+isbn+">Click here
         to view additional information about this
         book</A><br>";
128:     document.write(informationstring);
129:     BuyString="<A href='BookBuy.asp?BookTitle="
         +BookTitle+"&AuthName="+AuthName+"&fullprice=$"+
         fullprice+"&disprice=$"+disprice+"&available="+
         available+"&isbn="+isbn+"&subject="+subject+"'>
         Click here to buy this book</A><br><br><hr>";
130:     document.write(BuyString);
```

21

LISTING 21.2   continued

```
131:  }
132:  moveNode=moveNode.nextSibling;
133:  }
134: }
135: else
136: {
// We extract the contents of the keyword search textbox in
// order to perform the search.
137:    str1=form1.keywordsearch.value;
138:    if(str1!="")
139:    {
// We will be performing a search based on keywords.
// The first thing we must do is create an array of the
// keywords in the input field. This array
// will be filled by the keywords that are extracted from
// the string.
140:      keyarray=new Array();
// This identifier keeps a record of the next position in
// the array to be filled.
141:      arrayindex=0;
// We extract the number of characters in the string
// containing the keywords.
142:      slength=str1.length;
// This variable is the counter we use to move through the // string.
143:      counter=0;
// This variable stores the position in the string where
// the current keyword begins.
144:      lastposition=0;
145:      while(counter<=slength)
146:      {
// If the current position contains a comma, then
// everything from lastposition up to but not including
// counter is a keyword.
147:        if(str1.charAt(counter)==",")
148:        {
// The substring method extracts all characters starting at
// lastposition up to but not including
// the character in the counter position.
149:          keyarray[arrayindex]=str1.substring(lastposition,counter);
// Increase the location of the next entry to make.
150:          arrayindex++;
// Set lastposition to the location one past the position
// of the comma.
151:          lastposition=counter+1;
// Move the current character location counter to the
// position beyond the comma.
152:          counter++;
153:        }
154:        else
```

```
155:     {
// If we have encountered the end of the string, the what
// remains is a keyword. The process of the previous
// option is repeated, except that lastposition is not
// updated.
156:       if(counter==slength)
157:       {      keyarray[arrayindex]=str1.substring(lastposition,counter);
158:        counter++;
159:        arrayindex++;
160:       }
161:       else
162:       {
// If we have not encountered a comma or the end of the
// string, we simple move to the next position in
// the string.
163:         counter++;
164:       }
165:     }
166:   }


// Since we are looking for books having these keywords in
// their <Subject> entry, we need to search through
// the file of books.
167:     moveNode=RootElement1.firstChild;
168:     while(moveNode!=null)
169:     {
// Now we must, extract the string that contains the
// keywords listed for this book.
// To do this, we build another array. The algorithm to do
// this is identical to that used to extract
// the keywords from the entered string.
170:      str2=moveNode.firstChild.nextSibling.text;
171:      bookkeywords=new Array();
172:     bookindex=0;
173:     slength=str2.length;
174:     counter=0;
175:     lastposition=0;
176:     while(counter<=slength)
177:     {
178:      if(str2.charAt(counter)==",")
179:      { bookkeywords[bookindex]=str2.substring(lastposition,
          counter);
180:       bookindex++;
181:       lastposition=counter+1;
182:       counter++;
183:      }
184:      else
185:      {
186:        if(counter==slength)
187:   { bookkeywords[bookindex]=str2.substring(lastposition,
          counter);
```

21

LISTING 21.2 continued

```
188:        counter++;
189:        bookindex++;
190:        }
191:      else
192:        {
193:        counter++;
194:        }
195:      }
196:    }

// We now have two arrays containing keywords. keyarray[]
// contains the keywords entered by the user
// and bookkeywords[] contains the keywords for this
// specific node. It is now necessary to check
// each entry of one against each entry of the other. If
// there is one single match, this book
// is selected. The boolean identifier MatchFound stores
// whether a word match was found in the search.
197:    MatchFound=false;
198:    outcounter=0;
199:    while((outcounter<arrayindex)&&(MatchFound==false))
200:      {
201:      incounter=0;
202:      while((incounter<bookindex)&&(MatchFound==false))
203:        {
204:        if(keyarray[outcounter]==bookkeywords[incounter])
205:          {
206:          MatchFound=true;
207:          }
208:        }
209:      }

// The search loop has been exited. If a match was found,
// the output is the same as that for the previous
// three search criteria.
210:    if(MatchFound==true)
211:      {
212:      BookTitle=moveNode.firstChild.text;
213:      document.write("Title: "+BookTitle+"<br>");
214:      AuthName=moveNode.firstChild.nextSibling.nextSibling.
              firstChild.text;
215:      document.write("Author: "+AuthName+"<br>");
216:      subject=moveNode.firstChild.nextSibling.text;
217:      available=moveNode.lastChild.text;
218:      disprice=moveNode. lastChild.previousSibling.text;
219:      fullprice=moveNode.lastChild.previousSibling.
              previousSibling.text;
220:      pubDate=moveNode.lastChild.previousSibling.
              previousSibling.previousSibling.text;
```

```
221:     isbn=moveNode.lastChild.previousSibling.
         previousSibling.previousSibling.
         previousSibling.text;
222:     document.write("ISBN: "+isbn+"<br>");
223:     document.write("Publisher Price: "+fullprice+"<br>");
224:     document.write("Our price: "+disprice+"<br>");
225:     document.write("Availability: "+available+"<br><br>");
226:     informationstring="<A href=AdditionalInformation.asp?
         isbn="+isbn+">Click here to view additional
         information about this book</A><br>";
227:     document.write(informationstring);
228:     BuyString="<A href='BookBuy.asp?BookTitle="
         +BookTitle+"&AuthName="+AuthName+"&fullprice=$"+
         fullprice+"&disprice=$"+disprice+"&available="+
         available+"&isbn="+isbn+"&subject="+subject+"'>
         Click here to buy this book</A><br><br><hr>";
229:     document.write(BuyString);
230:     }
231:     moveNode=moveNode.nextSibling;
232:     }
233:     }
234:   else
235:     {
// This is the message is all the textfields on the form
// are empty.
236:     alert("All fields are blank, no search performed");
237:     }
238:   }
239: }
240: }
// These links allow the user to go back to the other
// pages.
241: document.write("<A href='xmlhour20-6.html'>
     Go back to main page</A>");
242: document.write("<DIV align=center><A href='SearchData.html'>
     Go back to search page</A></DIV>");
243:}

//-->
244:</SCRIPT>
245:</head>
246:<body onLoad="StartUp()">
<!--The code of Listing 21.1 goes here. It is eliminated for brevity. -->
</body>
</html>
```

21

The section within the <body> tags is the HTML code that presents the text boxes described earlier in Listing 21.1. Once the search criteria are entered in the proper text box, clicking the button will activate the search.

When files are to be loaded, there are many reasons why the access could fail. Therefore, the purpose of the StartUp() function is to verify that the XML data file to be accessed is available and can be parsed properly.

If a failure occurs, a message is displayed allowing the user to go back to the main page of the bookstore. Note that the StartUp() function is called when the load event for the page occurs.

Once the proper data is entered into the text boxes and the button is clicked, the SearchTheData() function is called. The code is a set of nested if/else constructs in which the contents of each text box are examined to determine if they're empty. This process starts with the title text box and moves sequentially down the list until one is found that's not empty. When such a text box is found, a simple loop is performed through all the nodes of the XML file to look for a match with the search criteria. A match generates a series of output lines in which the data of the book are displayed. The same code skeleton is used to search the file for each of the different options of the search data type.

LISTING 21.3   Moving Through the List of Nodes

```
1: moveNode=RootElement1.firstChild;
2:   while(moveNode!=null)
3:   {
4:    // Search and display code here
5:     moveNode=moveNode. nextSibling;
6:   }
```

The code to display the relevant data in the node is the same for each of the different search criteria. The data for the <Title>, <AuthorName>, <Subject>, <ISBN>, <GivenPrice>, <DiscountPrice>, and <Availability> fields are extracted and written to the page after a suitable message is attached. This is done in lines 210 through 230.

The informationstring and BuyString strings are used to call Active Server Page files. This is a topic that will be further explained in the next hour.

The code is significantly more complex when the search criteria is a list of keywords. After you extract the contents of the designated text box, it must be split into the distinct keywords. Since the comma is the separator, start at a position that's stored in lastposition and move until either a comma or the end of the string is encountered. All the characters from lastposition up to the current position are then copied as a complete string into an array. This is done in lines 140 through 166.

The preceding section of code extracts the keywords from the string input into a text box reserved for keyword entry. You also need to parse the keywords out of the <Subject> field, and the same algorithm is used to do that.

Once the keywords are parsed out into their respective arrays, a simple set of two nested loops is used to determine if there's a word that's common to the two arrays. The boolean identifier MatchFound stores whether a match has been found. If it's true when the loop structures are exited, the book data is output. This is done in lines 197 through 209.

When the search is done for "Teach Yourself XML in 24 Hours" in the title text box, the result is illustrated in Figure 21.2.

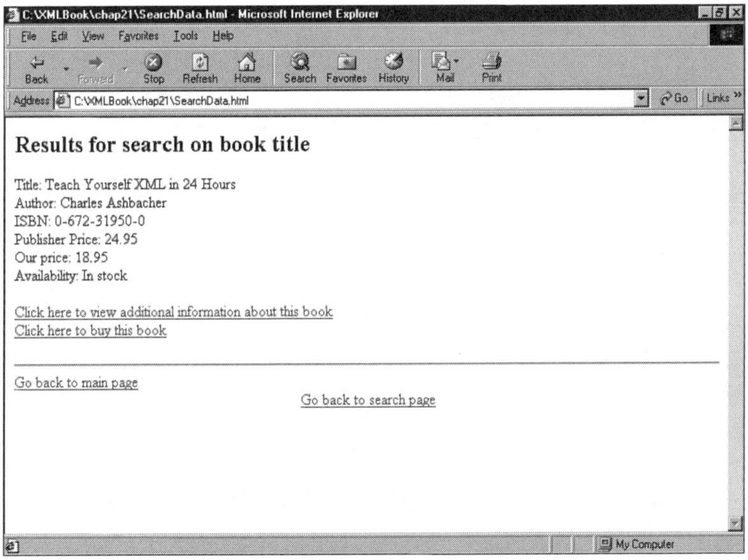

FIGURE 21.2

Search results for the input string "Teach Yourself XML in 24 Hours".

The result when "computers" is entered into the keywords text box is illustrated in Figure 21.3.

21

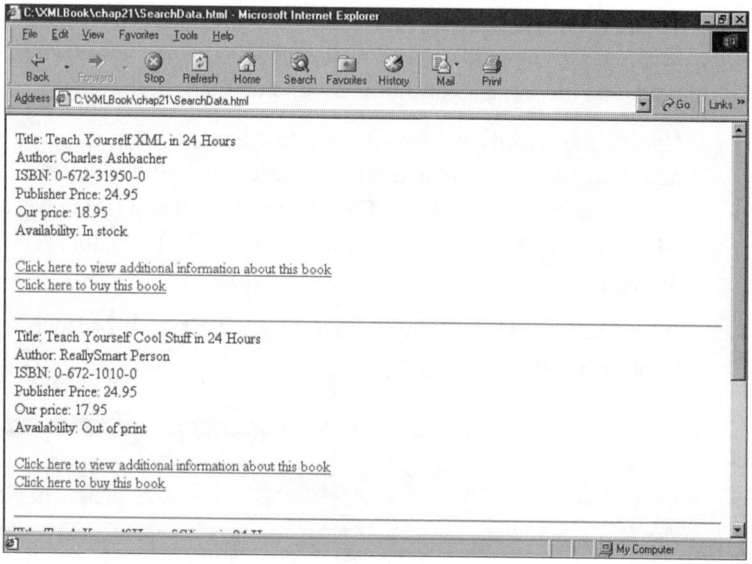

FIGURE 21.3

The result when a search is done for the keyword "computers".

Displaying the List of Purchased Books

For the purposes of illustration, assume that Listing 21.4 contains the data for the books that you purchased during this session.

LISTING 21.4   XML File of Books Purchased During This Session

```
 1: <?xml version="1.0"?>
 2: <!-- This file is a demonstration of the purchased books
 3:      database. -->
 4: <BooksBought xmlns:mm="x-schema:xmlhour20-5.xml">
 5: <mm:PurchasedBook>
 6: <mm:Title>Teach Yourself XML in 24 Hours</mm:Title>
 7: <mm:AuthorName>Charles Ashbacher</mm:AuthorName>
 8: <mm:GivenPrice>24.95</mm:GivenPrice>
 9: <mm:DiscountPrice>18.95</mm:DiscountPrice>
10: <mm:Availability>In stock</mm:Availability>
11: <mm:ISBN>0-672-31950-0</mm:ISBN>
12: <mm:Subject>computers,XML</mm:Subject>
13: </mm:PurchasedBook>
14: <mm:PurchasedBook >
15: <mm:Title>Teach Yourself Cool Stuff in 24 Hours</mm:Title>
16: <mm:AuthorName>ReallySmart Person</mm:AuthorName>
17: <mm:GivenPrice>24.95</mm:GivenPrice>
18: <mm:DiscountPrice>17.95</mm:DiscountPrice>
19: <mm:Availability>Out of print</mm:Availability>
```

```
20: <mm:ISBN>0-672-1010-0</mm:ISBN>
21: <mm:Subject>computers</mm:Subject>
22: </mm:PurchasedBook>
23: <mm:PurchasedBook>
24: <mm:Title>Teach Yourself Uses of Silicon in 24 Hours</mm:Title>
25: <mm:AuthorName>Missy Fixit</mm:AuthorName>
26: <mm:GivenPrice>26.95</mm:GivenPrice>
27: <mm:DiscountPrice>26.95</mm:DiscountPrice>
28: <mm:Availability>Out of stock</mm:Availability>
29: <mm:ISBN>0-578-31950-0</mm:ISBN>
30: <mm:Subject>computers,silicon</mm:Subject>
31: </mm: PurchasedBook>
32: </BooksBought>
```

The code to read and display this data is straightforward, as shown in Listing 21.5.

LISTING 21.5 The HTML File That Will Display the Contents of the File of
Purchased Books

```
 1: <html>
 2: <!-- This code demonstrates how to read and display the
 3:      data of the books that were purchased during
 4:      this session. The name of the file is Yourbooks.html. -->
 5: <head>
 6: <title>This page is used to search for the books of interest</title>
 7: <SCRIPT LANGUAGE="JScript">
 8: <!--
 9:  var xmlDoc1=new ActiveXObject("microsoft.xmldom");
10:  var RootElement1;
11:  xmlDoc1.load("xmlhour20-7.xml");
12:
13: /* The purpose of this function is to filter out the
14:    situation where the data loading fails for whatever
15:    reason. If the XML data file does not conform to the
16:    schema or there is any other problem, RootElement1 will
17:    have the value of null. */
18:
19:  function StartUp()
20:  {
21:    RootElement1=xmlDoc1.documentElement;
22:    if(RootElement1==null)
23:    {
24:      document.write("<h2 align=center>Data load unsuccessful,
                terminating the search process</h2>");
25:      document.write("<A href='xmlhour20-6.html'>Go back to
                main page</A><BR>");
26:    }
27:    else
28:    {
```

21

LISTING 21.5　continued

```
29:     SearchTheData();
30:    }
31: }
32:
33:   function SearchTheData()
34:   {
35:   document.write("<h2>These are the books that you have
       purchased in this session</h2>");
36:   moveNode=RootElement1.firstChild;
37:   while(moveNode!=null)
38:   {
39:    title=moveNode.firstChild.text;
40:    document.write("Title: "+title+"<br>");
41:    AuthName=moveNode.firstChild.nextSibling.text;
42:    document.write("Author: "+AuthName+"<br>");
43:    fullprice=moveNode.firstChild.nextSibling.
       nextSibling.text;
44:    document.write("Publisher Price: "+fullprice+"<br>");
45:    disprice=moveNode.firstChild.nextSibling.nextSibling.
       nextSibling.text;
46:    document.write("Our price: "+disprice+"<br>");
47:    available=moveNode.firstChild.nextSibling.nextSibling.
       nextSibling.nextSibling.text;
48:    document.write("Availability: "+available+"<br>");
49:    isbn=moveNode.lastChild.previousSibling.text;
50:    document.write("ISBN: "+isbn+"<br>");
51:    subject=moveNode.lastChild.text;
52:    document.write("Subject: "+subject+"<br><br><hr>");
53:    moveNode=moveNode.nextSibling;
54:   }
55:   document.write("<A href='xmlhour20-6.html'>
      Go back to main page</A>");
56: document.write("<DIV align=center>
      <A href='SearchData.html'>
      Go back to search page</A></DIV>");
57: }
58: //-->
59: </SCRIPT>
60: </head>
61: <body onLoad="StartUp()">
62: </body>
63: </html>
```

This code is called by clicking on the View Your Purchases link on the introductory page of your online bookstore.

The code to display the data for the books and the purchased books works well, but in the real world it wouldn't be executed on the client side of the transaction. The databases for books and additional information are located on the server, so the searches would be performed there. This takes you into the realm of Active Server Pages (ASPs), which are HTML files that are created dynamically on the server based on the information that was received from the client.

Summary

This hour presented code for searching through a database of books is presented. The same code is used repeatedly, which makes the entire program easier to understand. You also looked at the code for reading the file that stores the purchases made during this session.

Q&A

Q Why is it more efficient to perform database queries on the server than on the client?

A In all but the most trivial of cases, the database of books will be very large. To manipulate the database, first you would have to download it to the client. This would take a great deal of time and bandwidth. It would also create multiple copies of the database outside the realm of the online company.

Q Why does it make sense to store the file of purchased books on the server?

A Making the data available will allow the seller to mine the data for any significant information regarding purchasing habits.

Workshop

Quiz

1. Why would you be reluctant to add a section called <Shipping and Handling> to the definition of a <Book> object?

   a. I wouldn't be reluctant at all; it's a natural part of an online order.

   b. Handling fees tend to be the same price for all items, so I would be more willing to include a shipping field.

   c. Shipping costs tend to vary by weight, and nearly all books are in the same weight range. Therefore, the shipping and handling costs tend to be the same for each book, so it can be computed on a per-item basis.

21

2. Where would you place a page count field for the books in the online database?

   a. I wouldn't include such a field in my database.

   b. In the main database for the books.

   c. In the database of additional information.

   d. In both the main and additional information databases.

Answers

1. c (In general, it's best to compute S & H costs rather than store them)

2. c (Many people aren't interested in the page count)

Exercises

1. Add a page number field to this project. Add the additional code so that it's included in the file of books purchased.

2. Create an XSL file that will read the data from the main Books database.

3. Create an XSL file that will read the data from the additional information database.

Hour **22**

Processing and Displaying Purchases in an Online Bookstore

The previous hour presented code that reads a database of available books and displays a list of purchased books. This code assumes that the data files are in the same directory as the HTML file that's being executed. In the real world of Web commerce, however, computers create and exchange files in what's known as the *client-server model*. The XML data files reside on the server side, which means that the code to search them also has to run on the server.

In this hour, you'll learn the following:

- The basics of the client-server model of data transfer on the World Wide Web
- How to send data from the client to the server using the Querystring environment variable
- How to obtain and use the Microsoft Personal Web Server
- How to work with text files at the level of the server

The Client-Server Model of the World Wide Web

When you're running a browser with an Internet connection and you enter a URL into the destination text box, you're really not visiting anything. The URL is a request to the Web directory computers for the location of a file. If that location has a valid address, the computer containing the file is contacted with a request for a file. That file is then sent over the Internet to your machine, where it's displayed. In this model, your machine is acting as the client and the computer that sends the file is the server.

> When two computers are communicating, the one that requests information is known as the *client*, and the one that accepts the request and returns the information is known as the *server*.

If you're running an online bookstore, the data files of the available books and additional information are available on your server. Because these files are large, it makes no sense to send them to the client before they're searched. Therefore, the code to perform the searches is placed on the server and is run when the HTML file executing on the client passes the appropriate message to the server.

A Microsoft Active Server Page (ASP) is a file that will dynamically create an HTML file on the server when a message is received from the client. That file is then sent back to the client for display. ASP files have the general form of *.asp.

The Querystring Environment Variable

When a process is running on the client machine, there's an environment variable known as Querystring that's part of the normal communication between the client and server machines. It contains a character string and can be assigned explicit values in your code.

Although it's based on named fields and the values assigned to those fields, it's a very dynamic entity because the names of the fields can be altered at any time. Consider the lines of code that appeared in the Searchdata.html file in the previous hour, as shown in Listing 22.1.

LISTING 22.1 Explicitly Building the Querystring Parameter

```
1: informationstring="<A href='AdditionalInformation.asp?
   isbn="+isbn+"'>Click here to view additional
   information about this book</A><br>";
2: document.write(informationstring);
3: BuyString="<A href='BookBuy.asp?
   BookTitle="+BookTitle+"&AuthName="+AuthName+"&
   fullprice=$"+fullprice+"&disprice=$"+disprice+
   "&available="+available+"&isbn="+isbn+
   "&subject="+subject+"'>Click here to buy this
4: book</A><br><br><hr>";
5: document.write(BuyString);
```

The purpose of this code is to create two lines of HTML code and then insert them into the file to be displayed. For the purposes of demonstration, assume that the current value of the isbn identifier is 0-672-31950-0. The first line of Listing 22.1 will create the following HTML code segment:

```
<A href='AdditionalInformation.asp?isbn=
0-672-31950-0'>Click here to view additional
information about this book</A><br>;
```

You're probably familiar with the standard notation for the anchor of a hyperlink. Clicking on the text between the opening and closing tags will execute the actions of the hypertext reference.

In this case, that reference is to an ASP file. The link presupposes that AdditionalInformation.asp exists on the server. If it does, it will be executed on the server. If not, the standard "file not found" error will be generated.

The section after the question mark is both the definition of a field name in the Querystring variable and an assignment of a value. The rules for the field names are essentially those of variables in general. If more than one field is to be defined and assigned, they're separated by an ampersand (&). For example, if the following variables have the current values

```
BookTitle = 'Teach Yourself XML in 24 Hours'
AuthName = 'Charles Ashbacher'
fullprice='24.95'
disprice = '18.95'
available = 'In stock'
isbn = '0-672-31950-0'
subject = 'computers,XML'
```

then this section of code

```
BuyString="<A href='BookBuy.asp?
BookTitle="+BookTitle+"&AuthName="+AuthName+"&
fullprice=$"+fullprice+"&disprice=$"+disprice+
"&available="+available+"&isbn="+isbn+
"&subject="+subject+"'>Click here to buy this
book</A><br><br><hr>";
```

will generate this HTML segment:

```
<A href='BookBuy.asp?BookTitle=Teach Yourself XML in 24 Hours&
AuthName=Charles Ashbacher&fullprice=&24.95&
disprice=$18.95&available=In Stock&isbn= 0-672-31950-0&
subject=computers,XML'>Click here to buy this book</A>
```

The `Querystring` environment variable will have five fields and will be passed along to the server, along with the request to run the BookBuy.asp file.

> The current values of the variables could have been entered by the user in several ways. Therefore, you have a mechanism for accepting data from the user and passing it on to the server.

Using the Querystring Environment Variable on the Server

Now that you've specified an ASP file to run and assigned values to the `Querystring` variable, the next step is to demonstrate an ASP file and how to extract the data from the `Querystring` variable. It's possible to use JavaScript, JScript, and VBScript in ASP files, but you'll use JScript. The reason is rather simple. JScript provides simple file functionality and compatibility with the management tools being used, making the process easier to demonstrate.

Given the assignments in the previous example, use the `Request.QueryString(FieldName)` method to extract the data from a field of the Querystring environment variable at the level of the server. It will examine the current value of QueryString and look for a field with the name matching 'FieldName'. If the field exists in the current value of Querystring, the current value assigned to that field is returned. For example, given the assignments of the previous example, consider if Listing 22.2 is executed in the ASP file.

LISTING 22.2 Extracting the Values of the Passed QueryString Parameter's Fields

```
1: Title=Request.QueryString("BookTitle");
2: Author=Request.QueryString("AuthName");
3: fprice=Request.QueryString("fullprice");
4: dprice=Request.QueryString("disprice");
5: avail=Request.QueryString("available");
6: ISBN=Request.QueryString("isbn");
7: subjects=Request.QueryString("subject");
```

The variables in the ASP file will have the following values:

```
Title = 'Teach Yourself XML in 24 Hours'
Author = 'Charles Ashbacher'
fprice = '$24.95'
dprice = '$18,95'
avail = 'In stock'
ISBN = '0-672-31950-0'
subject = 'computers,XML'
```

These values can then be used to create HTML files.

For example, the HTML file in Listing 22.3 is to be run on the client machine.

LISTING 22.3 Using Clickable Links to Pass Data to the Appropriate asp File

```
 1: <HTML>
 2: <!-- This file is a simple test of passing data to the server via
 3: a hypertext link. The name of the file is asplinks.html. -->
 4: <HEAD>
 5: <TITLE>This is a simple test of passing data to the server</TITLE>
 6: </HEAD>
 7: <BODY>
 8: <A href="AdditionalInformation.asp?
    isbn=0-672-31950-0">Click here to view additional
    information about this book</A><br>
 9: <A href="BookBuy.asp?BookTitle=Teach Yourself XML in 24
    Hours&AuthName=Charles Ashbacher&fullprice=$24.95&
    disprice=$18.95&available=In stock&
    isbn=0-672-31950-0&subject=computers,XML">
    Click here to buy this book</A><br>
10: </BODY>
11: </HTML>
```

When this is run in IE, it looks like Figure 22.1.

FIGURE 22.1

The hyperlinks to the asp files.

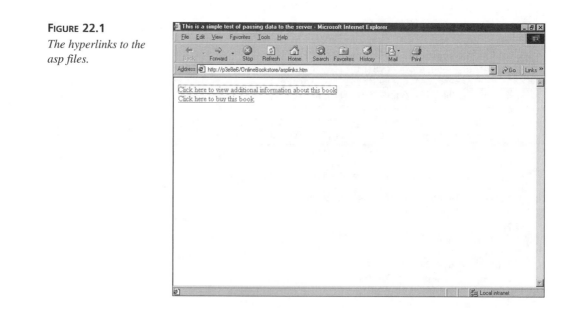

One of the ASP files that this HTML file refers to is AdditionalInformation.asp. This file simply captures the fields of the QueryString and uses them for output.

The file shown in Listing 22.4 is to be placed on the server. The name of the file is AdditionalInformation.asp.

LISTING 22.4   The asp File That Receives the Search for Additional Information

```
 1: <HTML>
 2: <!-- This is a simple ASP file used to demonstrate the
 3: transfer of data from the client to the server. The
 4: name of the file is AdditionalInformation.asp. -->
 5: <HEAD>
 6: <Title>This is a simple example of an ASP file</Title>
 7: </HEAD>
 8: <BODY>
 9: <Script Language=JScript Runat=server>
10: dim str1
11: Response.Write("<H2>This is a file that could search the
    XML database for a specific book</H2>")
12: str1=Request.QueryString("isbn")
13: Response.Write("Now that we know the ISBN to search for
    is "&str1&"<BR>")
14: </Script>
15: </BODY>
16:  </HTML>
```

Note that you're using JScript rather than JavaScript. Also note that you're informing the system that the scripting code is to be run at the server level rather than the client level.

Clicking the Additional Information link executes this ASP file. The result is demonstrated in Figure 22.2.

FIGURE 22.2

The file generated by AdditionalInformation. asp.

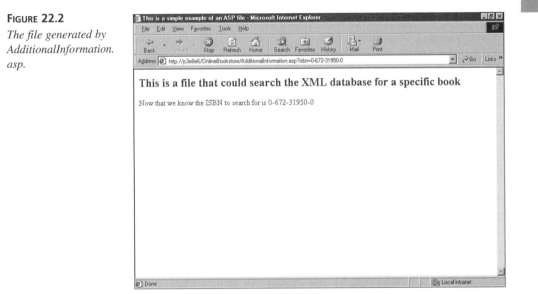

The key point is that the information passed from the client file is now available at the server level to conduct a search on the databases available there. This would include XML databases, of course.

When you're using HTML forms to capture data from the user, there are two possible assignments to the METHOD option:

`<FORM NAME=FORM1 METHOD=GET>`

or

`<FORM NAME=FORM1 METHOD=POST>`

This method corresponds to the GET method, which uses `QueryString` to pass the data.

To extract the data when the POST method is used, the function is `Request.FORM(FieldName)` rather than `Request.QueryString(FieldName)`. This is used for the data extraction only, and everything else is the same.

Microsoft Personal Web Server (PWS)

The client-server model of the World Wide Web generally requires two distinct machines, each of which assumes one of the roles. However, there's an inexpensive way to fully test the combination of HTML client and ASP files locally. Microsoft has developed a program called Personal Web Server or Personal Web Manager. This program will mimic the full client-server model on your computer without the need for an Internet connection.

Personal Web Server is available for free download from the Microsoft Web site at http://www.microsoft.com/windows/ie/pws/. PWS was used to test the combinations of HTML and ASP files used in this hour.

Microsoft Visual InterDev is part of the Microsoft Visual Studio package and is used to quickly build Web projects. It's also possible to link InterDev in PWS so that it's the server used. Visual InterDev contains features that allow for the easy addition of ASP files, automatically creating all necessary references between the files. Unfortunately, it's not free.

Creating Text Files on the Server

You certainly have all of the mechanisms you need to open and access the data from XML files. The final piece of your construction is the creation of new XML files and entries. Before you do this on the client, recall that XML files are nothing more than text files that conform to certain specific rules.

The premise that you'll use to create your new XML entries is the second link displayed by your file asplinks.html. The link is Click here to buy this book. This link is clicked when the information about a book is being displayed and the user wants to buy the book. Recall that listing20-5.xml contains the schema that defines the form that these entries are to take.

In this case, you're going to use JScript again to create a text file with an XML entry constructed by using the information passed to the ASP file.

The file shown in Listing 22.5 is to be placed on the server under the name BookBuy.asp. Note that it's the file called when the Click here to buy this book link is clicked.

LISTING 22.5   Creating a Node Representing a Purchased Book and Adding It to the File

```
 1: <HTML>
 2: <!-- This file is a demonstration of how to create a textfile
 3:     using the Stream ActiveX objects. The name of the file is
 4:     BookBuy.asp. -->
 5: <HEAD>
 6: <TITLE>Generating and saving an XML entry</TITLE>
 7: </HEAD>
 8: <BODY>
 9: <Script Language=JScript Runat=Server>
10: var ForAppending=8;
11: FileStreamObject=new ActiveXObject("Scripting.FileSystemObject");
12: WriteStream=FileStreamObject.OpenTextFile("WhatIBought.xml",ForAppending);
13: Title=Request.QueryString("BookTitle");
14: Author=Request.QueryString("AuthName");
15: fprice=Request.QueryString("fullprice");
16: dprice=Request.QueryString("disprice");
17: avail=Request.QueryString("available");
18: ISBN=Request.QueryString("isbn");
19: subjects=Request.QueryString("subject");
20: FileEntry="<mm:PurchasedBook>\n"+"<mm:Title>"+Title+"</mm:Title>\n";
21: FileEntry=FileEntry+"<mm:AuthorName>"+Author+"</mm:AuthorName>\n";
22: FileEntry=FileEntry+"<mm:GivenPrice>"+fprice+"</mm:GivenPrice>\n";
23: FileEntry=FileEntry+"<mm:DiscountPrice>"+dprice+"</mm:DiscountPrice>\n";
24: FileEntry=FileEntry+"<mm:Availability>"+avail+"</mm:Availability>\n";
25: FileEntry=FileEntry+"<mm:ISBN>"+ISBN+"</mm:ISBN>\n";
26: FileEntry=FileEntry+"<mm:Subject>"+subjects+"</mm:Subject>\n"+"
        </mm:PurchasedBook>";
27: WriteStream.Writeline(FileEntry);
28: WriteStream.Close();
29: </Script>
30: </BODY>
31: </HTML>
```

There are many well-known features of this file, but there are some new ones that require explanation. The following line is similar to the line you used to create an ActiveX XML object:

```
FileStreamObject=new ActiveXObject("Scripting.FileSystemObject");
```

What you're creating here is an object that allows for the creation of files from a segment of scripting code. As was the case with the XML DOM object, at this point only the creation has occurred. There's no file associated with the object yet. That's done in the line where the target text file is created:

```
WriteStream=FileStreamObject.OpenTextFile("WhatIBought.xml",
ForAppending);
```

The name of the file is "WhatIBought.xml", and a value of ForAppending for the second argument causes the system to append the data to an existing file.

The next set of lines extracts the data, and then there are the lines that build the string that will be written to the file. Note that you're surrounding the data with the tags matching those of the data schema.

The final two lines of significance write the string to the file and close the file:

```
WriteStream.Writeline(FileEntry)
WriteStream.Close();
```

When the appropriate link is clicked and this file is run, the WhatIBought.xml text file is opened. The entry written to the file is shown in Listing 22.6.

LISTING 22.6   The Node Written to the File of Purchased Books

```
1: <mm:PurchasedBook>
2: <mm:Title>Teach Yourself XML in 24 Hours</mm:Title>
3: <mm:AuthorName>Charles Ashbacher</mm:AuthorName>
4: <mm:GivenPrice>$24.95</mm:GivenPrice>
5: <mm:DiscountPrice>$18.95</mm:DiscountPrice>
6: <mm:Availability>In stock</mm:Availability>
7: <mm:ISBN>0-672-31950-0</mm:ISBN>
8: <mm:Subject>computers,XML</mm:Subject>
9: </mm: PurchasedBook>
```

Saving these entries to the XML file allows them to be read and processed by any of the mechanisms covered in this hour.

Summary

This hour demonstrated the remaining features needed to construct a simple yet complete online bookstore. Such a bookstore requires Active Server Page files, and you saw how some simple ones interacted with the HTML files residing on the server. Passing data to the ASP file via the Querystring environment variable was demonstrated as well. Finally, you saw the simple objects used to create text files that can be saved as XML files.

Q&A

Q **Why is it possible for Active Server Page files to create and modify files, but it's not allowed in HTML files on the client?**

A The ASP file is originated on the server and creates the files in storage managed by the server. Since the server manager is in control of everything, it's equivalent to a standalone program running on a computer. An HTML file is downloaded from a server to the client and runs on the client machine. This is considered to be unsafe and is prevented by the security features of the browsers. (At least most of the time.)

Q **Why is it possible for the programmer to define any number of fields in the Querystring environment variable?**

A The Querystring variable is a simple string. When field names and data are assigned, it's simply characters being placed in a string. The Request function parses through the string, searching for the name of the field.

Q **Why isn't it necessary to use XML functionality to add entries to an XML file?**

A An XML file is first and foremost a text file. Therefore, any functionality that modifies text files can be used to create and modify XML files.

Workshop

Quiz

1. Which of the following scripting languages can be used in ASP files?

   a. VBScript.

   b. JavaScript.

   c. Jscript.

   d. All of the above.

2. Active Server Pages are run at what location(s) on the World Wide Web?

   a. Client.

   b. Server.

   c. Both client and server.

3. When two computers are communicating via the Web, it's possible for them to dynamically reverse the client and server roles.

   a. True.

   b. False.

Answers

1. d
2. b
3. a

Exercises

1. If you have Visual InterDev and the Personal Web Server, use them to build the complete online bookstore.

2. Go back to "asplinks.html" and add another link to a file called "NewData.asp". Write the code so that this link will pass the entire collection of <Publisher> data to the server. Write the NewData file so that it captures the data and echoes it to the screen.

HOUR 23

Links in XML: XLink and XPointer

The hyperlink was one of the driving forces behind the development of HTML. It's hard to conceive of the World Wide Web being popular, or even existing, without hyperlinks. A hyperlink can point to another location in the current document, or it can access a document on a local drive or somewhere on the Web. The XML XLink mechanism is an extension of this, and it's based on the notion of linking to one or more resources. This is a significant difference from the HTML link, which links to only one location.

The pointer or memory reference is a fundamental concept of programming and is directly supported in many programming languages. It's a simple concept that's easy to use and even easier to misuse. So easy, in fact, that the direct use of pointers has been eliminated in some more recent languages. Java is the foremost language in which pointers are not supported.

The XML XPointer provides a way to access the internal structure of an XML document, and the terminology is similar to that used for traditional pointers.

In this hour, you'll learn the following:

- The various types of links available in HTML
- How to construct XLink connections to other locations
- The XLink global attributes
- How to write DTDs for XLink objects
- How to define XPointers

Links in HTML

The basic links in HTML are created using the anchor tag, <A>, and can be linked either to other files or to another location in the current document. To link to another document, place the HREF option inside the opening tag. Clicking on the item placed between the opening and closing anchor tags will cause the link to jump to the location assigned to the HREF option. For example, the following is a simple link to another file in HTML:

```
<A HREF="http://www.anotherplace.com">Click to go to another place</A>
```

If no internal location is specified, as is the case here, it jumps to the start of the linked file. It's possible to create a jump to a location inside the file by creating a position marker and then using that marker to qualify the jump.

Create the file shown in Listing 23.1 and save it as listing23-1.html.

LISTING 23.1   Defining Positions Inside a File Where the Link Connection Will Be Made

```
 1: <html>
 2: <!-- This file contains the positions that are the targets
 3:      of the jumps from another file. -->
 4: <head>
 5: <title>Demonstration of a link to an internal location</title>
 6: </head>
 7: <body>
 8: <A Name="StartPosition"></A>
 9: <h1>This is the start of the file</h1>
10: <br><br><br><br><br><br><br><br><br><br><br><br><br><br>
11: <br><br><br><br><br><br><br><br><br><br><br><br><br><br>
12: <br><br><br><br><br><br><br><br><br><br><br><br><br><br>
13: <br><br>
14: <A Name="MiddlePosition"></A>
15: <h1>This is the middle of the file</h1>
16: <br><br><br><br><br><br><br><br><br><br><br><br><br><br>
17: <br><br><br><br><br><br><br><br><br><br><br><br><br><br>
18: <br><br><br><br><br><br><br><br><br><br><br><br><br><br>
```

```
19: <br><br>
20: <A Name="EndPosition"></A>
21: <h1>This is the end of the file</h1>
22: </body>
23: </html>
```

The series of line breaks serves no purpose other than to give the appearance that the file is large when viewed in IE. In this case, you're defining three positions in the file: start, middle, and end. Those positions are the locations that you'll jump to when the links in the following file are clicked. Listing 23.2 contains links to the marked interior positions of Listing 23.1.

LISTING 23.2   The File That Contains the Links into listing23-1.html

```
 1: <html>
 2: <!-- This file contains three links to positions in the
 3:      file listing23-1.html. -->
 4: <head>
 5: <title>Demonstration of a jump to an internal link</title>
 6: </head>
 7: <body>
 8: <A href="listing23-1.html#StartPosition">Go to the start</A><br><br>
 9: <A href="listing23-1.html#MiddlePosition">Go to the middle</A><br><br>
10: <A href="listing23-1.html#EndPosition">Go to the end</A>
11: </body>
12: </html>
```

When you run the file in IE and click on each of the links, you'll jump to different positions in listing23-1.html.

There's another type of link that can be used in HTML, and it was demonstrated in Hour 11. In that hour, you created a Cascading Style Sheet (CSS) file and then imported it into an HTML file. The program you used to do that is shown in Listing 23.3.

LISTING 23.3   A Link That's a Connection to a File

```
 1: <html>
 2: <!-- In this file, we define four different interpretations
 3:      of the SPAN tag using style sheets in an external
 4:      file. That file is then imported into this one.
-->
 5: <head>
 6: <title>First Style Sheet Example</title>
 7: <LINK HREF="xmlhour11-2.css"
    REL=STYLESHEET TYPE="text/css">
```

LISTING 23.3 continued

```
 8: </head>
 9: <body bgcolor="ffffff">
10: <SPAN CLASS="red">
11: This text is rendered using the SPAN.red rule</SPAN><br>
12: <SPAN CLASS="purple">
13: This text is rendered using the SPAN.purple rule</SPAN><br>
14: <SPAN CLASS="blue">
15: This text is rendered using the SPAN.blue rule</SPAN><br>
16: <SPAN CLASS="silver">
17: This text is rendered using the SPAN.silver rule</SPAN>
17: </body>
19: </html>
```

In this case, the link to the other file is explicit, being defined by the <LINK> tag. However, this operation is the importation of the code in another file into that position, not a jump to another location.

Attribute Options in the <A> Tag

If you're like me, coding is a process that you should make as simple as possible, but no simpler. This is a paraphrasing of a quote from Albert Einstein, and like so much of what he said, a great deal of wisdom is packed into just a few words. However, reducing things to their simplest form also tends to create a bit of tunnel vision and needs to be reexamined on occasion.

In this case, you're going to delve deeper into the <A> (anchor) tag. In normal usage, we tend to forget that there are many attribute options to this tag. A complete list of those options appears in Table 23.1.

TABLE 23.1 The List of Attributes of the Anchor Tag

Attribute	Meaning
ACCESSKEY	In the Windows environment, press the letter assigned to it and the Alt key to trigger the link.
CHARSET	Character encoding of the material at the other end of the link.
COORDS	When the link contains an image, this attribute defines the coordinates of an area map.
DATAFLD	Maps the content of an entry in a remote data source to this object.
DATASCRC	Maps the ODBC data source to this object.
HREF	The URI destination of the link.
HREFLANG	The language code of the content at the other end of the link.
ID	An identifier assigned to the document.

Attribute	Meaning
METHODS	An attribute describing the functionality of the link's destination.
NAME	Used to denote a marker position in the file.
REL	Describes the relationship between the current location and the one the link will send you to.
REV	Defines a reverse link relationship.
SHAPE	Defines the shape of a server-side image map. Used with the COORDS attribute.
TABINDEX	The number of this element in the tabbing order of the objects.
TARGET	Used to specify the location of the document load when it's not to be the default window.
TYPE	An advisory concerning the content type of the resource.
URN	The uniform resource name of the resource assigned to the HREF attribute.

This book won't demonstrate these attributes in action. The purpose of Table 23.1 is to show that these attributes are available and prepare you for the similar list of items that can be used with the XLink.

XLink Construction

Given that XLink is a part of XML, it should come as no surprise that it's possible to write your own XLink tag names. To create such a link, start with the following outline:

```
<MyXLinkElement>
  . Body of the element
 </MyXLinkElement>
```

At the time this material is being written, XLink and XPointer are still in the draft stage and neither one is implemented in IE 5. Therefore, the examples presented here demonstrate the basic syntax and organization of XLinks and XPointers, but they cannot be run. To see the current XLink specification, go to http://www.w3.org/TR/xlink. To see the current XPointer specification, go to http://www.w3.org/TR/1998/WD-xptr-19980303.

There's an XLink namespace available at the URI http://www.w3.org/1999/xlink, and the declaration of this namespace is a required attribute. Therefore, the first thing that you'll add to your declaration is the specification of the namespace. The linking of the namespace is done as an option in the opening tag of the element.

The following will link the XLink namespace to the link that you're creating:

```
<MyXLinkElement
xmlns:xlink="http://www.w3.org/1999/xlink">

  .Body of the element
 </MyXLinkElement>
```

It's also possible to define a link that's part of a local, non-XLink namespace. The syntax to do this is the same as what you've already seen:

```
Namespace:ElementTag
```

If the link that you're defining is to be an element of the MyLinks namespace, the notation would be as follows:

```
<MyLinks:MyXLinkElement
 xmlns:xlink="http://www.w3.org/1999/xlink">

  .Body of the element
 </MyLinks:MyXLinkElement>
```

XLink Global Attributes

The XLink namespace provides a series of global attributes that can be used independently of the local namespace. However, these attributes need to be prefixed by the appropriate namespace qualifier.

Suppose that the content of the MyLinks namespace is found in the file "MyLinksDefs.com" and the data that you want to access is found in "MyData.xml". Furthermore, suppose that the definition of the MyLinks namespace contains an entry "DateLastEdit", which of course stores the day that some item was last edited. The following would be the proper namespace-qualified way to declare your growing link:

```
<MyLinks:MyXLinkElement
 xmlns:xlink="http://www.w3.org/1999/xlink">
 xmlns:MyLinks="http://MyLinkDefs.com"
 xlink:href="MyData.xml"
  MyLinks:DateLastEdit="05-01-2000"

  .Body of the element
 </MyLinks:MyXLinkElement>
```

The href entry is one of the global attributes provided by the xlink namespace and is the location of the resource. There are several other global attributes, and their names and meanings are summarized in the following sections.

type

This attribute is used to specify the type of the element and must be a value from this list: {simple, extended, locator, arc, resource, title, none}. For further information about this attribute, consult the XLink URL.

actuate

This attribute specifies how the link should be traversed, and the two possible values are {auto, user}. If the value is auto, the link should be automatically followed when the link is processed. If the value is user, some actual event (such as a mouse-click) is needed to execute it.

23

show

This attribute is used to specify how the resource is to be displayed. The values that it can be assigned are {new, replace, embed, undefined}. The following are the explanations of these values and are taken directly from the XLink document found at the Web site:

new	An application traversing to the ending resource should load it for display in a new window, frame, pane, or other relevant display context.
replace	An application traversing to the ending resource should load the resource for display in the same window, frame, pane, or other relevant display context in which the starting resource was loaded for display.
embed	An application traversing to the ending resource should load it for display in place of the starting resource.
undefined	The behavior of an application traversing to the ending resource is unconstrained by this specification. The application may use other cues, such as other markup options present in the link or environment settings, to determine the appropriate behavior.

href

This attribute provides the data used by the XLink application to find the remote resource. The resource must be in the form of a URI, although that restriction isn't qualified before processing.

role

This attribute is used to describe the function of the remote resource in a machine-readable fashion. If the element is an extended type, it serves as a resource category label for the rules of traversal.

title

This attribute is used to describe the function of the remote resource in a human-readable fashion. If used, it should be a string that describes the resource.

from and to

These attributes do exactly what their names imply. Used together, they make a two-way connection between resources.

Examples of XLink Global Attributes

One of the major advantages of the XLink syntax over that of basic HTML is the ability to define multiple links. This first example refers back to a data format that you used earlier. The <Catalog> database that you used in previous hours contained two parts, the <Author> and <Publisher> descriptions. In Listing 23.4, you link to the Catalog namespace in the outer tags and then to the author and publisher using internal <loc> or location tags.

LISTING 23.4   Creating a Multiple Link to the Interior of a File

```
1: <Multiplelink
2:   xmlns:Catalog="http://www.somewhere.net">
3:   <loc
4:     xlink:role="Catalog:author"
5:     xlink:href="http://www.somewhere.net/aut" />
6:   <loc
7:     xlink:role="Catalog:publisher"
8:     xlink:href="http://www.somewhere.net/pub" />
9: </Multiplelink>
```

For the next example, consider the <BookSeller> data type that you used in previous hours. A particular bookseller may want to maintain a database of the books and rankings that it assigns to an author. Therefore, when it receives a notice about a new book being published, deciding how many copies to order and how much shelf space to allocate is easy. As was the case before, <Author>, <Editor>, <Publisher>, and <Book> are complex data types. Instances of each are stored in distinct XML files.

LISTING 23.5   Defining a Set of Multiple XLinks Between XML Files

```
1: <BookSeller
2:   xlink:title="Name of the bookseller">
3:   xlink:type="simple"
4:   xlink:show="new"
5: <!-- This would be a series of links between XML files. -->
```

```
 6:    <go xlink:from="AuthorRank" xlink:to="RankDatabase" />
 7:    <go xlink:from="Author" xlink:to="Book" />
 8:    <go xlink:from="Author" xlink:to="Editor" />
 9:    <go xlink:from="Author" xlink:to="Publisher" />
10: <!-- The following are all links to the appropriate XML
11:      file. -->
12:    <Author xlink:href="Authordata.xml" />
13:    <Book xlink:href="SomeBook1.xml" />
14:    <Book xlink:href="SomeBook2.xml" />
15:    <Book xlink:href="SomeBook3.xml" />
16:    <Editor xlink:href="SomeEditor1.xml" />
17:    <Editor xlink:href="SomeEditor2.xml" />
18:    <Editor xlink:href="SomeEditor3.xml" />
19:    <Publisher xlink:href="SomePublisher1.xml" />
20:    <Publisher xlink:href="SomePublisher2.xml" />
21:    <Publisher xlink:href="SomePublisher3.xml" />
22:    <AuthorRank>6.5</AuthorRank>
23: </BookSeller>
```

The following set of lines all establish links between objects:

```
<go xlink:from="AuthorRank" xlink:to="RankDatabase" />
<go xlink:from="Author" xlink:to="Book" />
<go xlink:from="Author" xlink:to="Editor" />
<go xlink:from="Author" xlink:to="Publisher" />
```

<BookSeller> assigns a numeric value to the quality of the particular author. However, a number in isolation has little meaning, so to translate it, it must be compared to others. Hence the linking of the specific ranking contained in AuthorRank to the database of author rankings.

Clearly, each author can write more than one book, and each book could have a different editor and publisher. Therefore, while you've established the links between <Author> and <Book> and between <Editor> and <Publisher>, these are links between object definitions rather than links between instances.

The creation of links between specific instances takes place in the following lines:

```
<Author xlink:href="Authordata.xml" />
<Book xlink:href="SomeBook1.xml" />
<Book xlink:href="SomeBook2.xml" />
<Book xlink:href="SomeBook3.xml" />
<Editor xlink:href="SomeEditor1.xml" />
<Editor xlink:href="SomeEditor2.xml" />
<Editor xlink:href="SomeEditor3.xml" />
<Publisher xlink:href="SomePublisher1.xml" />
<Publisher xlink:href="SomePublisher2.xml" />
<Publisher xlink:href="SomePublisher3.xml" />
```

23

The ranking here is for a specific author, so only one such instance is allowed. If a book was written by more than one author, the entry for the other author(s) would be in a separate instance. Each book written by this author would have a corresponding link to the XML file containing the data. Different books could have different publishers and editors, so you need to have duplicate XML files for them as well.

Writing DTDs for XLink Objects

Given that these objects are instances of a data type, it's possible to create DTDs for them. The notation for DTD creation matches what you've used before.

Consider the following element, which is an instance of an XLink object:

```
<!ELEMENT MyLink (#PCDATA)>
```

You could write the following attribute list for it:

```
<!ATTLIST MyLink
 xlink:show (new |replace |embed |undefined) #IMPLIED
 xlink:actuate (onLoad |onRequest |undefined) #IMPLIED
 xlink:type (simple|extended|locator|arc|resource|title
      none) #IMPLIED
 xlink:title (CDATA) #IMPLIED
 xlink:href (CDATA)  #REQUIRED >
```

> This book has only scratched the surface of what can be done with the creation of links in XML. Once again, I encourage you to visit http://www.w3.org/TR/2000/WD-xlink if you're interested in learning more.

XPointer

In programming, a pointer is simply a location that contains a memory address. Generally, the pointer will contain the address of the first byte of a block of memory. Pointers are also often paired with an offset, which moves you a certain number of bytes away from the pointer in that block of memory. This basic organization is demonstrated in Figure 23.1.

The pointer is used to go to address number 1000, and then the offset is used to move from there to the actual location that's being accessed.

You can create an analogy to this if you're using objects defined in XML files. Consider an instance of <Book> in your catalog database. You could use any unique identifier to go to the specific instance of <Book> and then follow the <Author> offset to get the data concerning the author of that specific book. This direct access to the internal parts of an XML file is the primary purpose of XPointer.

FIGURE 23.1

A pointer and the companion offset.

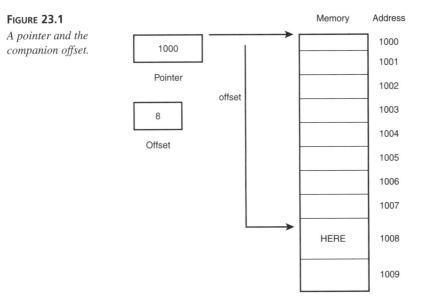

The following is the list of design principles governing XPointer, taken directly from the proposal document at `http://www.w3.org/TR/1998/WD-xptr-19980303`.

1. XPointers shall address into XML documents.
2. XPointers shall be straightforwardly usable over the Internet.
3. XPointers shall be straightforwardly usable in URIs.
4. The XPointer design shall be prepared quickly.
5. The XPointer design shall be formal and concise.
6. The XPointer syntax shall be reasonably compact and human readable.
7. XPointers shall be optimized for usability.
8. XPointers must be feasible to implement.

XPointer Absolute and Relative Location Terms

The keywords used to perform XPointer addressing are separated into two categories: the absolute location terms and the relative location terms.

Table 23.2 shows the absolute location terms.

TABLE 23.2   The XPointer Absolute Location Terms

Term	Meaning
root()	The source is the root element of the resource. If there's no absolute location term, this is assumed.
origin()	This term is used only if some application software is being used to perform the traversal. The location source is the subresource from which the user initiates the traversal.
id(Name)	The source is the object with assigned ID name 'Name'.
html(NameValue)	This tag uses the first instance of an anchor <A> tag with a value assigned to the Name option that matches NameValue.

Table 23.3 shows the relative location terms.

TABLE 23.3   The XPointer Relative Location Terms

Term	Meaning
child	Used to access a direct child node of the resource.
descendant	Used to access a descendant node of the resource.
ancestor	Used to access nodes higher in the hierarchical tree than the resource node.
preceding	Identifies the node that immediately precedes the resource node.
following	Used to access the node that immediately follows the resource node.
psibling	Used to access sibling nodes that appear before the resource node.
fsibling	Used to access sibling nodes that appear after the resource node.

All these keywords are used with inputs that are numbers and strings. Numbers are just counters, and strings are used to identify what's being counted.

Consider the node shown in Listing 23.6. Assume that the entries are all compatible with any associated DTD.

LISTING 23.6   XML Source File for Data Extraction Using XPointers

```
1: <?xml version="1.0"?>
2: <!-- This file is an XML file whose sole purpose is to
3:      provide the source for the extraction of data using
4:      XPointer notation. The name of the file is
5:      listing23-6.xml. -->
6: <Author ID="a12">
7: <!-- Standard name and address -->
8: <Name>Charles Ashbacher</Name>
9: <Address>119 Northwood Drive</Address>
```

```
10: <City>Hiawatha</City>
11: <State>Iowa</State>
12: <PostalCode>52233</PostalCode>
13: <Phone>(319)378-4646</Phone>
14: <!-- List of books authored. -->
15: <Book>Introduction to the Smarandache Function</Book>
16: <Book>Collection of Problems on Smarandache Notions</Book>
17: <Book>Pluckings from the Tree of Smarandache Functions and
    Sequences</Book>
18: </Author>
```

23

The following examples will extract the contents of various nodes from the file:

`id(a12).child(1,Book)`

This extracts the contents of the first <Book> node. Therefore, the value would be `'Introduction to the Smarandache Function'`.

`id(a12).child(3,Book)`

This extracts the contents of the third <Book> node. Therefore, the value would be `'Pluckings from the Tree of Smarandache Functions and Sequences'`.

`id(a12).child(2,#element)`

The #element notation is the generic one for a node in the entity. Since the entity starts at the point where the ID value matches, the counting of the child elements starts at the `<Author ID="a12">` position. Since the comment would also be an element, the second element in the list would be `<Name>Charles Ashbacher</Name>`. Therefore, the value would be `'Charles Ashbacher'`.

`id(a12).child(2,#comment)`

The #comment notation is used to select out a comment. Since you're extracting the second comment when starting at the <Author ID="a12"> position, the node in question is

`<!-- List of books authored. -->`.

Reopen listing23-3.xml and modify it to match Listing 23.7. Save it as listing23-7.xml.

LISTING 23.7   A Second XML File Used as a Data Source

```
1: <?xml version="1.0"?>
2: <!-- This file is an XML file whose sole purpose is to
3:      provide the source for the extraction of data using
4:      XPointer notation. The name of the file is
5:      listing23-7.xml. -->
6: <Author ID="a12">
7: <!-- Standard name and address -->
```

LISTING 23.7   continued

```
 8: <Name>Charles Ashbacher</Name>
 9: <Address>119 Northwood Drive</Address>
10: <City>Hiawatha</City>
11: <State>Iowa</State>
12: <PostalCode>52233</PostalCode>
13: <Phone>(319)378-4646</Phone>
14: <!-- List of books authored. -->
15: <BookList>
16: <Book Topic="Math">Introduction to the Smarandache
    Function</Book>
17: <Book Topic="Math">Collection of Problems on Smarandache
    Notions</Book>
18: <Book Topic="Math">Pluckings from the Tree of Smarandache
    Functions and Sequences</Book>
19: </BookList>
20: </Author>
```

```
id(a12).descendent (2,Book,Topic,Math)
```

This will search all descendent nodes of the node with the id 'a12'. The search is for the second <Book> node possessing the Topic attribute with an assigned value of 'Math'. Therefore, the value would be

```
'Collection of Problems on Smarandache Notions'
```

Reopen listing23-7.xml and modify the line

```
<Book Topic="Math">Introduction to the Smarandache
Function</Book>
```

to match the following:

```
<Book Topic="Computers">Introduction to the Smarandache
Function</Book>
```

In this case, the value returned by the XPointer notation will be

```
'Pluckings from the Tree of Smarandache Functions and Sequences'
```

The previous examples are only a small demonstration of the many ways that XPointer notation can be used to selectively extract data from XML files. To learn more, consult http://www.w3.org/TR/1998/WD-xptr-19980303.

Summary

There is little doubt that the ability to hyperlink is the single most significant driving force behind the popularity of the World Wide Web. Although the XML extension known as XLink hasn't been implemented yet, it promises to make hyperlinking even better. By allowing for more flexibility and description, the XLink notation lets you associate multiple XML files with a link, making all necessary resources available.

Although pointers are extremely dangerous if not used correctly, they're very powerful. If used properly, they allow for the examination and updating of memory locations anywhere in addressable memory. XPointers are used for the same purposes. They allow for the extraction of data from any node within the structure, so the construction of complex queries is often avoided.

23

Q&A

Q Should constructing a local namespace be done only as a last resort?

A No, it should be considered more of a first resort. When you write your descriptions, it's always easier to know precisely what's being referred to. The whole purpose of namespaces is to allow the same identifiers to be reused.

Q What's the analogy between a pointer-offset location descriptor and the absolute and relative location terms of XPointer?

A Since the pointer takes you to the start of the overall structure, it's equivalent to an absolute location term. Given a pointer, the offset then takes you to a certain location relative to that pointer. Therefore, the offset is equivalent to the relative location term.

Q Should a DTD be written for an XLink definition?

A Absolutely! The purpose of a DTD is to make sure that the particular instance of the data type is of the proper form. The more verification checks that are done, the more reliable your data will be.

Workshop

Quiz

1. Which of the following is an absolute location term?

    a. ancestor

    b. preceding

    c. root

    d. child

2. If an XPointer doesn't have a leading absolute term, which of the following is assumed to be present?

    a. root()

    b. html()

    c. id()

    d. origin()

3. Why would you want the href attribute to be CDATA rather than PCDATA?

    a. No reason; PCDATA will work just as well.

    b. PCDATA is actually preferred because the parser will be better able to interpret it.

    c. The form needs to be CDATA so that the XML parser won't convert it. That task must be left to the XML interpreter.

4. Which of the following best describes the function of the actuate global parameter?

    a. It tells the system what resource to use.

    b. It's used to turn a link on or off.

    c. It's used to tell the system whether a link should be followed automatically.

    d. If set to true, the system will check the file to verify that it's well-formed before processing.

Answers

1. c

2. a

3. c

4. c

Exercises

1. Reopen listing23-6.xml and modify it to match the following:

```
<?xml version="1.0"?>
<!-- This file is an XML file whose sole purpose is to
     provide the source for the extraction of data using
     XPointer notation. The name of the file is
     xmlhour23-4.xml. -->

<Author ID="a12">
<!-- Standard name and address -->
<Name>Charles Ashbacher</Name>
<Address>119 Northwood Drive</Address>
```

```
<City>Hiawatha</City>
<State>Iowa</State>
<PostalCode>52233</PostalCode>
<Phone>(319)378-4646</Phone>
<!-- List of books authored. -->
<BookList>
<Book Topic="Math">Introduction to the Smarandache
Function</Book>
<Book Topic="Math">Collection of Problems on Smarandache
Notions</Book>
<Book Topic="Math">Pluckings from the Tree of Smarandache
Functions and Sequences</Book>
</BookList>
<!-- List of awards won -->
<AwardsList>
<Award Date="05-07-2000">Book of the second</Award>
<Award Date="05-09-2000">Pointless book of the year</Award>
<Award Date="05-09-2000">Obfuscated math award</Award>
</AwardsList>
<!-- End of awards list -->
<? Another processing instruction here ?>
</Author>
```

Use this file to perform the following exercises:

    a. Write an XPointer expression that will return the value 'Obfuscated math award'.

    b. Write an XPointer expression that will return the value of the second processing instruction.

2. Write an XLink object that will link and properly label three data files: Bookdata23-1.xml, Editor23-2.xml, and Publisher23-3.xml. Assume that each file contains data about a book that will be published soon. The information about the author is found in another file called Authordata.xml.

23

HOUR 24

Additional Markup Languages

If the quality of an idea is measured by how universally it can be applied, the idea of the markup language is clearly of the highest quality. Besides HTML and XML, additional markup languages are being proposed at a rapid rate for everything from mathematics to real estate. There's even one for human resources.

To keep you abreast of current developments, this hour discusses some of the markup languages that are currently available or in the draft/standards stage.

When a markup language is created, a set of tags is defined that's used to produce the documents. This set of tags is known as the *vocabulary* of the language. You're already familiar with the vocabulary of HTML, of course.

In this hour, you will learn the following:

- How to program in Vector Markup Language
- The basic tags of Mathematical Markup Language and how they're put together to create expressions

- The purpose of Virtual Reality Markup Language and where to find resources to write programs in the language
- The basic structure of a DTD in Real Estate Listing Markup Language
- The purpose and uses of the Human Resources Management Markup Language
- The purpose and basic structure of VoxML

Vector Markup Language

Vector Markup Language (VML) is used to describe graphics and is implemented in IE 5. It allows you to use a fairly natural form of markup tags to draw shapes on a Web page, and it's a precursor to creating animations. Actually, there are currently three major specifications for XML graphics vocabularies: Precision Graphics Markup Language (PGML), Scalable Vector Graphics (SVG), and Vector Markup Language (VML). Since you're working exclusively in IE, this hour will demonstrate only VML, which is fully supported in IE 5.

To learn more about PGML, go to `http://www.w3.org/TR/1998/NOTE-PGML`. To learn more about SVG, go to `http://www.w3.org/TR/SVG/index.html`. Since VML is a proposal from Microsoft, the specification document can be found at `http://www.w3.org/TR/NOTE-VML` and additional information can be found at `http://www.microsoft.com`.

There are several tags that are available in the IE implementation of VML, as summarized Table 24.1.

TABLE 24.1 Vocabulary of Tags Available in the IE 5 Implementation of VML

Name	Usage
shape	The fundamental graphics element in VML.
path	A sequence of pen commands with related data such as points.
line	Draws a line from one point to another.
polyline	Draws a figure that's a series of connected lines.
curve	Draws a smooth curve from one point to another, where the smoothness of the curve is defined by control parameters.
rect	Draws a rectangle.
roundrect	Draws a rectangle with rounded corners.
oval	Draws an oval shape.
arc	Draws a segment of an oval.
group	Used to combine more than one element inside a declared draw region.

Before you learn how to use VML to draw these shapes, you need to understand the different ways in which images can be stored.

Bitmap Images Versus Vector Graphics

There are two ways to store images in a computer. In a *bitmap*, every pixel is assigned a color, and in a *vector graphic*, mathematical formulas are used. These mathematical formulas are then executed to create the image when needed.

Nearly all of the images that you see in Web pages are made up of pixels. However, the storage of those pixels can be done in two widely different ways. If you use a standard GIF or JPEG file, the color of each pixel must be stored. This leads to large files that are very slow to transfer and load. This is even more significant if you're creating an animation. Most animations are created by using a series of static images, each of which is a GIF or JPEG file.

A bitmap image also presents a problem when you *scale* the image, or change its size. Scaling causes fuzzy borders around any item where there's a sharp contrast. When a picture is scaled to a larger size, the computer is forced to fill edges with pixels of intermediate colors. Shrinking the image forces the elimination of these pixels, generally leading to a loss of clarity.

The second way is to store the image as a mathematical formula and then generate the image when it's requested. There's a bit of overhead in the computation, but not nearly as much as downloading a bitmap image from permanent storage or transferring it over a network. Since the formulas for most shapes are well-known, a markup language for inserting such shapes into a Web page is a natural.

Since these images are stored as mathematical formulas rather than pixels, there's little or no loss of clarity if the image is scaled.

A VML Example

When you're using VML, the first thing you must do is to make the proper namespace available. Do this by assigning a namespace qualifier in the opening HTML tag. The command is

```
<html xmlns:v="urn:schemas-microsoft-com:vml">
```

Once again, xmlns is an acronym for XML namespace, v is the prefix that will be used to qualify the namespace objects, and "urn:schemas-microsoft-com:vml" is the resource to use.

To use the functionality available in the VML namespace, you need to create an instance of the proper object. If that object is placed in the <HEAD> of the file, it's not necessary to specify the size parameters.

For example, the following would be a declaration of a VML object:

```
<OBJECT  id="VMLRender"
 classid="CLSID:10072CEC-8CC1-11D1-986E-00A0C955B42E">
</OBJECT>
```

The classid is the universally unique identifier of the VML object.

You've defined the namespace prefix as "v" and created the VML object. However, they're not linked together, and that operation must be done explicitly. To do it, define a <style> tag that uses the behavior qualifier.

For example, the following <style> definition will link the namespace to the VML object:

```
<style>
 v\:* { behavior:url(#VMLRender);}
</style>
```

The simplest of all objects that you can draw on your page is a line, and the following is a simple example of how to draw one:

```
<v:line style="width:300;height:300" from="10,10" to="200,200"
strokecolor="silver" strokeweight="1.5pt"/>
```

v:line is the namespace qualifier and the type of shape to be drawn.

style="width:300;height:300" defines the parameters of the box within which you will draw.

from="10,10" are the (x,y) coordinates where the drawing will begin.

to="200,200" are the coordinates where the drawing will end.

strokecolor="silver" defines the color of the line.

strokeweight="1.5pt" defines the width of the line.

Create the file shown in Listing 24.1 and save it as listing24-1.html.

LISTING 24.1   The Actions of the VML Elements

```
1:<html xmlns:vm="urn:schemas-microsoft-com:vml">
2:<!-- This is an example of using VML tags to draw figures
     from an HTML file. In this case, you are drawing
     several figures and using the group option to put all
     of them in the same drawing space. The filename is
     listing24-1.html. -->
3:<head>
4:<title>Testing VML</title>
```

```
5:<OBJECT  id="VMLRender"
6:  classid="CLSID:10072CEC-8CC1-11D1-986E-00A0C955B42E">
7:</OBJECT>
8:<style>
9:  vm\:* { behavior:url(#VMLRender);}
10:</style>
11:</head>
12:<body>
13:<vm:group style="width:1800;height:1800">
14:<vm:line style="width:300;height:300" from="10,10"
    to="200,200" strokecolor="blue"
    strokeweight="2.5pt"/>
15:<vm:polyline style="width:300;height:300" points="100,20
    120,50 150,95 190,146 140,35" strokecolor="red"
      strokeweight="1.5pt"/>
16:<vm:curve style="width:300;height:300" from="10,200"
    control1="100,100" control2="250,200" to="200,200"
      strokecolor="green" strokeweight="1.5pt"/>
17:<vm:rect style="width:100;height:150" fillcolor="yellow"
    strokecolor="blue" strokeweight="1.5pt"/>
18:<vm:arc style="width:200;height:200" startangle="30"
    endangle="100" strokecolor="purple"
    strokeweight="1.5pt"/>
19:</group>
20:</body>
21:  </html>
```

Run the file in IE. The output is illustrated in Figure 24.1.

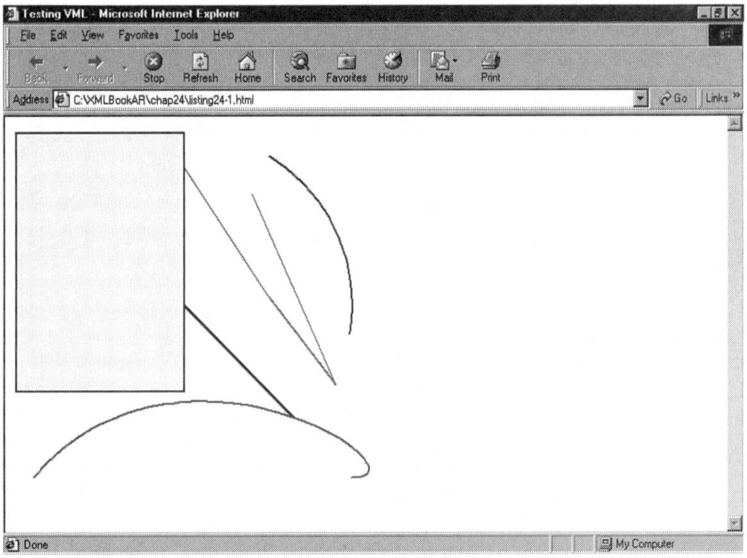

FIGURE 24.1

The actions of the VML tags.

Lines 5 through 7 insert an instance of the VML object into the Web page, and lines 8 through 10 set the namespace prefix to vm and the behavior to render. The combination of lines 13 and 19 define a group region that will contain the drawn figures. Placing the figures in a group will organize them into the area defined for the group.

Five figures are drawn inside the region reserved for the group: a line, a polyline, a curve, a rectangle, and an arc. The style qualifier is used to determine the appearance of the figure, and the color of each one is different.

For more information about VML, consult the VML section of the Microsoft Web site at `http://msdn.microsoft.com/standards/vml/` or the VML standard site at `http://www.w3.org/TR/NOTE-VML`.

Mathematical Markup Language

Mathematics has an extensive vocabulary of symbols that can be combined in many different ways to create problems and solutions. In the past, it was very difficult to accurately express mathematical expressions on a computer. Many symbols weren't supported, and the positions weren't rendered accurately. Since even slight changes in the positions could significantly alter the interpretation of the expression, many authors simply drew their formulas by hand when writing their papers.

That same problem is even more acute in Web pages, forcing many authors to use image files to display their formulas. Although this is a solution, it's a very poor one. Generally, the image files can be used in only one document because it's difficult to combine multiple images without creating a new one. Also, the image file itself doesn't impart any context about what's being displayed. Usually, the creator has to place explanatory text around the message or inside it to explain the image.

A very effective solution that's currently being developed and refined is the Mathematical Markup Language or MathML. This is a vocabulary of tag names that represent mathematical symbols and their placement. When the display device interprets the file, it renders the content in the standard mathematical style. For a complete description of the language, consult `http://www.w3.org/Math/`.

IE doesn't support MathML at this time, but there are some software packages that allow you to use MathML code. The foremost of these is Mathematica by Wolfram Research. This is the premier symbolic mathematics program, and it's truly amazing to use. You can read about it at `http://www.wolfram.com`. For a list of additional MathML resources, go to `http://www.webeq.com/mathml/resources.html`.

A MathML Example

This example will demonstrate the MathML code for displaying a simple algebraic expression. It might seem like a lot of effort just to create a simple expression, but keep in mind that segments can be reused. This reduces the overall cost of development. Also, the expression will be accurate no matter which browser is used to view it.

The basic or token tags in MathML mirror the different components used in mathematics:

TABLE 24.2   The Standard Delimiters of an Expression's Components

`<mo>`	Delimits a math operator, such as +, -, * and =.
`<mi>`	Delimits an identifier or variable, such as x or y.
`<mn>`	Delimits a number, such as 2 and 6.

24

To organize the components of the expression, you have these additional tags:

TABLE 24.3   A List of the Organizational Delimiters of MathML

`<mrow>`	Horizontally groups an arbitrary number of subexpressions.
`<mfrac>`	Forms a fraction from two subexpressions.
`<msqrt>`	Forms a square root.
`<mfenced>`	Encloses the content with a pair of parentheses or fences.
`<msup>`	Delimits a pair of expressions where the second is a superscript of the first.
`<msub>`	Delimits a pair of expressions where the second is a subscript of the first.
`<math>`	Delimits the entire expression.

For example, Listing 24.2 is the MathML code that describes the following mathematical expression:

$$(x - 3)^2 + x_n + x - 4 = 9$$

Once again, the line numbers are for reference purposes only and are not part of the code.

LISTING 24.2   The MathML Code to Display the Algebraic Expression

```
1: <math>
2:  <mrow>
3:   <mrow>
4:    <msup>
5:     <mfenced>
6:        <mi>x</mi>
7:        <mo>-</mo>
```

LISTING 24.2   continued

```
 8:        <mn>3</mn>
 9:      </mfenced>
10:      <mn>2</mn>
11:    </msup>
12:    <mo>+</mo>
13:    <msub>
14:        <mi>x</mi>
15:        <mi>n</mi>
16:    </msub>
17:    <mo>+</mo>
18:    <mi>x</mi>
19:    <mo>-</mo>
20:    <mn>4</mn>
21:  </mrow>
22:    <mo>=</mo>
23:    <mn>9</mn>
24:  </mrow>
25:</math>
```

Lines 2 and 24 delimit the complete expression, and lines 3 and 21 delimit the segment on the left side of the equals sign. Therefore, lines 22 and 23 are the equals sign operator and the number on the right side of the equals, respectively.

The subexpression

$$(x-3)^2$$

has a superscript as the second element, so those elements must be surrounded by an <msup> tag pair. The first element is surrounded by parentheses or fences, so the three interior items must be surrounded by the <mfenced> tag pair. Therefore, the MathML for this subexpression is in lines 4 through 11.

The subexpression x_n has a subscript as the second element, so each of the two items must be surrounded by an <msub> tag, which is done in lines 13 through 16.

Each of the operators is surrounded by <mo> tags. The rest of the code listing should be clear.

Virtual Reality Modeling Language

Virtual Reality Modeling Language (VRML) is a markup language that's used to model imaginary worlds. These worlds can be anything from approximations of the real world for training simulations to fantasy worlds for games. One of the elements needed to create an imaginary world is the data that defines that world. The Web is a natural medium for virtual worlds, so XML is a natural for describing them.

In early 1999, an initiative was put forward to migrate the features of VRML to XML. The name of this application is X3D. The initiative is still in the draft stages. For the latest information on this initiative and other proposals regarding VRML, consult `http://www.vrml.org`. For specific information concerning X3D, consult `http://www.vrml.org/fs_workinggroups.htm`.

Real Estate Listing Markup Language

If you've ever purchased real estate, you know that many different characteristics can be listed about a property. Furthermore, the goal of both buyers and sellers of real estate is to create a database that can be searched via the Web and in which new entries can be created by realtors that are generally computer novices.

The Real Estate Listing Markup Language, or RELML, is a set of four different XML vocabularies:

- Residential
- Commercial
- Vacant land
- Working land

The following is the initial section of the XML DTD for a residential property listing. This and all other DTDs can be found at `http://www.4thworldtele.com/public/design/rsdesign.html`:

```
 1: <Schema name="RELML"
    xmlns="urn:schemas-microsoft-com:xml-data"
    xmlns:dt="urn:schemas-microsoft-com:datatypes">
 2: <AttributeType name="VERSION" dt:type="enumeration"
    dt:values="19990523"/>
 3:     <AttributeType name="WIDTH" dt:type="int"/>
 4:     <AttributeType name="HEIGHT" dt:type="int"/>
 5:     <AttributeType name="SRC" dt:type="id"/>
 6:     <AttributeType name="NAME" dt:type="string"/>
 7:     <AttributeType name="DESCRIPTION" dt:type="string"/>
 8:     <AttributeType name="SECURITY" dt:type="enumeration"
    dt:values="MLS-Only Restricted Public"/>
 9:     <AttributeType name="CURRENCY-UNITS"
    dt:type="enumeration"
    dt:values="USDOLLARS CANDOLLARS PESOS"/>
10:     <AttributeType name="COUNTRY" dt:type="string"/>
11:     <AttributeType name="STATE" dt:type="string"/>
12:     <AttributeType name="COUNTY" dt:type="string"/>
13:     <AttributeType name="AREA-UNITS" dt:type="enumeration"
    dt:values="SQ-METERS SQ-FEET"/>
14:     <AttributeType name="LAND-UNITS" dt:type="enumeration"
```

24

```
        dt:values="HECTARES ACRES"/>
15:     <AttributeType name="TITLE" dt:type="string"/>
16:     <AttributeType name="RENT-PERIOD" dt:type="enumeration"
        dt:values="DAY MONTH YEAR"/>
17:     <ElementType name="RELML" content="eltOnly">
18:     <attribute type="VERSION" required="yes"/>
19:     <element type ="RESIDENTIAL-LISTING" minOccurs="0"
        maxOccurs="*"/>
20:     </ElementType>
21:     <ElementType name="RESIDENTIAL-LISTING"
        content="eltOnly">
22:     <element type ="GENERAL"/>
23:     <element type ="FEATURES"/>
24:     <element type ="FINANCIAL"/>
25:     <element type ="REMARKS"/>
26:     <element type ="CONTACTS"/>
27:     </ElementType>
28:     <ElementType name="GENERAL" content="eltOnly">
29:     <element type ="IMAGE" minOccurs="0" maxOccurs="*"/>
30:     <element type ="APN" minOccurs="0"/>
31:     <element type ="MLS" minOccurs="0"/>
32:     <element type ="TYPE"/>
33:     <element type ="PRICE" minOccurs="0"/>
34:     <element type ="RENT" minOccurs="0"/>
35:     <element type ="WHEN-BUILT"/>
36:     <element type ="LOCATION"/>
37:     <element type ="STRUCTURE"/>
38:     <element type ="DATES"/>
39:     <element type ="LAND-AREA"/>
40:     <element type ="STATUS"/>
41:     <element type ="OTHER" maxOccurs="1"/>
42:     <element type ="TERMS" minOccurs="0" maxOccurs="*"/>
43:     </ElementType>
44:     <ElementType name="IMAGE" content="empty">
45:      <attribute type="WIDTH" required="yes"/>
46:      <attribute type="HEIGHT" required="yes"/>
47:      <attribute type="SRC" required="yes"/>
48:      <attribute type="NAME" required="no"/>
49:      <attribute type="DESCRIPTION" required="no"/>
50:     </ElementType>
51:     <ElementType name="APN" content="textOnly"
        dt:type="int">
52:      <attribute type="SECURITY" default="MLS-Only"/>
53:     </ElementType>
54:     <ElementType name="MLS" content="eltOnly">
55:      <element type ="MLS-CODE"/>
56:      <element type ="MLS-SOURCE" maxOccurs="1"/>
57:     </ElementType>
58:     <ElementType name="MLS-CODE" content="textOnly"
        dt:type="int">
59:      <attribute type="SECURITY" default="MLS-Only"/>
```

```
60:    </ElementType>
61:    <ElementType name="MLS-SOURCE" content="eltOnly">
62:     <element type ="NAME"/>
63:     <element type ="PHONE" minOccurs="0" maxOccurs="1"/>
64:     <element type ="FAX" minOccurs="0" maxOccurs="1"/>
65:     <element type ="WEB" minOccurs="0" maxOccurs="1"/>
66:     <attribute type="SECURITY" default="MLS-Only"/>
67:    </ElementType>
68:    <ElementType name="TYPE" content="textOnly"
       dt:type="string">
69:     <attribute type="TITLE" required="no"/>
70:    </ElementType>
71:    <ElementType name="PRICE" content="textOnly"
       dt:type="fixed.14.4">
72:     <attribute type="CURRENCY-UNITS" default="USDOLLARS"/>
73:    </ElementType>
74:    <ElementType name="RENT" content="textOnly"
       dt:type="fixed.14.4">
75:     <attribute type="RENT-PERIOD" default="MONTH"/>
76:     <attribute type="CURRENCY-UNITS" default="USDOLLARS"/>
77:    </ElementType>
78:    <ElementType name="WHEN-BUILT" content="eltOnly">
79:     <element type ="ORIGINAL-STRUCTURE"/>
80:     <element type ="IMPROVEMENTS" minOccurs="0"
       maxOccurs="*"/>
81:    </ElementType>
82:    <ElementType name="ORIGINAL-STRUCTURE"
       content="eltOnly">
83:     <element type ="DATE"/>
84:     <element type ="DESCRIPTION" minOccurs="0" maxOccurs="1"/>
85:    </ElementType>
86:    <ElementType name="IMPROVEMENTS" content="eltOnly">
87:     <element type ="DATE"/>
88:     <element type ="DESCRIPTION" minOccurs="0"
       maxOccurs="1"/>
89:    </ElementType>
90:    <ElementType name="LOCATION" content="eltOnly">
91:     <element type ="ADDRESS" minOccurs="0" maxOccurs="1"/>
92:     <element type ="CITY" minOccurs="0" maxOccurs="1"/>
93:     <element type ="ZIP" minOccurs="0" maxOccurs="1"/>
94:     <element type ="ROUGH" minOccurs="0" maxOccurs="1"/>
95:     <element type ="GEO" minOccurs="0" maxOccurs="1"/>
96:     <attribute type="COUNTRY" required="yes"/>
97:     <attribute type="STATE" required="yes"/>
98:     <attribute type="COUNTY" required="yes"/>
99:     <attribute type="SECURITY" default="Public"/>
100:   </ElementType>
101:   <ElementType name="ROUGH" content="textOnly"
       dt:type="string">
102:    <attribute type="TITLE" required="no"/>
103:   </ElementType>
```

24

```
104:    <ElementType name="GEO" content="eltOnly">
105:     <element type ="LATITUDE"/>
106:     <element type ="LONGITUDE"/>
107:     <attribute type="TITLE" required="no"/>
108:    </ElementType>
109:    <ElementType name="LATITUDE" content="eltOnly">
111:     <element type ="DEGREES"/>
112:     <element type ="MINUTES"/>
113:     <element type ="SECONDS" minOccurs="0" maxOccurs="1"/>
114:    </ElementType>
115:    <ElementType name="LONGITUDE" content="eltOnly">
116:     <element type ="DEGREES"/>
117:     <element type ="MINUTES"/>
118:     <element type ="SECONDS" minOccurs="0" maxOccurs="1"/>
119:    </ElementType>
120:    <ElementType name="DEGREES" content="textOnly"
        dt:type="int">
121:    </ElementType>
122:    <ElementType name="MINUTES" content="textOnly"
        dt:type="int">
123:    </ElementType>
124:    <ElementType name="SECONDS" content="textOnly"
        dt:type="int">
125:    </ElementType>
126: <-- Additional material left out -->
```

The general realtor wouldn't see this DTD. Its purpose is to define a common language for all realtors to use. By using it as a common template for the data in a real estate listing, it's possible to use any form of data entry to accept the data as long as it conforms to the standard. This not only makes it easier to create the data records, but it also eliminates the need for any custom tweaking of the records, either by the creator or user.

Human Resources Management Markup Language

At many companies, much of the non-proprietary information on job openings and personnel is now being posted on company intranets, and the more generic information appears on the Internet. There are many Web sites that contain job listings and allow the posting of resumes. This means that standards for data and display must exist, and that's why the Human Resources Management Markup Language (HRMML) was created. As is the case with RELML, HRMML is built from a set of DTDs for the various documents that make up the human resources system. The preliminary set of definitions can be found at http://www.hr-xml.org/schemas.html.

As the world becomes more economically interlinked, there's a paradoxical increase in both cooperation and competition. This is no more apparent than on the Web. Suppose you want to post your resume on the Web. Of course, it's to your advantage to display it for as many people as possible. If there's a standard resume DTD that you follow, you can post it on all sites that use that DTD. Many companies that post resumes also have cooperative agreements with other companies, which necessitates the use of a standard.

The same goes for a company that's advertising a position. The more people that read the job posting, the higher the probability that attractive candidates will respond. Therefore, the ideal situation would be to write the posting in a standard form that's conformed to by all job sites. An XML DTD satisfies that requirement.

Although employee benefit programs vary more than the previous two examples, there's enough commonality to justify the use of a DTD to describe the benefits. However, employee compensation is generally considered secret information, so the site would probably display a pared-down version.

24

VoxML

VoxML is a vocabulary of XML DTDs that is used for interactive speech applications. Many predict that voice-controlled computers will be the next big thing, so the significance of VoxML should be obvious. For more information on VoxML, consult `http://www.voxml.com/voxml.html`.

A VoxML document is created by using two fundamental elements, DIALOG and STEP. The DIALOG element is the outer container, and STEP refers to each of the steps in the operation. The STEP element is itself a container, so generally an assignment is made to the NAME attribute of each STEP element. The NAME option of the STEP element is used to assign a unique ID reference to a STEP. Therefore, a skeletal VoxML document will look like the following:

```
<DIALOG>
 <STEP NAME="initial">
 </STEP>

   ...
 <STEP NAME="CleanUp">
 </STEP>
</DIALOG>
```

For output, two elements are used, PROMPT and HELP. The text inside the PROMPT element is the text that's spoken to the user, although it also can contain audio. You include an audio file by using the audio element, which has a required src attribute. That attribute would be the name of the sound file. Once this text is spoken, The user can ask for further information by saying the word "Help." Then the text in the HELP element is spoken.

For example, the following could be spoken at a fast food restaurant:

```
<STEP name="HamburgerPrompt">
  <PROMPT>Do you want sauce on your hamburger</PROMPT>
  <HELP>The sauce is similar to a tangy ketchup</HELP>
 </STEP>
```

The HELP element is an optional one. If it's not present, the default message "No help available" is spoken.

To define what's considered acceptable input from the user, use the INPUT tag. This is done in the TYPE attribute, the options for which are summarized in Table 24.4.

TABLE 24.4 Valid Type Attributes for the INPUT Tag

Value	Function
NONE	No input. Go to the next step.
OPTIONLIST	Input must be a selection from a list of options.
YORN	Input a yes or a no.
DATE	Input a calendar date.
TIME	Input a time of day.
DIGITS	Input a series of digits.
NUMBER	Input a number.
PHONE	Input a telephone number.
MONEY	Input a monetary amount.
RECORD	Input an audio recording.
GRAMMAR	Input a voice input grammar.
HIDDEN	Assign a value without user interaction.
PROFILE	Input a user profile (hidden).

If OPTIONLIST is used, the syntax is similar to that of an OPTION tag in HTML.

For example, the following demonstrates how to use the OPTIONLIST input type:

```
<STEP NAME="size">
 <PROMPT>What size pizza would you like?</PROMPT>
 <HELP>The Pizza Spot makes three sizes: small, large and
jumbo</HELP>
 <INPUT TYPE="OPTIONLIST" NAME="ConfirmOrder">
  <OPTION VALUE="small">small</OPTION>
  <OPTION VALUE="large">large</OPTION>
  <OPTION VALUE="jumbo">jumbo</OPTION>
 </INPUT>
</STEP>
```

Summary

In this hour, you were exposed to some of the additional languages that are constructed using markup tags. If you explored some of the URLs, you probably encountered other languages that are currently being proposed, developed, or implemented.

You've learned a great deal in this book, and now you're ready to use XML productively. As this last hour should have made clear, XML is a very powerful language that can be used in many different contexts. RELML and HRMML are simply sets of XML DTDs that define the forms of the data. Even the languages that weren't defined using XML—VML, VRML, and VoxML—are constructed using the same principles as XML. Because it's a data markup language and everything is data, it's hard to think of an area where XML won't be used.

24

Q&A

Q In what ways are vector graphics superior to bitmaps?

A Vector graphics maintain their crispness when resized. Bitmaps become fuzzy when the computer either computes intermediate pixels to fill space or deletes pixels to reduce space. Vector graphics require very little data, whereas bitmaps need every pixel to be described.

Q If vector graphics are so superior, why do Web pages use bitmap files almost exclusively?

A There are two problems with vector graphics in Web pages: 1) Lack of support. Until recently, there was no language available for Web pages that could be used to define vector graphics. 2) All images can be represented as bitmaps, but it can be difficult to find the precise mathematical formulas to create a vector graphic.

Q What are the advantages of using RELML?

A It's a standard that everyone can use to describe their data. And because it's an XML DTD, browsers can understand it and display it. Therefore, a listing created by a realtor in one area can be transferred and viewed by a realtor in another area.

Q Can we expect additional markup languages or vocabularies to be created in the future?

A Absolutely! In fact, the future is now. Many other vocabularies are being created.

Workshop

Quiz

1. If the <HELP> tag doesn't appear in a VoxML STEP tag with a PROMPT, what's the response to a help query?

   a. "No help available"

   b. No response

   c. "Sorry, there's no response"

   d. "Sorry, we can't help you"

2. To use the VML namespace, you must qualify which tag?

   a. The BODY tag

   b. The HEAD tag

   c. A DIV tag

   d. The HTML tag

3. Which of the following languages is a set of XML DTDs?

   a. VoxML

   b. MathML

   c. RELML

   d. VRML

Answers

1. a

2. d

3. c

Exercises

1. Use VML to construct a filled rectangle.

2. Use VML to construct an octagon.

INDEX